Six Plays of the Israeli-Palestinian Conflict

Edited by Jamil Khoury, Michael Malek Najjar *and* Corey Pond

McFarland & Company, Inc., Publishers
Jefferson, North Carolina

ISBN (print) 978-1-4766-7590-9
ISBN (ebook) 8-1-4766-3475-3

LIBRARY OF CONGRESS CATALOGUING DATA ARE AVAILABLE

BRITISH LIBRARY CATALOGUING DATA ARE AVAILABLE

© 2018 Jamil Khoury, Michael Malek Najjar and Corey Pond. All rights reserved

No part of this book may be reproduced or transmitted in any form or by any means, electronic or mechanical, including photocopying or recording, or by any information storage and retrieval system, without permission in writing from the publisher.

Front cover artwork: *Semitic Commonwealth* by Andrew Skwish

Printed in the United States of America

*McFarland & Company, Inc., Publishers
Box 611, Jefferson, North Carolina 28640
www.mcfarlandpub.com*

Six Plays of the Israeli–Palestinian Conflict

Table of Contents

Acknowledgments	vii
Introduction (in three parts) by Jamil Khoury; Corey Pond; and Michael Malek Najjar	1

The Admission: A Play in Fourteen Scenes
— Motti Lerner — 9

Essay: Motti Lerner's *The Admission*: Accounting and Atoning for the Past
   Michael Malek Najjar — 11

Playwright Statement: Facing the Trauma of 1948 — 13

Playscript — 14

Scenes from 70* Years — Hannah Khalil — 45

Essay: Hannah Khalil's *Scenes from 70* Years*: Snapshots from a Seemingly Endless Occupation
   Michael Malek Najjar — 47

Playwright Statement: Humanizing the "Other" — 49

Playscript — 51

Tennis in Nablus — Ismail Khalidi — 91

Essay: Ismail Khalidi's *Tennis in Nablus*: Mining History for the Origins of the Conflict
   Michael Malek Najjar — 93

Playwright Statement: Writing Palestine's Invisible History — 95

Playscript — 97

Urge for Going: Trilogy Version — Mona Mansour — 133

Essay: Mona Mansour's *Urge for Going*: Dramatizing "Permanent Impermanence"
   Michael Malek Najjar — 135

Playwright Statement: The Unspeakable Loss of Displacement — 137

Playscript — 139

The Victims: Or What Do You Want Me to Do About It? — KEN KAISSAR 177

Essay: Ken Kaissar's *The Victims*: Sympathy for the Suffering
    MICHAEL MALEK NAJJAR 179

Playwright Statement: Who Are the Victims? 181

Playscript 182

The Zionists — ZOHAR TIROSH-POLK 227

Essay: Zohar Tirosh-Polk's *The Zionists*: Tracking Generational Trauma
    MICHAEL MALEK NAJJAR 229

Playwright Statement: The Zionists—A Reckoning 231

Playscript 232

Afterword by Jamil Khoury and Michael Malek Najjar 273

Chapter Notes 279

Acknowledgments

Editing an anthology like this takes a great deal of time and support. We wish to thank Chicago's Silk Road Rising for producing *Semitic Commonwealth: A Series of Staged Readings* (February 10–26, 2017) with courage and integrity, both artistic and political, and for supporting this anthology. We wish to thank Layla Milholen and McFarland for their desire to publish these plays. We also wish to thank the talented writers included here—Motti Lerner, Hannah Khalil, Ismail Khalidi, Mona Mansour, Ken Kaissar, and Zohar Tirosh-Polk—who have devoted their careers to dramatizing the experiences of Arabs and Israelis in their plays. Your works are truly inspiring and we hope this volume helps make more people aware of your talents.

Thank you to the agents and assistants who aided us with the contractual aspects of this work. To Airan Wright, the photographer whose work is included in this volume, thank you for your work in capturing those fleeting moments of theatre. Thank you Andrew Skwish, for your beautiful cover art, and for helping brand Silk Road Rising with your dazzling poster art designs since 2004. Thank you to Carol Ann Tan who provided additional proofreading. We would also like to thank the Oregon Humanities Center and the University of Oregon College of Arts and Sciences for subvention funds.

Malek Najjar would like to thank his wife Rana and daughter Malak, and his mother Samia and sister Dina for their continued love and support, and his colleagues at the University of Oregon for their guidance. Jamil Khoury would like to thank his husband, Malik Gillani, for moving heaven and earth to create a home for Asian American and Middle Eastern American theatre artists, and the entire Silk Road Rising community for helping build a movement that expands representation in American theatre.

Thank you to the funders who made Silk Road Rising's *Semitic Commonwealth: A Series of Staged Readings* possible, including: The Alphawood Foundation, The Bass Fund, and MacArthur Fund for Arts and Culture at Prince. Thank you to the many artists who talents brought the six plays to life on stage: Annelyse Ahmad, Kaiser Ahmed, Owais Ahmed, Anna C. Bahow, Rom Barkhordar, Raj Bond, Melissa Canciller, Robin Chaplik, Adrianne Cury, Luke Daigle, Adelina Feldman-Schultz, Jerry Galante, Kroydell Galima, Jonathan L. Green, Torrey Hanson, Mark Hines, Michael Holding, Sami Ismat, Leah Karpel, Anna Klos, Jacqueline

Marschke, Virginia Marie Martinez, Tommy Malouf, Jess McLeod, Jack Miggins, Monica Orozco, Lindsey Pearlman, Chris Popio, Adam Poss, Tyler Ravelson, Annalise Raziq, Amro Salama, Awate Serequeberhan, Londen Shannon, Brian Sheridan, Lucy Schuh, Steve Silver, Rachel Silvert, Clayton Stamper, Kaelan Strouse, Dana Tretta, Mark Ulrich, Janet Ulrich Brooks, Penelope Walker, Alex Weisman, Sean Wiberg, and Dexter Zollicoffer.

Introduction

An Anthology Defined: The State of Semitic Commonwealth • Jamil Khoury

Where politicians and diplomats fail, artists and storytellers may yet succeed. Not in ratifying a peace treaty between Israel and Palestine, but in building the social and political connectivity that enables resolution. Amid the persistence of Israeli occupation, Palestinian dispossession, and narratives that reproduce staticity, I have, alongside Michael Malek Najjar and Corey Pond, curated this collection of six plays that explore the human toll of the Palestinian-Israeli conflict. Not with timelines, statistics, and SWOT (strengths, weaknesses, opportunities, and threats) analyses, but instead a laser focus on the personal, material, and spiritual tolls paid by those most affected.

Originally produced from February 10 to 26, 2017, as *Semitic Commonwealth*, a festival of staged readings by Silk Road Rising, my Chicago-based theatre company, this project has brought together distinguished playwrights of Arab and Jewish backgrounds, including Motti Lerner, Hannah Khalil, Ismail Khalidi, Mona Mansour, Ken Kaissar, and Zohar Tirosh-Polk.

All six artists have written plays that propel the discourse beyond the predictable enmities and righteous posturing, the monotonous talking points and selective memories that have stifled progress for far too long. These plays do not march in lockstep; they are dynamic, original, challenging, provocative, complicated, funny, painful, and oftentimes controversial. These are stories that do not cling to nationalist orthodoxies or party lines, but rather explore themes of identity, justice, occupation, exile, history, and homeland with remarkable honesty and integrity.

In many respects, this project is about leaving one's comfort zone. It's about empathizing with characters who embody perspectives that conflict with one's own. It's about abandoning certainty and extending the benefit of the doubt. The plays range widely in place and time, in thematic content and dramatic structure; they pose difficult questions without presuming to offer answers. They encourage active dissent, enabling audiences to reach their own conclusions. We never set out to achieve balance or moral equivalency, nor to provide equal airing to "both sides" (as if there are only two sides!). This collection is not about rooting for one's team; there is no home court advantage, and no one is keeping score.

In fact, the only conscious parity exists within the identities of the playwrights. Three identify as Jewish and Israeli, and three identify as Arab (two are Palestinian, one is Lebanese). Three are women, three are men, and I imagine all six identify as politically progressive, judging from their adherence to the inquisitive, self-questioning, and humanistic traditions of the left. These artists find truth and humanity in characters with whom they agree *and* disagree, eschewing the didacticism, polemics, and thought-policing that we associate with the very worst of political theatre. No one is being force-fed a politic; propaganda finds no home in these plays.

This project, moreover, is not about legitimizing or delegitimizing. The legitimacy of Palestinian peoplehood and Jewish peoplehood we take as givens. That sliver of land lying between the Mediterranean Sea and the Jordan River hosts myriad narratives, both national and religious. Such utterances as "There's no such thing as a Palestinian," or "Jews have no connection to the land," or "My claim is greater than your claim," run counter to empathic discourse. There is no litmus test to determine indigenousness, nor to gauge one's span of continuous inhabitation. We detest the delegitimization efforts being undertaken by either extreme. This collection is not a competition over who has suffered greatest and longest, but neither is it a normalization campaign (normalizing military occupation and asymmetrical power) nor an anti-normalization campaign (opposing mutually beneficial relationships between parties on the ground).

So what, then, is this anthology? How do we define this ambitious undertaking, simply and directly? In my estimation, it is a series of thoughtful, well-written plays that can help us evolve. It is an antidote to the myths and omissions that characterize pop culture portrayals of this conflict. Looking for anti–Semitism and Jewish conspiracy theories? Anti-Arab racism and Islamophobia? Palestinian victim blaming or Holocaust denial? You had better look elsewhere. Similarly, if your wish is to see Palestinians conflated with terrorism, or Israelis with fascism, then we are not your storytellers. Ours is a space for neither the erasure of Palestinian displacement, nor what I call the "duality of Israeli exceptionalism" (Israel as exceptionally good or exceptionally bad). To borrow a popular adage from Silk Road Rising, Jews and Palestinians are "neither angels nor demons but real human beings," with all the hopes and fears, challenges and complexities, triumphs and failures, that characterize being human.

Let it be known that we are neither naive nor self-aggrandizing enough to suggest that six plays could suddenly alter the political landscape of Israel/Palestine—but woe to those who underestimate the potential ripple effects of this project. If culture is destiny, as many would argue, then we are sowing the seeds that will anchor the roots that will sprout new narratives and that will blossom into new realities. Not swords into plowshares, but rather plays into plowshares. And while there are many lenses through which to approach this conflict (mine is admittedly a human rights lens), drama and narrative arc storytelling provide entry points that unburden us of any preconceived or predetermined conclusions.

I'm proud that the space created by the staging of *Semitic Commonwealth* accommodates a broad spectrum of views. And I'm proud that Silk Road Rising's audience includes those in passionate support of both Palestine and Israel. In fact, I'm awed that such ideological diversity has converged at our intimate 85-seat theatre—it's hard-won affirmation that our mission is working. Over the years, countless conversations have galvanized an audience that includes Palestine solidarity activists, Jewish community leaders, Arab journalists, Israeli diplomats, and, of course, Arab and Jewish theatre lovers. Silk Road Rising's plays have been engaged by partisans of both the Birthright Israel and Palestinian Right of Return movements, by BDS (Boycott, Divestment, and Sanctions) organizers, and facilitators of Aliyah (Jewish immigration to Israel). Of course, our patrons even include those suffering from what I refer to, with tongue somewhat in cheek, as Israel/Palestine Pervasive Fatigue Syndrome. And who *hasn't* been afflicted at one time or another?

Yes, there has also been pushback. Some of it ugly. For example, the Jewish audience member who complained of there being "too many Muslims" in the house the night he attended a show, or the Arab audience member who left an angry voicemail berating me for "associating with Zionists." And I'll not soon forget the indictment of an Israeli Jewish playwright who was deemed insufficiently anti-Israel by some, insufficiently pro-Israel by others, and therefore "dangerous," "self-hating," and a "tool of the enemy" (could he have been a double agent?). But on the whole, we've witnessed overwhelming gratitude and relief that a theatrical space exists for the democratic exchange of ideas surrounding these difficult and contentious debates.

Perhaps it is the doggedness of the above-cited pushback that vindicates the urgency of projects like this one. To varying degrees, all six playwrights have combated efforts to censor and vilify their work. All the more reason to be producing them, I'd say. Furthermore, the cause of justice continues to be undermined by an absence of Palestinian voices in American theatre. As communities of theatre makers, we bear partial responsibility for perpetuating this deafening silence around Palestine, an inequity we should be addressing loudly and collectively. Many theatres are also reluctant to produce Israeli Jewish playwrights who question and challenge dominant narratives about Israel. The three Israeli playwrights who joined us on this journey care deeply about Israel and its future—and still, some have confused this patriotism for "disloyalty," even "treason." Not only do such allegations sabotage artistic freedom, they impede the robust dialogue we now so desperately need.

If experience has taught me anything, it's that theatre audiences are hungry for deliberation of the liveliest kind. It's a myth that audiences seek out "safe" plays that only serve to provide affirmation. Audiences have grown weary of echo chambers and either/or thinking. Despite indications to the contrary, the world is poised for a democratic renaissance with storytellers leading the charge. Consider for a moment that these six plays speak to those who envision peaceful, equitable coexistence, and those who envision a carefully managed truce; those who support Israel's expansion, and those who wish to dismantle Israel altogether; those with a vast knowledge of the issues, and those who demonstrate profound ignorance and blindness to facts. No one has cornered the market on love of homeland or depth of conviction. These plays demand that we hear this love and conviction, in all its wild variance and angst. This is the stuff of democratic interchange. It matters in Palestine and Israel and it matters in the United States of America.

Why forfeit an opportunity to learn and be challenged? Our art form is both inspirational and aspirational. When you create art from your own subjective experiences, your truth can elevate others and allow parallels to begin to emerge. Good theatre not only touches the heart and mind, but also the soul. On two unrelated occasions, I heard from a Jewish artist and a Muslim artist that the theatre is a "sacred space," that encountering a play is the spiritual equivalent of reciting prayers or attending a religious service. This is an interesting idea to ponder, and I'm rather inclined to agree.

For those interested in producing one or more of these plays, I think it important to consider the "constituent audiences." I say this not to diminish or negate "mainstream audiences" (whose participation is vital) but to illuminate the diversity within the Arab American and Jewish American communities. Using Silk Road Rising as a case study, I'd wager that our Jewish audience is considerably larger than our Arab audience. The former is primarily Ashkenazi (Jews of Central and Eastern European ancestry), includes a good number of Israelis, skews more culturally Jewish than religiously Jewish, and reflects Zionist, anti-Zionist, non-Zionist, and post-Zionist politics. Many have expressed either an ambivalence towards Zionism or a conditional embrace of Zionism. Obviously, Jewish audiences are going to differ from theatre to theatre and community to community, but responsible producing nevertheless demands that they be present at the proverbial table for dialogue.

The same invitation must also be extended to Arab audiences, and this includes intentional outreach and collaboration. Silk Road Rising's Arab audience continues to grow. Hailing primarily from Egypt, Syria, Palestine, Lebanon, Jordan, and Iraq, it includes immigrants as well as those born in the United States. It's comprised of Muslims, Christians, and Druze; religionists and secularists; progressives and conservatives; nationalists and pluralists. Most identify as Arab American, or by their country of origin (oftentimes both). In my case, I identify as a mixed blood Arab American of Arab (Syrian) and Slavic (Polish and Slovak) heritage.

In terms of long-standing struggles, Arab Americans pay widely divergent levels of attention to Israel/Palestine, and their relationships to Arabness and the Arab world vary endlessly. Quite understandably, many Arab Americans concern themselves more with U.S. politics than with anything related to the Arab world. Degrees of political consciousness notwithstanding, cultivating and expanding our Jewish and Arab audiences has been a high priority since our company's founding. Facilitating deeper engagement and greater interchange within and between communities is vital to our mission. Make no mistake, all Semites have a home at Silk Road Rising!

As a collection of plays, this anthology bears witness to the belief that storytelling serves as a pedagogical tool, an "alternative" idea platform, an instrument for social and political change. An emotionally compelling, well-crafted play can reach us viscerally, intellectually, and spiritually. These are qualities essential to those seeking to study the world in an integrative manner. Weaving together strands of theatre, literature, history, cultural studies, sociology, political science, international relations, religion, and geography, this collection is ideal for artistic directors, theatre producers, literary managers, dramaturgs, scholars, theatre departments, clergy, activists, as well as anyone interested in learning more about Palestine/Israel.

Most of all, this project provides a fresh perspective on a decades-long conflict that is all-too-often defined in modern times by animosity and antagonism. Representation may follow reality, but often the inverse is just as true: perhaps when we recognize that stories can unbind what ideology restrains, we will inch that much closer to our hoped-for Semitic Commonwealth.

Chipping Away at Ignorance • Corey Pond

I grew up in a small, Christian town in the Midwest. Before college, I had never met a Jew, an Arab, or a Muslim. In fact, there was only one non-Christian family in my hometown, and they were Hindu. I had no conception of Palestinians, or a land called Palestine, or a community of indigenous Christians still living there. Israel, on the other hand, I had learned about.

As a child I knew five things about Israel: (1) it's the promised land; (2) Moses led his people there; (3) King David ruled it; (4) Jesus, a descendant of King David, was born there; and (5) Jews live there now. Those five reference points span more than 3,500 years, from Old Testament, to New Testament, to modern day. My small-town, public-school education offered no counterpoints, and so my mind just assumed that only Jews have lived there all along.

I may have been ignorant, but I was at least aware of my ignorance. I'm sure somewhere along the way I heard mention of Palestine, but it was certainly not taught in school. I had heard murmurs of some "eternal" conflict in Jerusalem between Jews and Muslims over the Temple Mount. I knew there was a lot of this history that I was not taught. With every play I read for this project, those gaps closed a little.

I like to think that my ignorance was an asset throughout the curation process. My co-curators, Michael Malek Najjar and Jamil Khoury, brought lived experiences and years of research to the process. I saw myself as a sort of stand-in for the everyman. So while I was first and foremost reading for a good play with characters and plots that excited me, I was also looking to have my knowledge expanded and complicated. And hopefully our audiences have a similar experience.

Scenes from 70* Years and *The Zionists* provide an overview of the last century. They trace systemic dehumanization across decades and trauma across generations. *The Admission* and *Tennis in Nablus* choose specific moments in the past and examine co-existence, occupation, colonization, and who gets to write history. *Urge for Going* delves into a displaced Palestinian family in contemporary times, caught between a desire to return to Palestine and an inability to move forward. And finally, *The Victims* abstracts the conflict to inspect victim narratives and a corresponding lack of empathy.

Throughout the six plays, audiences encounter very human stories about people and conflicts transpiring in Palestine and Israel. These six playwrights lend their voices to varied perspectives on multiple sides and create more than fifty characters who live in these pages. Amid those fifty, audiences inevitably find at least one character who affirms their beliefs and opinions. But what excites me most is those roughly forty-nine characters who challenge preconceptions we all have.

If the feedback we received from the staged reading series is any indicator, this anthology will provoke and inspire. In addition to talkbacks after every performance (most of which included the playwright, either virtually or physically), audiences were emailed post-show surveys so they could also submit anonymous written feedback. It quickly became clear that the pieces were striking a chord, both in opposition ("Please have something to say the next time you make someone sit through two hours of stories that bring the basic understanding that most audience members already have.") and in favor ("It was refreshing to see the Israel-Palestine conflict reflected in theatre. Usually our only exposure to anything related to this region is in bloody news, so this was eye-opening.").

While I still remain surprised that anyone could find one of these plays to be "basic," I am comforted by the overwhelmingly positive remainder of the feedback. One audience member commented, "The series gave me new perspectives about the lives of Palestinians and Israelis. I learned more about the history of the conflict and how complex the conflict is." Another response read, "It was a privilege to attend this series. Thank you and nicely done! Having the playwrights in the talkbacks was a great part of the experience." One particular response seems to best summarize audience experience attending the readings:

"Whenever I attend a Silk Road event I feel more hopeful about the power (and the necessity) of art and of ordinary people to break down barriers."

These responses affirmed our belief that this kind of theatre was not only necessary, but also impactful for our audiences. And that is why we have decided to publish our anthology. I hope with this collection that we can all recognize our gaps in knowledge and perhaps unexamined biases and move past them with empathy and greater understanding.

Staging the Semitic Commonwealth • Michael Malek Najjar

Staging *Semitic Commonwealth* was an enormous undertaking, and one that could only be handled by a company like Silk Road Rising, whose mission is to tell stories through primarily Asian American and Middle Eastern American lenses. On their website they state, "In representing communities that intersect and overlap, we advance a polycultural worldview." This desire to tell stories about intersecting and overlapping communities was fully on display when they decided to present three plays by Arab American playwrights and three plays by Israeli Jewish playwrights that focused solely on one of the greatest political crises that has faced the world over the past seven decades: the Israeli–Palestinian conflict. Let's be clear—this conflict is considered the "third rail" of American theatre and politics. Many theatre companies that have attempted to stage plays about Israel and Palestine have been censored, shut down, de-funded, and heavily criticized for daring to dramatize the complexity of this situation or the overwhelming struggles those living the conflict face on a day-to-day basis.

The six plays chosen for *Semitic Commonwealth* provide a wide range of historical circumstances, diverse opinions, and difficult questions that must be grappled with if there is ever to be a lasting peace. The playwrights who have committed themselves to this kind of artistic work have often faced personal and professional consequences for doing so. Motti Lerner, who by most accounts is one of the most prolific and accomplished Israeli playwrights in that country's history, states that he often feels like an exile in his own land for daring to question and/or contradict the unequivocal pro–Israeli perspective or to tell humanistic stories about Palestinians.[1] His play *The Admission* was downgraded from a full production to a workshop run in 2014 at Theater J in Washington, D.C., when donors threatened to withhold their money until the play was withdrawn.[2] To date, only a few theatres have been brave enough to stage some of these works. Alliance Theatre staged Ismail Khalidi's *Tennis in Nablus* in 2010 and London's Arcola Theatre staged Hannah Khalil's *Scenes from 68* Years* (as it was called in 2016). At a time when plays like these can shed tremendous light on the human toll taken by this ongoing conflict, it seems that most theatres find such plays too much of a commercial risk to present on their stages.

Silk Road Rising has produced many plays in a manner they call "enhanced staged readings." Most theatre companies typically provide four to eight hours of rehearsal for a staged reading which means that there is little that can be done outside of reading through the play with actors, working certain key moments, and having actors stand behind music stands with scripts to recite the play before an audience. By contrast, Silk Road Rising has committed much more money, time, and effort to their staged readings by allotting each director twenty hours of rehearsal per play. This allows for more possibilities such as the addition of stage blocking, a deeper exploration of the scenes with the actors, and the introduction of other performance elements such as sound, props, and lighting. This extraordinary effort has led to plays receiving much more time, care, and attention than they otherwise would have. In addition, there were in-person and Skype interviews with the playwrights after each staging, audience talk-back discussions, a full website devoted to the reading series, and now this anthology of the plays and essays.

As lead director of *Semitic Commonwealth*, and charged to direct three of the six plays myself, I thought back to all the ethical dilemmas I've faced as a director when challenged to stage verbal and physical conflict. Staging plays that deal with life and death circumstances like war, holocausts, and occupations present great challenges. How can one possibly put into artistic terms such a long and violent history that marks not only the Palestinian-Israeli conflict, but also the antecedents to that conflict which include the horror of the European Holocaust, the occupation of Palestine by Ottomans and British, and the daily lives of Israelis and Palestinians living under difficult circumstances? What is abundantly clear when examining the past half century is the fact that this conflict did not begin in 1948; plays like Ismail Khalidi's *Tennis in Nablus* and Zohar Tirosh-Polk's *The Zionists* clearly illustrate that both peoples came to this historical moment with decades, if not centuries, of trauma imposed by outsiders that dehumanized and brutalized them. In his essay titled "Directing the Holocaust Play," Professor Robert Skloot writes,

> The argument that artistic representation of the Holocaust experience must necessarily trivialize and falsify the "truth" which those events carry has produced one very important if unintended result: it has tended to underscore the need to approach the subject with an inordinate amount of seriousness and care.[3]

In her analysis of Palestinian theatre performed under occupation, professor Susan Slyomovics writes,

> In each performance, especially since the beginning of the intifada, the act of creating theatre is understood by author and audience as a political act entailing complex analyses of a seemingly hopeless situation. Palestinian theatre is not merely a means of politically educating audiences or a way to present a range of aesthetic approaches to the stage that reflect life under Israeli occupation [...] For the Palestinian spectator who is also a participant in the performance of Palestinian self-expression, all performative gestures, though they appear futile and self-destructive, are part of the unfolding fabric of a collective destiny.[4]

Seriousness, care, political acts, self-expression ... these are some of the hallmarks of directing plays by, and about, people who are living under the cruelest of human circumstances. The director of these plays must strive to connect to their deepest humanity, even for characters who may have committed the most unspeakable acts. In "Playwriting as Resistance to War," Motti Lerner says,

> What do I expect from the production of the play? I'm not naïve. I know that it will change neither the fate of the Middle East nor the results of the next elections in Israel. It's very difficult to change people by plays in the theatre. We must be aware of that. But nonetheless, we mustn't lose hope. Books and plays and films do create change. Sometimes the change is very small. Sometimes the change is hidden. Sometimes the change is so deep that we can't see its traces on the surface. But even if this change is very minor, even if it's hidden, it's worth attempting.[5]

Looking back now, staging these six plays was very much worth attempting because it allowed us to see those who are embroiled in this conflict not as terrorists, religious zealots, or hate-mongering radicals but rather as human beings struggling with complicated histories, emotions, desires, and hopes. Although it was challenging to direct these plays because of the overwhelming gravity of their subjects, it was also a privilege to see audiences stay through the plays, focus intently on the words and actions, and have such emotional reactions afterwards. Instead of shouting, stomping out in rage, or boycotting the plays, we witnessed audiences stay afterwards and share their deep and moving stories about their own experiences with this situation and how painful it was for them to see this conflict portrayed on stage and to feel so very helpless to change anything. Given the evanescent nature of theatre, it's unfortunate that we, as artists, cannot find these audience members again and ask them all how they feel now that so much time has passed. Based on what we heard from audiences I must believe that, for many, the performances left a deep and resonant impact.

In retrospect I realize what a tremendous opportunity it was to spend time with such a fiercely committed and talented group of artists working on plays by devoted and thoughtful playwrights about a subject that needs more attention now than ever. In that one month we held our own peace process, taking the time to think deeply about this long and painful conflict that has taken and damaged so many lives. Silk Road Rising's commitment to staging these plays is a testament to their ongoing engagement with theatre that matters despite facing critics that attempt to silence them, audiences that sometimes boycott them, or organizations that refuse to fund them. With the publication of this anthology, our sincere hope is that these plays will continue to be produced widely at college, community, semi-professional and professional theatres nationwide, and that audiences everywhere can have the opportunity to encounter these amazing plays in the theatre while contemplating a better, and more peaceful, future. Salaam. Shalom. May peace prevail.

A Note About the Editing of the Plays

The plays that follow are written by six playwrights with distinct voices and styles. In an effort to honor that, we the editors have opted to make minimal changes to the formatting and punctuation choices of the individual playwrights rather than to enforce a universal style sheet. We have set a standard for stage directions being italicized and character names being bold and in all caps prior to lines of dialogue, but in terms of the rest of the formatting (line breaks, punctuation, use of languages other than English, etc.), we have done our best to remain true to the voice of each playwright.

THE ADMISSION:
A PLAY IN FOURTEEN SCENES

Motti Lerner

Translation from the Hebrew by Johanna Gruenhut,
Ari Roth and Motti Lerner

All dramatic rights in this play are fully protected by copyright and no public or private performance—professional or amateur—and no public readings for profit may be given without the written permission of the author and the payment of royalty. Communications should be addressed to the Author's representative: Susan Schulman A Literary Agency, 454 West 44th St. New York, New York 10036; tel: 212 713-1633; email: susan@schulmanagency.com

About the Playwright

Motti Lerner is a playwright and screenwriter who writes mostly about political issues. His plays include: *Kastner, Pangs of the Messiah, Pollard, Exile in Jerusalem, Passing The Love of Women, Autumn, Hard Love, The Hastening of The End*. His U.S. productions include: *The Murder of Isaac* (Baltimore Centerstage) *Pangs of the Messiah* (Theater J, Silk Road Rising, and other), *Benedictus* (Golden Thread, Theater J), *Paulus* (Silk Road Rising), *The Admission* (Theater J), *Hard Love* (TACT, NY), and *After The War* (Mosaic Theater). He wrote the screenplays for the films *Loves in Betania, The Kastner Trial, Bus Number 300, Egoz, The Institute, A Battle in Jerusalem, The Silence of the Sirens, Altalena, Spring 1941* and *Kapo in Jerusalem*. He won the best play award (1985), the Israeli Motion Picture Academy award (1995, 2004), and the Prime Minister of Israel Award for Writers (1994). He is the author of the books *According to Chekhov* and *The Playwright's Purpose*. He taught playwriting at Tel Aviv University, Duke University, Knox College and was a fellow at the Institute of Advanced Studies at Jawaharlal Nehru University, New Delhi.

— Essay —
Motti Lerner's *The Admission*: Accounting and Atoning for the Past

MICHAEL MALEK NAJJAR

Motti Lerner's searing drama *The Admission* is the attempt by a playwright of conscience to both account and atone for the past. The occupation and evacuation of Palestinian villages in 1948 has been well documented with over 400 villages depopulated during the process.[1] For some, these expulsions were the aftermath of violent battles between Arab factions and the Haganah[2] forces that began fighting one another shortly after the United Nations announced partition on November 29, 1947. Others believe Palestinians either left of their own volition or sold their lands to Jews. Still others believe this was a premeditated, Zionist strategy to rid the land of Palestinians. Regardless of these competing claims, the fact remains that during the 1948 War, up to 10,000 Palestinians and over 6,000 Israelis were killed, 80 percent of Palestinians became refugees, and the bulk of these lands comprised the new Israeli state.[3]

Lerner's play attempts to address one of the most contentious issues regarding the 1948 War of Independence: did Haganah and Irgun soldiers commit atrocities when overtaking Palestinian villages? Lerner, who was born in the village of Zichron Ya'acov, near the historic village of Tantura, remembers growing up hearing stories about a massacre of Arabs that happened there during the 1948 War. He says he changed the name of the village in the play to Tantur because the play is fictitious, and he did not want to blur the line between history and fiction.[4] The play revolves around the contested history of the Alexandroni Brigade that, during the Battle of Tantura on May 23, 1948, was accused of massacring 250 Palestinians. A scholar, Teddy Katz, wrote a Masters of Arts thesis about this event claiming the massacre occurred; however, after Alexandroni veterans sued him for libel and, through pressure from family and friends, Katz signed a statement declaring there was no massacre. Lerner read Katz's thesis and, based on stories he himself had heard and the thesis itself, he concluded that there are many narratives that differ from one another. His solution to untangle these narratives was to write a play.

> As I said earlier, we, theater artists, cannot bring about a solution for the Israeli–Palestinian conflict. Our challenge is to create a public discourse that will lead to achieving it. How do we do it if the public discourse is so superficial and if our spectators are so deeply prejudiced, so deeply defensive, so deeply resistant to even hearing the narrative of the Palestinians? In other words, how do we transform our stubborn theater-goers into open-minded spectators who are capable of listening to the narrative of the "other"?[5]

Like other playwrights of conscience before him (such as Ibsen, Miller, Soyinka and Fugard), Lerner is attempting to dramatize historical events not for the purposes of historical accuracy, but rather to illuminate these events in a way that personalizes them, opening them up for reflection by contemporary audiences. This extraordinarily prescient play forces us to look back into the horrors of the past so we may, perhaps, turn to see the future more clearly.

— Playwright Statement —
Facing the Trauma of 1948

The Admission was inspired by the Israeli Defense Forces' May 23, 1948, occupation of the Palestinian village of Tantura during Israel's War of Independence, and by the controversy between several Israeli historians[6] who propose that, during the assault on the village and subsequent expulsion of its inhabitants, soldiers perpetrated a massacre on unarmed villagers. The play, however, is not a documentary. All characters and events are a fiction of the playwright's imagination. The play doesn't attempt to determine the historical validity of any one narrative of the Tantura occupation, nor does it present unequivocal facts with regard to what took place during the battle.

Set in Haifa in 1988, *The Admission* centers around two families, one Jewish, one Palestinian. Through their story we explore the suppression of the village's occupation—a process that took place in both Jewish and Arab societies. We also examine the circumstances that led to the resurgence of this suppressed trauma in our consciousness 40 years later. This examination stems from the belief that coming to terms with the events of 1948 is imperative for all involved. Otherwise, the rectification so crucial to our continued existence will not be carried out on either the political, personal, or social level, and we will be unable to recover from the collective trauma we've undergone.

The Admission was written in the hopes that it might encourage more fair, open, and empathic discourse among us, and that it would generate honest, unifying, constructive dialogue between the different sects of Israeli society. Such dialogue about this shared trauma would accelerate the process of appeasement with the Palestinian people living with us and next to us. I hope that this dialogue promotes, even in a small way, the founding of a joint society in Israel whose sects live side by side, in mutual recognition and acceptance.

While writing was completed as early as 2006, all plans to produce *The Admission* were ultimately aborted in spite of the interest expressed by several theatres in Israel. These repeated cancellations likely had to do not only with the theatre managers' fear of potential sanctions by the Ministry of Culture, but their concerns over an enraged public's reaction to this "deviation" from consensus in showing the forbidden story of the 1948 war.

The Admission at last premiered in spring 2014 under the direction of Sinai Peter at Washington, D.C.'s Theater J. Following rave reviews, one of the largest theatres in Israel made plans to produce it in the 2015–16 season. But then, on March 17, 2015, the election of the Knesset took place—a new government was formed, a new minister of culture was nominated, and the production was canceled. However, in early 2016, the Jaffa Theater in Tel Aviv decided to produce the play (again with Sinai Peter directing) which premiered in September 2016 and has since been playing regularly and with great success, evoking intense public debates between Jews and Arabs striving to create a joint society in Israel.

— PLAYSCRIPT —
The Admission

THE TIME
The play takes place in the spring of 1988 in different places in Haifa. The prologue and the epilogue take place on a hill facing the Arab village of Tantur that was destroyed in 1948.

CHARACTERS
AVIGDOR—Colonel in the Israeli army during the 1948 War of Independence. In 1988 he is the owner of a big construction company (64).

YONA—his wife (60).

GIORA—Their son, lecturer at the University of Haifa. He was wounded in the Lebanon war of 1982. Both his legs are lame. He uses crutches (35).

NETA—His girlfriend, an architect (29).

IBRAHIM—A refugee from the Arab village of Tantur (58).

AZMI—His son, owner of a restaurant (35).

SAMYA—His daughter, lecturer at the University of Haifa (30).

THE STYLE
The play takes place in Giora's mind as he's lying on a hill facing Tantur, watching the bulldozers plowing in the *wadi*. This allows for the breaking of realism and the introduction of characters able to watch scenes in which they do not participate.

THE SET
The set is abstract and minimal to allow for quick changes of locations and to suggest that the events are taking place in Giora's mind.

PROLOGUE

A hill in the depth of the stage. Clouds of dust drift above. The sound of bulldozers plowing down the other side of the hill is heard aloud. Giora enters on crutches, trying to climb the hill; he falls and rises, falls again and now can't get up. Lights out on the hill. The sound of the bulldozer fades out.

SCENE ONE

An Arab restaurant in downtown Haifa. Afternoon. Giora stands in the doorway, leaning on his crutches. Azmi wears a suit, holding a mop and cleaning the floor, careful not to wet his shoes. Ibrahim, his father, is in the kitchen, unseen.

GIORA. Why are you never satisfied? This is the nicest restaurant in all of Haifa now. Look how much light comes in through the windows. You put in air-conditioning; new tables. I see you've changed the tiles too.

AZMI. How am I ever going to repay the loan to your father? In the past month, I've had one customer a day, and he orders hummus to go. That's not even half the salary of a cleaning-lady from Jenin.

GIORA. He won't say a thing. Even if it takes you two years to pay him back. Give me the broom. By the time he comes, everything will be clean.

AZMI. One more word, Giora, and I'm gonna dump this bucket on your head. *(Angrily)* This morning I asked Khaula to help me out a few minutes. Not for clients. For you. And she opened her big mouth: "I didn't marry you to be your maid." Her father's a lawyer. Not a cook like her husband. I washed floors in stinking restaurants when I was ten. But soon she'll see where tears come from. Tonight she's cleaning the bathrooms.

GIORA. You don't have to fight with her because of us. *(Takes a broom)* My father's never been bothered by a little dirt.

AZMI. *(Grabbing the broom from Giora)* Sweep in your own house. *(Notices the smell from the kitchen)* He's in there cooking for two hundred. Yesterday I trashed ten kilos of lamb. It smelled so bad, even the zoo wouldn't take it. The entire *Intifada*[7] is on our heads. What do they want from us? Did someone hang a flag here? Someone throw a stone? People whose weddings I catered hide from me on the street.

GIORA. Don't worry. I'll speak to him about the loan today.

AZMI. Don't tell him "two years." Tell him I'll start the payments as soon as this mess is over. In installments. *(He bumps into the bucket and the water spills)* Yil'an din'hu this bucket. *(To the kitchen)* Where's the rag, *yabba*? *(To Giora)* Now my shoes are fucked. *(To the kitchen)* Where's the goddamned rag?

Samya enters, dressed in an elegant suit. She finds the rag in the entrance.

SAMYA. Here it is.

AZMI. Glad you're here. This morning dad burned a pot of rice and broke four plates. Go help him with the fish. He's already cut two fingers.

SAMYA. *(To Giora)* Are you heading back to the university later? We have to talk.

GIORA. Something happen?

AZMI. *Ya'allah*, Samya, go already!

Samya turns to the kitchen. Giora uses the broom to push the water to the exit. Avigdor enters. Samya stops. Azmi grabs the broom from Giora.

AZMI. Hello, Mr. Avigdor. Welcome. How are you?

AVIGDOR. *(looking around)* How beautiful. Congratulations. *Mabruk*. *(Shakes Azmi's hand)* I see you've opened up especially for us.

AZMI. Today is the Grand Re-Opening. I've turned everyone else away. *T'fadal*. Sit. *(Cleans a chair and offers it to him)* I don't have busboys today. They were stopped on the way.

AVIGDOR. *(To Giora)* And I see that besides your position at the university you now have a part-time job cleaning floors. *(To Samya)* Hello, Samya.

SAMYA. Hello. I received your letter about the grant yesterday. Thank you very much.

AVIGDOR. You deserve it. *(Shaking her hand)* All the best.
AZMI. I'm bringing you something to start with. *(Pointing at the kitchen)* Dad's not feeling well. He's been talking to himself since early this morning. If he says anything strange, don't pay attention. *(To Samya)* Why are you still standing here?
Azmi and Samya exit to the kitchen. Avigdor lights a cigar.
AVIGDOR. How was it?
GIORA. Beautiful development. The houses already have electricity. Tenants are putting flowers in their gardens. Kids are walking to school. We could build two more blocks to the south. In another few years, it'll be a city.
AVIGDOR. You'll build it. I've built enough, Giora.
GIORA. Next week I'll tell the dean I'm stepping down.
AVIGDOR. Say it tomorrow at the management meeting. By the way, I cleared out the office next to Neta's for you.
GIORA. That's what she wanted? Did she say it?
AVIGDOR. She doesn't need to say anything. Every morning she walks into my office and what she wants is written all over her face.
GIORA. What does she want?
AVIGDOR. That you get married. That you start working with us. And that in April, we'll have a *bris*.[8]
GIORA. *(Laughs)* No doubt you've already gotten him a job in the company, too.
AVIGDOR. Of course. The management will approve it tomorrow.
Ibrahim, Azmi, and Samya, enter from the kitchen carrying platters and plates of appetizers, salads, drinks, etc.
IBRAHIM. *Salam aleykum.* How are you? *A'halan u'sahalan, Abu* Giora. This is just to wake the appetite. The first olives of the season. We opened the jars just this morning.
AVIGDOR. *Allah y'a'tik el a'afi,* Ibrahim. *Shukran.*
IBRAHIM. And don't be angry about the salad. Because of the curfew in Gaza, there are no cucumbers in the market, no radishes, no lettuce.
AZMI. Even the fish are under curfew.
GIORA. It's okay, Ibrahim.
IBRAHIM. And the tomatoes are from my garden.
AVIGDOR. I see you've already collected *za'atar*.[9]
IBRAHIM. Of course. After the rains, it tastes the strongest.
GIORA. Thank you.
IBRAHIM. It's all thanks to you, *Abu* Giora. For the help you've given us. With the renovations, the permits. And also for Samya.
AVIGDOR. *Mabruk,* Ibrahim.
AZMI. From now on, you're our guests. On the house. Whatever you want, as much as you want. Everything. The salads, the meat, the wine.
AVIGDOR. Out of the question, Azmi.
AZMI. This is my restaurant, Mister, and here *I* decide! *(Pours wine) L'chaim!*
ALL. *L'chaim!*
Everyone drinks.
IBRAHIM. About the *za'atar*, Mr. Avigdor. Yesterday I go to Tantur to collect some, and out of the blue I see people. I ask: "*shu hada,* who are you?" and they said they work for you. Surveyors. That you're going to dig there.
AVIGDOR. We're building there, Ibrahim.

IBRAHIM. What for? What's there to build for?

AVIGDOR. People need homes.

IBRAHIM. In Tantur?

AZMI. We're eating now, dad. Go put the fish on the grill.

SAMYA. I'll do it.

AZMI. He'll do it. *(To Avigdor)* Today we have grilled eggplant. Cooked mushrooms. Shrimps. Calamari. All fresh from this morning.

GIORA. *(to Avigdor)* Did you arrive thirsty, dad?

AVIGDOR. If you're not drinking, I'll finish the bottle myself.

IBRAHIM. *(Pouring wine to Giora)* About Tantur, *Abu* Giora. Why are you building there all of a sudden?

AVIGDOR. It's a small country, Ibrahim. People build everywhere.

IBRAHIM. I'm from Tantur, *Abu* Giora. I was born there.

AZMI. Enough, dad.

AVIGDOR. What are you saying? From Tantur? When I was a kid, I used to go down there with friends, with canteens and knapsacks, we would drink from the spring and rest under the fig trees.

IBRAHIM. But why *dig* there? It's forbidden.

AZMI. *Cha'las.* We've already heard this story. Go put the fish on the grill.

Lights up on Avigdor and Yona's house. Yona stands watching the restaurant.

GIORA. *(to Avigdor)* What is he talking about? We don't have the permits?

AVIGDOR. Of course we have them.

IBRAHIM. The earth won't *let* you dig there.

AZMI. We've already heard this, Dad.

SAMYA. Let him speak. They're building on his village.

IBRAHIM. *(Exploding)* It's forbidden to build there! I am saying "forbidden." The stones are screaming "forbidden." The skies are crying "forbidden." And you are not listening.

GIORA. We've been talking about it for five years already, Ibrahim. It's the neighborhood that will be named after my brother.

IBRAHIM. *(To Samya)* Tell him not to dig there.

AZMI. Let's go to the kitchen, dad.

GIORA. *(To Avigdor)* What's the problem? Why is it "forbidden?"

SAMYA. *(To Ibrahim)* Sit and drink a little water. *(She seats him, and turns to Avigdor)* His house was there. He goes there every week. Maybe you could show him the plans.

Azmi (Sami Ismat, left) holds back Ibrahim (Rom Barkhordar, center) from Avigdor (Steve Silver) in *The Admission* by Motti Lerner, directed by Michael Malek Najjar (photograph by Airan Wright).

AVIGDOR. We'll send them tomorrow morning…
IBRAHIM. *(Standing)* I'll die before he digs there.
AVIGDOR. *(Standing)* I think it's best if we go.
IBRAHIM. *(Barring him)* You will listen until I am finished.
AZMI. Be'chiatak, yabba. Dachil Allah.
GIORA. *(To Samya)* What's going on with him? What does he want?
IBRAHIM. Son of a bitch. Ten years I'm cooking for you. Ten years I'm putting food on your table, and this whole time my heart is bleeding!
Ibrahim grabs a knife from the table and lunges at Avigdor
SAMYA. Drop the knife!
GIORA. Leave him alone!
AZMI. Dad!
Ibrahim stabs Avigdor in the shoulder before Azmi and Samya pull him away. Blackout.

SCENE TWO

Later that afternoon. Avigdor and Yona's house. Avigdor's wound has been sutured and his shoulder bandaged.
AVIGDOR. What do you want from me? You know more than the doctor? He didn't say I need a transfusion.
YONA. *(To Avigdor)* Take a pill. In a few minutes the stitches are going to hurt.
GIORA. You don't think you need an X-Ray?
AVIGDOR. What for?
YONA. Give me your hand.
AVIGDOR. The moment I go there, the hospital will call the police. They'll be stopped, questioned. I have more important things to deal with right now. *(Swallows the pill)* The intifada has made him mad.
GIORA. He stabbed to kill. I saw it in his eyes.
AVIGDOR. Sit, calm down. You'd think it was *you* who got stabbed.
YONA. Maybe he was stopped by the Border Police. Maybe he got searched. Maybe a hot headed soldier killed a relative of his in one of the refugee camps. *(She places his arm in a sling)*
GIORA. Aren't you going to press charges with the police?
AVIGDOR. He's insane. He hallucinates. He hears the ground talking.
YONA. You want their restaurant shut down?
GIORA. I want the police to investigate. I want to understand why he did it. If we don't file a complaint today, the police won't take it seriously. *(Stands)*
YONA. Where are you going?
GIORA. If he doesn't go to the police, I will.
AVIGDOR. You've gone out of your mind?! We have a management meeting tomorrow. We have to go over next year's plans.
GIORA. You're not going to the office tomorrow, Dad.
AVIGDOR. We'll have the meeting here.
GIORA. You lost a lot of blood.
AVIGDOR. I have enough left.
GIORA. You want me to start running the company tomorrow? *(Stands)*
AVIGDOR. Sit.

YONA. Tomorrow we're naming the neighborhood after Udi. We've been talking about it since he fell.

GIORA. We'll name it next week.

He turns to leave. Neta enters. Lights up on Samya's house. Samya is watching the scene in Avigdor's house.

NETA. *(To Avigdor)* It looks like you're still alive. You're even smiling. How are you feeling? *(She hugs him)*

AVIGDOR. Now, excellent.

NETA. I thought I'd find you lying in bed hooked up to an IV.

YONA. He didn't let the doctor do it.

NETA. I hope you're not planning on eating there ever again. *(To Giora)* Too bad he didn't stab *you*. You'd have to stay in bed for a few days, and every morning I'd bring you coffee and cake. *(Kisses him)*

GIORA. We're going, Neta.

YONA. You're not going to the police, Giora. You know how much time you'll spend in investigations? In Court?

NETA. Wait a second. I'm coming with you. *(To Avigdor and Yona)* I was at the Dan Hotel this morning. They have two open dates for a wedding in June, on the ninth and the twentieth. I promised them an answer tomorrow.

YONA. Great.

GIORA. Maybe you and I should talk about it first?

AVIGDOR. We're happy to discuss it, too.

YONA. We'll do whatever they decide, Avigdor.

AVIGDOR. *(To Neta)* Take vacation next week to find a dress.

GIORA. You're talking to her instead of me? Talk. You still have blood on your shirt. *(He turns to leave)*

NETA. Wait a second. We have to decide.

GIORA. We've decided to get married in July.

NETA. You have that conference in Boston in July.

GIORA. Fine. We'll get married on the twentieth of June. You don't want to check with your mom?

NETA. I hope she'll live till then.

AVIGDOR. Leave your mother to me.

GIORA. *(Sees that Neta is hurt)* OK. The ninth is also good.

AVIGDOR. Excellent. Are we settled?

GIORA. We're settled.

AVIGDOR. That's how you settle?

Giora takes the hint, kisses and hugs Neta.

YONA. *Mazal Tov!*

AVIGDOR. Now go home and celebrate. *(To Yona)* We also want to celebrate a little. Right?

NETA. See you later.

GIORA. June 9th isn't too close to Udi's birthday?

YONA. It's perfectly fine.

GIORA. *(To Avigdor)* I'll call later to see how you're doing. You want me to speak to your lawyer tomorrow? You have some friends in the police department.

AVIGDOR. Bye.

Giora and Neta exit. Silence.

YONA. I hope Giora doesn't do anything stupid. We have to watch him. *(He's silent)* Does it hurt? It's best if you rest in bed. Your blood pressure's high. *(He's silent)* Don't you want to delay the groundbreaking a few days? Maybe until they remove the stitches. *(He's silent)* Udi has waited many years for us to build something in his name. He'll wait another week. *(He goes to the bar and takes a glass)* Don't drink. You just took a pill.

Avigdor drinks, puts the glass on the table and turns to the kitchen.

YONA. Where are you going?

AVIGDOR. I haven't eaten since this morning.

YONA. Wait. I'll warm something up. What about the surveyors you sent to the *wadi*? They'll continue?

AVIGDOR. Of course.

Blackout. The sound of bulldozers is heard louder.

SCENE THREE

The next day. Afternoon. Giora's office at Haifa University. Giora and Samya.

SAMYA. He was awake all night. Tossing in bed. Crying. Talking to himself. Only this morning, when he heard your father was alive, could he fall asleep.

GIORA. He's lucky my dad didn't go to the police.

SAMYA. I'm not sure he understands what he did. He can't explain any of it.

GIORA. He joined the Intifada. If that knife would've penetrated another millimeter, my father would be dead.

SAMYA. You know he didn't mean it. *(Giora is quiet)* What should I tell Azmi? He wants to visit your father. He wants to invite you over for a meal.

GIORA. My father's in bed. They're removing the stitches next week.

SAMYA. Good. Come next week. *(Giora isn't too excited. Silence)* I don't think my father joined the Intifada. I think he remembers your dad from the battle of Tantur in '48. You never told me your father had been the commander there.

GIORA. There was nothing to tell. They fought there like in other places. He took us to the monument on the hill once. Fourteen of his soldiers died there.

SAMYA. Dozens of civilians were killed, too.

GIORA. Is that what your father told you? Is that why he suddenly remembered to stab my father with a knife?

SAMYA. I went to the library this morning. *(She shows him a book and a notebook)* This is by a historian from Damascus. This is a dissertation that was done here, in the history department. According to his calculations, there were two hundred twenty dead in Tantur.

GIORA. Are you out of your mind?

SAMYA. Look. These are testimonies from soldiers who took part in the attack.

GIORA. I don't need to look. I know we have too many self-hating historians. How can you believe that my father was involved in anything like that? Do you know many people who've done for you what he has? Even after my brother was killed. Even after I was wounded. This year he built a school in Tamra at cost. He built six schools in Arab villages without any profit over the last decade.

SAMYA. I know.

GIORA. You don't know. Who do you think paid for the ad in yesterday's papers calling for an end to the violence and a start to negotiations?

SAMYA. I know that too.
GIORA. And you believe what's written here?!
SAMYA. I don't believe anything. But my father has always been a rational man. Suddenly he picks up a knife and stabs?
GIORA. He's never talked about it until yesterday?
SAMYA. Until yesterday he told us that they were expelled from Tantur. Yesterday he said his father and two of his brothers were killed there. Their names are in this book.
Lights up on Avigdor's office where Avigdor and Neta watch the rest of the scene.
SAMYA. I'm not accusing your father of anything, Giora. I know how rumors spread among us. But I also know my father.
GIORA. If your father recognized my father ten years ago, why did he wait until yesterday?
SAMYA. He doesn't want them touching the bones buried in the *wadi*. He wants to give them a proper burial and put up a memorial.
GIORA. A memorial for who? If there were bones buried there, someone would have talked about it. Five hundred soldiers have been quiet for forty years?! If you think my father did something like this, return the grant he gave you yesterday for your post-doctorate.
Samya moves to exit. He stops her.
GIORA. Wait a second. You can't run away like this.
SAMYA. I'm *leaving*. You're running away.
GIORA. Until yesterday you thought your grandfather and two uncles were expelled. You never asked where they were? You never tried to see them?
SAMYA. He told me they died in a refugee camp in Tul Karem.
GIORA. And today you believe him when he tells you they were killed in Tantur?
SAMYA. Today I don't know anything anymore.
GIORA. I've asked you about them several times, and you've always said they were expelled.
SAMYA. When did you ask?
GIORA. In the hotel in London. You shut yourself in the bathroom and locked the door. I begged you to tell me.
SAMYA. I seem to remember you begged for something entirely different.
GIORA. I don't think I had to beg.
Memories of London wash over them. He takes her hands. They embrace. Lights up on Yona in her house. She watches Giora and Samya. Giora wants to go further than Samya is prepared to go. She stops him.
SAMYA. You know why your father gave me the grant for the post doc?
GIORA. Because he believes in you.
SAMYA. Because I have to do it in London.
GIORA. What does that have to do with anything?
SAMYA. He wants to separate us.
GIORA. He knows that we're not seeing each other anymore.
SAMYA. That's what I wanted to tell you yesterday. He thinks you haven't married yet because of me. *(He is silent)* Are you getting married? *(He is silent)* You see me every day in the department and you don't tell me?
GIORA. You're right. It was very difficult for me to tell you.
SAMYA. You don't owe me anything. You can marry whoever you want.

GIORA. What happened in the restaurant is just the tip of the iceberg, Samya. Since the *intifada*, we hardly speak. You protest at demonstrations I can't attend, and you say things there I can't agree to.
SAMYA. You can't agree to ending the occupation?!
GIORA. Not with this kind of violence.
SAMYA. You know I'm against violence. You also know what price I've had to pay because of it. *(Pause)*. I guess I was too naïve. I hoped that I'd be living in London next year and one night I'd hear a knock on the door...
GIORA. And afterwards we'd come back here and keep on meeting in hotel rooms? *(Takes her hand)* I couldn't keep waiting for you.
SAMYA. Don't touch me.
Samya exits. In her haste she leaves the book and notebook on the table. Blackout.

SCENE FOUR

Evening. Avigdor and Yona's house. Avigdor and Neta enter. Avigdor goes to the sofa. Yona notices he's not well.
YONA. Where were you?
AVIGDOR. I'm just a bit dizzy.
YONA. I asked you not to leave the house.
AVIGDOR. It'll pass.
YONA. You want me to call the doctor?
AVIGDOR. I'm absolutely fine. It's because of the stairs. *(To Neta)* Tell her.
YONA. Drink. *(Serves him)*
NETA. *(To Yona)* We got the hotel.
AVIGDOR. Tell her the deal.
NETA. They're giving us the garden and the pool too. We were about to decide on the menu. Suddenly the wound started to hurt.
AVIGDOR. When I asked them about the garden and pool, the manager turned his back on me. But when *she* asked, he melted.
NETA. Because you offered to pay more.
AVIGDOR. Because of your smile.
NETA. *(To Yona)* When he wants something, he doesn't take no for an answer. *(To Avigdor)* I think you ought to stay home tomorrow.
AVIGDOR. I'll think about it.
YONA. I'll ask the doctor to hospitalize you!
AVIGDOR. Fine. I'll stay home.
YONA. This is for you, Neta. Congratulations.
She hands Neta a small box. Neta opens it and reveals a pair of earrings.
NETA. Diamonds!!
YONA. Put them on.
NETA. You didn't have to.
YONA. Who am I going to buy earrings for? Giora?
AVIGDOR. I'll put them on for you. *(He gets up)*
YONA. Sit.
Avigdor succeeds in putting the earrings on Neta.
AVIGDOR. *(To Yona)* I'm sitting.
NETA. *(Hugging them)* Thank you.

YONA. I called Giora this morning. He didn't answer.

NETA. His back was bothering him. Probably because of what happened in the restaurant. But he did his exercises, and left for the university. I hope we don't hear about this affair anymore.

YONA. I went to his orthopedist without him this morning. He has surgery next month.

NETA. He'll do it.

AVIGDOR. And remind him he has to send his letter of resignation to the university. I want to bring his appointment up with our board next week. *And* your promotion too. *Giora enters. Lights up on Ibrahim and Samya's house. Samya watches the scene in Avigdor's house.*

AVIGDOR. Congratulations!

GIORA. What happened?

NETA. We confirmed with the hotel.

GIORA. Nice.

AVIGDOR. That's all you have to say?

GIORA. I'm very happy.

AVIGDOR. Tell me, Yona'leh, who does he resemble? In my family, we knew how to celebrate!

GIORA. *(To Neta)* You got earrings. Very nice.

YONA. They're giving us the garden and the pool too.

NETA. *(To Giora)* I'll tell you on the way there. We still have to finalize the menu.

GIORA. *(To Avigdor)* How are you feeling? Still in pain?

AVIGDOR. Oh, a lot. I may die tomorrow.

YONA. Ha. Ha. Ha.

GIORA. I need to talk to you, Dad. I went to the library today. I found a dissertation that was written in our history department about Tantur.

YONA. I thought we put that affair behind us, Giora.

GIORA. There are some strange things in it. *(To Avigdor)* Look. *(Showing him the notebook)* He claims that more than two hundred people were killed. *(To Neta)* I almost lost it.

YONA. You did lose it.

NETA. You're sure you found that in the library?

GIORA. Yes. *(To Avigdor)* Read.

AVIGDOR. I know this "historian." Two years ago I took him to the village.

YONA. Daddy doesn't feel well, Guri. Don't bother him. *(Places the notebook on the table)* I saw that house down the street. They're prepared to sell.

AVIGDOR. He's not bothering me. *(To Giora)* Even then I saw that he doesn't let facts confuse him. The village blocked the main road. They attacked cars. Buses. Ambulances. We had no choice. At four in the morning, we attacked. The first company from the *wadi*. The second from the road. The third stormed down from the hill. Fourteen of our men were killed. They lost twenty.

YONA. Everything clear now? *(Continuing)* I want you to see this house. It's like new. No stairs. You can drive your car all the way up to the doorway.

AVIGDOR. At ten they surrendered. They knew that most of the Arabs in Haifa had run away. And rumors of the massacre at Deir Yassin[10] had already reached them. The *mukhtar*[11] requested they be sent to Tul Karem. At four they got on trucks. At six we returned to base and buried our dead.

YONA. *(Firm)* I think it's best you go lie down, Avigdor, before your blood pressure goes up.
GIORA. *(taking the notebook)* There are two hundred and twenty names in here, dad.
AVIGDOR. Are you sure there's a person for every name?
NETA. The manager of the hotel is waiting for us, Giora. We have a wedding in two months. There are a few things we need to do, besides standing under the *chuppa*.[12] See you later.
GIORA. And you counted only twenty?
YONA. We counted exactly twenty!
NETA. I don't understand why you're picking at this.
GIORA. It's outrageous that our university would print lies like these. *(To Avigdor)* Let's get testimonies from your officers and soldiers. *(To Yona)* From you, too. *(To Avigdor)* In a few months we'll publish a book to disprove all this.
YONA. Nothing happened that is worth writing about.
AVIGDOR. *(Laughing)* Now we're going to start writing books?! We have a management meeting next week. We need to be prepared.
GIORA. Everyone who reads this, Dad, will believe that these are the facts.
YONA. Who's reading it? Who will read it?
AVIGDOR. If this bastard had bothered to investigate, he'd have found these "dead" living in refugee camps in Jordan.
YONA. Why are you telling him all this? You want him to go find them?
AVIGDOR. Better he knows what went on there. How we fought. How we survived. How we earned our lives here. *(To Giora)* And then maybe you'll understand that after wars like these we have to gather all our strength to restore ourselves, to build homes, start families, have children. This wound is worse than I thought. I almost fainted in the car today.
YONA. After all you've been through, Guri, you can't waste your life on such nonsense.
GIORA. I'm wasting my life on nonsense?! Ever since I woke up in that hospital I've been trying to live it. *(To Avigdor)* And if I sit silent while you're being accused of such terrible things, it means I condone them.
Blackout.

SCENE FIVE

Same night. Ibrahim and Samya's house. Ibrahim, Samya, and Azmi enter after closing up the restaurant.
AZMI. You stood in front of him and told him that his father's a murderer?!
SAMYA. I told him what I know.
AZMI. For what? When I go there tomorrow to apologize, they won't even open the door for me. He's a murderer?! We almost murdered *him*. It's only because he has such a big heart we're not in jail.
IBRAHIM. I recognized him ten years ago, the moment he came into the restaurant.
AZMI. You recognized him and gave him food?
IBRAHIM. What could I do? Go to the police? To the court?
AZMI. Why didn't you tell us?
SAMYA. What difference does it make? If he thinks it's him, we have to check.
AZMI. For what? Don't we have enough to deal with because of the *intifada*? The policemen who see you at those demonstrations come to complain to me. When you begin looking into Tantur, I'll have to shut down the restaurant.

SAMYA. Don't be a coward, Azmi.

AZMI. You're right. I'm a coward. But because "I'm a coward" you never went hungry; not a single day in your life. Because "I'm a coward" you always got new clothes for school and a knapsack filled with books, and in it every day there was a pita with an omelet. Because "I'm a coward" you studied ten years at the university like a princess. Your brave brothers who ran away to America never once sent you a measly dollar for underwear. So don't look down on me and my fears.

SAMYA. No one is looking down on you, except you. You deserve to know who murdered your family.

AZMI. You're sure they murdered them?

IBRAHIM. Sure they murdered them, *Ibn El Kalb*.

AZMI. Who saw them being murdered, *yabba*? They ran away.

SAMYA. *(Scornfully)* One day they just got up and ran away?

AZMI. Like they did in Haifa. In *Yaffa. Akko. Tabariyyah. Safad.*

SAMYA. Gave up their sheep, their goats, their fields, their stores, their homes? They probably just got tired of living here.

Silence. Ibrahim is hurt. Lights up on Giora and Neta's apartment.

SAMYA. Come, I'll take you to bed, Dad.

IBRAHIM. *(To Azmi)* I'll tell you who saw them being murdered. Me. With these eyes. Who could I tell? For two days I hid there between broken buildings, in the ruins. Then I ran here. And here more soldiers in the streets. They shot at everyone returning. Anyone who wanted to take something from their home. All day long I hid under the floor of a store in the vegetable market. At night I'd go through garbage. You have no idea, that kind of fear. You have no idea, to have no one. No one in the entire world. That you're nothing. That if someone points at you on the street, you'll be shot. *(Angrily)* You want to know why I never told you? I didn't want you to live with such fear. So now let him be afraid. He deserved that knife. In his heart.

Ibrahim almost falls over, but rejects Samya's help and exit.

SAMYA. You can go. He'll be okay. *(Azmi is silent)* I'm leaving at the end of the semester. You're going to have to look after him yourself. Talk to Khaula. You might have to take him in.

AZMI. *That* bitch?

SAMYA. What happened? She threw you out of the house?

AZMI. I asked the kids to help me after school, and she started screaming. I should have thrown her out and taken the kids to America. Without Arabs, without Jews. Without their wars. *(Pause)* I don't understand why you're going all of a sudden. What are you running from? The *intifada*?

SAMYA. I'm not running from anything. I can't do much here. Even a little business strike in Haifa, so that soldiers stop breaking arms and legs in the West Bank. People are scared. Maybe from London we can exert more pressure. Maybe there we'll be able to talk about what happened in '48. *(She hands him a book)* Read it. There are some interesting things in here about Tantur.

AZMI. *(Looks at the book)* You believe a book that came out of Damascus?

SAMYA. *(Giving him another)* This came from Nablus.

AZMI. They're even bigger liars! When I hear the news on their radio, I'm ashamed. Look at the books that came out on Deir Yassin. Of course the Jews murdered there. Exactly one hundred and seven people. So why say they killed three hundred? Why say that women and girls were raped? Because of stories like that, people fled from all over the country.

SAMYA. That's why we need to find the truth about what happened in Tantur.

AZMI. I know they swallowed a lot of shit there. My father had to swallow a lot. His father and brothers had to swallow even more. I've got enough shit with this damn *intifada* on my head. I don't need any more.
Blackout.

SCENE SIX

That same night. Giora and Neta's house. He is on the sofa still holding the dissertation that Samya left in his office.

NETA. I've been working for him for three years, Giora. He trusts me.

GIORA. But why now?

NETA. Because his VP retired.

GIORA. Is it so impossible that even these earrings are a bribe?

She takes off the earrings. Lights up on Avigdor and Yona's house. Both watch the scene in Giora and Neta's apartment.

NETA. Your father doesn't offer bribes, Giora. He knows that generosity is much more effective.

GIORA. He never once asked you to convince me to work for him?

NETA. When did I have to convince you? You always wanted it. You've been waiting till the end of your surgeries.

GIORA. Until a year ago, I was sure I'd spend my whole life at university. All of a sudden I find myself in the company. I already have an office. I sit in board meetings. Udi was born to run the company. My father knows I'm not the right one to run it. He insists because he feels responsible for what happened to me. Every morning on the way to school we heard from him what to do when a war breaks out.

NETA. That's why you blame him? You phoned him from London when the war started. You decided you couldn't stay there while your soldiers were in Lebanon. You asked him to meet you at the airport.

GIORA. I called him so he'd tell me to stay there. *(She's silent)* It dawned on me today that I don't have to rush. Maybe we should move to Tel Aviv for a few years. I've got a much better offer from the university there. In a year, I'll be able to write the book on business crisis management

NETA. You know I can't move to Tel Aviv.

GIORA. I don't have his stubbornness, Neta. I don't have his shrewdness.

NETA. You'll run the company your way. *(Pause)* I'm not going to leave my mother all alone, Giora. She's already lost her family once. *(Pause)* You really want to move? And what about the house? We won't buy it? And what about the wedding? Postpone it again?

GIORA. I'm not postponing anything. I'm trying to figure out how I survive next to him. I can't live where he wants me to. I can't work where he wants me to. By the way, haven't you ever wondered why he introduced us?

NETA. He introduced us because *I* asked him to. Because I saw how you fought to get out of your wheelchair. Because I saw you—two days after your operation—trying to get back to work. Because I saw you standing with one crutch playing Ping-Pong.

Silence. He stands up and goes to her. She turns her face away. He knocks with his crutches on the floor, and manages to dance a few steps. He bows. She softens.

GIORA. I'm sorry. I don't know what I'm saying. Let's go to bed. In the morning I'll come with you to the hotel and discuss the menu. I'll help you try on your wedding dress, and we'll buy the house with no stairs, where we can drive all the way up to the door.

NETA. You're also trying to bribe me?

GIORA. I don't have much to offer.

NETA. You do. If you trusted that, we could've had the baby. He would have been one by now.

GIORA. I'd be so happy if you had a little belly under the *chuppah*.

He hugs her. She responds. They cuddle.

NETA. And tomorrow you'll resign from the university.

GIORA. Okay. *(Kisses her)*

NETA. Next week the board will confirm your appointment.

GIORA. Okay.

NETA. And from now on you'll come to the management meeting every week...

He pulls away from her suddenly.

GIORA. Is it possible I'm hearing *his* voice coming out of *your* mouth? Is this what he told you to say to me?

NETA. Leave it alone.

GIORA. Look at how much pressure he's putting on me. Since what happened at the restaurant, he won't stop talking about our wedding. Maybe he is trying to distract me from something.

NETA. From what?

GIORA. We're not naïve anymore, Neta. Maybe things like this did happen. Not just at Deir Yassin.

NETA. Are you mad? Is that what you think of your father? Don't force me to think that you're suddenly poking around in that affair in order to postpone the wedding.

He sits on the sofa and picks up the dissertation.

Giora (Clayton Stamper) and Neta (Adelina Feldman-Schultz) discuss wedding plans in *The Admission* by Motti Lerner, directed by Michael Malek Najjar (photograph by Airan Wright).

GIORA. This historian has testimonies from five different refugee camps.

NETA. If you want to know what happened there, you have to ask your father.

GIORA. I'm not sure he wants me to know. *(Gets up, takes his crutches)* I need to speak to Ibrahim.

NETA. Ibrahim almost killed him yesterday.

GIORA. I want to know why.

NETA. Now? In the middle of the night? On the day we set a wedding date you go to her?

GIORA. I'm going to her father, Neta.
NETA. What's so urgent? You know your father. He wouldn't do such a thing. Maybe what happened to him is like what happened to you in Lebanon.
Blackout.

SCENE SEVEN

Ibrahim and Samya's house. Fifteen minutes after midnight. Azmi, in his father's robe, just opened the door to Giora. The two enter the living room.

GIORA. I'm sorry I woke you.
AZMI. It's good that you did. I'm sure my wife is worried. What time is it?
GIORA. Quarter past twelve.
AZMI. Quarter past twelve?! What are you doing here at quarter past twelve?
GIORA. I have to speak to your father for a second.
AZMI. At quarter past twelve?
GIORA. I hope he didn't go to sleep…
AZMI. Did something happen? *(Worried)* What happened?
GIORA. It's about Tantur. I have to know what happened there. I asked my dad. He denies everything.
AZMI. Well, you can sleep tight. He's right. I'm not sure anything did happen.
GIORA. What makes you unsure?
AZMI. Because my father is also unsure. After so many years he doesn't remember a thing. He doesn't remember if he was there. He doesn't remember who died there. Who fled from where. The whole story hangs together on a feather.
GIORA. I'd be happy to hear that from him.
AZMI. You want me to wake him at quarter past twelve? Come to us tomorrow with your father and he'll tell you. We'll shake hands over good food. Good drinks. Good coffee. Good night.
Giora hesitates a moment. Samya enters. Lights up on Neta in her house.
SAMYA. My father told me some other things.
AZMI. Just a second, Samya. What are you doing here all of a sudden?
SAMYA. I live here.
AZMI. So, first of all put something on. *(He puts his robe on her and turns to Giora)* Dachilak, Giora. It's almost twelve thirty. *(To Samya)* You know what they'll say all over town if they see him coming to you at twelve-thirty?
SAMYA. If you don't like it, you can go home.
AZMI. Don't tell me to go home.
SAMYA. It's my house, Azmi.
AZMI. It's your house because I gave it up for you.
Enters Ibrahim who couldn't fall asleep. At first he doesn't notice Giora.
IBRAHIM. All your lives you've been blind. You have never seen fear and what it takes to conquer it. What it's like to wake up every morning and say: "I'm alive. I'm taking a wife. I'm making children." Even if they too could be killed. You don't know how much strength you need to waste on that. Until you don't have the strength to remain a human being. And then your children get up one day and go off to America and don't come back to visit. Not even for their mother's funeral. And they marry girls nobody knows, and their children don't speak a word of Arabic. They've never heard who we were or what happened to us. You have no idea how much strength it takes

to go there after the rain and see bones scattered between stones. Maybe my father's. Maybe my brother's. *(Notices Giora and turns to him anxiously)* Giora? What? Is your father…?

AZMI. His father's fine.

IBRAHIM. *(To Giora)* Is he really?

GIORA. Yes. He's at home.

AZMI. When he's recovered, he'll come to us and we'll make peace.

SAMYA. Sit. I'll bring you some water.

AZMI. Why did you get out of bed? It's twelve-thirty already.

IBRAHIM. Make some coffee for our guest!

Samya exits to the kitchen to make coffee.

GIORA. I spoke with my father today, Ibrahim. He doesn't remember much of what happened in Tantur. Do you remember? People were killed there? How? During the battle? Afterward? Were they armed?

IBRAHIM. Right now I'm not sure what I remember.

AZMI. *(To Giora)* See? *(To Ibrahim)* Ya'allah, go to bed.

GIORA. How many people were killed? Do you remember their names?

IBRAHIM. If he doesn't want me to remember, then he shouldn't dig there.

SAMYA. *(Entering)* You told me a few things today, dad.

AZMI. Cha'las!

IBRAHIM. If he doesn't dig, I don't remember.

SAMYA. You said you were hiding on the rooftop and saw how the soldiers lined them up and shot them. You said they forced you to dig a pit…

AZMI. He told you he doesn't remember.

GIORA. My father was there? Did he shoot too?

IBRAHIM. I'm telling you again. If he doesn't dig, I don't remember.

GIORA. How do you know it was him?

IBRAHIM. Same voice. Same eyes. He had a hat. A big leather hat.

GIORA. A big leather hat!?

IBRAHIM. And a small rifle that shoots fast.

AZMI. *(Impatient)* Dachilak, yabba. Let's go to bed.

IBRAHIM. Tell your father that I don't want more blood spilled on the ground. He should let me put these bones under a stone, so that the rains don't wash them into the sea.

Azmi takes his father's arm and exit with him.

GIORA. My father *had* a big leather hat. *And* a Tommy gun. *(Silence)* Looks like your father remembers something. *(Silence)* I must speak to someone else who was there. One of his soldiers. Or maybe one of your relatives…

She moves closer to him and takes his hand. They hug. Lights out on Neta who was watching the scene from her apartment. Azmi enters and sees the two of them embracing. They separate.

SAMYA. Why are you looking at us that way? Nothing happened.

AZMI. Of course nothing happened. A dog barked and ran away. That's it. Good night.

GIORA. I want to ask your father one more thing, Azmi.

AZMI. My father's asleep. I already told him good night.

GIORA. He probably knows people who were there.

AZMI. He doesn't know a soul. Good night.

GIORA. *(To Samya)* We'll talk tomorrow in the office.
AZMI. There's nothing left to talk about. Nobody's said anything. And no one will say anything. Good night.
GIORA. Good night.
Giora exits. Samya turns to exit to her bedroom. Azmi stops her.
AZMI. Where do you think you are? You swore to me there's nothing going on between you anymore.
SAMYA. It's not what you think, Azmi.
AZMI. You won't see him again, and you won't talk to him. Son of a bitch. When he was lying in the hospital, I sat with him for hours every day. I wheeled him down to the beach in his wheelchair, even after he told me about all those old people and children he killed in Lebanon. Every year I stand next to him at his brother's grave with a *kippa* on my head. Now I turn around for one second, and he stabs me in the back. If you want to go abroad so badly, you'd better leave now. Next time I catch you with him, I'll break your bones. And his, too.

SCENE EIGHT

Afternoon. Neta and Giora's apartment. Giora sits at the table. Neta enters. Silence.
NETA. Your father's on the way. He heard that you are trying to speak to his soldiers.
GIORA. He can relax. They deny everything. "We had fourteen dead. They had twenty. All in the heat of battle."
NETA. I'll tell you everything I heard. I'll go with you to see his soldiers. I'm ready to go with you to her father. But one thing needs to be clear, Giora…
GIORA. It's completely clear. We're getting married. We're buying a house. We'll have children.
The doorbell rings. Avigdor and Yona enter. Avigdor's shoulder is still bandaged, his arm in a sling. He is still in pain. Lights up on Ibrahim's house: Azmi, Samya, and Ibrahim watch the scene in Giora's house.
YONA. We want to put an end to this, Guri. You will stop looking for dad's soldiers. You will not call them or meet them. We have nothing to hide. Dad hasn't committed any crime. I don't want lawyers and trials. Certainly not against you.
GIORA. I don't want it either.
YONA. So make do with what Dad told you.
GIORA. He didn't tell much. You didn't either.
YONA. Because there's nothing to tell. It's all rumors. And the minute you start asking questions, there will be more rumors. His shoulder is swollen. He has a fever. And instead of going to the doctor, we're here begging you to believe us.
GIORA. Is that true? *(Avigdor doesn't answer)*
YONA. I was there. I treated the wounded. I saw the dead. Your father looked like a survivor. Not a murderer.
GIORA. It's not just Ibrahim. It's also the dissertation.
YONA. The bastard who wrote it didn't even try to listen to Daddy. It was a just war, Guri. No war was more just.
GIORA. Ibrahim remembers your Tommy gun and your leather hat.
YONA. Dad doesn't deny that he was there.
GIORA. So maybe there's something to the other things he remembers.
YONA. You believe him more than you believe us?

GIORA. I want to believe you. Just tell me how many were really killed. You also know. Why are you so evasive? What are you covering up?
YONA. We told you how many.
GIORA. *(Turning to Avigdor)* It's no secret that you helped Ibrahim's family, Dad.
YONA. *(Cuts him off)* We're human beings, Guri. You're busy with your own wounds, so you refuse to see ours. Two days before Tantur we lost twenty-two boys in a battle with the Iraqi army. *(She chokes up)* And Udi … who burned in his tank … and you … he's surely going out of his mind now.
GIORA. *(Angry)* He's going out of his mind because you're using him.
YONA. *(Angrily)* Next week we're laying a stone in his memory. You'll stand with us, and give him the respect he deserves.
GIORA. Mom. Enough!
YONA. We can grit our teeth and let you keep picking at our wounds. But after you listen to whoever will talk to you, and after you realize you're mistaken, then you'll come to us and beg our forgiveness. And I'm not sure we'll be able to forgive. Then you'll know what your Dad did. Then you won't have to believe us. And if you don't believe us, then there's nothing for us to do here anymore.
AVIGDOR. *(Rising)* I think it's time to end this game.
YONA. Sit, Avigdor.
AVIGDOR. I never thought you'd speak to my soldiers.
YONA. I'm talking to him.
AVIGDOR. But since you've already done it, you'd better hear from me too.
YONA. I asked you not to interfere.
AVIGDOR. I thought that if we build there, we'd bury this affair forever.
GIORA. So there was an affair?
AVIGDOR. I always wanted to tell you and Udi about it. I tried a few times. When I thought you were old enough to understand, I took you to the monument I built there…
GIORA. Tell me now!
YONA. He's already told you! *(To Avigdor)* Don't you see what you're doing to him?
AVIGDOR. We killed. Not two hundred twenty like the Arabs claim. And not even the hundred fifty that the Red Cross reported. Maybe seventy. There were probably some injured who died on the way to Tul Karem. All of them were shot during combat. When the trucks came, two bastards tried to stop the others from getting on. One threw a grenade that he had hidden under his shirt. Four of my soldiers were killed. Twenty years old. Just a month after getting off the boat. Survivors. The last remains. *(Pause)* So we shot these two bastards. The Arabs started screaming. Throwing stones. Fifteen hundred people surrounded us. No reinforcements. Nobody could rescue us. We continued shooting until they calmed down. If we hadn't, they would have finished us off and stayed in the village. And then they would have stayed in other villages too. And the war would have continued. Until today. And we wouldn't be talking about a few dozen dead. We wouldn't be talking about a few thousand dead. We'd be talking about hundreds of thousands dead. From our side. And from theirs. Would that have been better? Answer me. Would you pat me on my shoulder and tell me what a decent man I am? *(Giora is silent)* A week after the battle an officer arrived to investigate what happened. He also determined that it all happened during combat. All of it. *(Giora is silent)* I admit that we expelled. We were afraid that they'd join the Iraqis and Jordanians

who invaded the week before. *(Silence)* Now you know it. And now you have to live with it. Without hypocrisy. Without pretense. I live with it. I worked very hard to make sure that we didn't expel for nothing; that we didn't kill for nothing. That the killing and expulsion would allow us to continue living here; building here; repairing ourselves and those of them that stayed here. That's why I always helped them. After Udi was killed, I doubled my donations. Now you can go check. Ask whoever you want. If you find out I was wrong; that I spilled blood for no reason; that I expelled for no reason; I'll pay the price, 'til the very last drop … even though I've already paid … and you know how much I've paid. But if you find out I was right … that I did what I needed to.… What everyone expected of me … then I hope you'll…

GIORA. I don't understand. You shot seventy people to calm down the others? Couldn't you shoot up in the air? Aim at their feet? I've also been surrounded by mobs a few times. Seventy people aren't killed by stray bullets.

YONA. He shot in the air. He yelled at the soldiers. He tried to stop them.

GIORA. I don't believe you.

YONA. *(Angrily)* You won't accuse us of anything, Giora. If we were guilty of something we've already paid enough. All of us. You too. No one blames you, even though you killed too.

GIORA. I threw a grenade into a house, where there were terrorists hiding. In the middle of battle. I couldn't have known women and children would be there too!

NETA. *(To Avigdor and Yona)* I think it would be best if you left. *(Yona protests)* I'm sorry. Not now. *(Forcefully)* Please. Leave.

A terrifying idea suddenly crosses Giora's mind.

GIORA. All of a sudden I see the connection. Now I understand why it happened.

YONA. Why what happened?

GIORA. *(Pointing to his legs)* This didn't happen by chance.

AVIGDOR. What didn't happen by chance? That's madness, Giora.

GIORA. It happened because of what you did there.

Avigdor and Yona are stunned. Neta hurries and holds Giora. Blackout. The sound of bulldozers grows louder.

SCENE NINE

Two days later. Yona and Avigdor's home. Morning. Yona is in the living room. Giora and Neta enter. The sound of bulldozers fades out. They hug Yona.

GIORA. How did it happen?

YONA. When we left your house his fever spiked. That night I took him to the emergency room.

GIORA. What did he have?

YONA. That knife was filthy. An infection spread. They opened it. Cleaned it. And stitched him up again. In the morning, he ran home.

NETA. Why didn't you call us?

YONA. He didn't want you to know.

GIORA. He knows we're here?

YONA. No.

NETA. You shouldn't have let him go to the office.

YONA. He went to stay sane. He can't sleep. He drinks. Smokes.

GIORA. He needs to see a doctor today.

YONA. He doesn't need a doctor, Guri. He needs you. He loves you more than anything in the world. From the day you were born. He never tried to hide it. I never told you this, but that night, when those officers knocked on our door, we came down together to open it. We knew what they'd come to tell us. He was so afraid it would be you.

GIORA. Mom, Stop.

YONA. When you got injured he sat by your bedside day and night.

GIORA. I know.

YONA. You were always your father's son. Your first word was "Daddy." From then on you never stopped loving him. Always on his shoulders. Going to the beach with him. Playing with him. How can you hurt him like this now?

GIORA. I love him like always, Mom.

YONA. Then come back here tonight and tell him you understand why he did it, and that there's no connection between what he did and what happened to you. And that will end the discussion. And he doesn't have to know that you know he was hospitalized.

GIORA. Maybe just the opposite. Maybe he can't live with these lies anymore either.

YONA. So far we've lived very nicely with these lies.

Suddenly the door opens and Avigdor enters, his arm still in a sling. For a moment it seems like there might be a miracle and Avigdor and Giora will rush to hug each other. But the miracle doesn't happen.

AVIGDOR. *(To Yona)* What is he doing here?

YONA. He came to talk to me.

AVIGDOR. Behind my back?

GIORA. I want to talk to you, too, Dad.

AVIGDOR. *(To Yona)* I don't want him in this house.

YONA. He came to apologize, Avigdor.

AVIGDOR. When I left this morning, I could see it all over your face that you were waiting for him.

YONA. *(Forcefully)* He's thought about what you said. He understands why it happened. He knows it has nothing to do with what happened to him. This affair is over and done with. He's coming back to sit on the board at the company.

Avigdor understands what happened behind his back.

AVIGDOR. I see that a little bird told him I got sick and his heart broke.

GIORA. Please, Dad.

AVIGDOR. Look at my chart. I'm perfectly healthy. I don't need your pity.

GIORA. I'm not offering any pity. I came to listen. I came to understand.

AVIGDOR. If you wanted to understand, you'd have listened to me. Instead you pronounced your verdict, and tied a noose around my neck.

GIORA. I'm sorry about what I said, Dad.

YONA. Listen to him, Avigdor.

AVIGDOR. I've already heard him. Let him go home and think about what I've told him. Let him come back when he understands what happened there. *(Assertively)* This morning I met with four officers from my regiment. They confirm every word I've said. None of them had the slightest shadow of a doubt that there was another choice.

NETA. If you think he doesn't understand, explain it to him. That's why we came. We had no idea you were in the hospital.

GIORA. I think I understand pretty well already. I read the general staff's plan. I saw the command to deport villagers who opposed the takeover of their village. I assume those were the same orders you got from the brigadier.

AVIGDOR. You want me to tell you I was just following orders? Put the responsibility on the brigadier?

GIORA. You said the report from the investigating officer cleared you completely. I'd be happy to see it.

YONA. He'll show you.

AVIGDOR. I told him what's written there.

GIORA. I'd also be happy to read the report from The Red Cross.

AVIGDOR. The Red Cross report was written from Arab testimonies. They never even spoke to us.

GIORA. Fine. Show me whatever you want me to see.

AVIGDOR. You don't want to see anything. You want to accuse. I'm also responsible for what happened to *you*. It's my fault you got on the first plane out of London. I'm to blame for getting you to Lebanon.

GIORA. I don't blame you for anything.

YONA. Leave it now Avigdor.

AVIGDOR. You got injured because when you broke into that house, and saw the children and the old people who were killed by your grenade, you panicked, left your soldiers and ran outside.

GIORA. Maybe we could just not talk about this right now?

AVIGDOR. This is what you've been talking about since you got injured.

GIORA. Now I'm talking about something else, Dad. The dissertation I showed you has already gone to print. In another couple of weeks, it will be published. We need to be prepared. When the battle broke out there was a government already. There was an army. There are transcripts from its meetings. Orders to the front. We must expose them.

YONA. Nobody wrote transcripts in those days, Giora.

GIORA. Don't dismiss this idea so quickly. Why do you have to protect the government? The chief of staff? The brigadier? You don't have to carry such guilt.

AVIGDOR. I'm not carrying any guilt!

YONA. No one was guilty in that war, Guri. We killed civilians. Less than they killed of us. We expelled a few thousand. We were very surprised when hundreds of thousands started running away.

GIORA. If you don't publish your own account, this affair will become just like the massacre at Deir Yassin.

AVIGDOR. Like Deir Yassin?!

GIORA. I want to write a book with you and publish everything you tell me.

YONA. For what? Whose purpose is it going to serve?

GIORA. Not only to absolve you, dad. My injury puts certain responsibility on me…

AVIGDOR. Get out of here!

YONA. Enough, Avigdor!

GIORA. Only when we find out what happened there, will we know how to live here.

AVIGDOR. Get out of here now!

GIORA. *(To Neta)* Come.

NETA. I'll come later. Wait for me at home.

Giora turns to leave. But he loses his balance and falls. Neta and Yona rush to him and help him to his feet. Giora exit. Avigdor takes out a cigar. A long pause.

AVIGDOR. We fought for our lives. And he thinks that we slaughtered like those murderers at Deir Yassin.
NETA. He didn't say that.
AVIGDOR. That's what he meant.
NETA. That's not true. He loves you. He knows how much he hurt you. He's sorry about that. He wants to come to the board meeting next week. He accepts your account. He wants to publish it in a book.
AVIGDOR. He wants to write that it was a massacre.
YONA. He won't write that.
NETA. If you think he doesn't need to write a book, then sit with him and explain why. He won't argue with you.
YONA. And we'll finally bury this affair forever.
AVIGDOR. I'll think about it.
NETA. I need an answer now. *(Firmly)* I don't care about that war. I don't care who died in it. I don't care how they died. I don't care who's guilty or who isn't. I'm fighting for his life now. So that he won't give up. So that he'll want to have children. So that he believes he can raise them.
AVIGDOR. I said I'll think about it.
NETA. We don't have time, Avigdor. If you push him, he'll write the book without you. Don't make him settle accounts with you. *(Silence)* We'll come here tomorrow evening. I'm sure you'll know what to tell him. *(Exits)*
YONA. I don't think we should wait until tomorrow.
AVIGDOR. Let him write his book. No one will publish it.
YONA. You're playing with fire, Avigdor. Talk to him now, before he gets us all into trouble. Eventually he'll understand.
AVIGDOR. He doesn't want to understand. Didn't you see? He'll only forgive me if I confess I was following orders. If I place the responsibility on others. He's not prepared to consider the possibility that it was the right thing to do. That there was no other option. Didn't you see how he avoided me? He wouldn't even shake my hand.
Blackout.

SCENE TEN

Late afternoon. Ibrahim and Samya's house.

GIORA. Try to remember, Ibrahim. Where did you sleep that night in Tantur? In the house? On the roof?
IBRAHIM. On the roof?! There's wind on the roof. From the sea. *(He laughs)* When I was a boy we'd make kites. Out of paper and rags. And they'd fly in that wind. And then we'd let go of the string. Once I flew my kite at night, and the next morning I found it outside our store in Haifa. *(Laughs)*
GIORA. When did you wake up that morning? What did you see?
IBRAHIM. In Haifa we had a fabric store next to the port. A thousand square meters, and a storage room. People came to us from Jaffa, Ramallah, Lud. My father was a big merchant. With a belly like a mountain. After lunch he would lie down in the storage room and snore.
SAMYA. Yaba...
IBRAHIM. That night we didn't sleep. We knew they'd come. They had some Jews with

them who used to buy their vegetables from us before the war. They knew the way. The ducks heard them and started screaming… *(Silence)* Now my head aches.

GIORA. *(To Samya)* I have some pills.

IBRAHIM. This isn't a headache for pills.

Samya gestures to Giora to put the pill back in his bag. Lights up on Yona and Avigdor's house. They sit in the living room watching the scene in Ibrahim's house.

IBRAHIM. *Yil'an din'hu* this head of mine. I wish it were empty.

GIORA. Where were you when the shooting began, Ibrahim?

IBRAHIM. I was in the tower of the mosque. When they saw the fire coming out of my gun, they… *(Pause)* Better if you came tomorrow.

SAMYA. Baba, I also want to know.

IBRAHIM. What for? So the dead will come back to life?

SAMYA. So we'll know their story.

IBRAHIM. Nobody's interested in the story anymore.

Azmi enters.

AZMI. *(To Samya)* I told you I don't want him here anymore. *(To Giora)* Take your legs and get out.

SAMYA. *(To Azmi)* You're not kicking him out, Azmi.

AZMI. And you shut up. His father's heard you two are talking to him about a book, so now he's issuing a complaint against us for assault.

GIORA. How did he hear?

AZMI. And he wants a million in compensation.

GIORA. It's just a threat. He knows what'll be found out the minute he gets to court.

AZMI. He's not afraid of any court. He knows I'm a tiny little Arab and he's a big Jew. And no court will defend a tiny little Arab against a big Jew. If you were a tiny little Arab you'd know it.

SAMYA. I know a couple of good lawyers who…

AZMI. I'm not getting any lawyers and I'm not going to any court. *(To Ibrahim)* And you won't tell him another word.

IBRAHIM. *(To Samya)* So I shouldn't tell?

SAMYA. Yes, you should.

AZMI. There's nothing to tell.

SAMYA. His life fell apart that day, Azmi.

AZMI. He's making it up.

SAMYA. You know him. You know he's not making anything up.

AZMI. *(To Ibrahim)* And I'll tell you why you're making it up. Because you don't want us to know the truth. You ran away from there. All of you ran away. Like pecking pigeons who fly away the minute a kid chucks his apple core at them.

IBRAHIM. You don't know a thing, *ya ahabal*. They ran from Haifa. From *Akko*. From *Yaffa*. Like mice from a drowning boat. We fought for six months. With a hundred old rifles, and a few boxes of bullets. We shot them on the roads. In the fields. We put mines under their trucks. Even if we wanted, we couldn't run. Lebanon took in only the wealthy ones who could pay for visas. The rest of us stayed until the end and fired till our last bullet.

AZMI. Of course. Now you're all heroes at my expense. The moment you open your mouth they'll throw us out of the restaurant and weld the doors shut. Where would we go? To sell *za'atar* at a refugee camp in Tul Karem?

IBRAHIM. *Wallah el Azim.* You aren't such a fool as I thought, Azmi. I'm the fool. I never told you what happened there because I didn't want you to be afraid to live here. And look what's happened. You're more afraid than me.

AZMI. I'm afraid?

SAMYA. We won't do anything without you, Azmi.

GIORA. You've just been in his office. Haven't you? You told him that I'm here. All my life I've seen people leaving his office with an offer they couldn't refuse. Don't you understand that he's more afraid than you?

AZMI. I'm not afraid. I'm looking to see which way the wind blows. I know what happened in Tantur. I know everything. They killed. Not just there. Everywhere. And those they didn't kill, they expelled. From every city. From every village. We won't forgive it the rest of our lives. But I'm also not going to talk about it. *(To Ibrahim)* And you're not going to build any memorial there. Because I'm thinking of you. And her. And about the kids she'll have. And about my kids. I know that if we start settling accounts with those who killed, then we should forget about our lives. *(To Giora)* You think I don't know that your father was responsible for that mess? The day he came to the restaurant and arranged a permit for me and offered a loan, paid for her university and gave her a grant, that day I asked myself "what happened? How did I win the lottery if I never bought a ticket?" I didn't have to spend ten years in school to figure it out. The first jerk I sent to the library told me your father was the commanding officer in Tantur. So I understood what was cooking in his pot. Maybe they didn't kill two hundred twenty people like some of us say, and maybe they didn't rape women or girls. But hundred twenty people they did kill. I asked my aunt in Tul Karem. She knows everybody. They shot them like rabid dogs. But I wanted to live like a man. Not die like a dog. So I kept my mouth shut. *(To Samya)* And that's why you kept your mouth shut, too. You could've also checked why his father was paying for your studies. But you didn't. You didn't check because you didn't want to know. Because you wanted his money and you wanted his son. *(To Giora)* You too could have figured out what your father did there. But you also didn't want to know. If you knew, how could you eat with us? How could you look at her face? So don't teach me what to remember or what to forget. You're not the hero you think you are. Maybe against a few kids and some old people who were hiding under the steps in a ruined house in Lebanon. If you had to live my kind of life, you wouldn't only shut up. You would run away. And don't ever come to my restaurant again. I wouldn't give you stinking hummus on a rotten pita.

Azmi exits. Lights out on Yona and Avigdor.

IBRAHIM. Make him some coffee for the way home. *(Exits after Azmi)*

SAMYA. He's right. I could have known everything a long time ago. I should have known it a long time ago. Instead, I shut up. Just like him. When I talked, I lied to myself. I lied because I wanted to be with people like you, because I didn't want to upset people like you. That's why I always despised myself around people like you.

GIORA. Those days are over, Samya. We won't shut up any more... *(He embraces her)* Your father will also have to talk. He'll show us where the bones are. We'll bring a few students, give them some shovels and uncover them. We'll bury them, build the memorial that he wants. I'm not sure it will console him, but maybe it will make it easier for him to mourn. *(She is silent)* We'll write the book together, Samya. Together we'll understand what we don't understand alone.

He wipes away her tears

SAMYA. I'll return the grant to your father. I can't touch his money.

GIORA. Will you postpone the trip?

SAMYA. My family will need me here.

GIORA. I will, too. *(He embraces her)*

SAMYA. I want to know what's going on with us, Giora. I have already managed to give you up. Now suddenly you're back. Why?

GIORA. We're in this together. Aren't we?

SAMYA. Together? Here? What does it mean? I don't want to lie to myself anymore.

GIORA. You think we'll be able to live together knowing what happened here?

SAMYA. Precisely *because* we know. I saw how you dealt with what you did in Lebanon. I see how you're dealing with what your father did.

GIORA. His blood runs through my veins. Wherever you look, you'll see the writing on the wall. You'll never forget and never forgive.

SCENE ELEVEN

Night. Avigdor and Yona's house. Avigdor sits on the sofa, one hand in a sling, the other holding a drink. Yona stands opposite him. Light on Giora and Neta's apartment. He watches his parents.

AVIGDOR. He won't uncover any bones and he won't build any memorial. The guards won't let him in.

YONA. Forget the guards. If you withdraw the complaint to the police, he'll stop everything and meet with you.

AVIGDOR. That's what he told you?

YONA. Yes. Sit with him. Show him the orders you received. Tell him you regret it. That you're sorry you obeyed them. He'll listen and give up on the book.

AVIGDOR. I was there for the discussions of those orders, and I took part in writing them.

YONA. I know.

AVIGDOR. And I don't regret it.

YONA. I said that you'd *say* you regret it.

AVIGDOR. We did the right thing.

YONA. I know.

AVIGDOR. He also has to know. Where the Jordan Legion was. Where the Arab Rescue Army was. He has to understand that the Iraqi Army was planning to use Tantur as their base to attack Haifa.

YONA. And if he doesn't? You'll keep chasing him until he does something to himself? I don't want to return to those days in the hospital when he was hiding sleeping pills in chocolate boxes.

AVIGDOR. *(Drinks his whiskey)* I don't either.

YONA. But you're forcing us to return. I never blamed you for what happened to the children, Avigdor. I've blamed myself. Only myself. That I didn't know how to protect them from you. Udi had a shorter leg. He didn't have to enlist.

AVIGDOR. He wanted to.

YONA. You didn't give him a choice.

AVIGDOR. He wanted to be like his friends.

YONA. When he fell, Giora should have been released from his unit.

AVIGDOR. He didn't want to be released.

YONA. You didn't give him a choice either.

AVIGDOR. When he came home with his beret, you were proud just like I was.

YONA. You lit this fire in them both. Giora didn't have to go back to Lebanon. When he called from London, I begged you to tell him to stay in the hotel.

AVIGDOR. I told him that the decision was his.

YONA. You didn't. I should have locked the door so they couldn't get out of the house. But I was afraid of you. I was so afraid that I gave in to their lust to sacrifice themselves. They were still boys. What did they know?

AVIGDOR. I'm not prepared to hear such accusations. We're not to blame for what happened to them.

YONA. We can still save him, Avigdor. *(He doesn't answer)* If you don't go and show him all the orders you received, and tell him how sorry you are that you followed them, then I'll go and tell him what I know. What I saw with my own eyes. Everything you don't want him to know.

Avigdor throws his glass against the wall. A sharp pain in his shoulder.

AVIGDOR. I'm hiding it to protect myself? How can you accuse me of such a lie? It doesn't hurt me that Udi is dead? It doesn't kill me that Giora was wounded!? I wanted them to sacrifice themselves?! My hands are clean. In spite of what happened at Tantur. Even though I thought that Udi should enlist. Even though I waited for Giora at the airport. Even though I took him to his company. He didn't even want to stop at home to get his boots! Both of them knew very well that if we didn't win, we wouldn't live. Every night I see Udi burning in that tank … I see Giora getting hit with the bullet…

Long silence.

AVIGDOR. You think I don't want to talk to him? I went there. I knocked on the door. I said I want to listen. To find out what he thinks. Maybe there's something I don't understand. He wouldn't open…

Blackout. The Bulldozers sound becomes louder.

SCENE TWELVE

Neta and Giora's apartment. Morning. Neta enters.

NETA. Where are you going? They're on their way here. He's already dropped the charges against Ibrahim and copied all the documents in the archive.

GIORA. And what about the grave and the monument?

NETA. He wants more details.

GIORA. And about the book?

NETA. He'll give you an answer after you've looked at the documents. *(Pause)* I think it's worth listening to him. He's never talked this way about that war. About the fear. The despair. The doubt. He was sure they would be defeated. A hundred and ninety soldiers from his regiment died. He remembers their names. He showed me the total number of dead. They killed two thousand of our civilians in that war.

GIORA. I know.

NETA. The week before the battle in Tantur, they massacred two hundred and forty members of kibbutz Kfar Etzion who were waving white flags.

GIORA. And that justifies what he did?

NETA. It means you can't judge what he did. Not out of context.

GIORA. He also doesn't believe the context justifies what he did in Tantur. If he believed it, he would have told me what he did there years ago. And I would have thought a little deeper about what happened in our wars since then. And perhaps I wouldn't have returned to Lebanon.

NETA. You chose to return there.

GIORA. He programmed me to return.

NETA. He's running a very high fever, Giora. The infection's spread through his shoulder.

GIORA. So he should go to the hospital. *(Turns to leave)*

NETA. Wait. If you're going to look for bones now, you'd better hold on for a second. *(He stops)* I want to tell the hotel we're postponing the date.

GIORA. Postponing? Why?

NETA. Because you're scaring me. You're punishing the people closest to you because they want to live. Don't you see how you've become obsessed with this pursuit of justice? If they had expelled more, there wouldn't be an intifada today. If they had killed more, maybe their war would have been the last war. If you had killed more, you wouldn't have been injured. When I see what you're doing to him, I'm not sure what you would have done, if you were in his shoes.

GIORA. I don't know. I'm not better than him. Maybe I would have killed just like him.

NETA. You're right you're not better than him. You're ruthlessly hurting him. And you're mother. And me. I can't marry you if you keep persecuting him.

GIORA. It's not just me and him, Neta. Don't you see that something has gone wrong here?

NETA. When you hear him you'll realize that you're wrong. And if you still want to save what you've ruined, tell him you accept his every word. And you won't see them again, or eat with them anymore. You won't look for any of their bones in any grave, and you won't work with them on any book.

GIORA. So you'll only marry me if I accept every word he says? Haven't I accepted enough? Because of him, I fooled myself that I wanted to marry you. Because of him, I fooled you as well. I wanted, because he wanted. You too wanted because he wanted.

Neta grabs him by the shirt and shakes him in anger.

NETA. I wanted. Me. There was nothing in the world I wanted more. *You* didn't want. You waited until I had got you back on your feet before getting rid of me. The moment I saw how much I loved you I should have run away from you.

She lets go of him and exits. Giora turns as if to go after her but stops. Slowly, he reconsiders.

SCENE THIRTEEN

Ibrahim and Samya's house. Afternoon. Ibrahim sits next to the table.

GIORA. Where is the grave, Ibrahim? How far down the *wadi*?

SAMYA. In front of the mosque? In front of the school?

GIORA. If you don't remember exactly, say approximately.

SAMYA. Try to remember, *yabba*.

GIORA. He's evading again.

SAMYA. He doesn't feel well. He didn't sleep all night.

GIORA. He'll tell us and go to sleep. *(To Ibrahim)* In front of the mosque or the school?

SAMYA. Maybe he's afraid to remember?

GIORA. He's not afraid to remember. He's afraid of my father. *(To Ibrahim)* We can still

find the bones, Ibrahim. Tomorrow my father will build a city there, and we won't be able to dig underneath it.
SAMYA. He can't speak, Giora.
GIORA. *(Vehemently)* If you don't tell me where they are, I'll bring tractors right now and dig up the entire *wadi*.
SAMYA. Don't threaten him.
GIORA. He's going to tell us where they are!
Lights up on Avigdor and Yona's house. Avigdor, Yona and Neta are watching.
IBRAHIM. I don't even remember if there are bones, Giora. And if there are, I don't remember whose. Maybe there was a village. Maybe not. Maybe soldiers came and killed. Maybe not. Maybe it was someone who only looked like your father. Who can remember such things today?
GIORA. *(To Samya)* I don't understand what he's saying. If there are no bones there, then where are they?
SAMYA. I don't know.
GIORA. *(To Ibrahim)* We've already planned a memorial, Ibrahim. With names. With flowers.
SAMYA. We can't force him to remember. *(To Ibrahim)* Come, Dad.
Samya walks Ibrahim out, Giora blocks her way.
GIORA. This is our chance too, Samya. I told you. I'm moving out.
SAMYA. He can hear you. *(Takes Ibrahim by his arm again)*
GIORA. He's known for a long time.
IBRAHIM. *Min Shan Allah,* Giora. Forget the bones. The knife that stabbed your father cut my heart too. It's almost empty of blood now. Why spill more? Your father's heart is almost empty too. So tell him to come here tomorrow. We'll sit. We'll talk. We're old men. We want to rest. The bones lying there also want to rest. If someone digs there, a fire will come out from the stones and burn him. Your father understands it. He'll do whatever is needed to guard them from the rains, so that they won't be... *(Pauses and exits)*
GIORA. I see my father spoke to him.
SAMYA. He didn't speak to him. His lawyer came here last night, knocked on the door. I didn't let him in.
GIORA. Why didn't you tell me?
SAMYA. So you could think sensibly. Leave your father alone. We don't have a chance against him. My father won't talk either.
GIORA. And we'll go on living with this lie?
SAMYA. We don't have to find bones to expose the truth. Let's go to London. I'll get another grant. There's no writing on the wall there. We'll write a book. And publish it. Teach it in university. *(Hugs him)* In London we can live together. Without fear. Without shame. Without guilt. We've waited years for this moment. There's no need to wait any longer.
GIORA. My father will talk only after we find the bones.
He disengages from her and exits. Darkness in the house of Avigdor and Yona.

SCENE FOURTEEN

Afternoon. Giora's apartment. Avigdor and Yona sit and wait. Avigdor holds a bag in one hand, the other is still bandaged. He has a fever and is suffering pain. Giora enters, the events of the past few days have taken a toll. Lights up on Ibrahim's house where we see Ibrahim, Samya, and Azmi. Lights up on Avigdor and Yona's house, there we see Neta. All are watching the scene at Giora's apartment.

AVIGDOR. I brought you the documents. I'll be happy to show them to you. But first I think it best you tell your students to stay at the university.

YONA. And tomorrow we'll all stand together, with Neta, for Udi's ceremony. And the day after you'll come to the management meeting.

GIORA. We're only talking about a few hundred square meters, Dad. A stone with names. A flower bed. An olive tree and a bench. *(Showing Avigdor a plan)* Look. I'd need a bulldozer for two days and a pile-driver for another three to install pillars for the fence.

AVIGDOR. *(Rejecting the plans)* I don't understand why you are being so stubborn. Even Ibrahim and his family don't want it anymore.

GIORA. They will.

AVIGDOR. When they want it, we'll talk about it.

GIORA. I'm doing it for us too, Dad.

YONA. We definitely don't want it. *(To Avigdor)* Show him.

Avigdor opens his bag and takes out a stack of documents.

AVIGDOR. I brought you government plans, orders of the general staff and the investigating officer's report on Tantur. There was a general guideline to expel villagers who resisted the takeover. There were no written orders to kill so that other would flee, but there were winking eyes from commanding officers who made clear what was expected. I'm ready to tell you everything, but only you.

GIORA. This is not a private dispute between us, Dad.

YONA. Dad has come a long way to meet you, Guri. Meet him halfway. Stop your students and we'll begin talking.

GIORA. And what about the book?

AVIGDOR. When you hear me, you'll understand why these things must remain between us.

GIORA. Everyone who lives here must know what happened here.

YONA. You know very well what will happen when they know.

AVIGDOR. The responsibility on my shoulders was too heavy, Giora. I was a twenty-four-year-old construction engineer. I was taken to the war from my office. After a year and a half I became a regiment commander. All of a sudden I discovered that I'm responsible for the fate of hundreds of thousands. I couldn't always deliberate. Against fire. Under attacks. Under terrible fear. In helplessness. In despair. I couldn't always be reasonable. I didn't always know how to refuse what this war permitted.

GIORA. The war permitted such shooting?

AVIGDOR. Perhaps we were too quick to shoot. Perhaps we shot too much.

GIORA. Perhaps?!

AVIGDOR. Yes. I shot too much.

YONA. Enough, Avigdor.

AVIGDOR. Yes. In rage. In revenge. In madness.

YONA. Avigdor!

AVIGDOR. Yes. We rampaged through the streets. Between the courtyards. Yes. I got swept away by my soldiers. I couldn't control them. Yes. I couldn't stop either. Yes. We shot those who hid in their houses, Yes. Those who were just throwing stones. Maybe even some women and old men who just peeped from their windows. Yes. Those who were trying to get away. But even so, it was a battle. Not a massacre. And two days later there was another battle. We killed there too. We got killed there too. And then there was another one. But we never slaughtered. Yes. Never slaughtered. I will not lie to you. I did not mourn their dead. Nor ours. We buried them and wiped away the sweat and the dust. And the blood. Yes. To mourn was a luxury… *(Pauses)*

YONA. *(To Giora)* What else do you want to hear?

GIORA. That you're sorry. That you regret it. That the killing was unnecessary.

YONA. Of course he regrets it. That affair soured our lives.

AVIGDOR. You'll only be satisfied when I put a gun to my head?

YONA. Avigdor, please.

GIORA. I'll be satisfied when you come with me to the *wadi*, and dig with me until we uncover the bones, and we erect a stone.

AVIGDOR. You know that's impossible.

GIORA. And you'll explain in the book what you did there. You'll ask for forgiveness. You'll atone.

AVIGDOR. All my life I've struggled to atone, Giora.

GIORA. You struggled to deny. To hide. From me too. And I closed my eyes. I always knew this village was destroyed and its people were expelled. I never asked why. Never checked how. And when my turn came, I also killed. Just like you.

AVIGDOR. You didn't have a choice either.

GIORA. Maybe I did?

AVIGDOR. If we learn to live with them, the wounds will heal.

GIORA. You promised me that before I was born.

Giora turns to leave. Yona blocks Giora's way.

YONA. Wait. We're willing to uncover those bones.

AVIGDOR. We're not uncovering any bones!

YONA. How much longer will we be able to keep them underground, Avigdor? It's better we dig there ourselves, while we can still explain what we did.

AVIGDOR. There's no point in going there. There is no *wadi*. The tractors went out today. They flattened the hill. Filled the *wadi*. You won't find a thing there.

Giora stops, shocked. Yona, too, is stunned.

YONA. *(To Avigdor)* How could you do that? Stop them! Stop them!

GIORA. *(To Avigdor)* You will never succeed in hiding the dead that you buried there. Even if you build skyscrapers on top of them. I'll dig for them with my hands and fingernails. Until they're found. Then maybe the wounds will begin to heal. *(He exits)*

EPILOGUE

The three houses are still lit. Lights up on the hill of Tantur. The sound of bulldozers is heard in the distance. Giora is crawling to the top of the hill. When he reaches it he begins to dig with his hands until strength gives out. In the distance, above the bulldozer's sound, we hear Yona.

YONA. Today we place this groundbreaking stone in memory of our eldest son, Udi. Udi was a company commander in the armored forces. He fell in the Yom Kippur War. His tank was hit. He died on the spot. His light went out. Before he could savor the fullness of our love. Before we could savor the fullness of his. The neighborhood he wanted to build here will be built in his memory by his younger brother, Giora … his younger brother Giora … whose light has filled our lives ever since…
Yona's voice dies out. Lights out on all the homes. Lights out on the hill.

END OF PLAY

SCENES FROM 70* YEARS

Hannah Khalil

© Hannah Khalil, 2018, *Scenes from 70* Years*, and Bloomsbury MethuenDrama, an imprint of Bloomsbury Publishing Plc.

All rights whatsoever in this play are strictly reserved and application for performance, etc., should be made before rehearsals begin to Curtis Brown Group Ltd, Haymarket House, 28–29 Haymarket, London, SW1Y 4SP. No performance may be given unless a license has been obtained.

No rights in incidental music or songs contained in the work are hereby granted and performance rights for any performance/presentation whatsoever must be obtained from the respective copyright owners.

About the Playwright

Hannah Khalil is an award-winning Palestinian-Irish writer. Her stage plays include critically acclaimed *Scenes from 68* Years*: "confirms Khalil as a dramatist of compelling potential"—*Daily Telegraph* (Arcola Theatre, London, 2016), *The Scar Test*: "Political theatre at its best" (Soho theatre, London), *Bitterenders* (winner Sandpit Arts' Bulbul 2013), *Plan D* (Tristan Bates Theatre, nominated for the Meyer Whitworth Award), and *Ring* (Soho Theatre London's Westminster Prize); as well as *Last of the Pearl Fishers* and *The Deportation Room* for BBC Radio 4. She was the Bush Theatre London's writer on attachment in 2016/2017 as part of Project 2036. She was also the recipient of the Arab British Centre's Award for Culture in 2017. Her work is published in the UK, U.S. and Canada.

— Essay —

Hannah Khalil's *Scenes from 70* Years*: Snapshots from a Seemingly Endless Occupation

Michael Malek Najjar

"You cannot like the word, but what is happening is an occupation—to hold 3.5 million Palestinians under occupation. I believe that is a terrible thing for Israel and for the Palestinians.... It can't continue endlessly."—Ariel Sharon, 2003[1]

How does one encapsulate 70 years of the Palestinian/Israeli conflict in one play? That is the momentous task Hannah Khalil has undertaken in her far-reaching, theatrical collage of scenes spanning the decades since the state of Israel was created, and the post-1967 occupation of Palestinian territories. Like her first major play titled *Plan D*, Khalil utilizes historical situations to create the dramatic backdrop for her dramas. "Plan D" was named after the Israeli "Plan Dalet" which, in the words of historian Walid Khalidi, "entailed the destruction of the Palestinian Arab community and the expulsion and pauperization of the bulk of the Palestine Arabs ... calculated to achieve the military *fait accompli* upon which the state of Israel was to be based."[2] In *Scenes from 70* Years* (the asterisk denotes that the number can/will change with each passing year of the conflict) Khalil provides snapshots of various scenes based on Palestinian survivor stories. Her patchwork assembly took years of development, workshops, and readings. Ironically, if not sadly, the play began as *Scenes from 62* Years*. The intervening eight years have most likely provided even more stories from which to create scenes.

Khalil includes shopkeepers, children, translators, charity workers, taxi drivers, Palestinians in the West Bank, Palestinians living in the diaspora, and Israeli soldiers. This diorama of the occupation gives audiences glimpses into the lives of Palestinians of all walks of life, desperately attempting to live through an occupation that is crushing their society. It also demonstrates that Israelis are also affected by this stagnating state of limbo where nothing changes except a constant hardening of positions, confiscation of lands, proliferation of checkpoints, and crushing of spirits.

Despite the serious topic, Khalil infuses her play with colorful characters, exciting and mundane situations, thoughtful dialogues, and static scenes of everyday people waiting in line at checkpoints. She knows that decades of this ongoing situation leads to a wide variety of situations from shockingly violent to monotonously boring, some with dialogue and others only silent action. She provides us with portrayals of human interaction that refuse to sensationalize or exaggerate the daily lives of Palestinians. Like Caryl Churchill's play *Love and Information*, Khalil takes us into the smaller, intimate moments that define a society.

Like the old keys Palestinians keep from their lost homes, or the maps that remain proving Palestinian claims to the land, Khalil's desire to transform Palestinian stories into these dramatic vignettes is an act of testimony—a desire to not let the small and seemingly insignificant events of this ongoing occupation be forgotten or lost to history. Her method of storytelling is by way of postmodern pastiche—fleeting moments compiled in a way to allow audiences to both see the details of the smaller pictures while simultaneously zooming outward to gain a perspective on the entire work. What is the importance of this play? Perhaps a line uttered during the final scene says it all: "…so we know that you remember—so you don't forget—so you can tell everyone."[3] Given all of the death, suffering, and destruction of the past 70 years, the least we can do is memorialize this ongoing strife.

— PLAYWRIGHT STATEMENT —
Humanizing the "Other"

I'm sick of seeing Arabs on stage. Don't get me wrong; I love Arabs—hell my dad's Palestinian, but why are we always portrayed in the narrowest way? Crying mothers, stone-throwing resisters, dead martyrs.

I saw a poster for an Arab American comedian's show, the tag line: "I'm not a terrorist—but I have played one on TV." Smart, I thought, expose the stereotypes. Those same clichés got me writing in the first place: my heart ached for the fantastic Arab actors I knew who had to don a suicide vest at every audition.

Palestinian filmmaker Elia Suleiman's *The Time That Remains* further inspired me. In it an old Palestinian man, depressed by life under occupation, routinely runs into the street in his PJs and douses himself in gasoline. His neighbors take turns to gently take the matches away and lead him home. It's sad but, believe it or not, darkly funny too.

So, suitably fired (!) up, I started penning scripts showing very "normal" Arab characters and I'm not alone, the other great writers in this Semitic Commonwealth series and Arab writers like Hassan Abdulrazzak and Hanan Al Shaykh reveal a common desire to myth bust.

Then, my first play about Palestine: *Plan D* was put on in London in 2010. It was based on testimonies of Palestinians who lived through the creation of Israel in 1948 and tells the story of what happens to one fictional family.

The thing that surprised and delighted me the most about that production was the fact that many people approached me afterwards—Palestinians in the diaspora—to tell me their story: what happened to them, their family, what happens to them now, every day, living under occupation.

And what stories they were, full of pathos and drama and dark, dark, wry humor. What a resource I'd been gifted. But how to tell all these tales? So many.... If I were to write each into a play that would be my life's work.

I decided to try a patchwork approach, and undertook the joyous task of writing each of these stories as a scene. That was the easy part. More complicated was the assembly job that followed; placing the scenes in a structure that would give the sense of journey to an audience despite not having one central character and objective to follow. This shaping was a long and detailed endeavor, the work of five years of development, workshops and readings. Beautiful scenes that I loved were cut, the order changed and changed.

The title however was easy: the first draft of the play was titled *Scenes from 62* Years*, the number denoting the time that has passed since 1948, the asterisk signifying that the number will change. By the first production in 2016, it was called *Scenes from 68* Years*. If you attended Silk Road Rising's reading you saw *Scenes from 69* Years*. In this anthology, being published in 2018, the title becomes *Scenes from 70* Years*. Of course my hope is that one day, when occupation ends that the number will become fixed.

That's one of my hopes. Another is that, in the future, I won't be sick of seeing Arabs on stage because they'll be portrayed as actual, real people—as opposed to terrorists—at last.

— Playscript —
Scenes from 70 Years*

Please note, the dates in the stage directions are for the performers' information and it's possible but not necessary to include them in performance, at the discretion of the director.

SCENE

(2010) The stage is in complete darkness, everything is still. Perhaps we hear a gentle sigh or the sound of a body turning in a bed.
Pause
Suddenly everything changes.
The sound of a door being broken down with one hard smash
The sound of feet moving and voices—but the stage should still be in complete darkness throughout this scene.
VOICE 1. *(Shouting)* Get up, get up now, where is he, where is he?
VOICE 2. *(shouting)* Move!
We hear a child scream and begin to cry, it's not clear if this is from this house or next door
VOICE 3. My wife is not dressed
VOICE 6. I have no clothes on—
VOICE 2. HE SAID GET UP GET UP NOW GET UP GET UP GET UP
VOICE 4. We are civilians—
The sound of a door opening and a gun being cocked then a child screaming and crying in fear, the child continues to cry throughout the rest of the scene.
VOICE 4. Don't point that at him he is a child
VOICE 5. Get him out then
VOICE 1. Where is he? Tell us!
VOICE 2. Move, we want to talk to your husband
VOICE 6. I'm not leaving him alone with you
VOICE 2. Get the fuck out and take your—
VOICE 3. We don't know anything
The sound of someone falling over, the soldier has kicked the man to the floor.
VOICE 6. Leave him!
VOICE 4. I'm filming this
VOICE 5. What?
VOICE 4. I have a camera and I'm going to show the world

VOICE 5. PUT THAT DOWN IMMEDIATELY
VOICE 3. Please calm down
VOICE 5. STOP FILMING
VOICE 3. I'll come with you—let my wife and child-
VOICE 2. GET THEM OUT
VOICE 5. IS HE STILL FILMING?
VOICE 1. Where is he?
VOICE 2. WHO? WHO's filming
VOICE 5. Him
VOICE 2. WHO THE FUCK IS FILMING!
VOICE 5. Him

Suddenly a film projection appears of what the cameraman sees as his night vision comes into focus, a soldier in full army fatigues right in front of him, pointing a gun at him

VOICE 2/SOLDIER. PUT THAT FUCKING CAMERA DOWN I'LL SHOOT YOU

SCENE

(1948) In the middle of the space there is a body—it is a boy. His face and hands are both bandaged, as is one of his legs. One arm is in a sling.

Pause

BOY. Mama!

A beat

BOY. Mama! Come here! I need you!

A beat

The boy's father rushes in

FATHER. What is it?
BOY. Where's Mama?
FATHER. She's hanging the washing—why are you shouting—be quiet!
BOY. I need her, I can't breath—you did it too tight
FATHER. Let me see

He examines the bandages on the boy's face and moves them around his nose area

FATHER. Is that better?
BOY. Not really.
FATHER. Breath through your mouth
BOY. I'm hot. When are they coming?
FATHER. Any minute
BOY. You said that half an hour ago.
FATHER. They will be here. They said they would and they will. You know it's not easy for them to move around.

A beat

FATHER. Now please stop shouting, be a good boy. They will be here. Be good.
BOY. What can I do? I want to play but I can't like this
FATHER. Then think. Think about how lucky you are. To have both your parents here with you, about what you want to do with your life, what you will study at university. I think you should be a doctor don't you?
BOY. Because you are a doctor, right?
FATHER. Not only because of that, but because you have an instinct for it. Remember the bird you found, made the bed for him, kept him warm

BOY. It died
FATHER. Comfortably. And dignified. Thanks to you
BOY. But a Doctor should make people better, not help them die
FATHER. If things are beyond help then it is better to make it easy to go.
BOY. Like Sayed?
FATHER. Yes
  A beat
FATHER. Now be good and quiet, I'll bring them here when they come OK?
BOY. Ok
FATHER. And don't call your mother, she has a lot to do
BOY. She doesn't know they are coming does she?

SCENE

(2003) A pavement. A man sits outside his shop on a folding chair. He is smoking a cigarette. Either side of him is a tank.
He shifts his chair a little to the left to move out of the shadow cast by one of them.
He sees the soldier looking at him and smiles.
SHOPKEEPER. Hello my friend. I'm just getting the sun. Very good for you, you know. Healthy. Vitamin D.
He sits finishes his cigarette and enjoys the sun a little more. Then he takes out his mobile. He dials a number.
SHOPKEEPER. Where are you? I've got nothing to do here. I'm sitting in the sun. I know but a shop with no food is like a blunt pencil—pointless.
  A beat
Come on have a sense of humour! I know. I know. How long have you been there? No. You can't have been. That's bad even for Huwara. Are there lots of people? Really. I hope you locked the car. People could steal the things. They're desperate. And you know what the soldiers are like.
As he says this he looks up at the tank, wary they may have heard him, they haven't.
I know it's not your fault, I'm not blaming you—but I don't want it all to go bad in the heat, why don't you try another way—how about you turn around and try Awarta checkpoint? I know it's meant to be for trucks but your car is full isn't it? So tell them it's a mini truck … try it—you may as well. What have you got to lose? I need those things—maybe I should ask Fouad next time eh? He'd manage to sweet talk his way through, Yulla Awarta, try it—. Ok ok bye
He hangs up the phone and leans back in the chair again.
FRIENDLY SOLDIER FROM TOP OF TANK. Well?
SHOPKEEPER. He's stuck at Huwara checkpoint. So no coca cola for a few hours … you should call one of your friends down there—he's the one with the blue hatchback.
FRIENDLY SOLDIER. Sorry mate, I'd help if I could—but I'm just a lowly Turai—a Private
  A beat
FRIENDLY SOLDIER. Shame, I could kill a coke…
SHOPKEEPER. I know—these checkpoints hurt everyone eh? I tell you what, how about a nice shay bin nana? That will refresh us?
FRIENDLY SOLDIER. Well—I wouldn't say no
SHOPKEEPER. I make it really good—I have a pot of mint on the back step and it tastes

so fresh. You wait—you have to try it to believe it. We'll all have a cup. It will make us feel refreshed and revived. The best. Trust me.

FRIENDLY SOLDIER. Ok, thanks

He gets up and goes into the shop to make the tea.

SCENE

(2005) We are outside a house, it is old but well kept. There is a small gate and front garden, outside which stand two men.

TRANSLATOR. Are you sure about this?

A beat

The Man nods

A beat

TRANSLATOR. And it's definitely this one?

The man nods

TRANSLATOR. OK. But I'll warn you again—you must be prepared for—well you know

The man nods

TRANSLATOR. Right then—you stay here. I'll go.

The Man stands by the gate, the translator walks up to the door and knocks. He looks back at the man and smiles weakly.

Eventually the door is opened by the Resident.

RESIDENT. Hello

TRANSLATOR. Hi, I'm sorry to bother you, I'm a translator, I'm working with the Orchestra, you know the

RESIDENT. Oh yes, they are wonderful—I have tickets for tomorrow night

TRANSLATOR. Oh, that's good. Well this man here

He points to the man

TRANSLATOR. is one of the musicians and, believe it or not, his mother used to live here

RESIDENT. In Jerusalem

TRANSLATOR. In this very house

RESIDENT. Oh. I see.

TRANSLATOR. And well, he wondered if he could have a quick look inside,

Pause

The Resident looks at the Man who stares back—he doesn't smile, nor does he frown. He wears a blank expression on his face. The Resident considers this face

RESIDENT. And he's a musician?

TRANSLATOR. Yes. A very good one. The best.

RESIDENT. Of course he can come and have a look, come on,

Gesturing to the Man

RESIDENT. Come in

The translator gestures to the Man who tentatively approaches the front door. They all go in and the door closes behind them.

SCENE

(2016) A girl in Palestine has left a message on Skype.

RULA. Ya Nadia—not there? Shoo? It's 10:20 with me, we agreed … oh right—the time

difference ... yes you're two hours behind me. Imagine Palestine being ahead of the West in something. I'll try you later. I'm waiting for you cousin...
She blows a kiss to the screen.

SCENE

(2003) Huwara checkpoint. A huge group of people stand waiting in the heat. People with cars have got out and are milling about. They are all looking at one female soldier, stood there. A man approaches her.

BLUEHATCHBACK MAN. What's the situation?

SOLDIER. Step back please

BLUEHATCHBACK MAN. How long will we have to wait here?

SOLDIER. Step back please. I'm waiting for orders.

BLUEHATCHBACK MAN. I have a car full of food, it's going to go bad in this heat. That's my one there—see? The blue hatchback? I've got coca cola—want one?
The soldier doesn't reply

BLUEHATCHBACK MAN. I just want to know if you think it's worth me waiting. I don't want to leave if it's going to be 15 minutes, but I don't want to wait if it's going to be closed all day. I need to get to Ramallah. With my supplies. I'm delivering them. It would be a shame if they went bad.
A beat

BLUEHATCHBACK MAN. So what do you think? I know all this isn't your fault—should I stick it out a bit longer or go?
No answer
The man looks despondent, he's not sure what to do. He takes out his mobile and moves away from the soldier—he makes a call.
A young woman in a hijab walks forward and hands her papers to the soldier.

SOLDIER. What's this?

WOMAN. My papers

SOLDIER. The checkpoint is closed.

WOMAN. But it's 3 o'clock

SOLDIER. and?

WOMAN. You told me yesterday
A beat

WOMAN. To come back—remember? I'm the student. I study here and my parents live over there—10 minutes walk. I haven't seen them for a month because this checkpoint is always closed on the days I'm not studying.
A beat

WOMAN. You told me to come back here with my papers today at 3 and you would let me go and see my parents
A beat

WOMAN. They're old
A beat

WOMAN. I miss them.

SOLDIER. I think you have me mixed up with someone else. You probably think we all look the same.

WOMAN. No, I know it was you. I remember

SOLDIER. You must be mistaken.

A beat
WOMAN. Please.
SOLDIER. Step back. This checkpoint is closed.
WOMAN. But-
SOLDIER. Step back
The man has finished his phone conversation and approached again
BLUEHATCHBACK MAN. Is it worth trying Awarta? I know it's usually for trucks but—?
No answer
BLUEHATCHBACK MAN. We don't want to bother you—really just let us know if it's worth us waiting or not.
The soldier turns her back on them. The two rejoin the throng of people, watching and waiting to see if the checkpoint will open.

SCENE

(1948) A group of male soldiers are inside a house. The house is empty but there are signs that it has only recently been vacated, the table is laid for dinner. The Soldiers look at the things in the house.
SOLDIER 1. Look at this picture
SOLDIER 2. It's very nice isn't it?
SOLDIER 1. It is. Colourful. Do you want it?
SOLDIER 2. No—no you saw it first—you can have it
SOLDIER 1. Are you sure? Do you think it will get ruined in the jeep—that would be a shame.
SOLDIER 2. I tell you what—lets take it out of the frame and roll it up—then you can get it reframed when you get home.
SOLDIER 1. Good idea
The two men very carefully take the picture down and proceed to remove it from the frame and roll it up.
SOLDIER 3. *(From off stage)* They've got a gramophone! I haven't seen one of these for ages! Listen!
Umm Kulthum's Fakarouni plays
The soldiers stop and listen
The sound of the needle sliding off the record
SOLDIER 3. *(Still off stage)* Sorry about that
SOLDIER 2. What a racket!
SOLDIER 3. Try this
On comes Eric Satie Gymnopodie no 3
SOLDIER 1. That's more like it.
Soldier 3 comes on
SOLDIER 3. It's in really good condition. We should bring it with us, give it to the captain for the mess
SOLDIER 2. Good idea.
SOLDIER 3. And the kitchen is fully stocked—try this jam—it's delicious
SOLDIER 1. What kind?
SOLDIER 3. quince—it's lovely
SOLDIER 1. It's heaven—is there much there?

SOLDIER 3. I'll collect up the jars, I've never tasted anything like it
He goes back next door
SOLDIER 2. There's some lovely embroidered bedding next door as well, I'll pile it up to bring.
SOLDIER 1. See if you can get something to wrap it in, we've got to be careful with this stuff on the jeep. It could get ruined,
SOLDIER 3. *(From off)* Chaps there's a whole cake in the larder—get in here!

SCENE

(2002) We are in a small studio flat, a woman is there, with a dressing gown on. She sits on the bed applying make up. The sound of a buzzer. The woman gets up, hurriedly puts away her make up and turns off the radio and answers the entry phone.
WOMAN. Hello? Come up
She checks her hair and face in the mirror.
She takes off her dressing gown to reveal a modest, but sexy negligee.
There's a knock at the door
She opens it, there is a man there. He is the friendly soldier from the tanks outside the shop scene.
FRIENDLY SOLDIER. Hi.
WOMAN. Hi, come in. How are you?
FRIENDLY SOLDIER. Oh, fine, a bit better
WOMAN. And your mother?
FRIENDLY SOLDIER. Getting worse
WOMAN. I'm sorry to hear that.... Would you like something to drink?
FRIENDLY SOLDIER. No, thank you
WOMAN. What's the matter?
FRIENDLY SOLDIER. Nothing, I'm sorry I'm late. The traffic was a nightmare. Almost a standstill on Ayalon. There was a bomb scare. Then I had a run in with this taxi driver
WOMAN. Arab?
FRIENDLY SOLDIER. No, Israeli
WOMAN. What happened?
FRIENDLY SOLDIER. I clipped his tail light—it was an accident—you could hardly see it—but he went crazy asking me where I was going. He wanted my number
WOMAN. What did you do?
FRIENDLY SOLDIER. Drove off. I couldn't give it to him. You know I'm signed off for stress—I have to avoid anything like that...
A beat
FRIENDLY SOLDIER. Did you get my message?
WOMAN. No I didn't—but it's ok. When you are coming I normally clear my afternoon.
FRIENDLY SOLDIER. I didn't know that. You didn't get my message?
WOMAN. No. But I don't mind. You're here now.
A beat
WOMAN. You seem really shaken. You're not yourself.
A beat
WOMAN. Did the taxi driver bother you that much?
FRIENDLY SOLDIER. Check the message I left you

WOMAN. Why?
FRIENDLY SOLDIER. I asked you something in it. Check it.
WOMAN. Why don't you just-
FRIENDLY SOLDIER. Check it.
WOMAN. Ok, ok
She gets up and finds her mobile.
WOMAN. Are you sure you won't have a drink?
He shakes his head.
She listens to her voicemail. She hangs up.
WOMAN. I see.
FRIENDLY SOLDIER. Is it OK?
WOMAN. What do you mean?
FRIENDLY SOLDIER. Do you mind?
WOMAN. Why would I mind? If it's what you want
FRIENDLY SOLDIER. It is. Very much
WOMAN. I'm a little surprised.
FRIENDLY SOLDIER. So am I—but I thought I should be honest with you. If I can't be with you then—
WOMAN. Yes. But I'll need you to be more specific.
FRIENDLY SOLDIER. What?
WOMAN. You need to tell me what you want.
FRIENDLY SOLDIER. Oh. Well. Perhaps I—hold on.
He takes a jotter and pen from his pocket and writes for a moment or two.
He then hands the paper to the woman.
She reads, nods.
WOMAN. What does that say?
FRIENDLY SOLDIER. Wall.
WOMAN. Oh.
She continues to read.
WOMAN. Ok. Well it's not exactly—I mean it's unusual.
FRIENDLY SOLDIER. If you are uncomfortable—
WOMAN. No, no it's ok. But it's going to be double.
FRIENDLY SOLDIER. I'll pay you triple.
WOMAN. Do you want me to change?
FRIENDLY SOLDIER. Would you mind?
WOMAN. What shall I wear?
He goes to her drawers and looks at the clothes. He takes out a pair of dark tracksuit bottoms and denim shirt with a faint military air.
WOMAN. Really?
He nods
She takes off the negligee and puts on the tracksuit bottoms and shirt and faces him.
FRIENDLY SOLDIER. Good. Do you have any boots?
She takes out a pair of heeled boots
FRIENDLY SOLDIER. they're a bit trendy
WOMAN. It's all I have
She puts them on.
FRIENDLY SOLDIER. Can you tie your hair back, and take off your make up.

She shrugs and does so. He looks around the space for the props he wants. He brings a chair centre stage and takes some of her tights out of the drawer. He's warming to the task, getting into it.

He takes a pillow off the bed.

WOMAN. Ready

FRIENDLY SOLDIER. Great. Now here's what I'm thinking.

He whispers into her ear, she raises an eyebrow but nods

FRIENDLY SOLDIER. Understand?

WOMAN. Understand.

He takes off all his clothes except for his underpants

FRIENDLY SOLDIER. No talking.

WOMAN. Understand.

A beat

FRIENDLY SOLDIER. Go!

She pushes him into the chair and ties his hands to it with a pair of tights. He is acting scared. She then takes another pair of tights and stuffs them into his mouth so he can't talk. Finally she takes a pair of black tights and blindfolds him.

A beat

She stands on his foot. He moans loudly.

She then pushes the chair so it falls backwards—he cries out.

She gets a small table and throws it upside down on his chest, he yelps in surprise. She sits on it crushing his torso, again he makes a noise.

Woman (Monica Orozco) gags Friendly Soldier (Mark Hines) in *Scenes from 70* Years* by Hannah Khalil, directed by Jess McLeod (photograph by Airan Wright).

She bounces up and down a little, knocking the wind out of him.

Finally she hesitantly picks up the pillow from the bed and holds it above his face for a moment. Then she presses it down hard.

He moans and struggles a little.

She silently counts to four, then lifts it up

A beat

He is breathing hard and moaning.

She presses the pillow down on to his face again, more moaning and gentle struggling ensues. Again she silently counts, this time to five, then lifts the pillow up.

A beat. More hard breathing and moaning from the Man.

She gets the pillow and presses it harder still on his face—she's getting a taste for this.

He moans and struggles.

She silently counts to 4, 5, 6, 7—the moaning and struggling has stopped. She is frightened. She casts the pillow aside

WOMAN. Are you alright?

She pulls the gag out of his mouth
FRIENDLY SOLDIER. I told you NO TALKING.

SCENE

(1992) A group of women sit on a rug outside, they have a bag with food in it and are sharing a picnic.

WOMAN 1. Right has everyone got a glass of tea? I want to say congratulations to Fatima, we wish you a very happy healthy married life

WOMAN 2. Here here

WOMAN 1. With lots of children

Laughing

WOMAN 1. Boys!

WOMAN 2. Why boys?

WOMAN 3. Thank you. This is such a nice idea.

WOMAN 1. Did you see the house yet?

WOMAN 3. No, not yet. Why?

WOMAN 1. Everyone's saying that Fouad has gone to so much trouble to make it perfect for you.

WOMAN 3. Really?

WOMAN 1. I heard he got a new mattress, imported from Italy

The women laugh, Woman 3 looks embarrassed

WOMAN 2. You mean from Abu Riyad's warehouse!

WOMAN 3. I feel very special

WOMAN 1. You even got to choose your own husband—lucky girl

WOMAN 2. And such a handsome one eh?

Two soldiers who are passing stop

SOLDIER 1. Good afternoon ladies

WOMAN 1. Good afternoon.

SOLDIER 1. What are you doing here?

WOMAN 3. We're having a picnic

SOLDIER 2. Nice day for it.

SOLDIER 1. On your own?

WOMAN 1. Yes. As you see.

SOLDIER 2. What's in the bag?

WOMAN 3. Just some pastries and mezza,

SOLDIER 1. And the flask?

WOMAN 2. Tea. With mint.

SOLDIER 1. Would you mind opening the bag?

Woman 1 opens it

Soldier 1 peers in

SOLDIER 1. Looks nice eh?

SOLDIER 2. Wish my wife could cook like that

A beat

SOLDIER 1. Enjoy your afternoon

They move off.

WOMAN 2. Pass me the tea.

SCENE

(2003) Inside the shop, it looks pretty empty. The Friendly Soldier and the Shopkeeper sit drinking tea, the soldier is on the folding chair the shopkeeper on an empty olive oil can.

FRIENDLY SOLDIER. Then my father died

SHOPKEEPER. Yaboyay, what bad luck. How did he die?

FRIENDLY SOLDIER. He had a heart attack, in his sleep, so it would have been completely painless they said.

SHOPKEEPER. And your mother? How did she take it?

FRIENDLY SOLDIER. That's the worst part, she was devastated, crying and crying. But when I went back the next day she was fine, then I realised she'd forgotten—that's the disease you see, so I had to tell her again, and her reaction was exactly the same, awful. This happened every day for a week until the nurse said "don't tell her anymore, it's not worth it."

SHOPKEEPER. Poor woman

FRIENDLY SOLDIER. And now I have to lie to her, she says why hasn't that bastard come to see me, tell him I'm getting a divorce. And I say he's busy with work, or he's at the dentist or anything that comes into my head. It makes me feel really bad. I got signed off work for stress last year you know

SHOPKEEPER. That's bad, how old is your mother?

FRIENDLY SOLDIER. 70

SHOPKEEPER. And to think my old mum is 87 and still climbing olive trees, I am blessed…

FRIENDLY SOLDIER. You are mate, you are.

A beat

FRIENDLY SOLDIER. Does she really climb—

An Arab man comes into the shop then sees the soldier and turns to go

SHOPKEEPER. Yusef, hello! How are you my friend, yulla come and try don't be shy!

NERVOUS MAN. I'm in a hurry

SHOPKEEPER. What are you after?

NERVOUS MAN. Nothing. *Looking pointedly at the soldier* Nothing.

FRIENDLY SOLDIER. I better be going, thank you for the shay

SHOPKEEPER. It's ok, you don't have to go

FRIENDLY SOLDIER. I better—don't want anyone to steal my tank.

Soldier goes

NERVOUS MAN. What was he doing here?

SHOPKEEPER. Drinking tea, probably going to buy something until you came in like a ticking bomb

NERVOUS MAN. What do you mean?

SHOPKEEPER. Look at yourself Yusef you are a twitching mess. A bundle of nerves

NERVOUS MAN. What the hell do you expect there's bloody tanks parked in the streets!

SHOPKEEPER. We've all got our problems my friend, my supplies are stuck at Huwara! What's the matter?

NERVOUS MAN. I've only got a few hours before they re-impose curfew but how will I know when they do it?

SHOPKEEPER. You'll know

NERVOUS MAN. How?

SHOPKEEPER. When everyone else disappears
NERVOUS MAN. Every other Palestinian in Ramalllah seems to have an inbuilt clock—they instinctively know when the curfew is starting—except me
SHOPKEEPER. Just look around to see who's about
NERVOUS MAN. I do that but then by the time I've realised, I'm the only one left, it's too late and those sons of bitches start taking pot shots at me
Shopkeeper is laughing
NERVOUS MAN. It's not funny—look
He pulls up his shirt to show a bandage in his stomach
SHOPKEEPER. Shit—you were shot?
NERVOUS MAN. Yes I was shot. Why are you surprised! There are men with guns, tanks!
SHOPKEEPER. You should be careful—get inside when there's a curfew
NERVOUS MAN. I KNOW ! That's what I try to do but I never know when it is.
SHOPKEEPER. Relax, what can I get you? Tea?
NERVOUS MAN. I'm in a hurry—but I need …
SHOPKEEPER. Yes?
NERVOUS MAN. You know—
SHOPKEEPER. Oh. I don't have any
NERVOUS MAN. Don't lie! Before all this they were as common as olives, now you can't find them anywhere. Please
SHOPKEEPER. What do you want it for?
NERVOUS MAN. Why does it matter? Do you have any or not?
SHOPKEEPER. I have but it depends what you want it for
NERVOUS MAN. Do you have any or not? Stop wasting my time
SHOPKEEPER. How many do you want?
NERVOUS MAN. One, two
SHOPKEEPER. Well it can't be for cooking then
NERVOUS MAN. What difference? Is there one kind for cooking and another kind for—?
SHOPKEEPER. No they are all the same but the price is different. I'll get them
He goes to the back of the shop and comes back with two onions
NERVOUS MAN. Thank you
He hands over a note, the shopkeeper gives him change
NERVOUS MAN. What's this?
SHOPKEEPER. Your change
NERVOUS MAN. Where's the rest?
SHOPKEEPER. Prices fluctuate my friend—it's the economy
NERVOUS MAN. Two onions!
SHOPKEEPER. They're in demand at the moment
NERVOUS MAN. You've charged me 3 times the regular price
SHOPKEEPER. Because I know you—anyone else would have to pay 5 times. Do you want them or not?
NERVOUS MAN. It's a lot of money
SHOPKEEPER. I'm the shopkeeper I can charge what I like
The man gives him a cross look
SHOPKEEPER. If you don't want give them back

NERVOUS MAN. Let me think
SHOPKEEPER. You better hurry up, the curfew is not far away
NERVOUS MAN. What? How do you know?
SHOPKEEPER. Can't you tell? The street sounds different
NERVOUS MAN. Oh my god. I'll take them, this time.
SHOPKEEPER. Send my regards to your wife—tell her she'll get a better price if she comes in
NERVOUS MAN. Why?
SHOPKEEPER. Because she uses them for cooking.... Get home safely
The man exits.

SCENE

(1948) The boy covered in bandages sits centre stage. There is a group of young men around him, and his father stands behind him.
FATHER. Mohammed, what is that?
MAN 1. My gun.
FATHER. I told you I didn't want guns in my house
MAN 1. But I might need–
MAN 2. No—go and put it by the door with the others
Man 1 goes off to dispose of his gun
FATHER. If my wife saw that, with the boy,
MAN 2. I'm so sorry. It won't happen again.
A beat
Man 1 returns
MAN 2. You were saying?
As the father speaks he undoes the bandages from the boy's head and then his hands and leg
FATHER. I was finished actually. I just hope you were all listening. I know some of you will think that this is women's work, but it's 1948, not 1928. This is the modern world. A new era for us and it is vitally important for all of you to understand the principles of first aid, it may make the difference between life and death. You need to practise so why don't you pair up, as there's an odd number one of you can use my son here, the rest of you work on each other, just pick one part of the body to bandage and have a go, I'll come back in 10 minutes and let you know how you've done. There's more supplies in this box here.
The father leaves the room.
The men get in pairs, Man 1 goes to the boy.
MAN 1. Do you mind if I bandage you up again?
BOY. No just so long as it's not my head.
MAN 1. How about I do your arm and sling it?
BOY. Ok.
The man starts
The boy watches him critically
The man notices
MAN 1. What is it? Too tight?
BOY. No, not nearly tight enough. Remember what he said, it has to stop the swelling and the flow of blood so it needs to be really tight. Start again.

MAN 1. Right
He does
BOY. That's better
The man continues to work
MAN 1. So I suppose you are going to be a doctor like your father?
BOY. Why do you say that?
MAN 1. You seem to know what you are doing.
BOY. Only because he always uses me as the test dummy
A beat
BOY. I don't want to be a doctor.
MAN 1. No?
BOY. No. Ask me what I want to be
MAN 1. No.
BOY. Why?
MAN 1. Because I already know. And it's a bad idea
BOY. Why?
MAN 1. It's too dangerous. And you are too smart.
BOY. I'm not. I want to help. Let me hold your gun
MAN 1. No.
BOY. Please! Why?
MAN 1. Because you are a boy. But according to them you are a man.
BOY. What do you mean?
MAN 1. Their law says any one of us over the age of 10 with a weapon will be treated as an adult
BOY. So?
MAN 1. So maybe you aren't as smart as I thought. You'd go to prison, maybe even be executed. Just for being caught holding a gun. Understand?
The man has finished and looks at his handiwork. It's a bit messy but does the job
BOY. I'm not afraid.
MAN 1. You should be.
BOY. I want to help.
MAN 1. How's your counting?
BOY. I can do it
MAN 1. How many can you count to?
BOY. As many as you like
MAN 1. Well if you want to help maybe you could count some bullets for me
The boy smiles
BOY. What happens if they catch me with bullets?
MAN 1. What use are bullets without a gun?
The father re-enters the room
FATHER. Right let's see how you are doing.
He goes to two men, one of whom has a bandage on his head.
FATHER. What's this?
MAN 2. He has a head wound,
FATHER. He'd be dead by now if that's the best you can do. Come on, all of you, I keep telling you, this is life and death. You need to pay attention. Right wallad, come here, I need your head

BOY. Oh!
FATHER. You're saving these men's lives. Now everyone watch
He begins to bandage up his son's head again.

SCENE

(2005) We are now inside the house where the Man and Translator are being shown round by the Resident.

RESIDENT. And finally this is the kitchen, which is pretty much as it would have been in 1948, in your mother's time.
TRANSLATOR. This is the kitchen, similar to how it would have been in 1948,
RESIDENT. The windows have been re-done obviously. And I think there used to be a wall here which was demolished to give the place more space, open it up and make it lighter
TRANSLATOR. There are new windows and a wall may have been removed here
RESIDENT. Oh he's looking at those tiles? They have been here as long as the house, I think that wall was covered in them once. Most of them fell off, but those four clung on somehow, refused to fall off, my wife hates them, wanted me to remove them but I insisted we keep them. They are authentic.
TRANSLATOR. He saw you looking at the tiles and says that they are originals, most have fallen off
RESIDENT. Would you like a glass of wine?
TRANSLATOR. We wouldn't want to impose on you any more—you've been extremely kind—
RESIDENT. Nonsense come on, have a glass with me.
The Resident takes out three wine glasses and a bottle from the fridge, pours wine and ushers them to sit at the table. The three drink for a moment in silence.
TRANSLATOR. I'm very surprised you let us in. Do you mind me asking how long you have lived here?
RESIDENT. 7 years, we came from the Loire Valley, in France.
TRANSLATOR. Oh it's beautiful there—all the vineyards
RESIDENT. That's right. But my family were only there for a generation, they were originally from Krakow in Poland.
TRANSLATOR. I see
RESIDENT. So you know what happened to them. Except my grandmother, she got out. Hid in a suitcase. Only got as far as Paris and then the war ended.
A beat
I still have that suitcase, it's an heirloom. You wouldn't believe someone could fit in it. She must have been so small. Desperate.
TRANSLATOR. Yes.
RESIDENT. My grandmother always wanted to come here, but she didn't make it. So my wife and I brought the suitcase here, a kind of pilgrimage and fell in love with it. You know when you feel you belong somewhere? We decided we should move here. To Jerusalem, my mother was furious, she said "don't you want a quiet life?"
A beat
RESIDENT. I'd like him to know that we love this house. We loved the place as soon as we saw it. We stood outside and put our arms around one another and thought, this is it, ok maybe my father, or grandfather or great grandfather didn't live here, but my ancestors did and that's in the bones, you know. This is the end of the journey started

by my grandmother. And now we, she, can have peace. It's like it was built for us. Home.
A beat
RESIDENT. Maybe don't translate that—it might seem insensitive.
Pause
TRANSLATOR. You feel at peace? Even with everything that's going on?
RESIDENT. Peace comes from inside you. If I didn't feel peace I wouldn't have let him in would I? But I'm not surprised, that he came. I knew he would
TRANSLATOR. How?
RESIDENT. It's like the final bit of the puzzle: this house has always had a feeling, a presence
TRANSLATOR. A ghost?
RESIDENT. No not that—it's like it has a memory. Sometimes you feel it in some of the rooms—a breeze like the echo of someone who was once there. It sounds stupid I know. My wife says I'm crazy, but I'm not. I knew it. I knew someone would come, sometime,
TRANSLATOR. And he did.
RESIDENT. I've looked forward to it actually, knowing that would be the full stop. The end, he'd see we belong here, and he could move on with his life and us ours, be at peace.
Pause
RESIDENT. Do you want to translate that?
The Translator drains his glass awkwardly.
TRANSLATOR. Perhaps later, thank you so much for your hospitality, we really should go, there's a rehearsal in a while and he can't be late
RESIDENT. Ok, well I hope that he's—you know he could have taken photos if he'd wanted
They get up and move towards the door. The Man and the Translator step outside.
RESIDENT. Good bye then, I hope the concerts go well, I'm really looking forward to them
TRANSLATOR. *(to man)* He hopes the concerts go well. *(to resident)* Thank you
RESIDENT. Oh hold on, wait a minute. Just wait there.
The Resident closes the door on the men and goes inside
TRANSLATOR. He told us to wait for a moment
Pause
The Resident opens the door beaming
RESIDENT. I found it—look, it's one of the tiles from the wall. I threw most of them away but I remembered I kept one. Maybe he'd like to have it. *(Directly to the man)* Here—take this—it would have been on the wall when your mother was here
The Resident looks directly at the man and hands him the tile which the man takes and stares at
TRANSLATOR. Thank you.
RESIDENT. I thought he'd like it. Goodbye then,
TRANSLATOR. Goodbye, thanks
The Resident shuts the door.
The man stares at the tile, then looks at the house. He continues to stare at the house until the Translator gently takes him by the arm and leads him away.

SCENE

(1960) There is a long queue of people from one side of the stage to the other, waiting, smoking, looking bored.

SCENE

(2010) Inside an office. A male Western charity worker is talking to a an Israeli female official. Both hold lists in their hands which they consult periodically.

OFFICIAL. What else?
CHARITY WORKER. toilet cleaner
OFFICIAL. OK
CHARITY WORKER. baby wipes
OFFICIAL. OK
CHARITY WORKER. female hygiene products
She looks at him he's a little embarrassed, she smiles a little
OFFICIAL. Tampons?
CHARITY WORKER. And sanitary towels
OFFICIAL. OK
CHARITY WORKER. toothpaste
OFFICIAL. OK
CHARITY WORKER. toothbrushes
OFFICIAL. OK
CHARITY WORKER. bath sponges
OFFICIAL. OK
CHARITY WORKER. candles
OFFICIAL. OK
CHARITY WORKER. blankets
OFFICIAL. OK
CHARITY WORKER. mineral water
OFFICIAL. OK
CHARITY WORKER. plastic combs
OFFICIAL. OK
CHARITY WORKER. sticks for brooms
OFFICIAL. OK
CHARITY WORKER. tea
OFFICIAL. OK
CHARITY WORKER. coffee
OFFICIAL. ummmm oh yes here—OK
CHARITY WORKER. Canned tuna
OFFICIAL. OK
CHARITY WORKER. Canned beans
OFFICIAL. OK
CHARITY WORKER. canned pineapple
OFFICIAL. No sorry
CHARITY WORKER. What?
OFFICIAL. You can't bring that in
CHARITY WORKER. Why?

OFFICIAL. It says so here
CHARITY WORKER. I can't bring in canned pineapple?
OFFICIAL. Nope
CHARITY WORKER. What about canned peaches
OFFICIAL. No sorry—no canned fruit
CHARITY WORKER. Oh. Right. Ok. So the canned Tuna and beans is ok, but not the canned fruit
OFFICIAL. you got it. No canned fruit.
CHARITY WORKER. Right. OK so I'll—
OFFICIAL. You'll have to off load it. Anything else
CHARITY WORKER. A few other things yes
OFFICIAL. go on then
CHARITY WORKER. tahini
OFFICIAL. yes
CHARITY WORKER. zaatar
OFFICIAL. yes
CHARITY WORKER. olives
OFFICIAL. yes
CHARITY WORKER. pasta
OFFICIAL. yes
CHARITY WORKER. sesame seeds
OFFICIAL. yes
CHARITY WORKER. black pepper
OFFICIAL. yes
CHARITY WORKER. Salt
OFFICIAL. oh—wait—I can't—no I can't see that here
CHARITY WORKER. no salt?
OFFICIAL. I don't think so—hm odd one—I can check on that if you like
CHARITY WORKER. Please. What about chicken stock powder?
OFFICIAL. yes that's ok
CHARITY WORKER. and I've got some clothes
OFFICIAL. of course
CHARITY WORKER. Shoes
OFFICIAL. fine
CHARITY WORKER. and some chocolate and toys and that's it
OFFICIAL. No
CHARITY WORKER. No?
OFFICIAL. No. You can't bring those last two things in. I'll check on the salt
CHARITY WORKER. I can't bring in chocolate or toys, why?
OFFICIAL. Not on the list I'm afraid
CHARITY WORKER. Why?
OFFICIAL. I didn't write it friend, I'm sorry
CHARITY WORKER. But why—in your opinion—why would the state want the children of Gaza to be denied toys?
OFFICIAL. Good place to smuggle guns I guess
CHARITY WORKER. What about chocolate?
OFFICIAL. I understand your frustration but please, I'm just doing my job

CHARITY WORKER. You realise that there are 1.5 million people who are effectively imprisoned in Gaza and half of them are children—it's going to be your problem when they all come of age don't you think?

OFFICIAL. Don't take that fucking tone with me—you Westerners, you're so fucking self righteous. Wake up! We're just doing your dirty work—the shit you don't have the courage to do yourselves.

Pause

CHARITY WORKER. I'm sorry. I—it's hot and it was a long drive. I'll, I'll off load the toys, chocolate and canned fruit. Would you check the salt situation for me?

OFFICIAL. I've just remembered—salt's off the list too. So you better off load that as well. Then you can be on your way.

SCENE

(2016) A girl in Palestine waits in front of a computer.

RULA. *(quietly)* Bastana el daw el akhdar.... Waiting—for the green light, for the little noise it makes. To show she's there. Waiting. Everyone here is watching me so I'm pretending I'm already talking to her. But there's no one there yet. She's not online. No one is listening. There's no audience. Or is there? Maybe I'm being watched ... by those Anonymous guys ... or the secret service ... or someone else. Well I don't care. I'm going to talk anyway. And my English is better than any of the hameer in this library so they don't understand what I'm saying. Yalla Nadia! Weinik inti? I hate waiting. I will never get used to waiting. Waiting. Don't you make me wait too. Come on! I'm getting nervous. For the question I need to ask you. Nervous! Silly isn't it! To talk to my cousin, on the other side of the world. England. While I'm here in Palestine. I shouldn't be nervous of her. There's nothing to be scared of. Just a little question—she can say yes, she can say no—I hope she says yes ... but it can't hurt me. There are more dangerous things. There are more dangerous things to be scared of. I should be scared of the dark. That would be smart. At night. Outside. It's dangerous. But I go out anyway. Wait until everyone else is in bed. And then I sneak out. In my black hoodie. Armed. Sneak down the backstreets. My hair is hidden, so is my face. I want them to think I'm a boy. A ghost. A phantom. I go looking for my spot. My target. I always know where it will be. I plan in advance. I'm organised. Decide the best way to get there without being spotted. And once I arrive and make sure no one is around I take out my weapon and start. Spraying. Red. Green. Black. White. Those are my colours. You can guess why. I have one picture—logo—tag. Not like Handala the barefoot Palestinian boy—mine is a tree. I use a stencil. It was sent to me by a woman in Syria. She used it there. This tree's branches spell out words—whatever I want them to say—so this way it's an original and a copy at the same time. I like that. Sometimes I write "tahrir." Freedom. Sometimes I write the names of people in prison—people who everyone thinks are forgotten, sometimes the names of the dead. It depends. On what's happening. But the most exciting part is the next day when someone discovers this new drawing on the wall. They all start talking and wondering who is the new Palestinian Banksy! Khally wally Banksy.... His pictures are considered art. No one would dare touch them ... but mine are gone by the end of the day. Painted over. Gone but not forgotten. I need to make sure they're not forgotten So, I'm waiting for my cousin Nadia to call me ... to ask her...

She turns to someone nearby who has said something to her.

No I'm still using it—sorry this is an important call—from London.

SCENE

(2002) An attractive woman stands outside Tel Aviv airport, she is waiting for a taxi. She sees the Taxi driver in his car and approaches him

WOMAN. Are you free?

TAXI DRIVER. Depends—where you going?

WOMAN. Home

TAXI DRIVER. Where's that?

WOMAN. Ramat Aviv

TAXI DRIVER. Oh—OK, I should warn you the traffic's a nightmare today—there was a bomb scare in town and everyone's acting crazy

WOMAN. I don't care how long it takes—I just want to get back to my house

TAXI DRIVER. Let me help you with your bag

He lifts it into the boot

WOMAN. What happened to your taillight?

TAXI DRIVER. Like I said there are crazy people out today.

They get in the car—she in the front seat. He starts the engine and they drive a little while in silence

TAXI DRIVER. So you been on holiday? Lucky you

WOMAN. Sort of

TAXI DRIVER. Where were you?

WOMAN. Poland

TAXI DRIVER. No wonder you don't have a tan

WOMAN. It was cold.

TAXI DRIVER. Should have gone to the red sea—that's where I always go

WOMAN. It wasn't just a holiday

TAXI DRIVER. No?

WOMAN. I had to go—for my service

TAXI DRIVER. Oh, oh right. I did that—years ago—I remember they took my fingerprints on the first day and pictures of my teeth—I thought—hey I'm not the prisoner here!

WOMAN. Where did you serve?

TAXI DRIVER. Ended up a driver! All over. Chauffeuring Generals—all sorts. What I'm good at.... Poland—so did they make you go to?

WOMAN. Auschwitz

TAXI DRIVER. Ah. Have you been before?

WOMAN. No

TAXI DRIVER. That's a tough one eh? Seeing the actual place ... what happened there.... Really gets you. Never affected my family—they came here in the 1920s, but it's a terrible place. Eerie ... you can feel the presence of all those poor people, don't you think?

A beat

TAXI DRIVER. I kind of also always wondered why? You know why send us there? It's a terrible thing and it's important to remember, but it's too late to change that now. I mean did you feel it was relevant to you?

WOMAN. What do you mean? Of course it's relevant

TAXI DRIVER. Excuse me, I mean to your day-to-day work—on the front. I mean it's important to remember like you say, that people want to destroy us and all that, but when you are in the service you are reminded of that every day aren't you? When you live here you are reminded of that every day. Why send the young people to Auschwitz, or Belsen, it's depressing.
WOMAN. That's offensive.
TAXI DRIVER. Oh I don't mean to offend you—I'm just trying to say it's a shame a nice young girl like you has to go and experience all that. See it. I dreamt about it for months afterwards.
A beat
WOMAN. So what happened with your taillight?
TAXI DRIVER. Oh nothing much—some guy was in a real hurry—you'd think his pants were on fire, and he clipped it. But when I got out and asked for his number he just drove off... what's the world coming to eh?
WOMAN. Arab?
TAXI DRIVER. No Israeli. People are so disappointing aren't they? Israeli and Arab, there are good ones and bad ones and this one was a bad one,
The woman begins to sob
WOMAN. Stop the car
TAXI DRIVER. we're in the middle of traffic—do you feel sick?
WOMAN. I need to get out, I can't breathe.
TAXI DRIVER. What is it? You're white
WOMAN. Just STOP
TAXI DRIVER. I think you're having a panic attack
WOMAN. STOP THE CAR
He stops the car and she gets out. We hear other drivers beeping at him
TAXI DRIVER. HEY HEY Easy pal! She's not well! Same to you!
While the taxi driver waits for the woman to sort herself out this scene bleeds into the next and we simultaneously see.

SCENE

(2002/2007) A man is shown into a room where he sits down on a chair to wait. He is the man who had the blue hatchback in the checkpoint scene. He is alone. He goes to light a cigarette but sees a no smoking sign. He puts away the packet and waits. He hums a few bars of Umm Kulthum Fakarouni.
As both taxi driver and blue hatchback man wait they say in sync:
TAXI DRIVER/BLUEHATCHBACK MAN: What a day. All I want is drive around but there's always something in the way. Imagine to be in America. The open road, route 66, miles and miles of clear road as far as the eye can see. No traffic jams, check points, road blocks, diversions, nothing. Just a straight clear road all the way to the horizon. Not even another car. You could fall asleep at the wheel and nothing bad would happen. Imagine. Driving off into the sunset.... A dream.

SCENE

(2010) A Woman with a camera and a bag stands outside another house, she knocks on the door.
WOMAN. Haitham, come on—it's time. Are you ready?

VOICE FROM INSIDE. No—I can't I can't come today
WOMAN. What do you mean? Open the door are you ok?
VOICE FROM INSIDE. I'm busy—not well
WOMAN. But it's Friday—and it was your idea—it's great come on open the door
VOICE FROM INSIDE. I think it's a bad idea
WOMAN. It's not it's brilliant—open it—everyone else is waiting for you. They all look fantastic honestly
VOICE FROM INSIDE. Really?
WOMAN. Really. Open up.

The door opens a little then more and a man stands there looking sheepish. He is dressed up as one of the characters from Avatar and his skin is painted blue. He has false pointy ears and a long black wig in plaits.

Woman looks at him and nods encouragingly then starts to laugh

MAN. I knew you would laugh
WOMAN. It's just—you look—great. Come on. It's a great idea—it'll definitely get the world's attention
MAN. You think so?
WOMAN. Of course, come on they're waiting.
MAN. I'm not the only one dressed like this am I?
WOMAN. No—Mohammed, Kamila and Hameed—loads of people.
MAN. Ok—hold on a minute

He gets his Palestinian flag from inside the door.

MAN. Let's go then.

They begin to walk to the bottom of the street, as they do more people join them, some dressed as Avatar characters, some with their faces covered with scarves, others in more traditional western clothes. Woman with her camera begins to take photos. Nervous Man appears

MAN. Yusef! What are you doing here?
WOMAN. You said you weren't coming again
MAN. What did the doctor say?
NERVOUS MAN. That my stomach ulcer is worse than the bullet wound,
WOMAN. That's the third time you've been shot in as many years—you are so unlucky
NERVOUS MAN. What do you mean unlucky—I'm alive aren't I?
MAN. You shouldn't be here, you aren't even from Bel'in
WOMAN. You're like a dog with a bone, always back for more
NERVOUS MAN. I have to stand in solidarity with you
MAN. What did Hanan say?
NERVOUS MAN. She thinks I'm visiting my mother, if she knew I was here she'd really kill me, seriously—Hanan is scarier that the whole of the IDF, so no photos please? Eh?

They approach a barrier where there is a partition marked by barbed wire and metal girders. Several people put on gas masks including Woman with camera. We do not see the soldiers but they are on the other side of the partition. The villagers of Bel'in begin their peaceful protest chanting:

"No wall in Bel'in"

They wave their Palestinian flags and a couple of men begin to shake the barrier with their hands

Suddenly a tear gas grenade is fired at them it lands at the feet of Woman with camera.

MAN. Shit! I knew I forgot something—

Nervous man takes an onion from his pocket and a small penknife and cut it in half

NERVOUS MAN. Here

The two men hold the onions to their noses

Avatar man picks up the canister and throws it back in the direction it came from.

Woman begins to take photographs.

More tear gas canisters are thrown as someone shouts from the crowd

"Shame on you! This is a peaceful protest!"

The protestors scatter to avoid the tear gas

The stage is now empty but covered in smoke.

Man (Tommy Malouf) and Woman (Annelyse Ahmad) ready themselves for a protest in *Scenes from 70* Years* by Hannah Khalil, directed by Jess McLeod (photograph by Airan Wright).

SCENE

(2011) A little boy is in bed sleeping, it is dark, the early hours of the morning. He is young. His mother enters the room and gently tries to wake him up.

MOTHER. Majeed, Majeed—wake up. It's time.

BOY. Huh? He's mine…

MOTHER. Darling

BOY. I'm taking him home

MOTHER. Majeed, wake up darling…

The boy stirs

BOY. Oh, Maama. I was dreaming.

MOTHER. Not bad ones again?

BOY. Is it time for me to get up?

MOTHER. It is, my boy it is.

BOY. But it's too early.

MOTHER. The bus is coming soon, now come on, up you get.

She encourages him to get up and fetches his clothes. He talks as she does this, and begins to dress himself, she helps him a little now and then.

BOY. It was such a nice dream. There was a cat. A kitten. He was tiny, I could pick him up in my hand. He was a tabby and he liked to be grabbed by the back of the neck because that's what mummy cats do isn't it? But his wasn't there. His mummy. She was gone somewhere else and I found him in the car park, just wondering about. And I put him inside my jacket and he was all warm, and I could feel him moving as he breathed next to my heart. And I showed Sami and Lamia and they were jealous, they tried to take him away but I said you can't because he's mine. He's my cat now.

MOTHER. Did you give him a name?

BOY. No, you woke me up, I didn't get that far.
The mother is now beginning to brush his hair.
MOTHER. Now you remember what you have to say today?
BOY. Yes. Are you coming Maama?
MOTHER. Darling we've been over this. You know I'm not allowed. You have to go. Be a brave boy. You've done it before.
BOY. I know.
A beat
MOTHER. There—you look all smart, now go and brush your teeth
The boy goes to brush his teeth the mother brings out several bags for him to take with him.
MOTHER. So in this one is your breakfast, try and have a little sleep on the bus first, then when you wake up at the first checkpoint eat something ok?
A beat
MOTHER. Aren't you excited?
BOY. I want you to come.
A beat
BOY. Sami says Daddy is in Israel
MOTHER. What—when?
BOY. He said the bus takes so long because I have to travel to a whole nother country
MOTHER. Did he?
A beat
MOTHER. I can't come. You know they don't let me. That's why you have to go. You are the man of the family now, what are you going to say?
BOY. "Mother sends her love and devotion, we both think of you every day and before we eat a meal we say a silent prayer."
MOTHER. Good, what else?
BOY. Sitti is healthy, the olive oil is nearly ready, Farouk is engaged and I got 10 in my English test
MOTHER. Bravo—clever boy
BOY. But why can't you come. I don't like the check points alone
MOTHER. You are with the other children and Mr Red Cross. Come on now—you have to be brave. What would your father do if you didn't visit?
BOY. What will happen when I'm 16?
MOTHER. That's a long way off—why?
BOY. Sami says when I'm 16 I can't go and see him any more—who will see him then?
MOTHER. Oh, don't worry about that you silly billy—daddy will be home long before that. Now come on I think the bus is here.

SCENE

(1960) The long queue of people reappears from one side of the stage to the other it has moved slightly. People continue to wait, smoke, looking bored. A man whistles Umm Kulthum's Fakarouni.

SCENE

(2002) A traveller stands outside Tel Aviv airport he has a couple of suitcases and is waiting for a taxi. The taxi driver approaches him

TAXI DRIVER. Looking for a taxi?
MAN. Yes please
TAXI DRIVER. Over here, that's my car, let me take your bag
MAN. That's kind thank you
TAXI DRIVER. No problem, where you going to?
MAN. It's a bit of a journey
TAXI DRIVER. Where you headed?
MAN. Nazareth
The taxi driver stops and puts down the bag
TAXI DRIVER. Are you kidding me? I can't believe this day
MAN. No. Nazareth, it's where I'm from
TAXI DRIVER. It's another country
MAN. Its only 100 Kilometres
TAXI DRIVER. 102
MAN. I'll pay you whatever you like
TAXI DRIVER. I don't go there.
MAN. Please—there are no other drivers around—I'm in a hurry
TAXI DRIVER. I'll need protection money
A beat
MAN. I need to get home to see my father. He's not well.
A beat
TAXI DRIVER. I think you need an Arab driver. I just don't know that area at all. I never get fares out of Tel Aviv. Besides the traffic's bad today and there are loads of crazies about
MAN. Please. I need to get there.
TAXI DRIVER. But I told you I don't know the way
MAN. I do, I'll show you
TAXI DRIVER. I don't have a map that goes that far
MAN. I have it all up here *(gesturing his head)*
TAXI DRIVER. How can I trust that? When was the last time you were in Israel?
MAN. 1988
TAXI DRIVER. Well it has changed a lot since then. You won't remember
MAN. I can't forget—honestly, it's etched on my memory, this is my home
A beat
TAXI DRIVER. I really think you should wait for an Arab driver. You know what's been going on—there was almost a bomb today. Nazareth isn't safe for me.
MAN. You'll be with me
TAXI DRIVER. How can you protect me? What if we are pulled over by gunmen?
MAN. You keep quiet and I'll talk. In Arabic, to them. I'll tell them who I am, that my Father is unwell. We will be fine.
A beat
MAN. It'll probably never happen anyway
TAXI DRIVER. That's the trouble with you Arabs, you always look on the bright side—don't see the bad things that could happen
A beat
MAN. I'll pay you double what it says on the metre
TAXI DRIVER. Danger money

MAN. Danger money
A beat
TAXI DRIVER. And you are sure you know the way?
MAN. Like the back of my hand. Don't be afraid.
A beat
MAN. Trust me
TAXI DRIVER. Oh all right then, come on, before I change my mind.
MAN. What happened to your taillight?
TAXI DRIVER. Don't ask
The two men move to the car, and we hear the engine starting, then a radio comes on with a news report which we hear as the car drives away.
BBC NEWS READER: Tomorrow is Israeli Independence day and the one day a year when the Israel government allows Palestinians to visit the sites of their former homes, Israel says it will put the IDF on alert for any terrorist activity that may occur...
Static as the driver retunes the channel
TAXI DRIVER. Is that the real reason you're back then? To visit the site of your former home? Cause trouble?
MAN. No, I told you I'm from Nazareth, my father's sick
More static as the taxi driver tries to tune it
TAXI DRIVER. And now I can't find any music ... come on you piece of crap
More static.

SCENE

(1978) Inside a very very basic house, almost a shack. An old man holds a radio, it is battered and the batteries are taped to the back. He is trying to get a reception to hear the news.
  He keeps trying.
  Nothing but static.
  It begins to get something—it is a recording Umm Kulthum's
  Fakarouni he smiles, and begins to slowly sway and mouth the words. He gets into it, and puts down the radio to dance more, but as he does so it loses the signal and becomes static noise again.
  He tuts, annoyed, and turns it off. He then moves to a stool and sits down. He takes out a cigarette and begins to smoke it. Suddenly he moves his hand to his head, something has dripped on it. He looks to the ceiling, there's another drip. He moves his chair to one side and looks at the floor to see if he's right—if there's a drip from the roof. He watches, he waits, he's right there is. He watches one, two, three drips. He gets up and takes a cooking pot and puts it under the drip. He sits smoking and watching it.
  Pause
  Suddenly his young grandson runs into the room
BOY. Seedi Seedi did you hear the news? They've liberated our lands!
GRANDFATHER. What?
BOY. We are free we can go home! Anytime we like! They've liberated/
GRANDFATHER. Thanks be to god (*he jumps up and grabs the radio*) when did you hear that?
BOY. Just now—come on—we can go back
GRANDFATHER. I knew it was coming—patience—that's what I said

He gets a bag and begins to fill it with his clothes and things Didn't I tell you all, I knew it. It couldn't last forever, liberated … free at last
The boy begins to laugh
GRANDFATHER. What?
The boy is laughing hysterically now
BOY. You believed it!
GRANDFATHER. What! You little bastard … come here
The man picks up the stick and chases the boy—he hasn't a hope in hell of catching him
GRANDFATHER. You little bastard
The boy runs away from his Grandfather still laughing and then runs out of the room. The old man stands, out of puff.
GRANDFATHER. You little bastard.
He lowers himself back into his chair and lights another cigarette. He watches the drip again as his breathing gradually returns to normal.
Pause
A man walks in
MAN. You didn't fall for that again?
GRANDFATHER. He's a little bastard
MAN. He knows you will always go for it.
GRANDFATHER. The next time it'll be true and I won't believe him
MAN. You will.
A beat
MAN. There's a drip?
GRANDFATHER. I know—that's why I put the pot
MAN. You can't continue to live like this its been 30 years—I'm going to get some iron from Mohammed, lay it on the roof and
GRANDFATHER. No. Leave it
MAN. You need a proper roof dad
GRANDFATHER. No.
MAN. Please—let me—I worry about your health…
GRANDFATHER. No.
MAN. Having a proper roof doesn't mean anything—
GRANDFATHER. This is not where I live. It's temporary.
MAN. But it's been temporary for—
GRANDFATHER. What would your mother think eh? Defeat? Not yet
MAN. It's just a roof dad.
A beat
GRANDFATHER. Tell that boy of your's next time he pulls that stunt I'll be ready—and if I catch him he won't be able to sit down for a week
A beat
GRANDFATHER. Nothing better to do…

SCENE

(1960) The long queue of people from one side of the stage to the other reappears. The order has changed slightly—it has moved a little. More waiting, smoking, looking bored. Suddenly a man jumps forward and breaks into a loud and fevered rendition of Fakarouni his wife clips him round the ear to shut him up. More bored waiting in line.

SCENE

(1992) The women sit on their rug outside, continuing their picnic.
WOMAN 2. Can you believe Hanan has been married 10 years
WOMAN 3. Really?
WOMAN 1. It's true, I have.
WOMAN 2. What a wedding!
WOMAN 1. It wasn't a wedding
WOMAN 3. Why?
WOMAN 2. Curfew.
WOMAN 3. Oh yes
WOMAN 1. You were just a girl so you wouldn't remember, but we had to be indoors
WOMAN 2. And the bastards cut the electricity too.
WOMAN 1. That's right
WOMAN 2. Well at least your first time was in the dark—just like you!
They laugh, Woman 3 looks embarrassed
WOMAN 1. And my mean mother-in-law was pleased because she didn't have to feed the guests all night!
The soldiers are passing again and stop
SOLDIER 1. Good afternoon ladies
WOMAN 1. Good afternoon.
SOLDIER 1. Still here?
WOMAN 3. We're having a picnic
SOLDIER 2. Nice day for it.
SOLDIER 1. What's in the bag?
WOMAN 1. Just some pastries and mezza,
WOMAN 2. Just like before
SOLDIER 1. And the flask?
WOMAN 2. Still tea.
SOLDIER 1. Would you mind opening the bag?
Woman 1 opens it
Soldier 1 peers in
SOLDIER 1. Nearly finished it all
SOLDIER 2. Didn't leave any for us
A beat
SOLDIER 1. Enjoy your afternoon
They move on
WOMAN 3. Shall we go?
WOMAN 2. No
WOMAN 1. Fadia
WOMAN 2. What? I haven't finished my tea.

SCENE

(2010) A kitchen where a woman puts the finishing touches to dinner and puts it on the table. Her son is watching TV in the next room, there is a news story about the protests in Bel'in and images of the men dressed as the characters from Avatar.
MOTHER. Come on everyone—dinner is ready!

The family come into the kitchen, there's a young son, a father and mother and a teenage daughter. They all sit and the table and begin to pour glasses of water

FATHER. Shall I serve tabbouleh?

DAUGHTER. Not much for me.

MOTHER. If you aren't eating meat anymore you need to eat vegetables

DAUGHTER. I've changed my mind

MOTHER. What do you mean you've changed you mind? I bought some really expensive vegetarian cheese for you

DAUGHTER. It doesn't seem right

MOTHER. That's what you said—and we respected that but Raquel if you want us to take you seriously as an adult you have to—*(to her husband)* speak to her

FATHER. Your mother's right. We respect your choices, you are nearly an adult, but—

DAUGHTER. I'm sorry it just seems wrong to choose not to eat meat when there are people not a million miles away who don't get any choice about what they eat
Pause

FATHER. That's fine. You must do what you think is right—but try and take your time to make a decision—particularly when it affects the rest of the family.

DAUGHTER. How does me being a vegetarian affect—

MOTHER. If you cooked occasionally you'd understand.
A beat

DAUGHTER. Ok. Sorry Mum.

SON. So you're not a veggie any more?

DAUGHTER. No

SON. Oh. Did you see the news dad?

FATHER. What news?

SON. There were some crazy people dressed up as that movie

FATHER. Which one?

SON. The 3-D one?

DAUGHTER. Avatar

MOTHER. What's that?

SON. They painted themselves blue—isn't that funny!

MOTHER. Mm. Do you want more chicken?

SON. And they were all sniffing onions but that's not in the film

MOTHER. Eat your food

DAUGHTER. The onions help with the tear gas

SON. How?

FATHER. Anyone want water?

DAUGHTER. Tear gas makes you feel like you can't breath but the onion helps

SON. Awesome I'm going to do that for Yoav's party! It'll be really funny

MOTHER. Do what?

SON. Dress up as one of those blue guys

FATHER. I think it's best to stick with your cowboy outfit

SON. But—

FATHER. It's already up there in the cupboard, otherwise you're mother will have to find blue paint
Pause

FATHER. I noticed the envelope's still there on the counter

MOTHER. I can post it for you if you like?
DAUGHTER. No—I'll do it.
FATHER. Just remember there is a deadline.
DAUGHTER. I know
FATHER. Don't imagine you are the only girl in the world who wants to go to Oxford
DAUGHTER. I don't

A beat

DAUGHTER. I don't want to go to Oxford
SON. Uh oh

A beat

SON. I've finished—can I go to my room
MOTHER. Don't you want more tabbouleh?
SON. No
MOTHER. Dessert?
SON. What is it?
MOTHER. Ice cream
FATHER. What do you mean you don't want to go? We spent a month on your personal statement
MOTHER. Let's talk about this later
FATHER. Did you know about this?
MOTHER. I had a feeling…
FATHER. But if you stay you'll have to do military service.
MOTHER. You are not doing that.
DAUGHTER. I don't want to leave
FATHER. What are you saying? You want to stay here, go to university here, over my dead body
MOTHER. It's not safe.
DAUGHTER. Yes it is
MOTHER. What about the rockets?
DAUGHTER. How many people have died from the Hamas rockets mum?
SON. Can I go upstairs?
DAUGHTER. How many? You don't know do you? I tried to find out—I looked on the IDF website I know how many rockets have fallen here—but there's no record of how many people have died
SON. Why?
FATHER. Go upstairs
SON. Why?
DAUGHTER. Because they didn't kill anyone
MOTHER. What about Mrs Silverman's niece?
DAUGHTER. She's alive
MOTHER. Thank God—but she was in hospital for 2 days
DAUGHTER. That's because she threw herself down in the middle of the road when she heard a car backfiring
FATHER. We live in a climate of fear—they've made that. That's why we want something better for you.
MOTHER. Where is she getting all of this from? Who have you been talking to?
DAUGHTER. No one. There's a thing called the internet

SON. Can I take some ice cream upstairs?
FATHER. So what exactly is your plan for your life?
DAUGHTER. I don't know. I just don't want to go to Oxford.
FATHER. I dreamed of going to Oxford, but we couldn't afford it, I've saved all my life so—
DAUGHTER. Let him go
SON. Me—no! I don't want to go to England
MOTHER. No one's going to send you there
DAUGHTER. Yet—you better watch out
FATHER. Go upstairs
The boy goes from the room
DAUGHTER. I haven't even got in yet. It'll probably never happen
FATHER. Is that what this is about? Of course you will get in
A beat
DAUGHTER. I'm not going to Oxford, I'm going to the West Bank to see for myself
FATHER. the West Bank?
DAUGHTER. Maybe Gaza too—you can't stop me. I'm nearly 18. I need to know what is going on.
MOTHER. Don't go there look on the internet … watch TV. It's too far
DAUGHTER. Further than Oxford?
MOTHER. Yes.
FATHER. Go upstairs
DAUGHTER. I'm not a child you can order around.
FATHER. You are still my daughter. And you are still underage.
She goes
A beat
The father stands up and picks up the envelope.
FATHER. I'm going to post this.

SCENE

(2016) We hear a skype ring tone then see two faces on the screen. They are cousins. Rula is a 20-year-old Palestinian woman living in the West Bank and Nadia is a 30-year-old mixed-race Palestinian British woman living in the UK. When the picture comes up both women scream and wave madly at each other
RULA. Marhaba Nadia
NADIA. HI hi! Oh my god I can't believe we managed to Skype, yay we did it!
More maniacal waving
NADIA. Where are you?
RULA. At University! What about you?
NADIA. In my house—do you want to see it?
RULA. Sure
NADIA. Ok, I'll just pick up the laptop and show you around. Don't get excited it's a tiny flat! So here's the kitchen area, you see, all my herbs and things, the fridge,
RULA. You have a washing machine in the kitchen?
NADIA. That's a dishwasher actually. Then this is the sitting room, tv, sofa and the sofa opens into a bed, it's where I sleep. And then through here the bathroom, that's it! Tiny isn't it?

RULA. It looks so clean and lovely. Everything is so new and shiny. Modern
NADIA. Enough about me, how are you doing? How's your studying going?
RULA. Good, although I hate Shakespeare
NADIA. What? Say that again I can't hear you properly
RULA. I can't speak too loudly I'm in the library—I said I hate Shakespeare
NADIA. WHY? He's amazing
RULA. Very hard to understand
NADIA. It's easier when you see it on stage.
RULA. Did you lose weight? Your face looks so thin
NADIA. Not at all. What about you—how are you? *(low voice)* Why are you covering your head? I didn't know you did that? Your mother doesn't does she?
Rula types a message at the bottom of the screen which her cousin can see it says:
My father thinks it's safer for me to cover when I'm out
NADIA. I understand.
A beat
NADIA. It's so nice to see you! To speak to you!
RULA. You too!
NADIA. It was such a good idea of yours! I didn't even know you had access to Skype!
A beat
RULA. Actually there's something I wanted to ask you, that's why I wanted to do this, it's nicer face to face than the phone isn't it?
NADIA. Much nicer, what did you want to ask?
RULA. I'm shy—but my mother told me I should ask…
NADIA. You can ask me, come on what is it?
Pause
RULA. I don't want you to feel like you have to—oh I'm embarrassed to ask
A beat
RULA. Oh I wish you could speak Arabic
NADIA. I think I know what you are going to say…. Is it about coming here Rula? Because I don't have the space really or any money it's just really really hard for me. I want to help but you know its-
RULA. No no it's not that. Uncle Hameed said you had a new iPhone 6 and I wondered if I could have your old one—
NADIA. Oh. Oh god.
RULA. But maybe you still need it
NADIA. No, no, I'm sorry. I'm embarrassed of course you can have it—
RULA. Only if you don't need it
NADIA. I'd love you to have it—shall I post it?
RULA. No, a friend of my fathers is in London in 2 weeks can I give him your number? Then he will meet you and bring it for me, it's much faster. You remember when we used to write to each other and it would take months
NADIA. And we had to write in our special code
RULA. Exactly. Is it ok?
NADIA. Of course. It's a bit scratched
RULA. But the camera works?
NADIA. Perfectly
RULA. Oh my god I'm so excited! Mahmoud is going to go crazy with jealousy

A beat
NADIA. I'm sorry I thought you-
RULA. Don't worry—when will you come to visit? We would love to have you here
NADIA. I want to—but my mum says it's too danger- *she stops herself*
RULA. What did you say? You cut out
NADIA. It's too expensive
RULA. Too what I can't hear you? Hello
The image of Nadia has frozen, Rula's internet connection has gone
RULA. Hello? Hello? Nadia? *(to someone who is waiting)* No I'm not finished, I got cut off … you have to wait.

SCENE

(1960) The long queue of people from one side of the stage to the other reappears. But now we can see the front of the line. There is a man at a desk.
Pause
Eventually the man at the front has been dealt with and the second man moves to the desk
OFFICIAL. Just a minute
Pause
OFFICIAL. Ok, give me your form
The man hands it over
OFFICIAL. You want a passport?
MAN. Yes. This is the right line?
OFFICIAL. Yes.
He looks over the form.
OFFICIAL. Your name?
MAN. Saeed.
OFFICIAL. Full name
MAN. It's on the form
OFFICIAL. Full name
MAN. Saeed bin Hameed Al Hassan bin Ibrahim al Faisal Walleedi
OFFICIAL. Too long
MAN. Sorry?
OFFICIAL. Too long.
He draws a line across the paper
MAN. Why did you do that?
OFFICIAL. I just told you—it's too long. So I've cut the last few words—your passport will be in the name Saeed bin Hameed al Hassan,
A beat
MAN. But that's not my name
OFFICIAL. Listen son, five names are enough for anybody
MAN. But it's not my name
The official eye balls him
OFFICIAL. You've been waiting 5 hours. 1 name per hour. I thought you wanted a passport
MAN. I do.
A beat

OFFICIAL. So what's your name?
MAN. Saeed bin Hameed … al Hassan …
A beat
OFFICIAL. Good. NEXT

SCENE

(2007) The interior of a house, IDF soldiers destroy everything (there should be male and female soldiers here), overturning tables, scattering things from drawers, breaking crockery may be even putting a bullet or two into the cushions so feathers fly everywhere. It should feel like wanton, deliberate destruction, not an act of rage.

SCENE

(1992) The women sit on their rug outside, packing up from their picnic.
WOMAN 3. You went to so much trouble—thank you I've had a lovely time.
WOMAN 1. Good. Well it's too important an occasion to miss—engagement, a wedding … babies
WOMAN 3. Stop talking about babies! You make me embarrassed. You know Saleh's mother put her hand here and said she thought I would be very fertile
WOMAN 2. She didn't! Old witch
WOMAN 1. Mothers-in-law!
The women laugh, Woman 3 looks embarrassed
WOMAN 2. How dare she, god they just think we are baby machines don't they? It makes me sick
WOMAN 1. I quite like it
WOMAN 3. What?
WOMAN 1. Making babies!
WOMAN 2. Stop it, you're embarrassing Fatima again
WOMAN 3. Stop raising your voices
The soldiers are passing again and stop. The women stop packing up
SOLDIER 1. Good afternoon ladies
WOMAN 1. Good afternoon.
SOLDIER 1. Still here?
WOMAN 2. Still here
SOLDIER 2. Nice day for it.
SOLDIER 1. Bag empty yet?
WOMAN 1. More or less
SOLDIER 1. And the flask?
WOMAN 2. Empty
SOLDIER 1. Would you mind opening the bag?
Woman 1 opens it
Soldier 1 peers in
SOLDIER 1. Nearly all gone
SOLDIER 2. Didn't leave any for us
A beat
SOLDIER 1. Are you going soon?
WOMAN 2. Why, shouldn't we be here?
SOLDIER 2. It's a free country. We're just asking.

WOMAN 1. We are just talking.
SOLDIER 1. Well you've finished your picnic so you must be going home soon … enjoy your afternoon
They move on
WOMAN 3. Shall we go then?
WOMAN 2. Sit back down. We'll go when we are ready.

SCENE

(2013) A kitchen where a woman puts the finishing touches to dinner and puts it on the table. Her 19-year-old and 13-year-old sons sit at the table.
MOTHER. Ok. It's ready. Go ahead.
SON 2 (13). Tabbouleh again? I'm sick of tabbouleh
SON 1 (19). *hits him across the back of the head* Eat it.
They sit in silence eating tabbouleh with bread
SON 1. Is there Zaatar?
The mother gets up and fetches some, putting it on the table.
MOTHER. I was thinking of making mousakkan on Friday, Umm Mazin said we can have a chicken in return for some of my soap
SON 2. Brilliant!
SON 1. I won't be here.
MOTHER. Why?
SON 1. I've got Uni
SON 2. On a Friday?
SON 1. Yes.
MOTHER. We'll wait till the following week then
SON 2. Oh! Can't we do it without him. Leave him leftovers?
MOTHER. No. A family meal needs to be the whole family
SON 2. It's never the whole family though is it?
Son 1 clips Son 2 across the back of the head again
SON 2. You better stop that you know!
SON 1. Or what?
SON 2. I'll pay you back
SON 1. What you going to do shortie?
SON 2. You wait.
A beat
SON 2. I've put you in hospital before
MOTHER. STOP you know you're not to bring that up
SON 1. Be careful.
A beat
SON 2. Are you scared?
MOTHER. Stop it!
SON 1. Of a few grape seeds?
SON 2. The doctor said if I'd pushed them in any further you'd have been permanently deaf
SON 1. At least I wouldn't have to listen to your singing
SON 2. I'm good. Everyone says I'm good. I'm good aren't I Mum?
Son 1 starts a rendition of Mohammed Assaf's Al Keffiyeh it's a mocking imitation of

his brother singing it and when he has finished he puts his hand out like he is begging for money

SON 2. MUM!

MOTHER. *(she's trying not to laugh)* Stop—Wallah stop! He's good

SON 2. Umm Mazin said I'm even better than Mohammed Assaf

SON 1. Did she.

Pause

MOTHER. So. University on a Friday?

SON 2. He's lying, look at his eyes! I bet he's seeing a girl—is it Samira—with the big/

MOTHER. Shut up or I'll tell your brother what happened yesterday

A beat

SON 1. What happened yesterday?

SON 2. You promised

A beat

SON 1. What happened? Huh?

MOTHER. Your brother was brought home by the police

SON 1. What?

SON 2. Don't tell him, you said you wouldn't

A beat the younger son appeals to his mother with a look

SON 1. What happened?

MOTHER. He was selling things

SON 1. What things? Not guns—I told you to stay away from Hussein

MOTHER. Guns? In God's name, guns! Who said anything about guns? What do you know about guns?

SON 2. There were no guns—tell her Khalid

SON 1. It's OK mum, but what was it then? Bootleg booze? Records? Cigarettes?

MOTHER. Flowers

SON 1. *Laughing* Flowers?

SON 2. Shut up! I told you not to tell him mum!

SON 1. Where did you get them? Where did he get them?

MOTHER. He persuaded Saleh and Jamal to collect wild flowers with him—he said they were for Sitti—and then he sold them at the side of the road

SON 1. Flowers?

A beat

SON 1. Quite the little entrepreneur! Asda price

SON 2. Fuck off!

MOTHER. Raheem—watch your mouth!

SON 2. I told you not to tell him, I told you he'd just laugh at me.

A beat

SON 1. No—it's inventive

MOTHER. But he had no permit so the police brought him home.

A beat

MOTHER. I told him in this day and age it's not safe to go walking in fields that don't belong to you

SON 1. It's true. No more scavenging eh?

SON 2. Well what else am I supposed to do—I can't live on tabbouleh forever!

He storms out of the room

SON 1. He'll cool off. Always had a hot head.
MOTHER. I do worry about him though. What will he do?
SON 1. Think up another scam to make money
MOTHER. In future I mean. I can't see him getting a scholarship and going to Birzeit University like you.
A beat
SON 1. Birzeit isn't everything
MOTHER. It's a huge achievement. The first person in our family to go to university, and with no father to support you
SON 1. I know you are proud
MOTHER. Proud! You have no idea. You always make me proud and happy I don't know what we would do without you,
SON 1. You'd be fine.
A beat
MOTHER. Are you really going to university on Friday?
SON 1. Of course
MOTHER. Your brother's not right about Samira?
SON 1. Don't be silly! She's a child!
A beat
MOTHER. What is it then … what's the lecture?
SON 1. Oh it's something about international law
MOTHER. You're lying, oh my God, what are you doing? Talk of guns at my table and now you are lying to me, yaboyay! What have I done to deserve this!
SON 1. Stop mother
MOTHER. My son lying to me,
SON 1. I'm not lying
MOTHER. You are, you are, oh what will I do if something happens to you, I can't bear to think of it
SON 1. Nothing's going to—
MOTHER. My own son, lying to his mother—who has made you do this? Yes, you have been sneaking around—I pretended it wasn't happening? Ya Allah! I can't bear any more tragedy in my-
SON 1. Stop stop I'll tell you—I'm not lying I am going to Uni but it's not a lecture.... It's an interview. On Skype. The internet. With UCL
MOTHER. UC?
SON 1. University College London. I've applied for a transfer to do my final year there.
MOTHER. London?
SON 1. Yes. If I can go and study there then/
MOTHER. But it's so far away … for a whole year
SON 1. Well I was thinking once I'd finished my course I could get a job there—the pay is really good—then I could—
MOTHER. Move there?
SON 1. Yes. My English is pretty good
MOTHER. But you are Palestinian—
SON 1. There are plenty of/
MOTHER. don't you know what that means?
SON 1. Of course. I've lived here all my life…

MOTHER. So you understand you have to be here. What if everyone left? They'd win
A beat
SON 1. Mum there are more Palestinians living outside of Palestine than in it—it's not our fault—this happened to us, there's nothing we can do
MOTHER. What are we doing then? Come on, lets go—all of us, lets tell everyone in the street, its too late we've lost, all the years of hardship, being murdered, imprisoned, having our homes taken, our jobs, our fields, our olives, our ability to move from one place to another—everything we have endured has been for nothing. They've won. So let's just leave it to them, disappear. It's what they want. You are doing what they want. You are an educated young Palestinian man. We need you here. Stay.
SON 1. I can't. I can't bear it any more. I need to go.
A beat
SON 1. I'll come back—to visit
MOTHER. They won't let you. It's a one-way door.
SON 1. They will. They'll have to. I'm Palestinian.
MOTHER. If you leave you won't be.
SON 1. Yes I will. I'll achieve more out there for us than I can in here—this is suffocating me.
A beat
SON 1. Do you understand?
MOTHER. No.
SON 1. I have to go
MOTHER. No you don't, you want to.
SON 1. It's impossible
A beat
SON 1. I shouldn't have told you … anyway I've got to pass the interview first. It'll probably never happen.

SCENE

(2002 and now) People approach a clearing. They position themselves in a formal grouping facing on point in the space, like a congregation in a church. A formal pre-theatre hush goes over the crowd and a middle-aged man stands up to address the crowd. He is the man who was trying to get home in the taxi scene.

MAN. Welcome everyone on this, the sad occasion of Nakba day. Take a good look around at what once was our village and retain every sight, smell and detail of our home, because, as Israeli law states, we will not be permitted to re-enter this place until Nakba day next year. This is our one day to reflect and remember our past, what happened in this place. The things we must none of us, ever forget. I'd like to welcome Abu Zaman, who is the oldest living member of our community. Abu Zaman.
An old man gets up and stands in front of the crowd.
OLD MAN. Our village. Stood here. We had a simple but prosperous life, four main farming families for whom everyone worked or was associated. There was no records office—we didn't need one, everyone knew who owned what where the borders of land lay these things were ingrained, in the blood and the hearts of every man woman and child from this place. Over here in the centre of the village was the communal taboon oven. Each house would take turns to make the bread for the village. We all shared.
A beat

I was born in 1925, in June. My mother was working in the fields, she came back to the house which stood over there, gave birth, handed me to my grandmother and returned to the fields.
A beat
When I was 23 everything changed. Of course there had been rumblings beforehand, suggestions, the wind was changing.... But here, so close to the border we felt safe and protected. Then on 25 April 1948 soldiers entered this village. They went from house to house and ordered everyone out, into this central square. Where you are standing now, that is where we all stood. Waiting. We were not afraid. We had nothing to hide. They could turn our houses upside down, they would only find oil, blankets, bread and chickens, we had no guns or bullets. We waited. Here
A beat
Once everyone was gathered they took men of age to one side, over there, the women and children were on the other side, there. They were told to go. Walk. Everyone looked confused. When this woman's grandmother—Umm Hameed tried to go back to the house to get another blanket for her baby daughter the soldier hit her in the face with the butt of his gun. She had a scar for the rest of her life, god rest her.
A beat
So the women and children began to walk, the men were taken to a field to the west—over there—and left to sit in the sun, with no water or food. We sat and sat. Then we began to get angry. We were hungry and thirsty and worried about our women. One of the village elders tried to speak to the soldiers. They were all going into the houses, we couldn't see what they were doing. The soldiers wouldn't listen to him. Then Fareed Khalili stood up—he was 18. He went to the soldier who was guarding us by the gate. He said this is enough. Fine you are in our village, do what you want but let us go—we have families, mothers and children who need us. The soldier took out a gun and shot him in the head. They wouldn't let us bury him, they threw his body into the well by the fourth field.
A beat
Two days later we were all put into a van and taken south—the opposite direction from our families. We were driven for seven hours and then let out. We did not know where we were. We did not know how to contact our families. We began the walk home.
A beat
He is overcome.
The Man who introduced him gets up to help him
Sorry—no I'm ok.
Beat
We began the walk home.
A beat
We are still walking.
He sits down there is a silence and a pause
MAN. Thank you Abu Zaman. Thank you very much. Now I need Kamil al Samuh
A beat
MAN. Where are you Kamil?
MOTHER. *(whispering)* Go on, do you want me to come with you?
LITTLE BOY. No
He gets up and moves to the front

MAN. Ok Kamil?
LITTLE BOY. Yes.
MAN. This, as you all know, is Kamil Al Samuh—the youngest speaking member of our community. Now Kamil you understood everything Abu Zaman said didn't you?
LITTLE BOY. Yes.
MAN. Well we need you to tell us what he said so we know that you remember—so you don't forget—so you can tell everyone
LITTLE BOY. OK.
A beat
The man steps back to give the boy the floor.
LITTLE BOY. This is where our villages was before the Nakba. There were lots of farmers. And here in the middle was the oven, which everyone shared to make the bread. In 1948 the catastrophe happened. On 25 April 1948 soldiers came and made everyone go out of their houses and stand in the middle—like you all. All the boys went over there. All the ladies had to leave or the soldiers would shoot them—her granny was hurt by a soldier. She's dead now. But not cause of that.
Pause
The soldiers shot a man for asking to go to his family. He was put in the deep well. Then all the boys were put on a truck and driven far away from here and their families.
Pause
The boy looks like he is about to cry
MAN. Are you ok—don't get upset
LITTLE BOY. They were driven far away from their …
A beat
LITTLE BOY. They were driven away from their…
A beat
LITTLE BOY. They …
He begins to sob
LITTLE BOY. I can't remember any more! Mum—sorry I can't
MAN. It's ok
The Mother begins to get up but the old man gets up first and goes to the boy and whispers in his ear
LITTLE BOY. Shall I say that?
The old man continues to whisper
LITTLE BOY. They began the walk home. *(he listens)* We are still walking. *(he listens)* And so will our children, and our children's children, until we are back in this place, our home, for good.
A beat
The old man has stopped whispering to him.
The boy looks at the old man
LITTLE BOY. Is it finished?
The old man smiles at him sadly.

TENNIS IN NABLUS

Ismail Khalidi

Copyright 2018 by Ismail Khalidi. Representative: Ron Gwiazda, Abrams Artists Agency, 275 Seventh Avenue, 26th Floor, New York, NY 10001; tel: (646) 486–4600

About the Playwright

Ismail Khalidi was born in Beirut and raised in the U.S. His plays include *Truth Serum Blues* (Pangea World Theater), *Tennis in Nablus* (Alliance Theater), *Foot* (Teatro Amal), *Sabra Falling* (Pangea World Theater), and the co-adaptation of Ghassan Kanafani's novella *Returning to Haifa* for the stage (commissioned by the Public Theater).

He has previously been a Many Voices Fellow at the Playwrights Center in Minneapolis, as well as an Emerging Writers Fellow at the New York Theater Workshop. His writing has appeared in *The Nation, Mizna, Guernica, The Daily Beast, American Theatre Magazine, Remezcla,* and *Words Without Borders*. He is the coeditor, along with Naomi Wallace, of *Inside/Outside: Six Plays from Palestine and the Diaspora* (TCG, 2015).

Khalidi writes plays on commission for Noor Theatre and the Actors Theatre of Louisville, and is an artist-in-residence with Teatro Amal in Chile. He holds an MFA from NYU's Tisch School of the Arts.

— Essay —

Ismail Khalidi's *Tennis in Nablus*: Mining History for the Origins of the Conflict

Michael Malek Najjar

Ismail Khalidi's *Tennis in Nablus*, labeled a "tragipoliticomedy," views the Israeli-Palestinian conflict through the lens of historical fiction. The play, set in 1939 British Mandated Palestine, relies on hindsight for much of its effectiveness. In many ways, viewing the Palestinian situation during this period of time can bring clarity to this extremely complex issue. Although Jews and Arabs (Christian and Muslim) were being dominated under British rule, Palestinians believe it was a decidedly pro-Zionist British Mandate which both trained and armed Jewish immigrants.[1] Set in Nablus, the play offers a view of Palestine when Arab resistance was focused squarely upon the British during the period that Jews were emigrating from Europe at the onset of World War II. If there was any doubt about how the British administration viewed the citizens of their Mandated Palestine, British General Sir Walter Norris Congreve once wrote, "I dislike them all equally. Arabs and Jews and Christians, in Syria and Palestine, they are all alike, a beastly people. The whole lot of them is not worth a single Englishman!"[2] It is Khalidi's view that British colonial rule was ultimately replaced by Zionist settler colonial rule and, later, Israeli occupation.[3]

The crux of the politics of the play is found in the British struggle to maintain control over Palestine, the European Jewish desire for a homeland during their persecution at the hands of the Nazi regime in Europe, and the Palestinian quest for freedom, dignity, and self-determination. From the European Jewish perspective, as voiced by Hirsch in the play, the situation for the Jews in Europe had become completely untenable. For the Palestinians of the time, embodied by Tariq, there is the burning question "Can we both live here? Or is it going to be one of us?" Neither ultimately finds satisfaction.

All of the characters have compelling reasons to fight and die for Palestine during this period, yet peaceful coexistence is nearly impossible when radicals rule the day and when an imbalance of power denies the rights and freedoms of one side to ultimately benefit another. The moderates of the play are silenced by those who wish to seize power through violence and deception rather than coexistence. The playwright manages to humanize both sides through an intentionally Palestinian position. In the preface to their edited anthology *Inside/Outside: Six Plays From Palestine and the Diaspora*, Ismail Khalidi and Naomi Wallace write about the fact that Palestinian plays are often "culturally delegitimized, derailed and delimited by the Israeli–Palestinian 'conflict' wherein the Israeli perspective is always/already privileged." It is their view that presenting both sides of this conflict in anthologies, for instance, is problematic because to do so limits and shapes free speech about Palestine, depriving the work of its right to be judged by its own merits, and because there is already an imbalance in the conflict that adversely affects the Palestinians due to their being the weaker party in this struggle.[4]

The play's decidedly melancholy ending presages the actual historical events following the failure of the Arab uprising which, according to Palestinian historian Rashid Khalidi, led to 5,000 killed, 10,000 wounded, and over 5,000 detained. Khalidi writes, "the suffering was considerable in an Arab population of about a million: over 10 percent of the adult male population was killed, wounded, imprisoned, or exiled."[5] *Tennis in Nablus* sets the stage for the events of 1948 known as *al-Nakba* or "the catastrophe" by Palestinians. By dramatizing the situation that preceded the establishment of the State of Israel, Khalidi provides the historical context for the intractable situation we see now in Palestine and Israel.

— Playwright Statement —
Writing Palestine's Invisible History

Growing up, the period of the Arab Rebellion in Palestine (1936–1939) was always of great interest to me, both in terms of my own family's involvement (several of my relatives were imprisoned and/or exiled by the British for political activities during this period) and also in terms of its importance to the history of Palestine. In my research for what would become this play, I came upon a passage in a book by an Israeli historian in which he documents an instance of Palestinian prisoners chained at the feet and used as ballboys for the tennis matches of the British authorities. This image was striking to me in that it spoke to the cruelty, absurdity and overall mindset of the British Empire in particular, and imperialism more generally. It also struck me as echoing the brutality of occupation and incarceration today, whether in Palestine, Iraq or the U.S. Most importantly, perhaps, the image conjured a situation brimming with dramatic potential.

I knew almost immediately that this was the image and dramatic situation which I wanted to build my play around. How then, I asked myself, were the two prisoners in this scenario related? Did they like each other? Did they agree on what their predicament meant and how best to extract themselves from it? Ultimately the two prisoners/ballboys, as they came into being in *Tennis in Nablus,* are indeed related by blood, and yet very much at odds. This circumstance seemed especially relevant and timely considering the infighting that has long plagued the Palestinian national movement. Working outwards, a host of other characters entered into the world, from the British overlords to the Irish and Indian conscripts; the fearless Anbara, the kind but troubled Samuel Hirsch, and even the wandering ghost of Emiliano Zapata.

As I began to construct the play, the year 1939 struck me as a unique and meaningful entry point into the conflict, especially for an American audience that is totally unfamiliar with the real history of the Palestinian struggle for self-determination. In fact, for most Americans, Palestinians, if they exist at all, only do so in opposition to Israel and therefore as a post-1948 phenomenon at best. At worst we are one-dimensional terrorists. To set a play before the creation of Israel and the accompanying dispossession of the Palestinians, seemed to me to be a crucial way to convey an important truth about Palestine: namely, that Palestinians did exist and were in fact struggling to achieve their freedom from a colonial power in the early part of the last century.

It was telling to me, for example, that in the U.S. the Irish and Indian struggles for independence in the 20th century are looked upon favorably and celebrated in art and mainstream culture and politics. Why then should the Palestinian struggle against the same British colonialism during the same period not be afforded such consideration? To set a dramatic story infused with tragedy and comedy and peopled with compelling characters against this historical backdrop was hard to resist, and for me served, in part, as an act of reclamation and solidarity.

For at the heart of the question of Palestine are a plethora of issues that go far beyond Palestine. They include settler colonialism, white supremacy, imperialism, ethnic cleansing, human rights, international law, refugee rights, anti-Semitism and Islamophobia among others. It is my hope then that this play can be one part of a larger conversation in the theater, not only about Palestine and Israel, but about much more.

— PLAYSCRIPT —
Tennis in Nablus

ACT ONE

PROLOGUE
Darkness. A summer night. Nablus, Palestine, 1939. The creaking of wheels on a donkey-drawn cart can be heard, then the cocking of a rifle.
SOLDIER *(offstage)*. Halt! Now step down from the carriage. With your hands in the air, old man.
Out of the darkness, Waleed, an old man in a peasant's robe, enters with his hands raised. From the opposite direction, a British soldier.
SOLDIER (CONT'D). What's in the carriage, Methuselah?
WALEED. Bidenjan, your…. Highness.
SOLDIER. What?
WALEED. Eggplants sir. Aubergines. I want to take them to the early morning markets up north.
SOLDIER. Eggplants, huh?
WALEED. No relation to eggs though, sir. They are related to the potato and tomato, however. Who would have known that such a dark elegant purple orb was related to the fat lumpy white potato, eh? The world is a mysterious place, sir, and God has a way of making a kind of poetry with his creations, no?
SOLDIER. I prefer to be called "your highness," old man. Now let's see what's in the cart.
WALEED. The word Aubergine, for example, "your highness," derives from the Spanish "Berenjena" which comes from the Arabic "Bidenjan," which in turn is from the Persian "Badin-gan," all derived originally from the Sanskrit, "Vatin Gameh."
SOLDIER. Bloody fascinatin'.
WALEED. Yes, I think so too.
SOLDIER. Why don't you tell me why you're driving up in the dead of night? There's a curfew you know.
WALEED. Well, because eggplants are in the nightshade family, sir, so it is their custom to move at night. They rot under the sun. But when they travel in darkness they arrive at the market pregnant with the night; full of the whispers of their friend the moon…. And this way I sell twice as many as the farmers who transport their produce in the morning heat! Shall I tell you about the harvesting of the eggplant sir? It really is/fascinating.
SOLDIER. Jesus, please don't! Just piss off, old man. Be on your way, and stay off the main roads!
Waleed bows and exits into the shadows.

SCENE ONE

Later that night in an old Palestinian house: There is a table with a typewriter on it. On the back wall hangs an Ottoman sword.

Yusef Al Qudsi enters quietly. He wears a British Officer's uniform. He removes oranges from his various pockets. One after another.

Anbara enters from behind Yusef. She silently grabs the sword off the wall and places the blade on his neck as he is about to sit down. He raises his hands.

YUSEF. Have you escaped from your harem to seduce a British officer such as myself, young lady?

ANBARA. It doesn't suit you.

YUSEF. Or am I being knighted?

ANBARA. You were about to sit in my chair.

YUSEF. This chair belongs to His Majesty King George! I…

ANBARA. Yusef.

Anbara touches his face. He rises.

YUSEF. Anbara. You…. Two years…. It's been two—

Anbara pushes him into the chair.

ANBARA. Two years. Yes. I know.

YUSEF. …And I've gotten older.

ANBARA. But you've been giving the Brits hell since they released you. At least that's what everyone in Nablus is talking about.

YUSEF. Seven days, non-stop. What are they saying?

ANBARA. After two years apart, it took you seven days to make your way to your wife?

YUSEF. Blame the British, not me.

ANBARA. I do.

YUSEF. Anbara, I was arrested and exiled because I fought. And I fought because they occupy us.

ANBARA. Simple.

YUSEF. And if it weren't for them, I'd be playing the 'oud for you every night.

ANBARA. I'd like that.

YUSEF. Like I used to. But that life is gone Anbara. So as soon as I was released I went to work. The revolution can't wait—

ANBARA. Spare me the speech. And don't talk to me like some young recruit from the hills.

YUSEF. I came as soon as I could.

ANBARA. I've been waiting.

YUSEF. Well. I had to see if I still had it in me.

ANBARA. Of course. And? Do you still have it?

YUSEF. Naturally.

ANBARA. I've missed you.

YUSEF. Naturally.

ANBARA. And still so modest. Naturally. *(beat)* So you've come home? To me?

YUSEF. In the flesh.

ANBARA. And who said you could come here, anyway?

YUSEF. You are my wife. This is my house.

ANBARA. And what if I have a guest over and this isn't a good time? Did you think about that?

YUSEF. I can leave.
ANBARA. A younger man perhaps. To keep me company. A man fleeing out the bedroom window at this very moment.
YUSEF. Somehow I imagined this homecoming differently.
ANBARA. That my clothes would fall to the ground the moment I saw you?
YUSEF. For instance.
ANBARA. Well perhaps you should be the one stripping down for me.
YUSEF. You haven't changed.
She lights a cigarette, takes a drag, and then hands it to him.
ANBARA. It's dangerous, Yusef, they'll be after you.
YUSEF. Hence the disguise.
ANBARA. You look ridiculous.
YUSEF. But I bet you're dying to hear how I got it.
She ignores him.
YUSEF (CONT'D). The English, as you know, are formidable opponents, Anbara. They're ruthless, callous, and greedy.... But!
ANBARA. Tea? Or a drink?
He nods to the bottle and continues.
YUSEF. But ... they have one weakness which allows a quick-witted opponent in need of a disguise to get their uniforms off their backs quicker than a Turkish prostitute.
ANBARA. And you have experience with such women?
YUSEF. It's a figure of speech, Anbara. Please. Ask me how I did it!
ANBARA. No.
YUSEF. Simple. Costume parties. The British will drop everything at the mere mention of a themed costume ball.
ANBARA. I've noticed.
YUSEF. I got the idea when I arrived with the other prisoners to Haifa last week. We docked before dawn and on shore I could see half the officers' corps in costume, returning from a night out. By mid-morning they'd released us. I made my way down the coast and then inland, village to village, town to town.
ANBARA. Like the old days.
YUSEF. Except half of my men from before are dead or in prison.
ANBARA. I've been to my share of trials and funerals while you were gone.
YUSEF. You hate funerals.
ANBARA. Almost as much as I hate trials. And stories that drag on.
YUSEF. Right. So yesterday, finally I arrive in Nablus.
ANBARA. Not to see me, however.
YUSEF. Not yet. To see the general, actually. Falbour. But he wasn't in. Off playing cricket. Or tennis. With Lord so and so.
ANBARA. But you went in anyway.
YUSEF. Disguised as a servant of the house I enter through the kitchen and up the back stairs, where I convinced none other than Lieutenant Douglas Duff that he was terribly late for the India-themed ball at the High Commissioner's house in Jerusalem. The man was in costume and out the door before you could say "his majesty's a royal ass!"
ANBARA. Ah. Leaving his uniform for the taking.
YUSEF. Precisely. And with it I was able to borrow from the Nablus armory forty brand-

new 1939 edition Enfield rifles, enough ammo for a month's campaign, and a supply of dynamite to derail British trains. *(a bow)* Thank you, thank you very much.

ANBARA. Impressive. *(beat)* And where is all of it now, Yusef?

YUSEF. Safe.

ANBARA. Not here I hope.

YUSEF. Hajj Waleed's taken it up to the fighters in Jenin ... hidden under his eggplants.

ANBARA. You shouldn't make the old man run your errands! He won't last if they catch him.

YUSEF. Waleed's been with my family for years. He was fighting the Turks before you finished grade school!

ANBARA. Exactly.

YUSEF. And if all fails he can bore anyone to death with the details of the eggplant or the olive harvest.

ANBARA. How they must regret the day they set the famous rebel Yusef Al Qudsi free.

YUSEF. Imagine! They wanted to send me to London for the negotiations.

ANBARA. But you refused. I heard.

YUSEF. They really thought I'd scurry off to England to beg them for terms with the others.

ANBARA. Don't underestimate them, Yusef.

YUSEF. Trust me, I know the Brits; I know precisely what they're about.

ANBARAL. I suppose you want me to ask you to go on.

YUSEF. They're after the sun! They want to conquer everything south of their dreary little island in order to kidnap the sun and brighten the bloody place up a bit.

He starts to shed the uniform.

YUSEF (CONT'D). Look at me, I'm sweating like one of them. Like a sweaty fucking Brit!

ANBARA. Take a breath.

YUSEF. I'm babbling?

ANBARA. Yes.

YUSEF. I still get nervous every time I see you.

ANBARA. Like a little schoolboy. In love with his teacher.

YUSEF. Or like a handsome rebel made speechless by a beautiful peasant girl.

ANBARA. Your fantasies are predictable.

Yusef kisses Anbara for the first time. A beat.

ANBARA (CONT'D). Drifting in at the strangest times.

YUSEF. *(pointing to the typewriter)* And you, writing away at the strangest hours.

ANBARA. Who knows if you would ever have become the dangerous revolutionary you are today if it weren't for my writing.

YUSEF. When's your deadline?

ANBARA. Before noon. Arabic and English editions. I want it published before the British release their report on the London meetings.

YUSEF. And what's the nom de plume these days?

ANBARA. Mohammad Ali Baybars. At your service.

They shake hands.

YUSEF. A pleasure Mr. Baybars. I hear you're quite a thinker. But you also have a lovely smile and divine—

ANBARA. Go. I'll follow. When I'm done. *(She gathers the clothes from the ground)* And your costume?

YUSEF. Waleed will make sure it's put to use. Give it to him when he gets back.
She throws the uniform at Yusef.
ANBARA. Give it to him yourself.
YUSEF. Fine. But one more kiss, Mr. Baybars. Please.
A kiss.
ANBARA. Away, beast!
He starts to leave but turns.
YUSEF. Exile is not fun, you know. It's incredibly lonely.
ANBARA. I know. You see, my husband was imprisoned on an island at the end of the earth for six hundred and thirteen days … but I almost got used to being alone.
YUSEF. You got used to being alone?
ANBARA. Almost … and the oranges?
YUSEF. Stole them from a grove on the road from Jaffa to Tel al Rish.
ANBARA. Your family's land?
YUSEF. New ownership: It's a Jewish farm now.
ANBARA. Tariq.
YUSEF. He's been busy while I was gone.
ANBARA. There's a killing to be made on real estate these days and your nephew isn't one to miss out.
YUSEF. We're becoming thieves in our own land. When Waleed returns I'll have him fetch Tariq for a friendly breakfast. I'll have a word with that boy.
ANBARA. They'll follow him here, Yusef.
YUSEF. He'll listen.
ANBARA. He didn't get the message last time.
YUSEF. I'm his uncle, I'll make him listen.… You better finish that article before the old man returns from Jenin.
He exits. Anbara begins to type. She stops, gets up, and follows him. Lights fade.

SCENE TWO

A Western-style office. Tariq sits at the desk. He wears a European suit. He reads the paper. It is early morning. The call to prayer is heard. Tariq turns on the radio.
RADIO (V.O.). "And from Palestine, British commanders hailed the success of anti-terrorist measures against the 'Arab Revolt,' which has raged on since 1936. High Commissioner MacMichael announced that: 'the violent unrest of the Arab population is in its last throes.' His assessment was confirmed by commanders of the Jewish units fighting alongside British troops. On the European front, escalating tensions between Germany and Britain—"
A knock is heard. Tariq turns the volume down.
TARIQ. Come in.
Reggie enters.
REGGIE. Mornin' Rik! Here early.
TARIQ. Couldn't sleep. You?
REGGIE. Haven't slept since I got here. All that chanting from the mosque at five in the bloody mornin'. Dublin was a shit post but the most you'd hear from the Irish was a fiddle or a flute or a brawl outside the pub. Or an explosion or two.
TARIQ. You'll get used to it.
REGGIE. Hope I'm gone before then. When did you get back from Alexandria?

TARIQ. Late last night.
REGGIE. Business as usual then?
TARIQ. Everything in order, yes.
REGGIE. Well it's good to have you back, Rik.
TARIQ. Good to be home. Any news?
REGGIE. No, just talk of war back home and how to get the Arabs on our side if we fight the Huns.
TARIQ. Let's hope for the best.
REGGIE. *(lowering his voice)* Though it's no secret that war is good for business, ey. Oh, almost forgot. That Hirsch fellow came by while you were gone to finalize the deal on that land in … uhh … Beiyt … Beiyt something or other. He said you'd know the place.
TARIQ. I know it, yes. I just have to convince the owners to sell.
REGGIE. They're a stubborn lot, them Arabs…
TARIQ. Indeed. We are.
REGGIE. Alright then, cheers man.
Reggie exits then pops his head back in.
REGGIE (CONT'D). Last thing: Party at the Governor's place Friday night. You gonna come along?
TARIQ. I hadn't planned on it but I might drop by.
REGGIE. You don't want to miss it. I'm gonna dress as a Bedouin Chieftain of the Hijaz. Fantastic, man! I make Lawrence of Arabia look like an amateur when I put this one on, yeah.
TARIQ. Weren't you a Bedouin Chieftain last time, Reggie?
REGGIE. No! Last time I was a Maharaja of the Mogul Court. Get it straight, man. Not all Orientals are the same.
TARIQ. Right. Thanks.
REGGIE. Actually I am using a bit from the maharaja costume, but I can lend you the rest. If you like.
TARIQ. I might just throw on the old Venetian mask again. Keep it simple.
REGGIE. Boring!
Reggie exits then pops his head in once again.
TARIQ. Yes, Reggie?
REGGIE. Sorry, you got someone out here, waiting to see you.
TARIQ. Is it Hirsch?
REGGIE. No. It's an older bloke. An Arab.
TARIQ. Oh. Send him in.
Reggie exits…. Tariq picks up an Arabic newspaper then picks up the English paper then switches again. As the door opens, he has one in each hand. As Waleed enters, Tariq pretends to read both at the same time.
WALEED. Good morning Tariq effendi.
TARIQ. And to you, Hajj Waleed.
WALEED. I never knew you were such a two-faced man, young Tariq.
TARIQ. And what is that supposed to mean??
WALEED. Well you are reading two newspapers at the same time. It is very impressive.
TARIQ. How can I help you this morning?
WALEED. I came to let you know you're invited to your uncle's house.

TARIQ. My uncle? Yusef? Here?
WALEED. Yes. He's back.
Tariq springs up, making sure no one is outside.
TARIQ. In Nablus? Since when!?
WALEED. He wants to see you immediately. He's cooked you breakfast.
TARIQ. I'm busy. Until later this afternoon. Send him my lukewarm regards.
WALEED. He insists. It must be now, he said. It's important.
TARIQ. It's not even 8! I haven't read my papers or, or had my tea.
WALEED. He's your uncle, Tariq.
TARIQ. Uncle!? He had my store in Jaffa looted and burned to the ground and then made my workers strike. My own workers! Some uncle he is.
WALEED. So what should I tell him … "Rik?"
TARIQ. What did you call me?
WALEED. "Rik." It's what the English one out there called you no? I thought maybe you had changed your name to "Rik."
TARIQ. It's just a nickname. At the office. That's all. I didn't even—
WALEED. Fine. Shall we go then?
Tariq, deep in thought does not answer.
WALEED (CONT'D). …Tariq!
TARIQ. No. Yes. You go ahead Hajj. Tell him I'll be there around nine. I have an urgent matter I have to attend to first. Is that all?
WALEED. Since you ask, I wonder if we could talk about this land sale in Beyt Naqquba? That land has been in my family for hundreds of years and—
TARIQ.—Thank you Hajj Waleed! Your reservation has been noted. I assure you I have everyone's best interests in mind, including your cousins,' when I conduct my business. Now if you don't mind…
Waleed exits. Tariq picks up the phone.
TARIQ (CONT'D). Get me Lieutenant Douglas Duff please.

SCENE THREE

Later that morning at the house. Yusef prepares food. Hajj Waleed reads.
WALEED. It gives me hope. A manifesto for revolution. Who wrote it?
YUSEF. A friend of ours. Mohammed Ali Baybars. A draft of his latest piece.
WALEED. Never heard of him. Where's he from?
YUSEF. The Galilee. From a small family. A recluse really—a shy man.
ANBARA. But no push-over.
WALEED. Well, it's very mature. Reminds me of the writing of that other boy who used to write for the weekly journal, before they shut it down. What was his name?
ANBARA. Mustafa el Badawi…. I believe. No, Yusef?
YUSEF. Similar styles, yes, but I think this Baybars is even better.
WALEED. He's a damn genius if you ask me.
ANBARA. Agreed.
YUSEF. Yes, and pretty, too.
WALEED. Did you say/pretty—?
YUSEF. I mean pretty likely the most important thinker between Cairo and Baghdad.
A knock at the door…. Yusef draws the pistol and melts into the shadows. Anbara lets Tariq in. Yusef emerges from behind him.

YUSEF (CONT'D). You look richer, nephew.
TARIQ. Yusef. Still carrying a gun, I see. Unreformed, even after all these years.
YUSEF. And unrepentant. Now give your uncle a hug.
Yusef grabs Tariq and hugs him.
YUSEF (CONT'D). You're late. I made ful. Still the best beans this side of the Sinai.
They sit. Yusef puts his pistol on the table near his plate.
TARIQ. *(calmly)* Um, excuse me but, are you … threatening me, uncle?
YUSEF. Um, are you threatened by me, nephew?
TARIQ. No need to mock me as if I were a little boy, you're only ten years older than me.
YUSEF. Eleven, actually.
TARIQ. Could you please just put that thing somewhere else?!
Yusef slides the gun a couple of inches away.
TARIQ (CONT'D). Further maybe?
Yusef slides it another couple inches away.
TARIQ (CONT'D). Further! Like NOT within reach. Like in another room perhaps!
YUSEF. Well maybe you'd like to hold it? Is that it? Take it!
Anbara takes the gun and tucks it into her robe.
ANBARA. Now, who would like some food? Tariq?
TARIQ. Thank God your wife is more civilized than you, uncle.
YUSEF. I'll take that as a compliment. To her. Unless, of course, you are referring to British "Civilization."
TARIQ. And so what if I was?
YUSEF. Then I would consider it an insult, since they were painting their bodies blue and drawing on caves when we were building fountains and universities and inventing mathematics!
TARIQ. Oh, such an example of refinement you are, sitting at the table with a bloody revolver on your plate.
YUSEF. In case you didn't know, I am a hunted man, so I have to be careful. Look at how they got Zapata in Mexico, and—
TARIQ. Oh no.
YUSEF. Don't "oh no" me. He was betrayed in his own territory. Ambushed!
TARIQ. Still comparing ourselves to dead "revolutionary" heroes, are we?!
YUSEF. Well, my dear nephew, I'm simply protecting myself from the death they wish upon me. I don't know who I can trust after all.
TARIQ. Spare me your suffocating self-indulgence Yusef! You're a petty thug.
YUSEF. And you are a petty little capitalist. But believe it or not, I've missed you Tariq … or is it "Rik" now?
TARIQ. It's Tariq! Let's please not confuse my business with who I am as a person.
YUSEF. Fine.
TARIQ. Though, such a notion surely didn't cross your mind as you sent my investments into flames in '36, dear uncle!
YUSEF. Yes. Well…. I wanted to … apologize. For that incident. It was. Unfortunate.
TARIQ. It was an insult!
YUSEF. It was not how I would have wished for it to happen, no!
TARIQ. It was a betrayal Yusef. It was utterly foolish and unjust./It was—
YUSEF.—It was a rebellion Tariq! There was a rebellion going on! Your people. You

remember who your people are?!? And that business of yours was breaking the boycott.

TARIQ. I was making a living for myself, not to mention my workers; our fellow countrymen!

YUSEF. You see this Anbara? I try to apologize and explain it to him but he's thick!

ANBARA. Calm down. Both of you. A patrol could hear you shouting. Don't give them an excuse to come in.

YUSEF. Listen to me Tariq, your "business as usual" helped the British to undercut the revolt! Is all this lost on you, boy?

TARIQ. I'll tell you what I lost. I lost years of hard work! I lost contracts, employees, investments, and thousands and thousands of pounds.

YUSEF. And I lost friends. I lost two years of freedom.

A moment of charged silence.

TARIQ. You must understand, I am not a little boy anymore.

YUSEF. Oh just shut up and eat your food!

Tariq gets up from the table.

TARIQ. I'm sorry to leave, Anbara, but I won't take his abuse.

YUSEF. I'm sorry. Sit ... it's important.

TARIQ. Make it quick.

YUSEF. It is precisely because you are not a boy anymore that I'm asking for your help. I am asking you as a fellow Palestinian. We need you Tariq. I need you.

TARIQ. No. The answer's no.

YUSEF. The Brits think they've won but if we can make one push—

TARIQ.—And what do I have to do with this?

YUSEF. We need a man of your standing, with your knowledge of the British.... If you were to support the revolt we could maybe hold our ground. But this is our last chance.

TARIQ. It's already over. You're practically the only one still fighting.

YUSEF. But if you joined me others would follow. You are my last hope Tariq.

TARIQ. Our leaders went to the London conference. Give it up.

YUSEF. The Brits kill thousands of us, imprison thousands more, and now they want to negotiate. They will use us and then throw us aside. Help me! Help us!

TARIQ. Tell me, uncle: What would I need to do to help save your little revolution? Carry a gun around, mugging people like you?

YUSEF. You could start by not selling off our lands to the Europeans.

TARIQ. You mean I'd have to stop selling to Jews, is that it?

YUSEF. No, I said Europeans. They are Europeans to me. I have no interest which way they talk to God. We've always had Jews among us, but they were Arabs, like us. These Zionists, they are Europeans, fighting side by side with the British Empire.

TARIQ. I happen to be friends with some of them and find they are equitable, kind business partners.

ANBARA. They are not just buying summer homes, Tariq! They're building a country right on top of ours while the British hold us down.

TARIQ. That's a matter of opinion.

YUSEF. Opinion!? Those aren't toy guns they're carrying around! Wake up Tariq! The days of looking the other way are over. They want it all for themselves.

TARIQ. Goodbye. I suggest you make yourself scarce for a while. You are a hunted man after all.

YUSEF. Tariq, wait!
ANBARA. Let him go.
A crash. The door is kicked open and a British soldier enters with his rifle pointed at Yusef. Lt. Douglas Duff enters behind him with a pistol drawn. He wears a full Maharaja costume.
LT. DUFF. Breakfast's over! Hands where we can see them. *(to Yusef)* Well, well. Hello again. I've been looking for you.
YUSEF. Good morning your Maharaja-ship.
LT. DUFF. Have this man cuffed and arrested.
SOLDIER. I think we arrest him and then cuff him sir. Technically.
LT. DUFF. Technically I don't care which order you do it in. He is a rebel and a thief! Cuff him!
The soldier cuffs Yusef.
YUSEF. In case no one's told you, it's an excellent costume, lieutenant.
Lt. Duff slaps Yusef.
LT. DUFF. Well in case no one's told you, I don't need my uniform to arrest you and have you exiled to some God-awful island, or better yet: executed. Now, if I hear one word out of you I'll have you all lashed and then gagged … or gagged and then lashed. Soldier, search the house.
TARIQ. Sir. Lieutenant Duff, please. There is nothing here I assure you, upon the King's throne. You've got who you came for, now leave these people alone.
LT. DUFF. And you are?
TARIQ. I don't believe we've had the pleasure. My name's Tariq Al Qudsi. Here's my card.
He hands Lt. Duff his business card.
TARIQ (CONT'D). I'm in the import-export and real estate business, sir.
LT. DUFF. Yes. I've … heard of you. Surprised to find you in the company of such a lawless bandit as this.
TARIQ. Family, sir. One can't choose them.
LT. DUFF. I'll take your word on that. *(to Yusef)* My uniform. I'd like it back.
YUSEF. It seems I misplaced it last night, your Excellency.
LT. DUFF. Take him away!
Anbara draws the pistol, cocks it, and holds it to the back of Lt. Duff's head.
ANBARA. You'll be taking no one out of my house. Unless you want a hole through the back of your turban, sir!
LT. DUFF. *(to the soldier, unable to see her)* Is that thing … real?
SOLDIER. Uh yeah, it looks pretty real to me sir.
LT. DUFF. And I thought they were supposed to be timid and docile in the Orient?
ANBARA. I'm very outgoing sir, and this gun is quite real. I could show you, if you'd like.
LT. DUFF. That's quite alright lady. *(beat)* Shoot her.
YUSEF. Wait!
LT. DUFF. I said shoot the bitch!!! Ready!… Aim!…
The soldier prepares to fire.
YUSEF. Anbara, put it down!
ANBARA. I won't let them take you, not again.
YUSEF. I'll be fine. I'll be free in no time.
LT. DUFF. *(to Yusef)* You'll hang!

YUSEF. Go to Baybars. What he writes in the papers makes a difference.
LT. DUFF. Silence!
YUSEF. If he can't free me, at least he won't let me die in vain.
LT. DUFF. Shut up, everyone shut up or I'll have you all shot!
YUSEF. Put the gun down, Anbara.
Anbara pushes the gun deeper into Lt. Duff's turban but after a moment lowers it.
LT. DUFF. Very good…. Now arrest her and confiscate that weapon.
The soldier grabs Anbara and the gun.
LT. DUFF (CONT'D). On second thought, give me the gun.
Lt. Duff now holds two pistols.
LT. DUFF (CONT'D). Ahh that feels better. I quite like the whole Wild West Cowboy feel. How do I look man?
SOLDIER. Really great/sir…
YUSEF. Duff, let her go. I'll give you names, just leave her. She's a woman, sir.
ANBARA. No. Take me in. Yusef, shut up!
LT. DUFF. *(intrigued, up in Yusef's face)* I want the financiers behind the revolt. Can you give me that, boy?
YUSEF. Yes.
LT. DUFF. Very well. Release her. Move out.
The soldier and Lt. Duff leave with Yusef in tow.
TARIQ. He was irresponsible to come here, to put you in danger Anbara. The one place they'd know to look! He acts recklessly. But, don't worry, I'll put my reputation and connections into play to free him. I'll go at once to straighten this out. And you'll see that my name and my way can achieve more than mere thuggery. Negotiations, compromise, and deal-making! A calm discussion between responsible, reasonable and reputable adults!
Lt. Duff re-enters, seen by Anbara but unbeknownst to Tariq.
TARIQ (CONT'D). You must assure me, however, that when I get Yusef out, you will make him see things my way. For it is only with restraint and cooperation that we can help our cause more. I call it "rational nationalism." The revolution, Anbara, is really about evolution! You'll see, I'll take care of this. And make the Brits pay for their arrogance. Everything is under control.
LT. DUFF. Bravo. Very inspiring. You were done, no? Or is there more?
TARIQ. No, Sir. Yes. Thank you, sir. I was. Done.
LT. DUFF. I must inform you, then, that you're under arrest by the Mandatory Authorities of His Majesty, King George of England.
TARIQ. For what!?
LT. DUFF. For your clandestine role in assisting, financially and materially, the treasonous rebellion against the British Mandate in Palestine.
TARIQ. There's been a terrible mistake, sir—
LT. DUFF. Evidence doesn't lie, Mr. Qudsi. *(beat)* And if it does, oh well.
TARIQ. What evidence!? This is an outrage, lieutenant! Not your fault per se, of course, sir, but a misunderstanding nonetheless. Please, I demand to speak with the general.
LT. DUFF. Yes. Perhaps you could give him your card.
Lt. Duff slips the card Tariq gave him into Tariq's front pocket.
LT. DUFF (CONT'D). Cheers.
Lt. Duff exits, leading Tariq out with him.

WALEED. God works in mysterious ways, Anbara. It's in his hands now.

Waleed exits. Anbara retrieves her typewriter and begins to write. She stops and slams her fist on the table.

SCENE FOUR

The courtyard in the British Compound. Rajib and Michael O'Donegal play cards and drink tea.

MICHAEL. Two kings. What do you have?

RAJIB. Two threes!

MICHAEL. Shite! Your hand. Again.

RAJIB. I've never been this lucky at cards, Michael, I swear.

MICHAEL. How do I keep drawing fuckin' face cards? It's a curse. A bad omen. Damn useless royalty!

RAJIB. Agreed. A worthless lot the Kings and Queens. *(beat)* You owe me a pound O'Donegal.

MICHAEL. I don't have it Rajib, but I'll pay you back Friday, I swear.

RAJIB. Jut don't go gambling away more money you don't have. At least until after you've paid me.

MICHAEL. At this rate I'll never slip back to Ireland.

RAJIB. It was your idea to change the rules, Michael; "Bolshevik poker" was your idea!

MICHAEL. Oh come on, we were both equally fond of that bloody inbred bastard on the Thames. I didn't hear you complainin' when we made the change.

RAJIB. That's true. And I'm not complaining now.

MICHAEL. I couldn't even buy a king before our glorious little revolution!

RAJIB. Also true.

MICHAEL. Right! So one would then surmise that I'd keep drawing low cards and be winning under the new rules. But no. Now that I don't bloody want 'em, I'm drowning in high cards!

RAJIB. Technically the high cards are low cards and the low cards are high/but—

MICHAEL. And who the fuck are you? The Commissar of the People's Republic of Poker!?

RAJIB. Just a poor comrade like yourself, Michael, trying to get out of this powder keg before it blows. I don't want to die in Palestine either. I'd prefer Calcutta or Karachi any day.

MICHAEL. It's all shit.

LT. DUFF. *(from offstage)* Guards!

Rajib and Michael pause, then continue as if they heard nothing.

MICHAEL. Another cup of tea?

RAJIB. Yes, why not. Thank you. Another hand perhaps?

LT. DUFF. *(still offstage, louder)* Privates Rajib and O' bloody fucking Donegal!!!

RAJIB. Sugar?

MICHAEL. Two spoons please. Whiskey?

Michael takes out a flask of whiskey, pours some, and offers Rajib.

RAJIB. Too early for me.

Soldier enters, winded.

SOLDIER. Lieutenant Duff is back. He's been screamin' his head off for you two.

MICHAEL. Really? I didn't hear a thing. Did you, Rajib?

RAJIB. I think I heard a dog barking maybe.

MICHAEL. No. That was a jackal. Or a hyena. *(to the soldier)* Did his head really come off?
SOLDIER. No O'Donegal. His head's still there. And he's still a pain in my arse.
RAJIB. One can always hope.
SOLDIER. Your orders are to report immediately. Says he's got a job for the two of you.
MICHAEL. Wonderful.
RAJIB. Maybe it's not too early. If you don't mind.
Rajib extends his cup. Michael serves the whiskey and they both gulp down their drinks, then grab their rifles and exit.

SCENE FIVE

The prison holding area. Tariq and Yusef cuffed. Lt. Duff, still in Maharaja-wear, sits at the desk writing. Rajib and Michael enter.
LT. DUFF. Well thank you for coming soldiers. I'm sure it was quite a struggle to follow orders and walk all the way here. Remind me to commend you to the general.
MICHAEL. Really sir?
RAJIB. That's very kind of you sir
LT. DUFF. No, it's not! I was being … never mind. At ease.
Rajib stares at Lt. Duff's outfit. Lt. Duff notices, to Rajib.
LT. DUFF (CONT'D). Yes?!?
Michael subdues a laugh.
LT. DUFF (CONT'D). Is there something you want to say Private O'Donegal? No? Good. Now button your uniform, soldier!
Michael rests the rifle against Yusef and starts buttoning his shirt.
LT. DUFF (CONT'D). Private! I'd prefer you didn't hand the prisoner your rifle, thank you.
MICHAEL. You're right, sir, you're right. It could have been a disaster; he might have shot you, sir.
Michael takes the rifle back.
LT. DUFF. One more insubordination from you, private, and I'll punish you. Understood?
TARIQ. Sir, I'd like to speak with the general, at once.
LT. DUFF. You'll get your chance to chat to General Falbour soon enough.
TARIQ. Thank you.
LT. DUFF. As it happens, he's the presiding judge of the military court you'll be standing in front of. *(to Michael)* Private, these two men are from a very well-respected clan of Palestine. And Arabs are quite fond of their honor, you know, so make sure they are treated accordingly.
YUSEF. You know lieutenant, our ancestors fought alongside Salah-a-Din when he defeated your Richard the Kitten Heart and his crusader hordes.
LT. DUFF. King Richard the Lion Heart, damn it! Lion heart! A little respect. Now shut up. All of you.
RAJIB. Sir? Any orders? For me?
LT. DUFF. Oh, you. Yes, actually. While this slow-witted paddy takes the brigands to their cell, you can hop on over to the tennis court and have it leveled and ready to go by eleven o'clock. Sharp. Dismissed.
Rajib salutes and exits.
LT. DUFF (CONT'D). Now that you look more like a soldier, O'Donegal, I'll ask you to

escort these two men to cell five. Not four. Not three. Five! And do remember these men are dangerous rebels and will gladly slit your throat. Though I suppose that'd save me the trouble.

Michael is about to respond but under Lt. Duff's gaze does not. Lt. Duff leaves.

YUSEF. What's your name young man?

MICHAEL. Well it's not paddy or Mick, I'll tell you that.

YUSEF. I quite enjoy being called "Arab beast," or just "Wog." I also like "damned Semite scum." It has a wider scope of targets for the discerning British gentleman.

MICHAEL. Is that so? You dirty Mohammatan!

YUSEF. Irish bastard!

MICHAEL. Bloody Bedouin goat-shagger.

YUSEF. Filthy Potato-eating pope-lover.

MICHAEL. Two-timin' camel-ridin' terrorist!

YUSEF. Tinker mick taig monkey son of a paddy whore!

Beat.

MICHAEL. Touché.

YUSEF. Yusef Al Qudsi. And this fellow next to me is my worthless, traitorous nephew Tariq. Say hello Tariq.

He doesn't.

MICHAEL. *(to Yusef)* Michael O'Donegal. Cigarette?

Michael shares a cigarette with Yusef who is still cuffed.

YUSEF. Any relation to Sean O'Donegal?

MICHAEL. It's me dad's cousin, yeah. You know him?

YUSEF. We know of him. Fought the partition, gave the Brits a hiding in 1918. An inspiration.

MICHAEL. Well he'd give me a hiding if he saw me wearing this uniform, but it was either this or rot in a Belfast prison for five years. This turned out to be much worse, of course.

YUSEF. The choices we're left with dear boy. I was conscripted into the Ottoman army; got a British bullet in my ass at Gallipoli. Now, whiskey's the only thing that numbs the pain.

MICHAEL. Well I've got somethin' for what ails you then.

Michael un-cuffs Yusef, gives him the flask.

MICHAEL (CONT'D). Not a pious Moslem I take it?

YUSEF. More of a pious rebel, Michael. It comes first these days.

MICHAEL. Amen. To the Empire!

LT. DUFF. *(offstage)* O'Donegal!

MICHAEL. Speak of the Devil. I'd best be off.

Michael puts cuffs back on Yusef and exits; another soldier enters to stand guard.

TARIQ. This is absurd.

YUSEF. Yes: An army of pink pig-eaters thousands of miles from their island telling us how to live. It's the height of absurdity.

TARIQ. That's not what I mean. You know what? I'm going to sit here in silence. I clearly can't have a conversation with you!

YUSEF. Fine. But know that communication with other human beings during imprisonment is the key to maintaining one's sanity. Learned that in the Seychelles. Ended up talking to a banana tree after one month in solitary.

TARIQ. You framed me! You gave Duff my name.

YUSEF. And you know the worst part?!... I had to eat them afterwards.

TARIQ. What are you talking about?

YUSEF. The bananas. I killed then ate my only friends; my confessors, my comrades. We were fed mostly bananas. Imagine. Like a bunch of captive monkeys.

TARIQ. You framed your own nephew, your flesh and blood.

YUSEF. I figured I'd return the favor.

TARIQ. Are you suggesting that I turned you in? You're insane.

YUSEF. Perhaps I am. And you are guilty. Banana sandwiches.... Banana kabab...

TARIQ. Guilty? Of what?

YUSEF. Stuffed bananas! They were the best.

TARIQ. What am I guilty of?

YUSEF. Doing monkey business, Tariq!

TARIQ. You know, you've always been jealous, Yusef. Because I built a fortune and a good reputation against all odds.

YUSEF. But despite your "reputation," to them, you are just another dirty Arab monkey. Guilty!

TARIQ. I am well respected by colleagues from Nablus to London!

YUSEF. And yet here you are, in jail.

TARIQ. Because you've framed me. Sullied my name.

YUSEF. Funny enough, being in prison is the one thing that can save your name from being truly "sullied." If only you were lucky enough to be guilty of fighting for your country.

TARIQ. So you admit it? I'm innocent.

YUSEF. If you mean naïve, then yes.

TARIQ. I actually think I'm the only one preparing himself realistically for the future of Palestine.

YUSEF. You're absolutely right. Because there won't be a Palestine to do business in before long! We'll be the foreigners soon enough and your business partners will be the citizens. *(pause)* But perhaps you'd trade it all for a flat in London? What a sight: A naïve, collaborating ape walking the rainy streets of the imperial capital in a nice European suit.

TARIQ. I am not a collaborator. And I am not going anywhere.

YUSEF. Banana juice with a little yogurt. That was my favorite.

TARIQ. And you wonder, you wonder why I would turn you in!?

Yusef (Rom Barkhordar, left) and Tariq (Amro Salama) debate the role of the British in Palestine in *Tennis in Nablus* by Ismail Khalidi, directed by Michael Malek Najjar (photograph by Airan Wright).

Beat.
YUSEF. I wonder how we are related, Tariq...
Tariq starts writing with a small pencil and a piece of paper.
YUSEF (CONT'D). What is that? What are you writing?
TARIQ. A note. A request for the prompt assistance of a respected man, a friend, who will vouch for my character and get me out of here. But not you I'm afraid.
Michael returns to lead Tariq and Yusef to prison cell.
YUSEF. That's true, your friends would have me rot in here while you run free.
TARIQ. You know what I think, uncle? I think you are the perfect example of why we need to be ruled. At least until we learn how to behave, to rule ourselves.
YUSEF. Tell me Tariq: What good is your pocket watch if you are nothing but a slave?
Both are led into their cell.

SCENE SIX

Later that morning, on the balcony of the British Compound: Standing over a map is General Allen B. Falbour with an elephant tail fly swatter in hand. He flicks away the occasional fly as he moves pieces around on the map. Lt. Duff enters. He wears a white tennis outfit. He holds a stack of files.
GENERAL. Bollocks Douglas! Damn you, man!
LT. DUFF. What is it sir?
GENERAL. Well, you've clearly withheld crucial information from me, Lieutenant Duff. Failed to remind me about the costume party this afternoon. Do you deny the charges?
LT. DUFF. No, sir! I mean Yes! No! Sir I ... think there's been a/misunderstanding.
GENERAL. I'll have to go and see if I can dig up my Zulu chieftain outfit from last year. *General exits.*
LT. DUFF. *(calling off)* Sir? Sir, I don't think that's necessary sir.
GENERAL. *(from offstage)* I could have sworn that party was Friday night. And now you'll show me up with that smart little sailor's outfit you've put together.
LT. DUFF. *(off)* But it's Wednesday sir. Remember. *(pause)* And I'm not a sailor, sir.
GENERAL. *(offstage)* Well what the hell are you supposed to be then?
LT. DUFF. A tennis player. Sir.
GENERAL. *(offstage)* Oh. Well done. Yes. You're missing the racket though.
LT. DUFF. That's because it's on ... well it's on the tennis court, sir. We play tennis together, Wednesdays sir, after the briefing. I got dressed a little early today. So there's actually no costume ball, sir.
General re-enters behind Lt. Duff. He wears a Zulu headdress and holds a spear. His face is covered in crude black-face/war paint.
GENERAL. No party then?
He exits before Lt. Duff can see him and returns quickly, without the costume, but his face still painted.
GENERAL (CONT'D). Tennis it is. Shall we carry on with the meeting then lieutenant?
LT. DUFF. Um, sir?
GENERAL. Get on with it Duff, so we can hit the court before it's too hot to play.
LT. DUFF. Your face, sir. You seem to have put on your Zulu ... um ... war paint.
GENERAL. Yes. *(beat)* Of course. Just a little ... prototype. We're testing it out. A sort of anti-wog camouflage, lieutenant, to blend in better with the natives. I wanted to get

your top-secret feedback before we put it to the test in the field. Maybe a shade lighter, but you get the idea.
LT. DUFF. Great thinking sir.
GENERAL. Thank you. Turns out I couldn't find the old Zulu costume after all.
LT. DUFF. Too bad, general. It was stellar. The Spanish Consul was quite convinced, you know.
GENERAL. Yes, yes. He was, wasn't he.
General wipes off blackface.
LT. DUFF. And when you did your war dance in the fountain in the High Commissioner's garden ... now that was pure genius sir!
GENERAL. I suppose it was quite good, wasn't it.
Lt. Duff studies the map.
LT. DUFF. I see you're strategizing, sir. Studying the battle field of the Levant to give us the upper edge. Tell me, what's on your mind, general. Why have you moved this regiment here for instance?
GENERAL. No, this is actually a miniature recreation of the Battle of Waterloo, lieutenant. Arrived yesterday from London. Even that mad little midget Napoleon was a more honorable foe than these Arab hostiles.
LT. DUFF. Most definitely sir. Indeed. Shall we get on with the briefing?
GENERAL. Yes, yes. I'll be right back.
General exits. Lt. Duff looks at his watch then calls out off the balcony.
LT. DUFF. Rajid! O'Donegal! Report to the courtyard at once!
Michael and Rajib enter.
LT. DUFF (CONT'D). Didn't I tell you two to have this raked and smoothed over by eleven AM?
MICHAEL. Definitely not me sir. Sorry.
Lt. Duff points at Rajib.
LT. DUFF. And what about you?
RAJIB. I don't recall you telling me anything sir?
LT. DUFF. Are you certain?
RAJIB. Yes sir. I do remember a very odd looking Maharaja told me something about tennis courts but I have not seen him since.
MICHAEL. Oh I've seen him too, sir. He was wiping the general's arse for him just this morning.
LT. DUFF. I warned you O'Donegal. *(He calls offstage.)* Soldier!
Soldier runs onstage.
LT. DUFF (CONT'D). Administer five lashes to private O'Donegal for being a smug, Fenian bastard. *(to soldier)* On my count...
Michael removes his shirt. The soldier, with a whip, stands over Michael. With every count, Michael is struck on his back.
LT. DUFF (CONT'D). One ... two ... three ... four ... and five! This isn't Dublin or Belfast or wherever your whore of a mother spawned you. You will follow orders and act civilized even if it is against your nature. And that goes for you too Vikrum! I'll deal with you later.
RAJIB. It's Rajib, sir.
General re-enters in his tennis outfit.
GENERAL. Now. That's much better. Proceed.

LT. DUFF. Gladly sir. Ahem. As you know, the European front looks increasingly, well, warlike, sir. But here in Palestine our tough response to the "Arab Revolt" has paid off. We are within reach of crushing the terrorists.

GENERAL. Good, lieutenant; and what of the "prison situation?"

LT. DUFF. As of this month we are down from nine to roughly 7,000 Arabs in custody. Also, the decision to bring the anti-terror experts from the Irish and Indian campaigns has been effective: Confiscation of weapons is up, as is the suppression of agitating publications.

GENERAL. Good, good.

LT. DUFF. Similarly, the pattern of executing convicted rebels in the military courts has clearly sent a message to the average Arab. Just as you predicted sir.

GENERAL. Damn it's hot.

LT. DUFF. And last but not least sir, I am happy and proud and excited and deeply honored to announce to you here, that just this morning we've apprehended a most foul and dangerous renegade. His name is Yusef Al Qudsi.

Lt. Duff removes a file and hands it to General.

LT. DUFF (CONT'D). As you can see, he was behind the strikes in Jaffa, Haifa and Nablus in '36, and he fought us to a standstill in Tulkaram in '37. He was captured, exiled and recently released. Which turned out to be a bad idea. But he's in our custody again now.... I personally oversaw the operation, sir.

General has tracked a fly on Lt. Duff's shoulder and swats Lt. Duff.

GENERAL. Well done!!!

LT. DUFF. Thank you sir.

GENERAL. You're welcome. Now what do you say we bring the Arab out to the court today?

LT. DUFF. I believe in swift justice as much as the next man, sir, but we do need time to prepare for the trial.

GENERAL. I mean the tennis courts, lieutenant. For our match.

LT. DUFF. Oh, well, yes, it's just I'm sure he's not up to our level of play sir, and with the chains—

GENERAL.—No, not to play. To fetch our balls.

LT. DUFF. Ball boy, sir?

GENERAL. In Rhodesia and Tanganika, Douglas, we'd march the Pygmy prisoners to our cricket matches. We'd have each one stand in as the wicket. Then the batsman would miss on purpose so the bowler could really knock one right on the blackies' jewels. I thought Africa was hell until I came to Palestine. There was water there at least, and not an Arab or a damned Jew in sight.

He leans confidentially towards Lt. Duff.

GENERAL (CONT'D). And the problem with the Jews, lieutenant, is that I don't quite know whether to fear them or have contempt for their groveling and jockeying. They're not as simple as the Arab.

LT. DUFF. Nor quite as short as the Pygmies, sir.

They enjoy the joke as SAMUEL HIRSCH enters the courtyard.

HIRSCH. Hello, Gentlemen.

GENERAL. Oh.... Hello there.

HIRSCH. May I?

GENERAL. Of course, Mr. Hirsch, join us. We were just finishing up. *(To Lt. Duff, sotto voce)* Speak of the Devil.

Rajib enters with a tray of tea along with Hirsch.
LT. DUFF. Two sugars in mine. None for the general.
RAJIB. Yes sir, sugar sir. Two.
LT. DUFF. Next time do inform us beforehand if a guest arrives. Dismissed.
Rajib exits.
GENERAL. How can we help you Mr. Hirsch?
HIRSCH. Well sir, I've come by to follow up on our last meeting. I've also brought our counter-proposals in regard to the Jewish immigration and land purchase quotas, as Lieutenant Duff requested.
Lt. Duff takes the document.
LT. DUFF. ...By the way, thank your comrades in the special night squads for their assistance in suppressing the Arab rebellion. Quite a job they've done.
HIRSCH. That isn't really my doing sir. It's frankly not my field of expertise or my responsibility. But I'll be sure to pass on your thanks if I get the chance.
LT. DUFF. *(to General)* The Jewish units have proven quite competent and fierce fighters actually, sir. It's been quite a shock, really.
HIRSCH. What is that supposed to mean lieutenant?
GENERAL. Oh, don't take it badly Mr. Hirsch, it's a compliment. Anything else we can do for you?
HIRSCH. There is one other matter, which is the worsening situation in Europe this summer, sir. Our community is deeply worried and I hoped you could pass on our growing concern to/your superiors.
GENERAL. Yes, yes. We're all very concerned Mr. Hirsch.
HIRSCH. You can call me Samuel, sir, or Sam if you'd like.
GENERAL. And I assure you, Samuel, that we in England are vigilantly watching Mr. Hitler.
HIRSCH. Thank you sir/but
GENERAL. And we are deeply committed to the plight of the Jews, in Europe and everywhere, as I believe we have proven time and again in Palestine.
HIRSCH. That's very reassuring, thank you sir. I simply wanted to convey to you that it is of the utmost importance that something is done at the highest levels to stop the coming/storm.
Lt. Duff sips from his tea and spits it out all over himself and Hirsch.
LT. DUFF. Good God, it's horrible!
GENERAL. What is it Douglas, what's gotten into you?
LT. DUFF. It's salty! My tea's full of salt, the bastard!
GENERAL. These servants, from God knows where! You can't trust them with anything. Shifty as a pack of ... *(He looks at Hirsch and stops himself)* ... Shifty as a pack of ... shifty things. If that's all, you must excuse us Mr. Hirsch. We have an appointment. Nice of you to drop by though; let us get a taste of each other's ... brains. As it were.

SCENE SEVEN

Yusef and Tariq sit on opposite ends of their cell. Tariq continues to draft his letter. Michael enters with food and the newspapers.
MICHAEL. Stole a bit of fish from the kitchen ... scraps off the master's table. And an old Arab out front told me to give this to you. He said the Arabic edition sold out.
He hands the newspaper to Yusef.

YUSEF. Here it is. Front page: "The Fork in the Road."
As Yusef reads, Anbara appears at her typewriter.
YUSEF AND ANBARA. By Mohammad Ali Baybars…
ANBARA. "This, people of Palestine, is the decisive moment. It is our fork in the road…"
YUSEF. "Our cry for freedom is once again threatened by the terrible sound of silence and servitude…"
ANBARA. "Our leaders have been exiled, killed, imprisoned, or co-opted. And the Arab Kings are far too comfortable under the tutelage of their Western masters to be of any use. Soon we will find ourselves/strangers in our own land."
YUSEF. "Strangers in our own land." My line. "The question then, is this: Why should we believe our British overlords who promise us morsels of a state that is not theirs to give or take?"
Tariq rips the paper from Yusef's hand.
TARIQ. Cheap words printed on cheap paper. People need food on the table. They need stability and progress, not your "revolution" with its funerals and famine and anarchy in the streets. And you can tell your friend Baybars I said that.
Yusef pushes Tariq and Tariq pushes back. The paper falls to the ground. Michael picks up the paper and reads on as they fight, which they do, off and on, throughout the scene.
MICHAEL. "The British promises of independence are empty: Their declarations and delegations; their mandates and solutions are nothing more than the crude tricks of magicians. And as long as they rule, they'll play the Arab and the Jew like so many chess pieces."
YUSEF. *(Yusef subdues Tariq)* See! You're a pawn, being played by the Brits and the Zionists. Resist boy, it's in you. I can see it in those beady little eyes of yours.
TARIQ. I do not have beady eyes!
Tariq breaks free.
ANBARA. "When the British do leave we will find ourselves out-gunned. Our Jewish cousins see their prize and they are armed and ready to take it by force. In the meantime, the British will promise us the moon to keep Palestine and to ensure our help in their coming battle with Germany."
Tariq pulls Yusef's mustache.
TARIQ. That's for burning down my store!
Yusef subdues Tariq again.
MICHAEL. "So let us look to the opponents of England elsewhere in the world for guidance: To the brave Irish strikers and to the mass movement of non-violent resistance led by Mr. Gandhi and Badshah Khan in India today…"
ANBARA. "And yet so many of our leaders have been neutralized by British foul play and violence."
MICHAEL. "Most recently, Yusef al Qudsi." Hey, that's you. He's talkin' about you! "Qudsi, returned from exile, was thrown back into British dungeons. It is our duty to free him and the others from their chains."
Yusef takes the paper from Michael, who keeps reading over his shoulder.
ANBARA. "The British believe that they have made us into a defeated people, but we are only defeated if the flame of resistance recedes into fear and doubt."
YUSEF. "If we are reduced to such a state then we are nothing but walking ghosts."
ANBARA. "So let us march to the gates of every British compound and show them that the resistance of the people of Palestine is eternal and just."

YUSEF. "Let them hear our voices rise above the thunder of their rifles and the crack of their whips: We will be free."
Anbara fades back into the darkness.
MICHAEL. Jesus. Give me a pitchfork and a torch and let's burn this fucking prison down.
TARIQ. Rhetoric and drum-beating. We can work with the British to get what we want. It's called "rational nationalism" and it's based on the premise/that—
Yusef shoots Tariq a threatening glance.
TARIQ (CONT'D). *(to Michael)* Listen, please just get this letter to Mr. Samuel Hirsch.
Yusef intercepts the letter.
YUSEF. Now here we have really cheap words on even cheaper paper!
TARIQ. It's very important.
RAJIB. Enough! You're needed on the court today boys and it's hot, so save your energy. The general and his little terrier await.
Michael takes Tariq's letter as they are led out of the cell towards the tennis court. General and Lt. Duff stand doing their stretches as the prisoners enter the court.
GENERAL. So which one is the rebel Yusef al Qudsi?
Tariq points to Yusef and Yusef points to Tariq. Lt. Duff points to Yusef.
GENERAL (CONT'D). Welcome back to hell, boy.
YUSEF. Thank you sir.
GENERAL. Maybe this time we'll send you to rot in Sarafand prison instead of the Seychelles. It'll make you miss those days of tropical bliss.
He looks at Tariq.
GENERAL (CONT'D). And you must be the financier? Definitely not the rebel type in any case.
TARIQ. Well, yes, that's precisely it general. There's been a grave misunderstanding. I would happily explain—
GENERAL.—Soldier, have these men shackled together at the feet.
The two men are chained together by their feet as General and Lt. Duff retreat, rackets in hand, to their playing positions in the wings.
LT. DUFF. *(offstage)* It's love all, sir.
YUSEF. What do you barbarians know about love!
The tennis balls starts flying back and forth across the net center stage.
TARIQ. Just keep your mouth shut, Yusef.
GENERAL. I won't be censored, not by you.
LT. DUFF. Balls!
Tariq jumps up and runs for the ball but runs out of chain and falls flat on his face.
GENERAL. *(from offstage, as they play)* I wonder if that Hirsch fellow has an ulterior motive lieutenant. A kind of hidden agenda, you know.
TARIQ. You know Hirsch, sir? Sam Hirsch is a friend and business partner. He'll vouch for my continued cooperation with the British—
Yusef pulls the chain, Tariq falls hard.
LT. DUFF. Balls!!!
Yusef hops on the court to one side of the net and throws the balls back at Lt. Duff as hard as he can while Tariq gently rolls the balls back to General. The game continues.
GENERAL. Balls!!!
Yusef does not get up but sits at the base of the net as Tariq runs from one side of the net to the other.

YUSEF. Tariq, look what they've turned you into. Their little monkey.

Tariq returns to the base of the net and sits with Yusef. He is out of breath. The two men let out a slight laugh as the stage darkens and the rumbling of thunder is heard, followed by a flash of lightning. It starts to rain.

GENERAL. Tea time Douglas.

General and Lt. Duff exit, soldiers carrying umbrellas above their heads. Tariq and Yusef remain, and as the lights fade their laughter is heard mixing with the storm.

ACT TWO

PROLOGUE

The dark cell. Steady rain. Tariq sleeps alone. A scream pierces the cell. Tariq is startled awake. He looks around. Yusef is not there.

TARIQ. Yusef?

Another scream; it is coming from a close-by room. Tariq moves around the cell trying to determine where it is coming from.

TARIQ (CONT'D). Yusef!?!

Tariq picks up the newspaper with Anbara's article. He reads it, trying to block out the cries from Yusef. The door swings open and Yusef, badly beaten, is thrown in. The rain outside slows as dawn breaks.

SCENE ONE

Anbara in her house practices jabs with the sword. She stops and writes something down. This is her writing routine. Waleed enters with a small sack in his hands.

WALEED. I brought soap from the factory, the latest batch.

ANBARA. You think we can wash the British off with that, Waleed?

WALEED. No, but this might work.

He pulls out a folded newspaper from the bag.

WALEED (CONT'D). The new Baybars article. He's something else, that man.

ANBARA. Yes.... I know.

WALEED. As soon as I read it I headed back to the newsstand and bought all the copies I could.

ANBARA. I thought the British raided the newsstands?

WALEED. That's why it's the grocer who sells the papers now. Keeps them hidden under his produce. My idea. I passed out copies for free on the way home ... as discreetly as possible of course. Listen to this: "Brothers! Have we still not realized that in order to truly liberate Palestine we must also liberate and elevate the Palestinian woman?" ... Ah! And here it is, the second to last paragraph. He's got balls this Baybars!: "If the High Commissioner is a buffoon, and he certainly is, then our leader the Mufti is at the very least marked by the unmistakable signs of opportunism, egoism, and above all, mediocrity." It's true, I've met him.

ANBARA. And what news on the streets?

WALEED. There's a British warrant for Baybars' arrest. And apparently our dear Mufti has sent word from Beirut that he wants Baybars "reined-in." *(He draws his finger across his throat.)* And the word from Tel Aviv is that the Jewish Agency fellows are looking for Baybars as well.

ANBARA. To...?

She draws her finger across her throat in a question.

WALEED. No. Apparently they want to pay him. To stop writing against the Zionists.

ANBARA. Really? Disgusting. *(a beat)* How much?

WALEED. No idea. They did the same thing with the editor of Filastin. A couple years back. He refused the money. Just like he refused to agree with the Mufti. Now he's a poor exile in Beirut...

ANBARA. Maybe he should have taken the money.

WALEED. Anyone low enough to take such money would have to disappear and start over, with a new name, a new everything.

ANBARA. And Baybars wouldn't stoop so low?

WALEED. Who knows. They can't even find the man. No one can. The money will just sit and rot in Tel Aviv.

ANBARA. Well, what if Baybars took the money and used it for a worthy cause?

WALEED. His ideas, my dear, are worth more than a thousand rifles.

ANBARA. This coming from a man who drove a cart full of guns up to Jenin just the other night.

WALEED. I didn't just take rifles up to Jenin. I took copies of Baybars' articles.... And it would be a shame if a bag of gold silenced his tip-tap-typing in the middle of the night.... Unless he had a really good plan. Though, if my memory serves me, he's not very good with money.

A moment. Anbara disappears into the bedroom. Waleed prepares a bag. Anbara re-enters and Waleed hands her the bag.

ANBARA. Watch the house.

WALEED. I take it you're going to Tel Aviv.

ANBARA. I hear they've made it look like Europe.

She exits.... Lights fade down on Waleed.

SCENE TWO

Lights up on Tariq and Yusef in the cell while unseen, from offstage, a tennis game is heard.

LT. DUFF. *(offstage)* Fantastic shot general!

GENERAL. *(offstage)* Thank you Duff.... Deuce!

YUSEF. I prefer football: More of a people's sport.

TARIQ. It's still a rather new game. Give it time.

YUSEF. It can have all the time it wants.

LT. DUFF. *(offstage)* Balls!

GENERAL. *(offstage)* Pick up the pace, Paddy!

TARIQ. I dreamt of eating Kunafi last night, Yusef!

YUSEF. *(calling to the court through the small window of their cell)* Hey general! Ever had kunafi? It's a Nablus specialty. Hot cheese with a crispy layer of pastry—

TARIQ. *(to Yusef)* Semolina.

YUSEF. *(to Tariq)* Not wheat?

TARIQ. Semolina. Just say—

YUSEF. Semolina! Then soaked in warm orange blossom syrup. A hell of a lot better than your lemon curd or you Bedfordshire clanger! Yukhhh!

LT. DUFF. *(offstage)* Balls!

YUSEF. Empire Biscuits are also predictably depressing!
LT. DUFF. I'm going to count to three O'Donegal. One! Two…
Rajib enters and shouts offstage towards the tennis court.
RAJIB. General, there is a telegram just arrived from London.
GENERAL. *(offstage)* Well what does it say Dipankar?
RAJIB. It's Rajib sir … and I don't know what it says. Strangely enough, I am fluent in Hindi, Bengali, Sanskrit, Tamil, Urdu, Punjabi, Malyalam, Gujarathi, Telegu—Dutch—and at least six more languages sir, but English is still a mystery to me. Perhaps you should come and read it yourself, sir.
GENERAL. We have to do everything around here, don't we. Here I come.
Rajib exits.
TARIQ. Perhaps I owe you an apology … for…
YUSEF. Turning me in?
TARIQ. I hope when we're old men we can laugh at all this.
YUSEF. Sure. If I don't hang, why not.
TARIQ. You won't hang.
YUSEF. I've seen plenty of men hanged for less.
TARIQ. While you were gone. Last night. I read Baybars' article.
YUSEF. Were you crying when I came in?
TARIQ. No! I was just overcome with … this sense of…
YUSEF. Guilt?
TARIQ. I heard you screaming and it made me/feel…
YUSEF. I wasn't screaming.… I was laughing.
TARIQ. I thought they were going to kill you in there Yusef.
YUSEF. I'm immortal kid.… But this revolt. Maybe you're right. It's done.
TARIQ. After all your grand speeches you've suddenly given up?
YUSEF. No.
TARIQ. So?
YUSEF. The problem with a revolt, Tariq, is that it's a reaction; a stand against something, right?
TARIQ. Sure.
YUSEF. But sometimes people forget that it also has to be a step towards something. We want independence, fine, but what's next? So we just fight to forget, to survive; and chaos and violence become the wine and the hashish of the oppressed.
TARIQ. You don't sound like yourself.
YUSEF. I haven't been myself for years. All this, it changes you. *(beat)* Tell me, what if we can't get back what we've lost?
TARIQ. Are you saying the ferocious rebel thief Yusef Al Qudsi doesn't have it in him to scare the Brits into concessions?
YUSEF. I am telling you that I don't want to be feared in order to be free. *(beat)* And as long as the Brits fear the Jews more than us, we will always be at the bottom, fighting over the scraps that are left to us by those more powerful.
TARIQ. You really think they fear them.
YUSEF. I think they look down on them and fear them at once. They see the Jews as plotting to rule the world. Nonsense but it's real to them. I see them differently, as our long lost cousins maybe. But changed. From all their years in Europe. They became the tribes of Berlin and Odessa, Vienna and Warsaw in that time. And now they come

here and they are intrigued. But also repulsed. So they change the land it to make it like Europe, to make it theirs. Mercilessly. Efficiently. And that … that is what scares me.

TARIQ. Not all of them think like that. I know them Yusef, personally.

YUSEF. I know not all think like that, but the ones that matter do.

TARIQ. You don't know how this will end.

YUSEF. What if I do? What if told you I know because the bananas told me. Or because I read history and watch people; their eyes, their hands. Because I read the coffee grounds every morning; because, Tariq, the other day I was forced to steal an orange from what had been my own family's grove. Or because there is a European city that has appeared on the coast of Palestine and it wasn't there 30 years ago. Because the air doesn't feel the same in the morning; because the olive groves speak to me at night and tell me they're scared. Because it rains in the summer…. Because I dream of vultures and I wake up with the urge to run and keep running! Because…. Because…

TARIQ. Yusef…

YUSEF. Because I dream of my unborn children and they do not know my language. And because the wind has told me secrets: …We will soon be the new Jews—wandering, hated, nostalgic nomads with anger and sadness in our prayers.

Thunder rumbles, then turns into the sounds of protest.

TARIQ. Well what if I told you that I have hope, Yusef? Me. Your worthless, traitorous nephew.

Protest sounds become louder and clearer.

TARIQ (CONT'D). Listen. There must be thousands. They've come to get us. They're calling our names, Yusef.

YUSEF. They've answered Baybars' call.

TARIQ. I've never heard so many people saying my name at the same time!

YUSEF. Whether you like it or not, you're guilty now little Tariq.

TARIQ. No! Yes. I like it. Give me a cigarette.

Yusef hands him one.

TARIQ (CONT'D). So this is what it's like, huh? To be a rebel?… I can do this.

YUSEF. But sip it. Sip it slowly. No need to get drunk. There's work to do.

TARIQ. You're right, you're right. You know, these people, they—

YUSEF. They're resilient.

TARIQ. They love me! Yusef, I can put my money behind the revolt. With certain caveats, I'm in.

YUSEF. Caveats?

TARIQ. Stipulations, requirements—

YUSEF. —Yes, I know what it means.

TARIQ. I can put money to strengthen and unify us. I can convince other businessmen too.

A raucous cheer from outside.

TARIQ (CONT'D). I can't let them down Yusef, not now. They came for us.

YUSEF. You have to love them back. I mean really love them.

TARIQ. Yes. But I don't have a clue what to do. I mean, now…. A memo perhaps. Or a manifesto?

Outside, shots are fired—screaming, chaos, more shots. The sound of a riot.

YUSEF. Just promise me something.

TARIQ. What?
YUSEF. That you'll always come back to them.
TARIQ. But I won't leave them. I'm here.
YUSEF. Just don't forget how they cheered for you today.
TARIQ. I won't.
Yusef is pulled violently out of the cell. The crash of thunder brings darkness.

SCENE THREE

Tariq sleeps. A bloodied Yusef is thrown back into the cell. A man stands in the shadows. Yusef sees him and removes a folded picture from his pants. He looks at it and then the man, as if to compare. It is Emiliano Zapata. The man hands him a bottle.
ZAPATA. Have a sip brother. It dulls the pain.
The two men drink in silence. Yusef smiles. Church bells ring in the distance as morning breaks. After a moment, it is just Tariq and Yusef. Zapata is gone.
TARIQ. Yusef. Are you ok?
YUSEF. Been better. Duff kept me up. Chatting away.
Rajib and Michael enter.
MICHAEL. Word is, your trial's been set for tomorrow morning, boys.
TARIQ. Trial?
MICHAEL. That's what they call them, at least.
TARIQ. Where's the evidence? Do we get lawyers? What about habeas corpus?
Michael and Rajib stare at Tariq.
RAJIB. *(to Yusef)* He's serious?
YUSEF. He's figuring it out. Until yesterday he thought he was equal to any Brit in the Empire.
RAJIB. Ah yes, one of those. *(to Tariq)* You'll adjust.
MICHAEL. And if you ever feel yourself drifting back into fairy land, just remember hopping around that court picking up tennis balls for those two baboons.
YUSEF. Michael, Rajib, I need a favor.
RAJIB. Anything, your rebelliousness.
YUSEF. You'll have to go to the Old City.
MICHAEL. Ahh but we're both fond of mingling with the riffraff, sir.
RAJIB. We feel right at home.
YUSEF. My house is at the end of Khalil Street, white stone, three arches and a fig tree in front. Give this to my wife.
He takes out the same piece of paper and writes something on it, then hands it them.
YUSEF (CONT'D). Tell her time is running out and to tell Baybars to think of something. Today.
RAJIB. Anything else, sir?
YUSEF. That I love her. And miss her. That I'm sorry.
MICHAEL. Do you want me to show her too? I mean, I could demonstrate to her the depths of your affection, sir, if you know what I mean. Humbly, of course, and with your permission.
Rajib smacks Michael across the back of his head.
YUSEF. No need, Michael. You Irish boys can fight but I hear you're not much as lovers.
MICHAEL. British lies and propaganda! They're threatened by our virility and romanticism, sir. They're quite insecure you know.

RAJIB. You should see how they turn beet red when they flip through the Kama Sutra. It's remarkable.
MICHAEL. And it does explain the British obsession with conquest and plunder.
TARIQ. What are you saying? That the Empire is fueled by sexual repression.
MICHAEL. More like feelings of inadequacy.
RAJIB. Some combination of the two, I would say.
MICHAEL. One day we'll get to the bottom of it.
RAJIB. I'd rather not, Michael. *(to Yusef)* We'll ship out first chance we get, sir.
Rajib and Michael salute and exit.
TARIQ. So the costume parties?
YUSEF. And the stripping and whipping. It makes sense when you think about it.
Lt. Duff and soldier enter.
LT. DUFF. *(to Tariq)* You have a visitor.
Tariq exits with Lt. Duff.

SCENE FOUR

Hirsch sits waiting in the prison holding area. He bounces a tennis ball, which he loses at the sight of Tariq.
TARIQ. I'm not picking that up.
LT. DUFF. You've got five minutes.
Lt. Duff exits.
HIRSCH. My God, what have they done to you?
TARIQ. They've made me a ball boy.
HIRSCH. Have they mistreated you?
TARIQ. I'm ok.
HIRSCH. I came as soon as I heard. I've already talked to the high commissioner and the general/
TARIQ. /How are you Sam?
HIRSCH. Tired, stressed, smoking like a chimney, nightmares, an ulcer ... the usual ... but good.
TARIQ. From here it looks ... different out there. Worse, you know.
HIRSCH. Of course it does, but when all this calms down a bit, some sanity will return and we can—
TARIQ. Sam, I think we both know it's not going to end the way we said it would.
HIRSCH. But two men like us. We can make a difference.
Beat.
TARIQ. You really look like shit, you know. How about one of those cigarettes?
Tariq takes one and Hirsch lights it for him.
TARIQ (CONT'D). It helps me wipe away a little of the bourgeois shine. I'm a rebel now.
HIRSCH. Yes, you're quite the star in the Casbah. You look good. Alive. Alive is good when you've been thrown in a British prison.
TARIQ. I'm not out yet.
HIRSCH. Not quite. But I've arranged for you to be released. By the afternoon. It's a matter of paperwork at this point.
TARIQ. And Yusef?
HIRSCH. No.
TARIQ. I see.

HIRSCH. Not him.
TARIQ. Tell me Sam, can we both live here, or is it only going to be one of us in the end?
HIRSCH. You're being released. Say something.
TARIQ. You say something. Answer me.
HIRSCH. I want to live in Palestine, as a proud Jew. Alongside the Arabs. Safe.
TARIQ. I don't feel safe, Sam.
HIRSCH. That's why I want you out of here.
TARIQ. And what about your leaders? The Ben Gurions and the Sterns, what do they want?
HIRSCH. There are always reactionaries as well as sensible folks, Tariq.
TARIQ. You're building an army. With British weapons. An army that will fight anyone in the way of an all-Jewish state, including the Brits.
HIRSCH. *(hushed)* The British are limiting our immigration now, so, yes, there is talk of a break with the Brits. But what does this have to do with anything?
TARIQ. It's everything, Sam. I just ask us to talk, as friends, honestly, while it is still possible.
HIRSCH. That way of thinking is winning. It's stronger every day. And every day the Arab Revolt is struck a blow, the stronger the hardliners get. On all sides!
TARIQ. I'm asking about your side.
HIRSCH. I'm not represented by those who dream of war and conquest Tariq. You know that.
TARIQ. And yet you do not oppose them. You do not oppose them when they speak of us as trash to be disposed of.
HIRSCH. When I can, I do. But as their strength grows, our population grows, our economy grows, our land grows!
TARIQ. And you have to take the good with the bad?
HIRSCH. We all do.
TARIQ. And I just gave it away to you. I sold off the land. Like it was a crop that could be re-grown the next year.
HIRSCH. Listen, all of Germany is mad!
TARIQ. And what do I have to do with Germany?
HIRSCH. There is talk of the Germans invading Poland by the end of the summer. There will be war and there will be nowhere for us to hide, Tariq. It's become intolerable for Jews, for anyone who thinks differently or looks differently. People are being shipped off in trains they say, a trickle now, but perhaps a flood tomorrow.
TARIQ. I am sorry for that. I am. I wish—
HIRSCH. It's going to make Palestine look like paradise. Even to the non–Zionists.
TARIQ. And what if your paradise turns into our hell, Sam? *(beat)* I don't think I can help you anymore. Not like before.
HIRSCH. Yes. I suppose that is how it must be now.
TARIQ. I've been a fool.
HIRSCH. It's an age made for fools.... I brought you the paper.
He hands him a newspaper.
TARIQ. Anything from Baybars?
HIRSCH. He's good; smart, fiery. He's awoken the Arabs.
TARIQ. And terrified the Brits.
HIRSCH. Not to mention the Ben Gurions and the Sterns. But between us, I don't think you'll be seeing any more articles from him.

TARIQ. How come?

HIRSCH. He was paid heftily by Tel Aviv to shut his mouth. So I've heard. I find it a bit disagreeable, throwing money around to silence opponents. But if he can be bought then it's his burden to bear.

Tariq is silent.

TARIQ. I ... should get back.

HIRSCH. You'll be released. It's the least I could do for a friend.

TARIQ. Thank you Sam. But I'll find my own way out of this. Goodbye.

HIRSCH. Tariq, please, you must reconsider—

LT. DUFF. *(entering)*—Time's up!

Tariq exits with Duff. Hirsch stands alone, then exits.

SCENE FIVE

Anbara sits at the table with several stacks of bills. She shifts the piles into different arrangements as she speaks.

ANBARA. Run. A ticket to Beirut. A villa, just me and Yusef.... No. *(She shifts the piles.)* Rifles, ammunition and.... Or... *(She shifts it again.)* Buy back land. Yes. Buy it back.... Plus a new typewriter and some books. Or a library. No. *(shifts the money)* A massive citrus grove hugging the coast and then cutting inland. An orange scented wall against the spread of Tel Aviv. No. It would never work. *(again)* Olive trees. Old thick twisted olive grove. Huge, endless, deep. *(...and again)* A car. Like the British generals. And a sail boat to zig-zag between Greek islands, sunbathing nude, no veil, no call to prayer.... Or... *(shifts the money again, into one huge stack)* A typewriter, 50 rifles, a small sailboat, 30 olive trees, 30 orange trees, a bicycle, books, a ticket to Beirut and a weekend in Alexandria. *(She knocks over the stack of money.)* Yusef where are you? I'm no good with money ... *(beat)* ...Yusef.

A knock at the door. Anbara covers the money with the table cloth, leaving a bulge. She grabs the sword from the wall.

ANBARA (CONT'D). Who is it and what do you want?

MICHAEL. We're looking for Yusef's wife. We've brought word from him. We're friends, ma'am.

She opens the door to reveal Michael and Rajib in Arab garb.

MICHAEL (CONT'D). I have a feeling our disguises are not entirely convincing, ma'am.

ANBARA. No. Come in.

RAJIB. You have a lovely sword, miss. And a beautiful house.

MICHAEL. And a very unique table as well.

ANBARA. What's your message?

He hands her the folded up piece of paper from Yusef.

MICHAEL. Well, what is it?

ANBARA. A picture of Emiliano Zapata. The rebel. My husband tore it from the newspaper years ago. He's written his name on it.

MICHAEL. Perhaps it's a secret message ma'am.

ANBARA. More like an autograph. The man has a terrible tendency to make a martyr of himself. How is he?

RAJIB. Holding up. We're quite fond of him. He asks that we tell you that/

MICHAEL. That he loves you very much ma'am. And that you're bloody drop dead gorgeous—

Rajib smacks Michael on the back of his head.
RAJIB. Their trial is tomorrow, ma'am. He said Mr. Baybars could help.
ANBARA. Can he escape before then?
MICHAEL. It'd be difficult ma'am.
ANBARA. Could you help him?
MICHAEL. Perhaps…. But…
RAJIB. We'd be…
MICHAEL. Done for ma'am. It'd be the gallows for us.
RAJIB. We'd need to disappear too, miss, for our own safety, and one needs resources for that/
MICHAEL. Funds.
RAJIB. Unfortunately, our Irish friend here is not lucky. Not least with the cards, and in serious debt with officers and cooks alike. He keeps drawing kings, Ma'am. In pairs. Tragic.
ANBARA. I thought that was a good thing in cards.
MICHAEL. Not in Bolshevik poker, ma'am.
RAJIB. Different rules
MICHAEL. Long story.
Anbara uncovers the money.
ANBARA. What if I were to say that half of this was yours?
MICHAEL. I'd probably say I could lose that in one night.
RAJIB. More like three hands. *(to Anbara)* Ma'am, have you thought this through?
ANBARA. Not really. Half. If you can get him out tonight…. I'd say this would take you as far as? Monte Carlo?
MICHAEL. Irish by origin ma'am, but a gambler by fate.
ANBARA. What do you say?
RAJIB. I'd say you have a deal.

SCENE SIX

In the cell. Yusef is praying as Tariq is let back in.
TARIQ. I didn't know you prayed.
YUSEF. Good for my back. It also softens my secular image into something more pious and sagely.
TARIQ. Maybe we could use God's help at this point.
YUSEF. What does God have to do with any of this? It's all about the pounds and dunams. Land leases, population registries, and business ownership ratios.
TARIQ. Numbers?
YUSEF. It's all just a complicated real estate deal.
TARIQ. I want to make it right.
Yusef finishes.
YUSEF. I know.
TARIQ. Then help me. Give me orders.
YUSEF. You know, I can almost see myself disappearing sometimes. Just now when I woke up, I couldn't even see my right arm! It flickers in and out of sight like a mirage on the horizon of my body.
TARIQ. Samuel Hirsch came…. Got me released. Everything arranged. Later today, he said.

YUSEF. That's good.
TARIQ. I said no.
YUSEF. Are you out of your mind? Get out, man. Go.
TARIQ. I won't leave you.
YUSEF. I'd leave you!
TARIQ. No. You wouldn't. Anyway, in here I'm a hero. Out there, I don't know, but I'm not that. I'm scared.
YUSEF. Why? Like I said, it's about numbers. And you're good with numbers.
TARIQ. They've paid off Baybars.
YUSEF. What?
TARIQ. He's taken money from the Zionists to shut up.
A beat.
YUSEF. How much? I mean, how much do you think a bribe like that will get you?
TARIQ. You're missing the point.
YUSEF. She's got something up her sleeve.
TARIQ. Who?
Rajib and Michael enter.
MICHAEL. From your wife sir.
Yusef takes the note.
YUSEF. It's signed Abdel Qader Salah-al-Din. Which must mean Mohammad Ali Baybars has been reincarnated.
RAJIB. As a very wealthy man.
YUSEF. So what's the plan?
RAJIB. *(quietly)* During the ball tonight, at midnight, while the general drinks and dances…
MICHAEL. …With a particularly pathetic creature at his side…
RAJIB. We, well-armed with cash for bribes, will unlock your gate and slip you out unnoticed…
MICHAEL. …Into the serene Palestinian night, full of gun shots and distant explosions…
RAJIB. Then…. We all disappear our own ways. There's enough to pay off one of the guards and get me and Monsieur. Monte Carlo as far away from the Britishers as possible.
MICHAEL. Be ready at midnight.
RAJIB. The signal is three knocks and a sneeze…
MICHAEL. And then another knock.
YUSEF. And how did she look?
MICHAEL. She's quite a stunning specimen sir, and sharp as a knife. Not to mention her—
Rajib smacks Michael again.
YUSEF. Stay. Have a drink.
Michael complies but Rajib stops him.
RAJIB. We have to prepare. And pack our things.
MICHAEL. In that case, a round later. On me. The other side of these stinkin' walls.

SCENE SEVEN
On the balcony. The same evening. Lt. Duff stands dressed as an Italian style clown.

GENERAL. *(offstage)* Ready.

LT. DUFF. Ahem. Ladies and gentlemen. Fraulines and…. Señores. I now present to you the man with the plan, and perhaps the most peculiar facial hair in the free and fascist worlds: the mad Chancellor, the freaky Fuhrer, Mr. Adolf crout-Hun Hitler.
General enters in a Hitler costume.

LT. DUFF (CONT'D). Oh bravo sir. You've really captured the gravitas, and all the stern, intense, demented energy of the man. Bravo, tut-tut, well done.

GENERAL. And you are supposed to be…?

LT. DUFF. A clown. Of the Comedia dell'arte genre. Of Italy sir. I had it sent from Florence.

GENERAL. I thought you were going to be a Nazi thug with me, Douglas?

LT. DUFF. Well sir, yes I was. But then I thought that one of our sharp and alert guards might spot my convincing outfit and mistake me for a German infiltrator, and then shoot me. I figured that you wouldn't want to lose me over a misunderstanding like that.
General doesn't respond.

LT. DUFF (CONT'D). Right sir?

GENERAL. No I suppose not Doug, I suppose not.

LT. DUFF. I also got to thinking sir, that the Nazi theme might upset some of our Jewish guests at tonight's party and that perhaps—

GENERAL.—Oh nonsense, it's a damn good joke; a witty piece of political satire as far as I'm concerned, and nothing more. And if all else fails, they'll laugh to please us and keep us on their side.

LT. DUFF. Right, sir. Of course.

GENERAL. Not that it matters much, since London will court the Arabs for the war effort now that the revolt has been crushed.

LT. DUFF. And what of this new journalist writing pamphlets against us? Mr. Saladin?

GENERAL. Dreadful bloke. If we can't hang him then at least the Jews will take care of him. You know what I tell people Douglas: I say that I'm neither anti–Arab, nor anti–Jew, but simply, utterly and eternally pro–British.

LT. DUFF. Well said, sir.

GENERAL.—Though that is a bit of a lie too. God help them and their wicked ways if the British Empire leaves Palestine and they're left to fight over it. But in the meantime, we have work to do. In the meantime—

LT. DUFF. —The Mandate is here to/stay!

GENERAL. In the meantime Lieutenant Duff, we have a fabulous party to attend and a busy day ahead of us tomorrow. Orders to execute, tennis to play, and a trial to get on with.

LT. DUFF. Yes sir, the case of Al Qudsi.

GENERAL. Right. Now remind me how they do their little thingy, Douglas.

LT. DUFF. What? Oh, no. I don't know sir…

GENERAL. C'mon, it's an order. Get me in the mood. Salute me.
Lt. Duff does a half-hearted Nazi salute.

GENERAL (CONT'D). Now don't let me see you do that again or I'll have you shot for treason!… Shall we then? Last one there's a foolish Italian clown.
General exits off the veranda with Lt. Duff following close behind.

SCENE EIGHT

Lights up on a soldier in the prison holding area. Rajib brings Tariq in.

SOLDIER. Sign this paper.

TARIQ. What's this?

SOLDIER. You're being released.

Tariq hesitates. Rajib nudges him to get on with it. Tariq signs the paper.

SOLDIER (CONT'D). Your things. And a note. You're lucky to have friends like Mr. Hirsch.

Rajib shakes his hand and Tariq steps forward, out of the prison. After a moment he opens the letter. As he does, Hirsch appears elsewhere.

HIRSCH. Dear Tariq,

I hope they've treated you decently and I hope you don't mind that I went against your wishes. It seemed the right thing to do. I hope to never see your freedom taken away, and hope that all this ends well. But perhaps that's naïve.

In my life I've seen capitalists turn to socialists, socialists to capitalists, and far too many people turn into fascists. I've seen men quoting the Torah in one hand and holding their still-warm rifles in the other. I've seen a whole country fall into line behind the devil dressed in a well ironed uniform. I've moved in and out of dozens of apartments on three continents. I've learned Hebrew, the few words of Arabic you've taught me, and now, I've fallen in love with Palestine, its past and its future. And yet I hope that none of us love it so much that we would smother and strangle it just to keep it all to ourselves. I am not that kind of lover and I don't think you are. That is not true love but possession.

So it is my hope that this place is big enough for us all. Either way, I will find solace in the knowledge that I have a friend who wished it otherwise before our future was stolen by men who follow a violent God. And I will remember that you welcomed an exile to these shores and made me feel at home when perhaps you had every right to do otherwise.

Take care of yourself friend,

Samuel

Tariq folds the letter and puts it into his jacket. The lights shift.

SCENE NINE

The cell. Yusef plays cards. Across from him sits Emiliano Zapata's ghost. They drink as they play their hands.

ZAPATA. It was smart to let the boy go.

YUSEF. I know.

ZAPATA. You never know. Or maybe you do.

YUSEF. It's a shame. What they did to you.

ZAPATA. Yes. The world is full of shame. And beauty, too.

YUSEF. They hunted you down.

ZAPATA. I know. I remember.

YUSEF. Stabbed you in the back. Fuckers.

ZAPATA. I went to Jerusalem. It's a sad city. The stones cry and the shadows whimper in corners. But the sky. Man, it's a special color when you're inside those walls. Jesus was a lucky bastard. To die with a view of that sky.

YUSEF. You know what Jesus was? A Palestinian-Jewish freedom fighter; an anti-imperialist leading a spiritual rebellion against the occupiers.

ZAPATA. That's good. I'm gonna use that.
They play their cards. Yusef loses.
YUSEF. That's three straight for you, compadre!
ZAPATA. I was riding in a valley today, just south of the walls, you know, and for a moment, for one moment, I could have sworn I was riding across plains of Northern Durango. Then I saw a camel.
They laugh. Church bells in the distance.
YUSEF. It's almost time. They'll get me out of this place. You think I have more fight left in me?
ZAPATA. Yes. I do.
YUSEF. This is my country, Emiliano. It's all of ours.
ZAPATA. But full of hunters these days. Beware how the prey can turn to predator, the hunters into the hunted and back again, until we don't know predator from prey, right from wrong, up from down.
YUSEF. I keep losing my hands. They flicker. On and off.
Zapata whips his head towards the door and watches it. It is silent for a beat.
YUSEF (CONT'D). Is it time?
Zapata turns to Yusef and nods. A loud knock and then darkness.

SCENE TEN

The prison holding area. Rajib waits. He has a small duffel bag. Suddenly Michael runs up out of breath, holding several bags.
RAJIB. Damn it Mike, you're late. It's almost midnight.
MICHAEL. I got caught in the market.
RAJIB. What the hell were you doing in the market?
MICHAEL. I had to pick up souvenirs. For me mum and me family.
RAJIB. Souvenirs?
MICHAEL. You know, crosses, olive wood virgins.
RAJIB. I know what souvenirs are!
MICHAEL. It took me an hour to find an open store at this hour. Then, you know, we sat for tea, and…
Rajib stares at him in disbelief.
MICHAEL (CONT'D). What? I can't come back from the Holy Land empty-handed.
RAJIB. Let's just go. It's time. We have a job to do.
They quietly make their way to the cell.
MICHAEL. So it's two knocks, a sneeze and then another knock right?
RAJIB. No, three knocks, then a sneeze … and then another knock. Definitely a knock.
Rajib finally knocks three times then coughs, then sneezes, and knocks again. No response.
MICHAEL. Fuck it.
They unlock the door and look in.
MICHAEL (CONT'D). Yusef.… Yusef.… Hello?
From behind them a soldier appears.
SOLDIER. What you fellas up to?
MICHAEL. Nothing. Just … nothing really.
RAJIB. Where's the prisoner?
SOLDIER. I was looking for you two. You missed the show.

MICHAEL. Was the general doing his belly dancing routine again? Gave me nightmares last time.
SOLDIER. No, the trial. The general decided to get on with it a bit early. Apparently the high commissioner's coming tomorrow, but the trial was scheduled when the general wanted to play tennis with him.... So he pushed the proceedings up a bit. Wouldn't have made much of a difference anyway, tonight or tomorrow.
RAJIB. ...It might have.
SOLDIER. Well at least you didn't have to clean up the mess. I was at it alone, so you owe me a pint.
MICHAEL. Mess?
The soldier turns and looks upstage and we see, in the dim light, the twisting silhouette of a limp and bloodied body hanging from the balcony.
SOLDIER. He wouldn't go easily. *(beat)* Tell you what. You two can have the job of taking him down tomorrow after the tennis game and we'll call it even.
RAJIB. After the tennis game?
SOLDIER. The general insists the Arab watch his tennis match. From the balcony.

SCENE ELEVEN

The sound of protests and rain outside. A knock at the door. Anbara opens it. Rajib and Michael stand in the doorway, their hats off.
RAJIB. We let you down, miss.
MICHAEL. We went in to get him like we planned.
RAJIB. But he just wasn't there, ma'am. Secret trial.
MICHAEL. You're not at the funeral? It's massive. You should see all the/people—
ANBARA.—I hate funerals *(beat)* ...He used to play the 'oud for me. The notes fit perfectly in the creases of my skin, and into the arches of windows; they just fit. But he sold that 'oud. To buy a gun.
MICHAEL. They say he fought to the end.
Rajib hands her the money
RAJIB. We can't take it. Not now.
ANBARA. It's yours. Go home.
Rajib and Michael bow and exit. After a moment there is another knock at the door.
ANBARA (CONT'D). Come in.
Tariq enters carrying a bag.
TARIQ. It's started to rain again.
ANBARA. It's unusual this time of year.
TARIQ. I'm sorry. For/everything
ANBARA. Shhh.
TARIQ. Your writing. Your writing. You should be ... careful.
ANBARA. I should. *(beat)* But I won't. I won't hide anymore.
TARIQ. I suppose if anyone can handle the times, it's you Anbara.
ANBARA. *(calmly)* That's nice.
TARIQ. I went to the rally. After the funeral. I walked up to the front of the crowd. I got up on the fountain and I spoke. I felt intoxicated, on fire. I was holding something, a flag maybe, or a rock, a gun, I don't even remember. It was as if...
ANBARA. As if Yusef was speaking.
TARIQ. And they cheered me, Anbara. They roared, and we marched, moving like a sea.

ANBARA. And then the shots.
TARIQ. Yes.
ANBARA. Always the shots.
TARIQ. And we ran. We scattered, screaming, bleeding, in every direction. I ran like a boy escaping a beating, not seeing or hearing anything, just the explosions echoing in my head. I was lost. In Nablus; lost in my own city. I made my way back. To where the shots were fired, and it was empty. I was sure it was a dream, Anbara. I told myself that it was a dream the whole way home. And it was in flames. The house of my great-grandfather. And I felt empty. On fire.
ANBARA. Who did it?
TARIQ. The British … the Zionists. Does it even matter anymore?
ANBARA. Yes. And no.
TARIQ. I have to leave. I don't want my hands to disappear in all this blood. At least until things die down…. I can't, Anbara … I can't live like this.
ANBARA. None of us want to live like this.
TARIQ. I'm going to Beirut. I came to say goodbye. To you.
ANBARA. Go.
He hands her a ring of three old iron keys.
TARIQ. I want you to take the keys for what's left. What I haven't sold or seen burn. Until I return.
ANBARA. Yes.
Tariq turns to leave.
ANBARA (CONT'D). Don't forget us. Don't forget how they cheered for you.
Tariq exits. From the back door, Waleed enters.
WALEED. Who was that who just left?
ANBARA. Just another ghost.
WALEED. Imagine, perfectly good vegetables. They were throwing produce at a pair of British soldiers. People have no sense anymore. No sense at all.
Anbara goes to the back wall and takes the sword down. In its place she hangs the keys. Waleed sits by the window and looks out. A kind of sunlight peeks through the windows.
WALEED (CONT'D). The sky is clearing. That strange rain has stopped. Perhaps things will start looking up.
Blackout.

Anbara (Monica Orozco) and Hajj Waleed (Torrey Hanson) reflect on the future of Palestine in *Tennis in Nablus* by Ismail Khalidi, directed by Michael Malek Najjar (photograph by Airan Wright).

END OF PLAY

URGE FOR GOING: TRILOGY VERSION

Mona Mansour

Copyright 2018 by Mona Mansour. For reading and performance rights please contact Jonathan Mills at Paradigm Agency, tel: 212.897.6400

About the Playwright

Mona Mansour is an Arab-American playwright. Her "The Vagrant Trilogy" premiered May 2018 at Mosaic Theater in Washington, D.C. (directed by Mark Wing-Davey). The trilogy was presented at New Dramatists in fall 2016 after a workshop at the Vineyard Arts Project with the Public Theater. Of the trilogy: *The Hour of Feeling* (directed by Wing-Davey) premiered at the Humana Festival at Actors Theatre of Louisville, and a new Arabic translation was presented at NYU Abu Dhabi, as part of its Arab Voices Festival in 2016. *Urge for Going*: Productions at Public LAB (directed by Hal Brooks) and Golden Thread (directed by Evren Odcikin). *The Vagrant*, the third play in the trilogy, was commissioned by the Public and workshopped at the 2013 Sundance Theater Institute. Her play *We Swim, We Talk, We Go to War* (directed by Odcikin), will premiere at SF's Golden Thread in winter 2018. *The Way West* received its New York premiere at Labyrinth Theater in April 2016 (directed by Mimi O'Donnell). Prior to that, the play was at Steppenwolf (directed by Amy Morton) and Marin Theatre Company (directed by Hayley Finn). Her other credits include: *Unseen*, Gift Theater in Chicago (directed by Maureen Payne-Hahner) and *In the Open*, a 16-character play for Waterwell (directed by James Dean Palmer).

Mansour was a member of the Public Theater's Emerging Writers Group and a Core Writer at Minneapolis' Playwrights' Center. She has written, with Tala Manassah, *Falling Down the Stairs*, an EST/Sloan commission. Their short play *Dressing* is part of *Facing Our Truths: Short Plays about Trayvon, Race and Privilege*, a collection of plays commissioned by the New Black Festival. Her television credits include: *Queens Supreme* and *Dead Like Me*. Her commissions include Playwrights Horizons, Old Globe Theater, La Jolla Playhouse and Oregon Shakespeare Festival's "American Revolutions." She has won the 2012 Whiting Award and the 2014 Middle East America Playwright Award. More information is available at monamansour.com.

— Essay —
Mona Mansour's *Urge for Going*: Dramatizing "Permanent Impermanence"

Michael Malek Najjar

Mona Mansour's *Urge for Going* is part of "The Vagrant Trilogy," which also includes the plays *The Hour of Feeling* and *The Vagrant*. While many writers have approached the situation of Palestinians living in Palestine, few have dramatized the situation of millions of Palestinians living in refugee camps scattered throughout the Middle East. These "permanent residences in exile"[1] began following the suppression of the Arab uprisings of 1936–1939, but was hastened by the founding of the State of Israel in 1948 and with the subsequent wars between Israelis and Arabs. According to BBC News, the Palestinians comprise "one of the biggest displaced populations in the world."[2] The resulting Israeli contention that refugees should relinquish all right of return has only aggravated an already desperate situation. According to the United Nations Relief and Works Agency (UNRWA), there are currently 450,000 Palestinian refugees living in twelve camps in Lebanon. Palestinians in Lebanon are denied the right to work in certain professions, are unable to claim the same rights as other foreigners living and working in Lebanon, and often live in abject poverty.[3] According to *Al Jazeera*, "Today, Palestinians in Lebanon continue to suffer from draconian measures which the Lebanese state claims are there to prevent them from becoming permanent guests."[4] To make matters worse, there has been wholesale slaughter of these refugees in their Lebanese camps, such as the infamous Sabra and Shatila massacre of 1982 and the suicide attack on the Burj el-Barajneh camp in 2015.

Urge for Going, set in an unnamed Palestinian refugee camp in southern Lebanon (just a thirty minute drive to the Israeli border), opens with Palestinians themselves debating how the crisis began, and with each citing historical facts to prove their position. Mansour's play highlights the fact that Palestinians in Lebanon and Syria's refugee camps are living in a state of limbo—unable to become citizens of the nations to which they've been displaced, and disallowed from returning to their ancestral homes in Israel and the occupied Palestinian territories. Regarding Jordan, prior to 1988, all Palestinian refugees were granted full Jordanian citizenship; however the 1967 refugees from Gaza were exempted from this citizenship. To make matters worse, many Jordanian Palestinians have lost their citizenship, thereby rendering them stateless.[5]

Urge for Going also focuses on the urge to flee the camps for a better life elsewhere.

This urge to leave is strong, given that life in the refugee camp is untenable: from lack of sanitation and electricity to beatings from Lebanese soldiers that have left family members physically and mentally injured. The only clear way out for this family is through academic opportunity—yet even Jamila knows that no matter how much one masters their intellect, "if you don't have the innate talent, you won't succeed."[6] For Jamila's father, Adham, the opportunity to escape came when he was invited to London in 1967 to lecture on Tennyson's "Lines Composed a Few Miles Above Tintern Abbey, On Revisiting the Banks of the Wye During a Tour. July 13, 1798." Although the lecture's reception grants Adham a fellowship to study in London, the defeat of the Arab armies in 1967 forces his return to a homeland that is seemingly lost, leaving him and his wife refugees in neighboring Lebanon. For his young daughter Jamila, however, the opportunity arrives thirty-six years later, when she tests for her Baccalaureate.

Palestinian American scholar Edward W. Said once said, "In a way, it's a sort of the fate of the Palestinians not to end up where they started but somewhere unexpected and far away."[7] The play ends with Jul and Jamila reciting statistics about the painful situation Palestinian refugees face. According to the website *Visualizing Palestine*, ninety percent of Palestinians in Lebanon were born there and most are third- and fourth-generation. Only two percent have an official work permit while the rest face "biased attitudes and discriminatory labor laws." Most are forced into precarious work and sixty-six percent live below the poverty line. Their average monthly wage is $369 for men and $305 for women.[8] "After more than 60 years, Palestinian refugees are barred from numerous professions in Lebanon—including medicine, law and engineering—because they are defined as foreigners."[9] Therefore, like many Palestinian families living as refugees for the past seventy years, the family in Mansour's drama have a Hobson's choice: either stay put in their refugee camps, or rely on the hope that a better life exists elsewhere. Mansour allows audiences to take a moment to empathize with those Palestinians who are living in the hopeless purgatory known as exile.

— PLAYWRIGHT STATEMENT —
The Unspeakable Loss of Displacement

The characters in *Urge for Going* are strangely closer to my heart now than they were when I first started working on the play. Now they live in two other plays as well; all three plays now collectively form "The Vagrant Trilogy." But *Urge* was the first time I "met" them officially; the first of the three I wrote.

Set in contemporary times (2003), in a refugee camp in Southern Lebanon, *Urge for Going* was written as my way of trying to understand the past and present of my father's home country, Lebanon. What did it mean that outside my father's village (near the city of Sidon), there were two Palestinian camps that had been in existence since 1948? What happens to those inside that kind of "permanent impermanence?" What happens to the family dynamic when someone tries to push against that enforced stasis? After finishing that play, I hadn't imagined writing anything more about those characters.

Then later, in the Public Theater's Emerging Writers Group, I was trying to decide what to write, and it occurred to me that I was very interested in the story Adham tells his daughter, Jamila, in *Urge* about his trip to London in 1967 as a young man just out of Cairo University, full of hope about his future. I knew I wanted that new play, called *The Hour of Feeling*, to end with Adham making the decision to go back to Palestine in 1967 as the war broke out. I *needed* the character to make that decision, so *The Hour of Feeling* would line up narratively with *Urge for Going*. But the younger version of Adham didn't want to "join up" with his future self, stuck in a refugee camp. He essentially refused to go back to that fate. So from there the third play was born, *The Vagrant*, which imagines Adham's life as it would be if he stayed in London and became a professor. There, he does well enough materially but has completely compartmentalized all connections to family, home and trauma, until all of that shatters and he simply can't anymore.

So it's a conditional trilogy. And I go into all this because seen together, what the plays speak to is the fundamental fact that there is a deep psychic cost of displacement. This is what has obsessed me through writing all of these plays about the imagined life of a Palestinian scholar: The place you escape to, if you're "lucky" enough to escape, will never be home; you will never fully be of that place. Nor will you ever be "of" your homeland again, once displaced.

I think about this more and more as the issue of migrants and migrations sets off elections, galvanizes the xenophobic right, and fuels visions of massive walls: At the beginning of every one of those journeys is an unspeakable loss. In *Urge for Going*, it's almost impossible for the characters to speak of this loss directly. Here, Wordsworth's poetry steps in as Adham and Jamila say their goodbye: "The picture of the mind revives again/While here I stand, not only with the sense/Of present pleasure, but with pleasing thoughts/That in this moment there is life and food/For future years. And so I dare to hope..." My hope is that that together, the plays will speak to the psychic effects of displacement not just for Palestinians, but for all of us.

— Playscript —
Urge for Going

> "Politics is the family at breakfast.
> Who is there, and who is absent and
> why. Who misses whom when the coffee is
> poured into the waiting cups. Where are
> your children who have gone forever
> from these, their usual chairs?"
> —Mourid Barghouti, *I Saw Ramallah*

The poem that Hamzi recites is an excerpt from "Abd Al-Hadi Fights a Superpower," from Never Mind, *by Taha Muhammad Ali, translated by Peter Coles. The Baywatch episodes are the playwright's fabrication.*

PART ONE

THE NOISE.

Setting: In and outside a dwelling in a refugee camp, Southern Lebanon. 2003, between wars. The adult characters enter: Hamzi, the uncle, large, 60s; Abir, the mother, 50s, sharp, perceptive; Ghassan, the other uncle, 60s; and Adham, late 50s, the father, handsome, intelligent.

What follows isn't completely direct address, nor is it completely to each other. It's a hybrid. It's important to note here and throughout the play: They argue vigorously, and they mean it all, but they love it—the arguing, and each other.

ALL. The noise.
HAMZI. The 1948 Palestinian exodus refers to the refugee flight of Palestinian Arabs during the last six months of British rule and the first Arab-Israeli war.
ABIR. I reject this interpretation of events.
HAMZI. There's nothing to interpret.
GHASSAN. Certainly there is.
HAMZI. How? Those were just facts.
GHASSAN. One man's facts are another man's fabrications.
HAMZI. It's right. I Wikipedia'd it. It's right.
ABIR. This description? Arab-Israeli War? There was no Israel before 1948, so the description is meaningless!
GHASSAN. British rule? It was an occupation.

HAMZI. Walak! The British created Palestine —
GHASSAN. "Created"? As if the lands weren't there to begin with?
HAMZI. The borders —
ABIR. Two men in a room with a map, drawing lines. That's all it was. That's/all it ever is.
GHASSAN. An Englishman, a Frenchman, boom-boom, it's done.
HAMZI. There were borders, okay? That were created in 1918, and again, in 1922—
ABIR. I disagree with this assessment as well.
GHASSAN. Let it be noted that two of us disagree with this assessment.
HAMZI. *(to Adham, who hasn't spoken)* You too?
Beat—they look to him.
ADHAM. Maybe.
GHASSAN. So three of us, at least, disagree with this assessment.
HAMZI. No one listens to anyone here.
GHASSAN. What's that?
HAMZI. I said no one listens!
GHASSAN. We listen.
ABIR. We just don't agree with you!
GHASSAN. Imagine that.
HAMZI. This is going to take all day! All right, we agree: 1948. We agree: Nakba.
GHASSAN. Catastrophe.
ABIR. Disaster.
HAMZI. The U.N. estimated almost eight hundred thousand refugees.
GHASSAN. Again, that's not right.
HAMZI. This is common knowledge, my friend.
GHASSAN. Everyone knows it was a million.
HAMZI. Whatever the number, we were forced to leave.
ABIR. Again, I disagree.
HAMZI. With what now?
ABIR. *(shrugs, enjoying this)* Your tone.
HAMZI. *(to Adham)* Can you rein in your wife a little?
Adham smiles.
ADHAM. Not so far.
GHASSAN. My sister likes to speak her mind!
HAMZI. I'm trying to tell a very basic story. It should take no more than two minutes, front to back!
He wipes his hands.
ABIR. If you tell it badly!
HAMZI. The point is, we left. We left, we left, we left. Okay?
ABIR. The point is, each and every point is open for discussion.
HAMZI. We left. The story begins there.
ABIR/GHASSAN. No.
GHASSAN. Not at all.
HAMZI. So we don't agree on the beginning.
GHASSAN/ABIR. No.
ABIR. You've left out centuries of our history.
HAMZI. *(to the audience)* We don't have time for that!

ABIR. You're too busy?
GHASSAN. I have plenty of time. I have nothing but time.
HAMZI. Can we agree on one thing? We're all the same here. Palestinians.
GHASSAN. Of course we are.
ABIR. I agree.
HAMZI. Thank God.
ABIR. But you haven't mentioned Deir Yassin.
HAMZI. I covered it! 1948, Nakba, Deir Yassin!
GHASSAN. *(to Abir, mocking Hamzi)* He covered it.
ABIR. He's moved on.
HAMZI. No!
GHASSAN. Deir Yassin was a massacre. Women, children, it didn't matter.
HAMZI. Yes. And after —
GHASSAN. Don't move on from there! Deir Yassin. Those people were terrorized.
ABIR. Terrified. The stories of what happened were enough to make everyone leave.
Hamzi steps downstage a little bit. He massages this next bit, knowing what he's saying is controversial.
HAMZI. There are those who have said that some of what happened at Deir Yassin may have been slightly exaggerated. According to a 1988 documentary, our leader at the time, Hussein Khalidi, admitted as much. He said the leaders, eh, well, inflated the story to bring the Arab armies in.
Joining him downstage, infuriated:
ABIR. No no no.
GHASSAN. Khalidi didn't say this! The Zionist BBC mentioned this! That's who said it! No one believes any of that!
HAMZI. I'm saying, this is what we face! A massacre they say we fabricated!
ABIR. You were a young boy in 1948.
HAMZI. Yes.
ABIR. And weren't your parents terrified?
Beat: He looks at Adham.
ADHAM. I barely remember it.
HAMZI. —They were.
I like to present every side.
ABIR. Why?
What's wrong with you?
(to Adham) What's wrong with your brother?
ADHAM. Mostly he just likes to hear himself speak.
HAMZI. This is our nature. We talk. I like to chat. It's healthy! I will chat with anyone.
ABIR. *(to Adham)* Why don't you talk to him?
ADHAM. I don't like getting involved in arguments like this.
GHASSAN. This is our life. Our history.
ADHAM. Political. I'm not political.
He smiles at Jamila, who has entered with a hardbound book.
JAMILA. You like literature.
GHASSAN. *(butting in)* Saying you aren't political is itself POLITICAL. You realize that?
ADHAM. I was interested in the politics of subject, verb, object. Or no verb and object. Of rhyme, or no rhyme. What are you reading?

JAMILA. William Wordsworth's "Tintern Abbey."
She hands him an old book. This private moment hangs in the middle of the argument, almost its own universe:
ADHAM. That was my book.
JAMILA. I found it with the others. I'll be careful with it.
ADHAM. I don't care. It's not a treasure.
Jamila nods. She opens the book, looks through, finds:
JAMILA. "Feelings too/Of unremembered pleasure: Such, perhaps,
As have no slight or trivial influence
On that best portion of a good man's life,
His little, nameless, unremembered acts
Of Kindness and—."
ADHAM. I know the poem.
JAMILA. I don't get the "unremembered" though. I looked it up. It means "allowed to drop out of mind." But if he's forgotten everything, how does he have any feelings about it at all?
ADHAM. ——I don't know.
HAMZI. *(resuming argument, to Ghassan)* You've misinterpreted what I've said as an approval of Zionism.
ABIR. *(to Hamzi)* No.
HAMZI. You say one thing critical, and you're a Zionist.
Their moment broken, Adham hands the book back to Jamila.
ABIR. Why are you smiling? Why is he smiling?
HAMZI. I have to! Who cares if I smile?
GHASSAN. And now he laughs!
HAMZI. At my own misfortune! This is my God-given right!
GHASSAN. *(to Abir)* He can't absorb the weight of it.
HAMZI. This is the weight of it. *(points to his body, his girth, etc)* Here is the weight of it. It's in my body my entire life! I was speaking of 1948. When I came to Lebanon, to live in a city of tents. I was a child. I thought it was an adventure.
GHASSAN. Not everyone came then.
HAMZI. I know, I know. 1967. When all of you left what remained of Palestine. And came to live with me.
GHASSAN. Agreed.
HAMZI. Okay. Good. We're almost done.
ABIR. And here we are in Lebanon.
GHASSAN. In temporary camps built sixty years ago.
HAMZI. Still here, still temporary. A refugee camp permanently impermanent.
They step into a small structure, shelter more than house. They are all there, crouched under it—one room, pillows and mattresses on the floors, two wooden tables. To the walls are pinned a few tapestries and small rugs.

BAYWATCH.

Jul, Jamila's brother, rushes in, carrying a small TV set. He places it downstage. He's a grown man, and physically fine, but something about him is off.
JUL. Sssh. It's. My show.
GHASSAN. The Baywatch.

HAMZI. The Baywatch is on now? Which one?

JUL. The girl's father visits. He goes in a dangerous part of the water.

GHASSAN. Yes, yes. And the girl rescues him. He doesn't want to accept her help, but he takes her hand at the end, and she pulls him into the boat.

HAMZI. I've seen it. Good. This is a beautiful story.

Jamila looks at the book.

JAMILA. It's actually in pretty good shape. I mean. A little frayed at the edges. It's fine. I need it for my test.

ADHAM. The Baccalaureate.

JAMILA. I have three weeks.

ADHAM. Ah.

JAMILA. One thing —

ADHAM. What?

JAMILA. I need some paperwork for the test. To show them we have, um, legal residency.

ADHAM. Show who?/The government?

GHASSAN. *(overlap)* Legal? Legal. Ha. What is legal about human beings living like this?/Kuz-ukhta.

HAMZI. Shi be kharree.

She nods.

ADHAM. Invite them here. Here is my residence.

JAMILA. I mean it, Baba.

ADHAM. Okay.

Jamila, looking through the book all this time, has found something—a small black-and-white picture.

JAMILA. What is this?

Behind them, a blow-up of the picture. It's Adham, circa 1967, young, handsome, speaking at a podium to a very Anglo audience.

ADHAM. Me in London.

JAMILA. You never showed me this before.

ADHAM. I haven't looked at that in thirty years. Put it away.

She studies the picture.

JAMILA. You wore a tie. You combed your hair!

ABIR. He didn't. I did.

ADHAM. She cleaned me up.

ABIR. Yes!

JAMILA. You look so … official.

ABIR. It was a lecture at a school.

ADHAM. University College. Darwin Lecture Theater, Gower Street.

JAMILA. Was he nervous?

ADHAM. Not at all.

JAMILA. Your English was good enough for everyone to understand?

ADHAM. Of course!

ABIR. Not everyone! I had no idea what he was saying. But he sounded good. He looked very relaxed.

ADHAM. I always look relaxed.

ABIR. No habibi.

JAMILA. Where did you sit?
ABIR. Fourth row. He didn't want me in the front.
Adham points to the left and front of him.
ADHAM. I knew she was somewhere … over there. I didn't want to know exactly. Didn't want to feel her eyes on me.
Adham's barely listening, caught in the memory.
JAMILA. Did you go to Harrods?…Were you hopeful?
He snaps out of it.
ADHAM. Put the picture away.
JAMILA. Why didn't you stay there?
Adham walks away.
JAMILA. (cont'd) Why didn't you stay?
Lights shift: We hear a 1960s Fairuz song: "Ya Ghozayel."

THE BOOK.

Another day. Adham sits down with the men on the floor, playing the card game Basra. Jamila's off to the side, reading and taking notes. Abir does housework, listening to the conversation, and Jul sits at Hamzi's side, watching the card game.
HAMZI. In the book—
GHASSAN. *(overlap)* Which book?
ADHAM. *(overlap) (Teasing him)* A book you read?
GHASSAN. He reads?
ADHAM. We didn't know this.
GHASSAN. Notify the authorities.
HAMZI. I read. Always!
GHASSAN. The back of a candy wrapper?
ADHAM. No he's too busy stuffing it in his mouth, the whole thing, paper and all.
HAMZI. Tuz feek, shut up! You see how they are, Jamila? They don't know how to listen!
A pause. Hamzi proceeds…
HAMZI. (cont'd) There is a book, "Who Move My Cheese." And it's right.
JAMILA. I think it's Who Moved. "D." There's a "d" at the end.
HAMZI. Who cares?
JAMILA. I'm just saying.
ADHAM. You're reading Hamzi's children's books now?
GHASSAN. I've seen this book. I was curious.
JAMILA. It was in the library. Next to "Andrew Morton, Diana: Her True Story."
ADHAM. This is what the U.N. puts on the shelves?
Jamila shrugs. Hamzi looks at them to make sure they both are done.
HAMZI. IN the book, there's two mice, Scurry and something —
GHASSAN. *(probing)* Scurry?
HAMZI. Yes.
GHASSAN. *(satisfied)* Okay.
HAMZI. And two people, named Haw and Hem.
GHASSAN. Ham like the Son of Noah?
HAMZI. No. Not Ham. Hem. Hem. Haw and Hem. These tiny humans. Everyone lives on cheese. Everyone enjoys cheese.

The group nods.
HAMZI. *(cont'd)* And the cheese means different things for different people. The mice love to eat it, they don't care about anything else. And the humans. It's their main happiness.
GHASSAN. They don't eat it?
HAMZI. They do, they do, of course, of course. But they don't notice that bit by bit, it's disappearing.
JAMILA. Why don't they notice?
GHASSAN. They're eating it.
JAMILA. Ergo: it disappears.
HAMZI. Yes, but more than it should!
Ghassan laughs at what he feels is "insight" into the book.
GHASSAN. Someone's lying then. Eating more than he should and not telling everybody.
HAMZI. No no no that's not it.
ADHAM. The two mice are overeating.
JAMILA. Very mice-like of them.
HAMZI. No—yes, the mice are eating it, but they can't eat this fast.
Beat.
HAMZI. *(cont'd) (emphatically)* It's not the mice. It's the Cheese Removers.
ADHAM. *(in spite of himself)* What are the Cheese Removers?
HAMZI. We don't know.
GHASSAN. I don't trust the tiny people, the Ham ones.
HAMZI. Not Ham. Hem.
ADHAM. Who gives a shit. Play.
GHASSAN. Ham, Hem…
HAMZI. *(to Adham)* We're talking, right? Analyzing? So he should get it right.
GHASSAN. I think the tiny people—Hems?—say they're just looking, but I think they're eating it.
HAMZI. Walak, they are eating it!
JAMILA. Are the Cheese Removers people or mice? I think they're taking extra and giving it to their counterparts in secret.
ADHAM. Ah ha.
GHASSAN. Wait. Which counterparts? I didn't hear him say that!
ADHAM. Well, it was implied.
HAMZI. No no no. I'm telling this story. The Cheese Removers are coming in at night, whenever, and taking it.
JAMILA. And. What. Are They. Doing. With. It?
HAMZI. WE DON'T KNOW.
The point is, nobody notices the cheese is diminishing until one day they see an empty space where the cheese should be. They look up and say, SHIT. IT'S GONE. Who Move My Cheese?
ADHAM. Hence, the title.
HAMZI. Meaning: "What happened? We got nothing left."
ADHAM. Then go somewhere else. Where they have cheese.
Hamzi's excited now. Thrilled. He's woven it all perfectly. Got them where he wants them.
HAMZI. That's the point of the book! "Go somewhere else!" Right. It's so simple, but we don't think of that!

JAMILA. He just did.

Jamila and Adham laugh at their minor victory. Hamzi grows more agitated.

HAMZI. We stay in one place and refuse to change until it's too late. We do nothing except shake our heads in wonder until we starve to death!

ADHAM. Well, they're idiots, these characters.

HAMZI. This is the Arab World, you see! The Arab World is refusing to change. We hold on to old ideas about our empire. "We were the highest form of civilization! We will be again." We've been here since 1948. Sixty-seven. Waiting to go home.

GHASSAN. We will. Maybe not you and me, but Jamila. It will happen.

HAMZI. This is what I'm talking about. Jamila: Do you want to go back to Palestine?

JAMILA. Wait. What?

HAMZI. Ah ha.

GHASSAN. *(schooling Jamila)* Palestine? Your father's homeland, thirty minutes away, depending on traffic.

HAMZI. Depending on traffic! Like he makes this journey every day!

GHASSAN. I will, okay! The Right of Return! United Nations One-Nine Four!

HAMZI. Which Israel does not adhere to.

GHASSAN. You wait.

HAMZI. He's gonna get in a taxi, and drive across the border! What a man!

GHASSAN. Jamila, answer.

JAMILA. Honestly, it's not like it'd be the first place I'd visit.

Everyone looks at her.

JAMILA. *(cont'd)* I mean. I was born here, I've never been anywhere but here, so…. There's lots of places I want to see. Paris, definitely. Prague. Iceland? I like the pictures.

Beat. No one's particularly happy to hear her say this.

GHASSAN. *(to Adham; total disapproval)* You see how you've raised her? No ideology.

ADHAM. What ideology was I supposed to raise her with?

GHASSAN. Maybe not ideology. But a sense of history.

HAMZI. Psh.

ADHAM. I see.

GHASSAN. Of our leadership!

HAMZI. Leadership? Haiwan *(pronounced HIGH-wahn)*, what leadership?

GHASSAN. She should know those who came before! George Habash *(pronounced HA-bash)*…

ADHAM. George Habash? What can he do for her?

HAMZI. He's not doing so well these days, so nothing,/God have mercy on him.

ADHAM. He can get my daughter a college degree? Is that it?

GHASSAN. She should know some of the story of the Struggle. Not just the Latin you taught her.

JAMILA. He didn't teach me Latin.

GHASSAN. Whatever the language. Useless. What's she gonna/do with that?

HAMZI. Ya khara, don't tell him how to raise his daughter. He wanted to raise his kids above all that. That's how my mother (God rest her soul in peace) brought him up.

GHASSAN. Why? What did this approach do for Adham? He still ended up in the shit like the rest of us.

If Adham is stung, he doesn't let on.

JAMILA. I take it back, okay? I want to go. I do. *(beat; then, simply, not heavy)* I just don't think ... it will happen.
Beat.
HAMZI. Well. So then. You see? Jamila is the only one who has seen what is really there and moved on.
JAMILA. *(back to teasing Hamzi, waving her hands in the air emphatically)* Who Moved My Cheese?
ADHAM. This conversation is ridiculous.
HAMZI. What would you suggest be done?
ADHAM. About what?
HAMZI. Our progress. How we move forward.
ADHAM. In the context of what you just said?
HAMZI. Yes, by God, yes.
Beat, as Adham ponders...
ADHAM. Let me think. Given the current political climate, and only if all diplomatic channels have been exhausted, I suggest we offer the Israelis a giant piece of gruyere and hope they get diarrhea.
Now Hamzi's furious.
HAMZI. What the Hell solution do you have? What do you offer?
ADHAM. Nothing. Not a damn thing!
Song: Fairuz: "Ya Helou Al Amar."

TALK SHOW.
Lights up. A dusty square of earth right outside the metal "structure."

Outside, the metal walls have been "fortified" with cardboard advertisements: one for Schwepps Limonade, the other for "The Matrix." Both are in Arabic.

Jul sits on a ratty beach chair, and holds up a fake "microphone" as Jamila comes outside to sit with him. Note: It's important that Jul not be any more "noble" than anyone else in the family. His interactions with Jamila can be playful, competitive.

JUL. The talk show.
Jamila's pissed.
JAMILA. Wait.
JUL. What's wrong?
JAMILA. I'm not even seated yet. You have to wait till the guest is seated.

Abir (Penelope Walker, left), Ghassan (Dexter Zollicoffer, second from right), and Adham (Rom Barkhordar, right) try to reason with Hamzi (Amro Salama, foreground) in *Urge for Going* by Mona Mansour, directed by Anna C. Bahow (photograph by Airan Wright).

JUL. Bossy.
JAMILA. *(smiles)* So? I'm the producer.
  She gets seated. The chair sags to the ground, precariously. Jul laughs.
JUL. Chair's gonna bust.
JAMILA. Just—go.
JUL. Hamzi's been sitting his fat ass on it.
JAMILA. No wonder it's all saggy. Poor chair!
  They both laugh. She readjusts.
  The fibers almost give way—but no. They hold her—for now.
JUL. Ready?
JAMILA. Yes.
  Beat. Jamila looks at Jul. Prompts him:
JAMILA. *(cont'd)* Welcome back…
JUL. Welcome back. We are sitting with…. What do I call you?
JAMILA. My name.
JUL. Jamila al-Awahni.
JAMILA. Keep going.
JUL. And you are…
JAMILA. Renowned author and child psychologist.
JUL. Both?
JAMILA. Yes. Tell me I'm so young.
JUL. But you're so young.
JAMILA. Well, not really. I look young because…. It's the expensive products I put on my skin.
JUL. And we are here in London. *(breaking out of it)* You said you'd write it down.
JAMILA. I will, next time. I didn't have time.
JUL. I can read.
JAMILA. I know. Of course.
JUL. Sometimes the words get.
Mixed up.
JAMILA. *(softening)* I don't want to play this.
JUL. You used to beg me to play all the time. All. The. Time.
JAMILA. I know, but —
JUL. And I did. Right? I was busy! I had studies!
JAMILA. I know.
  Jul speaks to the "audience":
JUL. Something happened to me when I was seventeen. *(matter-of-fact)* Two years ago! Recent! I left home one way, and came back another.
That is why I am…
And what do you do, Miss Al-awahni?
Go.
JAMILA. Thank you, I specialize in studying children who grew up in violent atmospheres.
JUL. Wow.
JAMILA. It's because of my background, of course.
JUL. Of course.
How did you get out of the refugee camp?

JAMILA. Well, it's a long story. I don't know if there's time…
JUL. You're the only guest.
JAMILA. Well. Basically what happened is, I was invited to attend a conference in Copenhagen —
JUL. By who?
JAMILA. A very prominent … organization.
JUL. Okay.
JAMILA. And after I spoke…
JUL. How many people?
JAMILA. Oh. Um. No one counted, but the lecture hall was packed, so I would say … approximately six-thousand, maybe?
JUL. Continue.
JAMILA. I spoke, and there was, you know, applause.
JUL. Whistling?
JAMILA. No. Just thunderous applause. But when I stepped off the stage there was an announcement that violent clashes and bombings had begun in Beirut.
JUL. That's typical.
JAMILA. Not to them. Everyone looked at me, thinking: How can we force her to go back to that? Before I even knew what was happening, several Danish teachers surrounded me, linking arms.
JUL. A human shield? That's corny.
JAMILA. So? It worked. No one could send me back after that.
JUL. I know how this is going to turn out.
JAMILA. No you don't.
JUL. You get four Ph.D.s and everyone wants you and you never come back here.
JAMILA. Not quite. This one's different: I get … five Ph.Ds. And go around the world, speaking to people about violence. Last year, the U.N. asked me to speak. And I sit between Angelina Jolie and … someone else.
JUL. Who?
JAMILA. I don't know yet. I'll decide.
JUL. Someone good?
JAMILA. It will be. And I'm sitting there, with these international bigwigs, and everyone is amazed at my wisdom. How much I have learned in spite of the worst set of circumstances. The funny thing is, the really funny thing is, I get so caught up in what I'm saying that I forget what language I'm speaking. I go from Arabic to French to English—
JUL. And Danish—
JAMILA. And Danish—all within one sentence, and everyone laughs and claps. I'm not even trying to be smart. It just comes out of me. Then they give me a huge party. Right there at the Copenhagen International Club.
JUL. Okay then.
JAMILA. Ask me if there's dancing.
JUL. Is there dancing?
JAMILA. It breaks out spontaneously. A DJ plays Arabic music mixed with disco. And during the party, everyone grabs me and puts me in the middle of the room. I've never danced in public before, so I just stand there. And I look stupid, but everyone loves me even more for my humility.

JUL. Huh?

JAMILA. I cry, and wipe tears away from my eyes, and brush the hair off my face, and then everyone copies me.

JUL. You create a dance move.

JAMILA. Exactly.

She does a move where she brushes hair from her face…

JAMILA. *(cont'd)* Then the DJ releases the song, and calls it "Jamila's Dreams." It's currently number two worldwide.

JUL. That's too much.

JAMILA. No it's not.

JUL. Number two?

JAMILA. Yes.

JUL. In the world?

JAMILA. It's possible. You have to think about what's possible.

Jul and Jamila dance, laughing at themselves as they do so. Lights shift, and Jamila is alone. She goes into the structure, reading from another old book:

JAMILA. *(cont'd)* "The woods decay, the woods decay and fall
The vapours weep their burthen to the ground,
Man comes and tills the field and lies beneath;
And after many a summer dies the swan…
Alas! for this gray shadow, once a man —."
(beat)
"Please discuss how grief fuels the sentiments behind Tennyson's Tithonus."

BAYWATCH 2.

Continuous. The group has finished eating and everyone sits around the table.
The tiny black-and-white television casts its glow on their faces.
The men play cards again while Jamila, having entered, sits on her bed/a chair separate from the group.

JAMILA. *(to no one in particular)* Grief is fueling MY experience of reading Tithonus.

ADHAM. *(correcting her pronunciation)* Tithonus.

JAMILA. That's how you say it? I didn't know.

HAMZI. Will this be on the examination?

JAMILA. I don't know. I have to be prepared. I just resent having to spend so much time on a writer I don't find inspiring. Baba hated Tennyson too.

HAMZI. What did he ever do to Baba?

JAMILA. *(horrified)* Nothing! He's a Victorian poet. He died like a hundred years ago.

HAMZI. I know that! I'm kidding! A man can't joke anymore?

JAMILA. *(to Adham)* Do you remember? How you hated Tennyson?

ADHAM. That sounds right.

ABIR. I remember.

JAMILA. See?

ABIR. I told your father once early on that I liked one of those poems.

JAMILA. You studied Tennyson? I thought you studied engineering.

ABIR. Well yes. But everyone studied the English writers, of course. Anyway, this poem, it sounded—well, pretty. I told your father this, and he thought I was such a peasant.

GHASSAN. How's that? Our family wasn't lowly.

ADHAM. I never said/"peasant"!
HAMZI. Nothing wrong with being called a peasant. We used to respect people/who worked the land.
GHASSAN. True, our village was in the middle of nowhere. But we moved to the city, eventually.
HAMZI. But you were farmers.
GHASSAN. Walak, until they took the farm!
ABIR. *(cutting them off)* He was incensed that I could possibly find Tennyson's words sublime. He spent three days lecturing me.
ADHAM. No I didn't.
JAMILA. Did you change your mind?
ABIR. No.
JAMILA. Look. You wrote in the margin. Just for a second. Look.
HAMZI. Don't interrupt him habibti.
GHASSAN. He's busy.
JAMILA. Playing cards!
ADHAM. *(mock serious)* This is a very important game we're in.
JAMILA. This is more important!
HAMZI. Consider yourself lucky! He's leaving you alone. He used to force you both to sit at the table and finish your exercises.
GHASSAN. He was running a jail.
HAMZI. Jul came home with a ninety-three one day, and Adham was furious it wasn't a hundred. He's not like that anymore.
JAMILA. I know. Why is that? It's like he doesn't care if I do my work or not.
ABIR. He does care, very much.
JAMILA. Why doesn't he show it?
ABIR. Adham, help her. She's asking.
Adham motions to Jamila.
ADHAM. Let me see.
She springs up, bringing the book, points to where he wrote in the margin—
JAMILA. "Excessive examination…"
ADHAM. "…of this poet is unwarranted." … Yes, I got very worked up about it.
Jamila lights up.
ADHAM. *(cont'd)* But not for the reasons you're mentioning.
JAMILA. Why, then?
ADHAM. Well. Yours is a very surface assessment of the poet.
JAMILA. Oh. Okay.
Tell me why then.
ADHAM. It's complicated.
Jul pops up.
JUL. The Baywatch!
HAMZI. The Baywatch.
JUL. The Bay. And the Watch. Equals Baywatch.
GHASSAN. It's on?
JUL. This is the one where it's very hot outside…
HAMZI. It's a quality show, it is. You can see the quality.
JAMILA. *(to Adham)* Tell me why it's complicated.

JUL. ...So everyone jumps in the water without their clothes on.
JAMILA. *(to Adham)* Can you? Complicated is a very catch-all word.
GHASSAN. Well don't tell us. Let us see it.
Jamila walks over to the TV, turns the volume down.
HAMZI. Don't do that! We can barely hear it as it is!
JAMILA. He just said he wanted to SEE it. You can see it. *(to her father)* They've watched this episode already.
ADHAM. Turn it back up.
She sighs, turns it up, makes a show of sitting down and opening her book. Over the sound of the TV:
GHASSAN. I remember this one: The president of the U.S. comes, but there's no one to make sure he doesn't drown.
HAMZI. It's not one of my top ten.
JAMILA. Wait. Can we have the show or the side commentary? One or the other?
GHASSAN. Walah...?
JAMILA. I'm trying to study!
ADHAM. You want a library, go to a library.
JAMILA. The UNRWA one closes at four!
And the commentary continues:
JUL. The president doesn't know how to swim. It's scary.
JAMILA. *(can't help herself)* The president doesn't know how to swim? That makes no sense.
HAMZI. It's not that unusual. Some people never learn.
GHASSAN. Me, it was easy. I was thrown in the sea, and just started paddling—done.
JAMILA. Even if it were credible, the fact that none of the Secret Service people know how to save him? That's bad storytelling. They have serious training, those guys!
HAMZI. *(overlap)* Okay, okay.
JAMILA. So why do they need the lifeguards?
HAMZI. It's the show. It's about the lifeguards.
ADHAM. You're analyzing this story too much.
HAMZI. Yes. You're taking it in the wrong direction.
JAMILA. You taught me to analyze stories. To be a critical thinker.
ADHAM. I taught you to know when the story isn't worth thinking about! It's a stupid story, let it go.
JUL. *(overlap)* It is?
JAMILA. *(overlap)* I'm the one who SAID it was a stupid story! I'm the voice of reason here!
HAMZI. *(overlap)* We know it's stupid. We enjoy it anyway!
JAMILA. I don't!
ADHAM. You have to learn to talk to people calmly!
JAMILA. I am!
ADHAM. You're yelling.
JAMILA. So are you!
Somewhere in all this, Jul goes to the set and turns it up. Ghassan nods in approval.
ABIR. Jamila, stop. You're making things hard for yourself.
ADHAM. She can't stand to be corrected, so she lashes out.
HAMZI. Every day at school we debated. Ten-year-olds!

JAMILA. *(trying not to cry)* Why do you give me such a hard time?
HAMZI. *(no one is really listening to him, but…)* Our own debates. We organized them…
ADHAM. You'll never make it, academics, anything, if this gets you upset.
JAMILA. *(cont'd)* I'M NOT UPSET.
JUL. You kind of are.
HAMZI. I'm not the smartest one, I'm not full of every single fact, okay, I know this, right, but I win. You want to know why?
JAMILA. Not right now.
HAMZI. I would stay calm. Breathe and look confident.
JAMILA. I can't do that here!
ADHAM. So go outside!
ABIR. Habibti, you're outnumbered. Do what your father says.
JAMILA. I don't want—
Suddenly, all power goes out: Everything goes black.
GHASSAN. Shit.
JUL. Oh no.
Barely skipping a beat, Abir calmly begins to light a few candles. As she does so, the men resume cards—this happens all the time.
HAMZI. *(good-naturedly)* See? No more show. It all worked out.
JAMILA. I still have to study.
Abir lights another candle, takes it over to Jamila.
GHASSAN. One thing I don't understand—
JAMILA. Can it please, please not be about "Baywatch"?
GHASSAN. No. It's about you.
JAMILA. Oh.
GHASSAN. Why take this examination? This, uh…
JAMILA. Baccalaureate? To go to college.
ABIR. *(to Ghassan)* You know that.
GHASSAN. But how will she be able to sign up for the test? She doesn't have I.D.
JAMILA. There's ways. *(to Abir)* Tell him.
ABIR. The PLO office is helping some students get into these tests.
GHASSAN. Bribing the government?
JAMILA. No.
HAMZI. Why not? That's how everything gets done in this country.
ABIR. We're not sure exactly. And we don't need to know.
HAMZI. You grease palms.
JAMILA. Stop saying that!
ABIR. All we know is they've got some kind of arrangement.
GHASSAN. *(skeptical)* Which is what? The students show up for the tests, and the Lebanese army arrests them when they get there?
JAMILA. No!
GHASSAN. You don't know for sure they don't.
ABIR. Enough, okay? She's already nervous about this.
JAMILA. *(re: Ghassan)* He's scaring me.
HAMZI. Your uncle is a conspiracy theorist.
GHASSAN. Because I happen to know some facts?
HAMZI. Very few. Which is a dangerous thing.

GHASSAN. You think our own people wouldn't sell us down the river? I've seen it happen. How do you think the Israelis swept in in 1948?
HAMZI. Forget 1948. It's happening now!
JAMILA. We were talking about me!
GHASSAN. So assuming you get into this test—
JAMILA. I will—
GHASSAN. What good does college do? Lebanon is a dead end.
HAMZI. Dead. Nothing here.
GHASSAN. They don't let us work here. What's the point?
JAMILA. I'm not necessarily staying in Lebanon for college.
HAMZI. Oh.
GHASSAN. I see.
Lights come back up. A sadness in the group, to have actually heard Jamila say this.
JAMILA. That's why I have to do well on the test. To go to another country. Where I can actually do something with my degree. *(to Adham)* Baba?
ADHAM. What?
JAMILA. I need you to take your papers. Remember?
Adham seems grim.
ADHAM. Yes, yes, my papers.
JAMILA. Your passport, anything you have.
GHASSAN. His passport?
HAMZI. It's ancient. "Hashemite Kingdom of Jordan," or some such nonsense.
GHASSAN. *(overlap)* What good is that going to do?
JAMILA. They need to get me started. They need something. With your picture on it, so they know you're you. It's totally stupid. I know. But everyone has to register. I told you this, remember? I know you remember.
Adham doesn't respond.
JAMILA. *(cont'd)* Okay?
DHAM. Okay.
JAMILA. So, you can do it this week.
ADHAM. I should be able to.
JAMILA. My teacher said it won't take long. Hopefully.
ADHAM. *(absently)* She did? Okay.
Beat.
JAMILA. Okay?
ADHAM. Fine.
JAMILA. I'm just reminding you, because sometimes you —
ADHAM. *(yells)* Stop asking me!
Jamila looks at him for a beat. She takes the book and candle and goes outside.

WHAT HAPPENED TO JUL.

Moments later. Moonlight.
Jul comes outside to join Jamila, who sits in one of the ratty beach chairs.
With him is a little cloth bag. During the scene, he takes out the contents—parts of a small wooden airplane—and starts to put it all together, painstakingly.
JUL. You got yelled at.
JAMILA. He yells at me all the time now.

JUL. He's whipping you into shape for your test.
JAMILA. No. He's just, mad. In general.
JUL. Well he can't yell at me anymore.
JAMILA. Not true.
JUL. His son who's—
JAMILA. Stop it—
JUL. Not a son anymore.
JAMILA. What? No!
JUL. A baby.
JAMILA. No.
JUL. Remember how he would go on?
He laughs.
JAMILA. So full of himself.
JUL. No kidding.
JAMILA. "You must learn to master the intellect…"
JUL. That's him.
JAMILA. "Even then, if you don't have innate talent, you won't succeed…"
JUL. I mean, that statement. Right there. Is not, uh, um. Logical! I told him that. Once.
JAMILA. "Trying to argue with me will leave you intellectually impoverished."
JUL. You're good at doing him.
JAMILA. I just shrug my shoulders.
JUL. You should show him. He'd like it.
JAMILA. I don't think so.
JUL. I want to help you with your test.
   He reads her response.
JUL. *(cont'd)* No?
   Now Jul switches into TV show mode:
JUL. *(cont'd)* Let me tell you about my life. What happened.
JAMILA. Are you sure?
JUL. It's my story.
JAMILA. I said okay.
JUL. I was in Jerusalem. I flew there. On a helicopter. I hovered but didn't land.
JAMILA. Fancy.
JUL. It's true.
JAMILA. Okay.
JUL. It's my story.
JAMILA. So go.
JUL. Would you chill?
JAMILA. You don't even know what that means.
JUL. Yes! It means "relax."
JAMILA. I'm relaxed.
JUL. You're never relaxed.
JAMILA. So say what happened.
JUL. I will. I was in Tel Aviv.
   She shakes her head. As his story progresses, she plays along.
JUL. *(cont'd)* It's my story. At the Ben and Jerry's. But it's called Benyamin and Yermiah's.
JAMILA. *(laughing)* You're crazy.

Lights shift as Jul tells his story. We're transported a bit.
JUL. And the first thousand people who get there get a free scoop, did you know that? All the Muslims and Jews and a few Christians tripping over each other for one brilliant scoop. Everyone praying to be THE FIRST. One woman spends the night with her children, just so she can be at the front of the line.
JAMILA. Wow.
JUL. But then a priest comes and goes to the front of the line, he's a priest, everyone should respect him. But the woman doesn't care, she hits him and tells him to fuck off—
JAMILA. Jul!
JUL.—It is mayhem.
JAMILA. So where are you in all this?
JUL. Using my jet pack, I land in the middle of the crowd. *("landing" sound)* Shooom. They clap for me, and my special powers! I am charged with keeping the peace. They give me a stick.
JAMILA. Oh no.
JUL. I am patient with people, I try to keep it orderly. But then. The woman's husband walks up, and he has a gun, and everyone screams. He says he is Ice Cream's holy warrior. And everyone scatters. It's just me, the gunman, and the Priest. I. I—I use my talents, and I knock the man down, took the gun. I fired it in the sky… *(as if it's a French name)* Like Charles Bronson.
JAMILA. Who?
JUL. Charl-es Bronson.
JAMILA. Charles Bronson. He's not French. He's American.
JUL. Shit. Is he.
JAMILA. If you want a French guy, you should use Jean-Claude Van Damme. Although actually? He might be Belgian…
JUL. That's not the story. I was telling the story. It's my story.
JAMILA. Okay, I know! I was right there with you!
Jul's face changes.
JUL. No you weren't. … What happened to me is. I. I went to Sidon one day. Near the souks. And I was …
He stops. Dead stops. Beat.
JAMILA. You don't have to tell it Jul. You don't.

VACATIONS.

Night. Everyone is inside. Jamila reads, and Abir works on an embroidery tablecloth. Jul is there. He has headphones on and plays with a small electronic device, while laying on a mattress.
The men play cards again. Hamzi has a bit of a coughing attack.
ABIR. That's not safe.
HAMZI. What's not safe?
ABIR. That. A pack a day. And it's expensive.
HAMZI. We're going to get our heads blown off one day tying our shoes on a corner in Beirut—
GHASSAN. It almost happened in '82, it all almost ended—thank God it didn't—
HAMZI. And she's worried about us smoking! The day I find out I got twelve months is

the day I praise God for giving me a long life and a peaceful death. I'll have a great time dying in the hospital. TV, magazines, good toilets.

GHASSAN. Good plumbing.

HAMZI. Me, or the hospital?

Hamzi and Ghassan laugh.

GHASSAN. The St. George in Beirut lets you have private shits.

HAMZI. That would be pure pleasure, my friend. I could finish all the books I've been meaning to read, no one bothering me.

JAMILA. *(laughing, in spite of herself)* Eeugh! Can you please stop? *(to Adham)* Make him stop.

HAMZI. You just have to wave your hands like this ... *(crossing himself like a Catholic)* ...And pray it doesn't make you late to the toilet.

Adham laughs, but—

ADHAM. Alright, enough.

ABIR. Please!

HAMZI. It's true. The St. George has crucifixes everywhere, even in the bathrooms.

GHASSAN. Why wouldn't they? If you're sick, that's where you spend the most time.

HAMZI. Good point. May God put me there at the end.

JAMILA. That's ambitious.

HAMZI. This is my vision, my future!

JAMILA. It's not funny.

HAMZI. But you're laughing! She is, but—

JAMILA. I'm serious.

HAMZI. Admit it, my niece, isn't this an achievable goal?

JAMILA. Having your own bathroom?

Hamzi clasps his hands together and prays, in full-on clown mode.

HAMZI. Please God!

JAMILA. That's your ambition.

HAMZI. Don't tell anyone!

ADHAM. *(joking)* Sounds good to me.

JAMILA. *(horrified; taking him at face value)* That's not what you want.

ADHAM. Oh no…

GHASSAN. The lecturer.

ADHAM. She likes to lecture.

JAMILA. I'm asking.

ADHAM. You don't know what you're talking about.

HAMZI. Come on, Jamila, habibti, tell me if I should hold onto this hand. That information will save my life.

They laugh again. This time, Hamzi's laugh turns into a cough that doesn't stop.

JUL. Is he okay?

ADHAM. Your uncle's fine, habibi. This is what happens when people talk too much.

Hamzi recovers; smiles.

HAMZI. I couldn't be better! The more I cough, the closer I am to my cancer vacances!

ABIR. Haram. That's a terrible thought!

GHASSAN. Give me a cigarette. I want to get there first.

Ghassan tries to grab Hamzi's pack.

HAMZI. Hey! These are expensive! You have a job.

GHASSAN. Barely!
Ghassan gets a cigarette, and both men light up.
JAMILA. That's what everyone's settled for? Wasting away in some Christian hospital?
ADHAM. Stop.
JAMILA. Just letting it all go?
ADHAM. Stop talking about things you don't understand.
JAMILA. Explain it to me.
ADHAM. Leave it.
JAMILA. I want to understand.
ADHAM. By God she can't shut up.
Jamila can't help herself—she lowers her voice, mirroring his inflection.
JAMILA. "BY GOD SHE CAN'T SHUT UP." I know. You taught me that.
The others laugh.
HAMZI. She's doing you, Adham!
JAMILA. *(still doing him)* YES I AM.
HAMZI. She's good at that!
JAMILA. BEING "GOOD" IS NOT ENOUGH. YOU MUST EXCEL AT WHATEVER IT IS YOU SET OUT TO DO.
Everyone, save Adham, loves this.
ADHAM. Stop it.
JAMILA. ACADEMIC INQUIRY, ABOVE ALL ELSE…
ADHAM. That's the respect you have for me now?
JAMILA. THAT'S THE RESPECT YOU HAVE FOR ME NOW?
ADHAM. *(bursts)* Stop it! Do you understand me? Shut your mouth for five seconds! You think you can behave like you did when you were twelve? Demanding attention like a child?
JAMILA. *(stung)* No.
ADHAM. Look at your brother! He doesn't even do that!
Beat.
ADHAM. *(cont'd)* Don't ever do that again.
She grabs her book and goes to her mattress, next to Jul's.
Hamzi looks at Adham, who waves him off. Adham picks up something that's fallen out of Jamila's book: the picture he'd shown her earlier.
Lights go down.

LONDON.

Lights up. All the adults assembled once again outside the structure. Adham comes downstage. He takes a beat to look out into the large, dark theater. He gives the first line of his lecture:
ADHAM. How does a man become what he becomes?
He takes a breath: in, out. Can he do this?
ADHAM. *(cont'd)* Lines Composed a Few Miles Above Tintern Abbey, on Revisiting the Banks of the Wye during a Tour. July 13, 1798. Mister Wordsworth writes this poem upon returning to England—here—after a five-year absence. He'd gone to France to witness the Revolution, full of excitement at this dawn of a new age, democracy.… But as things in France devolve, his ardor fades and he comes back to England. To the Wye.

From where they are, the other characters speak to the audience:
HAMZI. The Noise, part two:
The Six-Day War.
ABIR. Don't call it that.
HAMZI. That's the name it's known by.
ABIR. Not by us!
GHASSAN. That name's an insult to Arabs.
HAMZI. Who cares? The whole thing was an insult!
GHASSAN. I can't believe you'd call it that.
HAMZI. It's a description. Six days is all it took.
ABIR. The 1967 War.
HAMZI. Also known as H'arb a' Sabah wa Sitin.
GHASSAN. Also known as the Third Arab-Israeli War.
ABIR. Also known as An-Naksah:
ALL. The Setback.
ADHAM. Wordsworth returns to his childhood home, and what's the first thing he does? Exactly what we would expect of any great Romantic poet. He walks. And walks. *(making a little "joke," enjoying himself)* They like to walk.
And as he does, he takes in everything that surrounds him, again. This word—again—he uses four times in the first fourteen lines. This is because the poem is not, ultimately, about the river, the hedgerows, the landscape … it's about that which is gained when one comes back and sees it all again.
HAMZI. It's a pissing match the Arab world loses.
ALL. Again.
GHASSAN. We hear the president of Iraq, Abdel Rahman Aref, on the radio: "This is our opportunity to wipe out the ignominy which has been with us since 1948. Our goal is clear—to wipe Israel off the map." Israel takes that comment very seriously.
HAMZI. They usually do.
ADHAM. Wordsworth leaves England at twenty-three, and returns at twenty-eight. A man. And this makes all the difference. That which was "unremembered" is now felt. This word, unremembered. What do we make of this? It's as if during his time away, Wordsworth has been bolstered, held up, sustained by memories he didn't even know he had! One could devote years to this concept, and still not come to a full understanding.
HAMZI. We Arabs think it's all a success. And why not? Radio Cairo says, "We've pushed the Israelis back!"
ADHAM. With it, those "beauteous forms" transcend the world of the corporeal. They are carried here *(points to his head)* …and here *(to his heart)* available whenever Wordsworth needs them.
GHASSAN. Tuesday, June sixth, 1967: Bombs rain down in the distance, in what we assume is their part of the city. From what we assume are Arab jets.
ADHAM. It's not the leaving that has given Wordsworth this imprint. It's the leaving, and the coming back; the return.
ABIR. Tuesday, June sixth, 1967: I sit in the audience and watch my new husband speak in a language I don't understand.
ADHAM. I finish the lecture. A moment hovers, interminable. Did they enjoy it? Was I understood, completely? A young woman in glasses in the front row begins to clap. I

see her clap. I hear a huge booming noise. I jump just slightly, and then I realize it is everyone else, clapping. The claps bouncing off the walls and the ceiling of the huge theater. My professor in Cairo has coached me through everything, except for this moment.

ABIR. He does the tiniest of bows, and leaves the stage.

ADHAM. They throw a small party in my honor. A room of people, all looking at me, waiting for more.

ABIR. Adham tells me he is offered a chance to stay in London and continue his studies.

ADHAM. Yes,

ABIR. he says,

ADHAM. Yes.

GHASSAN. But it's over before it even begins. The entire Egyptian air force destroyed, just sitting in the desert.

HAMZI. Pieces of shit. All the commanders, such confidence!

ABIR. The next morning, we hear of this disaster in our homeland.

HAMZI. And suddenly our leaders are nowhere to be found, King Hussein's troops come too late, and all of Jerusalem is falling, blah blah blah, blah blah. All of it, a big failure.

ABIR. Adham's mother is there. We have to go back. Just for now.

GHASSAN. Everyone from our village is put on buses. Sent to the other side of the river. To Jordan. We'll go back. We just need to wait

HAMZI. And wait

GHASSAN. And wait

ABIR. And wait for something called the "family reunion program" to commence.

GHASSAN. But it never does. So we go to Lebanon, to the refugee camps—

HAMZI. And they arrive! The brother I haven't seen since I was eight years old!

Adham, back to his lecture:

ADHAM. Much has been said about the notion of maturity, of the poet's process of becoming a man.

And it is so: The return completes the cycle for the poet.

Without it, he is suspended in time. Stuck.

And now he's in the moment of leaving London:

ABIR. Lazim itrooH. *(You have to leave.)*

ADHAM. I don't want to leave London.

GHASSAN. Ana Asif. *(I'm sorry.)*

ADHAM. I need more time. I have work to do.

ABIR. La. Inteh khallasit. *(No. You're done.)*

HAMZI. Balash. *(Forget it, you're better off forgetting.)*

ADHAM. Khallas.

Blackout.

THE PASSPORT.

Late afternoon. Lights up on the structure, Adham and Hamzi napping on the mattresses that sit on the ground. Abir cooks. Jamila tears in.

JAMILA. Where is Baba?

ABIR. Sleeping.

JAMILA. Wake him up!
ABIR. Sssh!
JAMILA. I know it's really important he gets his rest!
ABIR. What's wrong?
JAMILA. Baba!
ABIR. Sit down!
JAMILA. So he lied to me. All this time. —Did you know? Did you know he was lying? (**ABIR.** No!) Everyone got their examination times today. Except me. I wasn't on the books! He never went to register me.
HAMZI. Habibti, relax.
JAMILA. I know you can hear me!
Adham wakes/comes in, startled.
ADHAM. Don't come in this house yelling like that.
JAMILA. Nothing else works!
ADHAM. What is the problem?
JAMILA. You didn't do the paperwork for my test.
ADHAM. *(giving away nothing)* Oh.
JAMILA. Do you not understand? If I don't get this all worked out, I have to wait until next year to take the Baccalaureate. If I don't do this now, I'm never going to do it.
Jul, who's been napping, now wakes up, upset.
JUL. Who's here?
ADHAM. No one. Nothing, habibi. Everything's fine.
JAMILA. No it's not!
JUL. Something happened.
JAMILA. I need this. You told me stop asking and I did! You won't help me study, you've completely gone away, and I don't know why, I, I don't. But that I can do alone, I can study. I can't do this without you. So let's go, okay?
ADHAM. It's not gonna work, this plan. It won't work.
JAMILA. Yes it will. My teachers said —
ADHAM. Your teachers, huh? Good for them. When I show them this passport I have, this thirty-year-old piece of paper, you know what they'll say? It's worthless! That's what they'll say.
JAMILA. Who's "they"?
ADHAM. All of them, all of them, DPRA,
ADHAM. *(cont'd) (overlap)* UNRWA, PLO.
HAMZI. *(overlap)* Crooks, liars, crooks.
ADHAM. To prove who I am, you know what I have to do? Go to the first place I became a refugee and get the passport renewed!
HAMZI. *(to no one in particular)* Our lives are ruled by pieces of paper
JAMILA. What? Go to the West Bank?
ADHAM. YES. Yes, go to the West Bank. That's right.
JAMILA. That's not right.
ADHAM. It is.
HAMZI. He can't leave the camp because he has no ID. But to get the ID he has to go to the West Bank! Perfect Lebanese logic!
GHASSAN. Khara this country, they hate us here.
ADHAM. So. It's utterly impossible.

JAMILA. No. NO. It's not! Nothing is impossible!
ADHAM. Is that right?
JAMILA. You have to work around it! Talk to the right people! Everything is like that here!
ADHAM. It won't work. Okay?
JAMILA. You have to just, I don't know, stand there and make them! Is that it? You can't stand in line like everyone else? It's so degrading? You're so above it all? Such a GREAT MAN OF LETTERS you can't do this thing that everyone else has to do all the time?
Impulsively, Adham reaches to her and slaps her face.
Stunned, Jamila pulls back.
HAMZI. Okay, okay...
ABIR. Adham!
JAMILA. Why would you do that? Why?
ABIR. Is that who you are now? Is that the man you are?—You're angry?—I'm the one who made us come back.
Adham doesn't have an answer. He leaves.
Jamila is devastated.
JUL. Can I help?
JAMILA. *(simply)* No.
GHASSAN. Come help me with this, Jul. Electronic soccer.
JUL. Nintendo?
GHASSAN. Yes. We sold three at the store this morning. I got an extra for you.
Jul goes over to him.
Long, long beat.
Abir goes to a small table. Opens the drawer, pulls out an envelope. Hands Jamila what's inside.
ABIR. We'll take my passport down there. It's supposed to be your father's. They'll use that. But we won't leave.—I don't know if it will work.

Hamzi (Amro Salama, left) and Ghassan (Dexter Zollicoffer) play cards while Jul (Awate Serequeberhan) consoles Jamila (Annelyse Ahmad) in *Urge for Going* by Mona Mansour, directed by Anna C. Bahow (photograph by Airan Wright).

Onstage, a black-and-white projection of the young Abir, looking right into the camera.
JAMILA. "Abir Najjar." ... I've never seen this before. You look...
ABIR. What?
JAMILA. Nothing.
HAMZI. Young.
JAMILA. Your face is different.
ABIR. It changed. I was nineteen.
JAMILA. You had makeup on.
ABIR. So?
JAMILA. Your eyes look like ... tiger stripes.
Abir takes the passport from her, looks.
ABIR. Everyone did her makeup like this then.

JAMILA. Cat eyes.
ABIR. We thought it was beautiful. We spent a day doing it. And we could spend hours on our eyebrows. Just looking and looking. You could never get it right. Ridiculous.
JAMILA. No.
GHASSAN. Let me see.
Abir hands it to him.
GHASSAN. *(cont'd)* I remember this. My sister looked like a movie star.
ABIR. You never said that then.
GHASSAN. So what?
ABIR. Every girl wanted to look like, what's her name? The actress? The blonde one.
GHASSAN. The Greek one. Melina Mercouri.
HAMZI. No: Julie Christie.
ABIR. Julie Christie. Like her.
Jamila looks at the picture she has no idea what Julie Christie looks like.
JAMILA. Did you?
ABIR. No!
JAMILA. You look beautiful though.
Abir grabs her hijab, starts to place it on her head.
ABIR. Y'allah. Let's get going.
JAMILA. What's this?
More photos fall out of the passport.
ABIR. Extras.
JAMILA. Why?
ABIR. He took more than one.
JAMILA. Because he thought you were beautiful.
ABIR. Because they always do. In case one doesn't turn out.
JAMILA. I would've used this one.
ABIR. I wanted to look professional. To be taken seriously. No one in our families had ever left the country before. Voluntarily. For a trip.
JAMILA. I still would've used the smiling one.
ABIR. Enough. Let's go.
Jamila stands up, holding tight to the picture. She can't quite believe her mother.
JAMILA. I'm coming.

UNKNOWN VARIABLES.

Next day. The sound of planes overhead.
Jamila enters the outside space. Jul is in one of the lawn chairs, putting together his small wooden airplane.
JUL. I can't talk right now.
JAMILA. Okay.
JUL. I would but—
JAMILA. It's okay. I'm busy anyway.
JUL. You're studying for the test. You got an appointment.
JAMILA. Yes.
Jamila watches him for a moment, then goes back to her work. She sits on the beach chair, places a heavy textbook on the ground, and a notebook on her lap. She opens the notebook, takes out a few pieces of paper—a practice exam—and stares.

JUL. You all right?
JAMILA. I'm fine.
She tries to dig back into the book.
It's not easy. Jul studies her.
JUL. You can't be like that the day of the exam.
JAMILA. I know!
JUL. Is it math? Tell me.
JAMILA. I'm embarrassed.
JUL. No.
JAMILA. It should be easy.
JUL. So...?
JAMILA. "Unknown variables."
JUL. I remember those.
She opens the big textbook and reads, a mix of sarcasm and dread:
JAMILA. "Arrange your equations so that the unknown variables (and the coefficients that multiply them) appear on the left-hand side of each equation. All constants should appear on the right-hand side of each equation." Isn't that stupid?
Beat.
JUL. I knew all of that. One time.
JAMILA. I know.
JUL. *(re: the book)* Can I see? Let me see. Please. I'll help you.
She hands him the book.
JUL. *(cont'd)* "Twelve plus A X equals sixteen." Easy. That is so easy.
JAMILA. So help me.
JUL. *(playing with her)* Hm.
JAMILA. Come on.
JUL. So easy.
JAMILA. So tell me.
She watches Jul and waits. He starts with enthusiasm, but it's difficult for him to stay focused, and gets painful.
JUL. You take the unknown. X. The unknown and you, uh, take the × and isolate it—it becomes...
He trails off, still looking at the book. Jamila shifts to talk-show mode.
JAMILA. I always go on about myself at these things. But the real story was my brother. He was the smartest. He knew all the algorithms. All. He knew how to isolate the unknown.
For a beat, Jul is clear, quick:
JUL. B X times B Y equals B times X plus Y. Once you've mastered this concept, you can go anywhere with it.
JAMILA. Professor Jul!
And then he falls back into "now" Jul.
JUL. Jul was minding his own business...
JAMILA. Do you want me to tell it?
JUL. Jul went into Jerusalem. No. Jul went to India with Gunga Din. And hung out.
JAMILA. You always loved Kipling.
JUL. When I was little.
I went to Sidon. The city. Near the souks. Something was happening in another city.

Closer to the border. But they were worried about us here. Keeping an eye on us. More than usual. This man…

Lights up on inside the house. From there, Abir, Hamzi and Ghassan speak in that direct address/hybrid way, but much more muted, gentle, than times prior.

ABIR. The noise, part three:

HAMZI. Jul.

GHASSAN. The problem was:

HAMZI. The problem was:

ABIR. The problem was some part of his brain got disconnected from another part of his brain.

HAMZI. The problem was:

GHASSAN. Can I finish?—the doctor was not specifically a neurologist. He's a general practitioner. He's guessing.

Back to Jul and Jamila. As Jul's story progresses, he starts taking apart the plane…

JUL. This soldier, Lebanese Army, says, why are you coming into the city? Is he serious? I mean, the Army guys. You can't imagine how stupid they are. Every last one of them. They couldn't even become lowly accountants. You know that right? But I don't say this. I'm polite. I answer: I'm getting the newspaper.
He says, "I didn't know you could read." Oh shit, really? But I keep cool. I say, I can read. I'm mega-talented that way. "And funny," he says. And he says, "Show me. Show me reading." And he holds up a picture, a man they want to arrest. Under the picture are words. "Read this. Tell me who's this. Maybe he's your cousin. Maybe he's your brother." And the words say: "This man is a dog," and so on. And I won't say it out loud. I won't. He pushes me. Has a stick. And he … says, "Come on. Read this." And now I'm getting mad. And I make—mistake.

HAMZI. The problem is, he's not even really a doctor. He started his studies 40 years ago, never finished.

GHASSAN. The problem is, they're always guessing anyway, even the professionals.

ABIR. There's something called the Glasgow Coma Scale to determine how far away he went. I hear this, and think Glasgow? We need the Scots to show us the problems in his brain?

JAMILA. No. You didn't make a mistake. You did nothing wrong.

JUL. No. I do. It's a, it's a, this is an error in judgment. No one knows this part, but I make mistake. What do you do when you're faced with idiocy? People below your intelligence? Rise above it! But I don't. And this makes all the difference. I take the can of coke out of my backpack, and I throw it. Mistake. I'm not even a good throw—

He laughs.

JUL. *(cont'd)* But this time, my aim is perfect. It makes it. Not too hard! Just his leg! His fat thigh! And then he is mad … more mad than I. And I start to run. And he gets on his bike, he's coming after me! Shit!
In the movies, I would jump into a trash can, and the halfwit would go by, and then I'd come out with flour on me, and it would be funny and heroic all at once. The ridiculous hero. Literature is filled with characters like this.

ABIR. He gives me a book, our friend, the doctor, the non-doctor. He says, "Here. Read this." And it's something about the orbitofrontal cortex—

HAMZI. Who can even read this?

ABIR. The lower surface of the frontal lobes, and the anterior temporal lobes. And he's compromised now, my son … he…
Long, long pause as she—
ABIR. *(cont'd)* And it's social behavior, emotion regulation, olfaction, and decision-making; and finally: aphasia. Language skills. We waited, to have children, you know? Let's see when things become stable. Then we realized, there is no "stable." We were so close with this one, getting him out, medical school. That was the plan. He should be making these diagnoses right now, for other people!
JUL. But I run…
ABIR. Why didn't I take him to Beirut? To a better hospital?
JUL. And I'm laughing…
ABIR. Just risked it? What's the worst they could've done, arrested him?
JUL. And he gets out off the bike. Shit. And I have nowhere left to run. I stand there, and he walks up. And that's that. He hits me. And only the first time hurts … and … so…
Long pause. Jul can't go on. He looks at the book again, and reads, laboriously:
JUL. *(cont'd)* Solving equations with one or more unknowns.
He tries to keep reading. Jamila comes over to him.
JAMILA. It's okay.
She tries to close the book. He stops her.
JUL. I want to help.
She gently closes the book. He cries. She puts her arms around him…
Lights fade.

IN HIS LIFE.

Morning sky. All are asleep. Hamzi comes in, unsteady on his feet. He stumbles, waking up Jamila first.
JAMILA. Hey.
HAMZI. Sssh.
She notices he's staggering.
JAMILA. What happened to you?
HAMZI. Nothing, Jamila. Beautiful niece. Go to bed.
JAMILA. Where were you?
HAMZI. Out.
He keeps walking, tries to get to his bed, knocks the table.
JAMILA. You're bleeding!
Abir springs up.
ABIR. What? Who's bleeding?
She sees Hamzi's head.
ABIR. *(cont'd) (to Jamila)* Go get a cloth.
Jul wakes up, sees Hamzi.
JUL. Oh no.
ABIR. *(to Jamila)* Go get the cloth!
(to Jul) It's okay, baby.
(to Hamzi) What happened?
Adham wakes up. Ghassan wakes up.
HAMZI. I got into a fight.

ABIR. With who?
HAMZI. The Lebanese government.
GHASSAN. What?
ABIR. Have you lost your mind?
GHASSAN. Yes.
HAMZI. They've been doing construction on Rue Fakhreddine. I grabbed some bricks that no one wanted.
ADHAM. What?
ABIR. Why would you do that?
HAMZI. Can I please speak uninterrupted?
JUL. *(upset)* Oh boy. He's gonna die?
ABIR. No.
HAMZI. No, no. I'm alive.
ABIR. Jamila. Take your brother outside.
JUL. I don't want to go out there.
ABIR. Just for a minute, habibi. You're okay. All right?

She looks him, touches him reassuringly. Jamila takes his hand, they go outside. She sits him down, keeps looking through the door.

ABIR. *(cont'd)* You throwing bricks at soldiers?
HAMZI. God no. What do you think I am, twenty-five? I wanted to fix this wall.
ADHAM. What?
HAMZI. The wall. See that?
ADHAM. Where?
HAMZI. There! There and there! Don't you see that?
ADHAM. Don't yell at me, old man.
HAMZI. I wanted three bricks to patch the hole.
ADHAM. Which hole?
HAMZI. That. Hole. There! You can't see it? This place is riddled with cracks!
ADHAM. So you stole a brick? What would make it stick together? Have you thought of that?
ABIR. No!
HAMZI. I grabbed the bricks. I didn't think. I put them here. *(he points to his stomach)* ...I figured they wouldn't notice. What's a few more pounds? They found them at the checkpoint.
ADHAM. You actually thought you'd get away with this?
GHASSAN. He thinks it's a James Bond movie.
ABIR. They beat you?
HAMZI. They ran after me, they laughed at the spectacle.

Meaning: him. He takes his hands and shakes his belly to demonstrate.

HAMZI. *(cont'd)* I dropped the bricks and took a swing.
ABIR. Oh God.
JAMILA. *(from the door)* He should see a doctor.
HAMZI. Thank God someone cares about me.
ADHAM. So you tried bringing those in here? You didn't think about the army?
HAMZI. Of course I did.
ADHAM. *(cutting him off)* I have a son who may never recover from what happened with the army—

HAMZI. Three bricks to fill the hole. That's all I wanted.
ADHAM. You're ridiculous. Making a fool of yourself.
HAMZI. I'm ridiculous? Dear brother, I am sorry to inform you, but this whole thing … *(meaning: where they are, where they live)* is ridiculous. Your house is a shithole. Did you realize that? We have nothing keeping us from the cold. Don't you see that?
ABIR. You're lucky they didn't arrest you.
JAMILA. *(to no one in particular)* I have my test tomorrow.
ABIR. They don't care how old you are, they got no problem locking you up. But that doesn't stop you, because you don't think!
ADHAM. *(to Abir, trying to calm her)* Ssh. It's okay.
And now Hamzi loses it, practically throwing punches in the air:
HAMZI. It is NOT okay, as you put it. We are in trouble!
ADHAM. I'm not saying—
HAMZI. We have been in trouble for years and years and years, and no matter how poetically you put it, we are still living in a shithole. Look at this wall. This wall is falling apart, and even though human beings aren't meant to live in here, I wanted to feel a modicum of civilized!
ADHAM. *(sarcastic)* Then do what I do. Have a cup of tea.
HAMZI. I can't, because every time I do, the smell of shit wafts through the room!
JAMILA. Would you stop saying that? It's making me sick.
HAMZI. It should. It should make you very sick. All of this should make you sick! We don't see it anymore. You want to see it, the hole?
He tears at the small hole in the wall, making it bigger.
ABIR. *(overlap)* Stop him.
GHASSAN. *(overlap)* You made your point!
ADHAM. You're going to give yourself a heart attack.
HAMZI. We don't vote, we can't build, we don't bury our dead! Do you see it now? Still don't see?
He tears again at it, exerting himself.
HAMZI. *(cont'd)* This is the home of a scholar! I can live in this, maybe, but the fact that you have to utter these words—this is my home—that is unforgiveable!
Adham tries to grab him, which sets Hamzi off even more.
HAMZI. *(cont'd)* At Nahr-al Bared they're begging them please, please when you rebuild our camp, our temporary home for sixty years, please, would you mind naming each corner of our palatial suite, every centimetre, after a village we left in Palestine, so we remember which part of the camp we're supposed to go to?
He takes the piece of metal that's loose, pulls at it, until the whole thing comes off.
HAMZI. *(cont'd)* Good, right? We like this idea? Good! Because we are never going anywhere but here.
He throws the metal piece to the ground. Jul, facing away from the house, outside with Jamila, speaks, almost in a whisper:
JUL. "He's had enough…. I think he's had enough."
JAMILA. *(gently)* Jul! Ssh…. It's okay.
Back inside, no one says anything for a beat. Then:
ADHAM. None of us can change anything.
Abir moves to pick up the cloth, which has long since fallen. She takes it to Hamzi. He takes the cloth from Abir. He wipes his forehead.

HAMZI. Look at me.
He laughs.
HAMZI. *(cont'd)* Sacrificing myself for the cause.
He holds up the bloody cloth. Laughs again. No one speaks.
ADHAM. That's enough. Let's go to bed.
He goes to the door, calls to Jul:
ADHAM. *(cont'd)* Son. Come here. It's okay.
He holds out his arms. Jul comes to Adham, who gently brings him inside.
ADHAM. *(cont'd)* See? It's all fine.
Jul stops and looks at Hamzi. Hamzi wipes his head, smiles, shrugs his shoulders.
HAMZI. *(to Jul)* Good as new.
Hamzi stays sitting up, and around him, everyone settles into bed, all laying down under the structure.

Lights go down, and against the structure, we see images of modern-day Palestinian slums in Lebanon, as we hear:
HAMZI. *(cont'd)* In his life
he neither wrote nor read.
In his life he
didn't cut down a single tree,
didn't slit the throat of a single calf.
In his life he did not speak
of the New York Times
behind its back,
didn't raise
his voice to a soul
except in his saying:
"Come in, please,
by God you can't refuse."
Nevertheless-
his case is hopeless,
his situation
desperate.
His God-given rights are a grain of salt
tossed into the sea.
LIGHTS OUT.
ON THE TARMAC.
Early, early morning. Adham comes from the other room, sees Jamila sitting at the table, studying by candlelight/lamp.
ADHAM. What are you doing?
JAMILA. What does it look like?
ADHAM. Studying. The test.
Beat. She says nothing.
ADHAM. *(cont'd)* Your uncle is snoring now. He's fine.
JAMILA. Uh-uh.
ADHAM. Hearing someone sleep soundly is uh, unsettling. Especially when one is … not. What time is the exam?
JAMILA. Nine-thirty.

ADHAM. That's in four hours. Go to bed. You need rest.
She ignores.
ADHAM. *(cont'd)* This thing called "cramming" is not a good idea, you know.
Beat.
ADHAM. *(cont'd)* You should be feeling confident.
But Jamila's attention is on her biggest fears—
JAMILA. Some people say you wake up, and it's just not your day. It's just like that. Tests. It could be just not my day.
ADHAM. That's only true for people who haven't been working hard all along.
JAMILA. Well maybe I haven't. Or maybe I have, but not in the right way. You hear all the time of people who panic, who sit down and get some kind of cramp in their arm that won't go away, and then literally can't write.
Or they get so nervous that they feel like they'll fall out of their chairs, which makes no sense, but that's it. They fail. You hear of it all the time. You don't want me to leave anyway, right? Just have me stay here. Right?
It's out. Out of her exhaustion, it comes out. She sits there, spent, on the precipice. Adham can see that.
Long, long beat.
ADHAM. I felt that way. Uh. Dizzy. Before I left for London. The night we left Qalandia airport—Jerusalem—I smoked a pack of cigarettes before we even took off.
JAMILA. Hm.
ADHAM. On the plane. Your mother too.
JAMILA. Mama never smokes.
ADHAM. Everyone smoked then.
Beat.
ADHAM. *(cont'd)* That feeling. I had it. In Cairo. I practiced with the English professor before I left, just me and him and a thousand empty seats. I looked out and thought, how do they expect me, a mortal man, to fill this gigantic space? My legs buckled. Everything was spinning.
JAMILA. Vertigo.
ADHAM. No. That's not what it was.
JAMILA. Sounds like that to me.
ADHAM. That's not what it was. There was no room for error. I was the face of the school.
JAMILA. You were the first to be invited to speak in London.
ADHAM. No. I never said I was. Still, the English professor didn't want the school to look bad. So. Somehow, I found a way to breathe. I pretended I was holding a cigarette. *(he laughs)* The tricks we play on the mind! Anyway, it worked. I got through it.
JAMILA. How did it all go when you got there?
ADHAM. Where?
JAMILA. London. Were you able to do it when it mattered?
ADHAM. When it mattered. Yes. I was. It happened very fast. I got up to the podium, took a breath, nice and soft, and everything worked: My voice, my hands, I was their version of the well behaved Arab. My English was impeccable, my understanding of and reverence for their poet was unequaled. This is the one time in my life I believed in God.
He barely knows she's there anymore. Long beat. Jamila has relaxed, finally—a little.
JAMILA. You got a drink after.

ADHAM. Yes. One.
JAMILA. At Harrods?
ADHAM. No. The home of one of the professors.
JAMILA. What did mama think?
ADHAM. She didn't go. Enough, go to bed.
JAMILA. A party with professors? That's the whole point of a trip like that!
He pats her on the head and starts to leave.
JAMILA. *(cont'd)* I hate that I only get one chance. Who creates a system like that? Someone who never needed a second chance. It all could go wrong.
Beat. She looks at him.
ADHAM. Go to bed.
And finally, just before going:
ADHAM. *(cont'd)* It won't.
Lights go to black.

THE EXAM.

Lights up on Jamila.
She sits at a big desk, in a large room. In front of her is the exam booklet.
For a moment it looks like she could jump out of the seat and leave. Then she takes a deep breath. Prays, sitting up, keeping her hands together and on top of the exam.
SOUND SYMPHONY: Baywatch theme, voices of her family, all that she's heard.... Jamila opens her eyes.
Then slowly, ritualistically, she opens her satchel and pulls out a pencil. She lifts it, and starts reading. She's in her version of heaven. Lights get brighter and brighter. She smiles.

KIPLING.

Later. Jamila with Jul, in their outside area. Inside, we see Abir packing a small bag for Jamila. She puts in one of the extra passport pictures Jamila looked at earlier.
JAMILA. I can't take you.
JUL. You said it's a special school. In Damascus.
JAMILA. It is.
JUL. So ask them.
JAMILA. Who?
JUL. The people at the school! The Headmaster!
JAMILA. Nobody's families come with them. That's not how it works!
JUL. They might learn better.
JAMILA. *(finds this funny)* I doubt it… *(softens)* It's just for the students. *(reaches into her knapsack)* I got you something.
JUL. A picture?
JAMILA. No. Who do you want a picture of?
JUL. Someone on TV. Anybody.
JAMILA. No. I didn't get you that.
She pulls out a book. Jul examines it.
JUL. "Land and Sea Tales for Scouts and Guides."
JAMILA. Do you like it?
JUL. It's by Kipling.
JAMILA. You liked him. When you were little.

Jul looks at the book.
JUL. It has an elephant on the front.
JAMILA. I know.
JUL. Can you take me?
JAMILA. I can't.
JUL. You'll never come back here.
JAMILA. Yes I will!
He hands her the book.
JUL. Here.
JAMILA. What?
JUL. Hit me.
JAMILA. What?
JUL. So I won't miss you. I can take it.
JAMILA. No!
He takes the book and hits his head with it a few times, quickly.
JUL. You see. I did before. I took it. I took it too good. It left me dull, but not dull enough.
Hits his head again.
JAMILA. No.
And again.
JAMILA. *(cont'd)* Stop.
JUL. Please. So I don't miss you.
She grabs him, takes the book, makes him hug her. He resists.
JAMILA. I won't do it.
She touches his face.
JAMILA. *(cont'd)* You have so much to live for.
JUL. So much!
The words sink in. They both laugh, suddenly.
JAMILA. *(cont'd)* Stop it.
But they both keep laughing. They can't help it. It moves into sadness.
JUL. The numbers are bad.
JAMILA. No.
JUL. No! This part I know! Give me some credit. Twenty in three hundred Palestinians will ever leave Lebanon.
JAMILA. More than that.
JUL. Of those, six will ever come back. One in eighteen makes it past age seventy-five.
JAMILA. Where are you getting these?
JUL. One in half a million will attend "American Idol" in person.
JAMILA. That's ridiculous.
JUL. I made that one up. But it's probably right.
One in three will leave school by age eight.
One in twelve will be jailed at least once.
One in six will die before sixty.
JAMILA. *(trying to stop him)* Okay—
JUL. One in a hundred will go to school past the age of sixteen…
Beat.
JUL. *(cont'd)* You're the one. See? I get it. I am smart.
She shakes her head. He takes the book back.

JUL. *(cont'd)* I will think of you when I look at night sky. You are the direction I want to go.
He sits down, opens the book. She watches him.

URGE FOR GOING.

Adham and Jamila, inside. She sits on the bed, her satchel in her lap.
JAMILA. So you know. I made it. I got in.
ADHAM. I knew you would.
JAMILA. Were you just not going to say anything to me? …The adjudicator said only seven percent of all applicants get into the school.
ADHAM. Uh-huh.
JAMILA. That's good, right?
ADHAM. Of course it's good. If you have to ask me that, you must not be ready.
Beat. Jamila says nothing.
ADHAM. *(cont'd)* Someone ready to accept his fate doesn't need to ask anyone what's good.
Beat.
JAMILA. She said my essay and oral exam scores were very high. My math leaves something to be desired.
ADHAM. Ah yes.
JAMILA. I got that from you. You never liked math either.
ADHAM. Ha.
JAMILA. They can put me in a supplemental class for that though. Math for the humanities majors. Did you know they do that?
ADHAM. No.
JAMILA. They want people to succeed.
ADHAM. You have one good day at a test, and you think you know everything about the world.
Beat.
JAMILA. Why did you come back?
ADHAM. The war happened. My mother was alone.
JAMILA. Did she tell you to come get her?
ADHAM. No.
JAMILA. Was she glad you came?
ADHAM. No.
JAMILA. Why do you stay?
ADHAM. Your mother! Our family! … I can't leave here.
JAMILA. Couldn't you try.
ADHAM. I have no identification. You know this.
JAMILA. Who cares? I'm so sick of it.
ADHAM. We have to stay. In case we ever get the opportunity to go back.
JAMILA. What?
ADHAM. It could happen.
JAMILA. The chances of that happening are very low. You said that over and over!
ADHAM. But still.
JAMILA. I didn't think you believed it.
ADHAM. You failed to read this story properly then.

JAMILA. No I didn't! You taught me how to analyze!
ADHAM. You think you're so great? Is that what you think? That you passed this one hurdle and now you're a great scholar?
JAMILA. I know it's going to be hard.
ADHAM. You have no idea.
JAMILA. You taught me how to be rigorous. To hold my own in any academic setting. When I was little, you taught me these things! Clarity of thought. Preparation. Mental fortitude.
ADHAM. I went to the bathroom and cried.
She stops.
JAMILA. When?
ADHAM. At the party. In London. After the lecture.
JAMILA. Did anyone know?
ADHAM. Of course not.
JAMILA. Why?
ADHAM. I don't know. I looked around at everyone. So light, smart. Making connections between this piece of literature and this piece of art. Talking about politics like it was a game.... I think I knew this was the beginning and the end for me.
Jamila looks at him, shakes her heads as if to say "That's not true." He nods.
Beat.
JAMILA. Tell me what you talked about in London.
ADHAM. No.
JAMILA. Just part of the lecture.
ADHAM. I don't even remember it.
JAMILA. Try.
ADHAM. Leave it alone.
JAMILA. Just part.
ADHAM. The theories I talked about have been replaced by much more sophisticated thinking.
JAMILA. So.
ADHAM. It doesn't stand up.
JAMILA. So. I want to hear it.
Beat.
JAMILA. *(cont'd)* You discussed William Wordsworth's "Tintern Abbey."
ADHAM. That's not the full title.
JAMILA. I know.
ADHAM. I hate when others choose to abbreviate. As if they're too lazy to utter twenty words.
JAMILA. I know.
ADHAM. It's not even his best work.
JAMILA. He had left England for a long time, and then came back.
ADHAM. Yes.
JAMILA. Tell me. Give me some of it.
ADHAM. "And now, with gleams of half-extinguished thought, With many recognitions dim and faint, And somewhat of a sad perplexity..."
He can't continue. He starts to cry.
ADHAM. I've wasted it all.

JAMILA. No you haven't.
ADHAM. Yes. I have.
JAMILA. No.
ADHAM. Yes.
JAMILA. Trust me, you haven't.
ADHAM. Trust me, I have.
JAMILA. Just say the rest of that first part. Please. *(helping him)*
"The picture of the mind revives again,
While here I stand not only with the sense
Of..."
ADHAM. "...present pleasure but with pleasing thoughts
That in this moment there is life and food
for future years.
And so I dare to hope,
though changed, no doubt, from what I was when first
I came among these hills";
Up under: Song: Joni Mitchell's "Urge for Going."

END OF PLAY.

THE VICTIMS
OR WHAT DO YOU WANT ME
TO DO ABOUT IT?

Ken Kaissar

© 2017 by Ken Kaissar. For licensing, please contact the playwright at kenkaissar2@gmail.com

About the Playwright

Ken Kaissar was born in Ramat Gan, Israel, and raised in Indianapolis, Indiana. His plays have been performed or developed by Philadelphia Theatre Company, Delaware Theatre Company, Mildred's Umbrella, Fusion Theatre Company, Urban Stages and Passage Theatre. His ten-minute play *Ceasefire* (written in response to Israel's war with Hezbollah in 2006) was an official selection in the 2012 New Works Festival at the Fusion Theatre Company in Albuquerque, and the 2015 ReOrient Festival at Golden Thread Productions in San Francisco. His adaptation of Geoffrey Chaucer's *The Canterbury Tales* was commissioned by Columbia University in 2008. His other plays include *A Modest Suggestion*, *A Leg Up*, and *Nude Study*. He holds a BFA in directing from Carnegie Mellon University and an MFA in playwriting from Columbia University. He teaches playwriting and theatre history at Rider University and Stockton University.

— Essay —
Ken Kaissar's *The Victims*: Sympathy for the Suffering

Michael Malek Najjar

The full title for Ken Kaissar's play is *The Victims: Or What Do You Want Me to Do About It?* This playful subtitle gets to the heart of the frustrations most feel regarding the situation in Palestine and Israel. As outsiders to this conflict, we are constantly barraged by stories of death, violence, and political intransigence. Kaissar's main theme is victimhood, and the play asks audiences to remember that everyone claims the role of victims—but the only thing that really matters is finding a way to achieve peace. According to Kaissar, "our sympathies should be with whomever is suffering.... We should be concerned with the good and welfare of all people. There can be no peace unless all live in peace."[1]

There are many identifiable characters in the play: innkeepers, restaurant owners, cell phone salesmen, soldiers, and police officers. However, there are also many ambiguous characters listed in the play: "Jadi, the frightened one," "Bassee, the tired one," "Paula: a peacemaker," and "Assav, the adversary." By providing these enigmatic descriptions, Kaissar refuses to allow directors, actors, and audiences alike the comfort of easily identifying who might be Israeli or Palestinian, protagonist or antagonist, right or wrong. The play forces us to see the characters as humans first, and as Israelis or Palestinians second. In his artistic statement for the play, Kaissar writes:

> The prospect of empathizing with the other is terrifying because we perceive that the needs of Israelis and Palestinians are mutually exclusive. Acknowledging that the other side has a legitimate point threatens to render our own narrative invalid. That fear tends to shut down all dialogue.[2]

In the play Kaissar also introduces a perspective not often heard in American plays about Israel—that of the Yemeni Jewish experience. The character David, a Yemeni Jew who was born and raised in New York, finds himself somewhat lost in Israel. He doesn't speak Hebrew well, doesn't know his way around Israel, and he learns that his outside perspective on this conflict is shaped more by the media than by facts on the ground. The character Mas'ud tells David,

> Do you know what we hate, David? We hate living under Israeli occupation. We hate that the Israeli government targets Palestinian civilians. We hate that there is not a moment of peace for us. That there is no freedom. That's what we hate.[3]

David is also attacked by his fellow Israelis. Yael berates him for being a "peacenik" and judging Israeli society from afar. He also meets Palestinian Christians, Israeli Arabs, and Israeli soldiers serving their compulsory military service. Elad even raises the specter of American intolerance of Jews, a frightful premonition given the current political climate:

> And where will you go when the Americans decide they've had enough of the Jews? ... It's happened everywhere else. Why wouldn't it happen in America? Because America is some magical place where everyone is equal. Except for Blacks. Oh, and Muslims. And gays. So ... you don't think the Jews are next?[4]

Is the play's ending hopeful or hopeless? As he has done throughout the play, Kaissar refuses simple answers to such difficult questions. By employing humor, a complex variety of characters, biting dialogue, and shifting perspectives, *The Victims: Or What Do You Want Me to Do About It?* provides a fascinating perspective on such a perplexing quagmire.

— Playwright Statement —
Who Are the Victims?

Fear is the great impediment to dialogue about the Israeli–Palestinian conflict. Jews and Arabs alike are loathe to bring up the question of Israel or Palestine in the presence of the other, for fear that they might—god forbid—disagree with one another.

Let me save you the suspense. When it comes to the history of the Middle East in the 20th century, Jews and Arabs are certain to disagree with each other, if not about the entire narrative then at least about some aspect of it. But why are we so afraid to uncover that disagreement and talk through it?

The prospect of empathizing with the other is terrifying because we perceive that the needs of Israelis and Palestinians are mutually exclusive. Acknowledging that the other side has a legitimate point threatens to render our own narrative invalid. That fear tends to shut down all dialogue.

But Israelis and Palestinians understand each other better than most outsiders think. Both sides share a common goal, the struggle for the dignity of their own nationalistic identity. Israelis are told that they are merely European colonialists who have no business dwelling in the Middle East. Palestinians are told that they are a fictitious people with a fabricated history. These narratives deny each side the dignity of their histories and are completely unproductive to achieving a peaceful resolution. So stuck we will be, until we find the wisdom to abandon both of these inaccurate narratives.

We should be able to agree that both peoples are entitled to the dignity of their identities. Both deserve to live in peace and security under a state whose government is dedicated to their basic needs for a free and prosperous life. This is a goal that unites not only Israelis and Palestinians, but the entire human race. Who would claim that anyone is undeserving of such a promise? All we need is the courage to empathize with anyone who struggles to achieve it.

The title of my play, *The Victims*, raises a great many questions, the most prominent being who are the victims—Israelis or Palestinians? My answer, without being flippant, is both. For the last 70 years Israelis have lived under daily threat of hostile invasion and terrorist attacks. On the other hand, the establishment of Israel 70 years ago displaced hundreds of thousands of Palestinians and rendered them homeless. Can't we acknowledge and empathize with both of these narratives? Does it really cost either side anything to acknowledge the suffering of the other?

— PLAYSCRIPT —
The Victims

CAST OF CHARACTERS

Jadi: the frightened one
Bassee: the tired one
Paula: a peacemaker
Assav: the adversary
Pilot Voice-Over, can be prerecorded or performed live by a male or female voice
David: 30s, an American traveling in Israel
Immigration Officer: an airport immigration agent
Motti: an innkeeper
Moshe: a guest
Shachar: a restaurant owner
Mas'ud: a cell phone salesman
Israeli Soldier #1: a soldier
Israeli Soldier #2: a soldier
Yael: late teens, a soldier at a checkpoint
Shlomo: late teens, a soldier at a checkpoint
Farmer: middle-aged, a Palestinian farmer
Elad: David's cousin
Bassam: Elad's employee
Police Officer: a police officer

CASTING SUGGESTIONS

While *The Victims* can be performed with a large cast, the play has been received successfully in readings with only 8 actors. Here are my suggestions for double-casting:

Immigration Officer/Yael/Police Officer
Motti/Shlomo/Elad/Soldier #2/Chasidic Man
Moshe/Shachar/Captain Voice-Over/Solider #1
Mas'ud/Farmer/Bassam/Arab Father
Paula/Arab Mother
Assav/Arab Child

ACT ONE

AT RISE: A beautiful garden in the center of the stage, with gorgeous fig trees. A bench sits in the middle of the garden. DAVID, 30s, stands in the garden.

Though the play will take place in other locations, the Garden never leaves the stage.

DAVID walks over to one of the fig trees. He pulls off a fig and eats it. It is clear from DAVID's reaction that the fig is incredibly delicious.

BASSEE, a disheveled creature, wearing rags and worn out shoes appears from behind one of the trees.

BASSEE. You've come back.
DAVID. How could I not?
BASSEE. And now?
DAVID. Peace.
BASSEE. The time has come to strike.
DAVID. No.
BASSEE. We have to fight back.
DAVID. Don't be stupid. It won't help.
BASSEE. Could it hurt?

JADI, another disheveled creature, appears from behind one of the trees.

JADI. Soon they will be back to beat us.
DAVID. You don't know that.
BASSEE. Stop lying to yourself.
JADI. They will push us into the sea.
DAVID. If they could, they would have by now.
JADI. Eventually we will be annihilated.
BASSEE. Just like before.
DAVID. Never again.
JADI. For whom.
BASSEE. We will fight.
DAVID. There has to be another way.
JADI. And when we're dead? What then?
DAVID. Stop it. You're only making matters worse.
BASSEE. I suppose we are the ones to blame?
DAVID. I have to go.
BASSEE. You can't run from this, you know. Wherever you go, we will always be with you.
DAVID. Then we'll see each other again, won't we?
JADI. This is the land of our forefathers. This is our homeland.
DAVID. You're not the only ones.
BASSEE. Our blood ... will be on your hands.

DAVID exits the garden. A suitcase rolls onstage to meet him.

We hear a voiceover of an Israeli airplane captain addressing his passengers. His speech is recited in Hebrew and then repeated in English.

PILOT (VOICEOVER). *Gveerotai v' rabbotai, boker tov. Medaber hakabarnit. Anachnu b'erech shloshim dakot minechita b'namal te'ufah ben Gurion. Hasha'ah b'Tel Aviv hee sheva vachetzi v'hatemperatura esrim v'shesh ma'alot. Na livdok she-chagurot hamoshav hadookot v'shemaga-shey' ha-achila hoochzeroo lamakom. Todah she-bachartem b'El-Al... hachi babayit ba'olam. B'ruchim haba-im l'Yisrael.*

Ladies and gentlemen, good morning. This is your captain speaking. We are approximately 30 minutes from landing at Ben Gurion Airport. The time in Tel Aviv is 7:30 and the temperature is 26 degrees. Please check that your seat belts are fastened and that tray tables are upright. Thank you for choosing El Al. Welcome to Israel.

Lights up on the immigration line at Ben Gurion Airport. There are two lines: one labeled visitors, the other labeled citizens. DAVID is in the line for visitors.

He looks over at the line for citizens. He sees a CHASIDIC JEW at the front, and an ARAB FATHER, MOTHER, and CHILD just behind him.

The IMMIGRATION OFFICER motions the CHASIDIC MAN forward. He stamps the CHASIDIC MAN's passport and motions the CHASIDIC MAN on.

The IMMIGRATION OFFICER then motions the ARAB FAMILY forward. He motions for them to step out of line. A SOLDIER with a large gun enters. The ARAB FAMILY puts their hands on their heads and spreads their legs while the SOLDIER pats them down. DAVID watches in fascination. Another IMMIGRATION OFFICER then calls DAVID forward. The IMMIGRATION OFFICER speaks in a thick accent.

IMMIGRATION OFFICER. Excuse me. Where are you coming from?
DAVID. New York.
IMMIGRATION OFFICER. Passport.
DAVID. Oh yeah.

DAVID takes a passport out of his bag and hands it to him.

IMMIGRATION OFFICER. Purpose of your visit?
DAVID. I was born here.
IMMIGRATION OFFICER. Where's your other passport?

DAVID hands over another passport.

IMMIGRATION OFFICER. Ahhh. You see? This is the passport I needed to see. This other one won't do you much good here. What's your religion?
DAVID. Excuse me?
IMMIGRATION OFFICER. Religion. You know Christian, Muslim.
DAVID. I'm Jewish.
IMMIGRATION OFFICER. What was the last holiday you celebrated?
DAVID. Passover.
IMMIGRATION OFFICER. You skipped Shavuot?
DAVID. *(nervously)* Uh …
IMMIGRATION OFFICER. Don't get nervous. I don't really care. Where were you born exactly?
DAVID. Bat Yam.
IMMIGRATION OFFICER. *(looking at the second passport)* It says here Ramat Gan.
DAVID. Oh yeah. Ramat Gan.
IMMIGRATION OFFICER. You don't know where you were born?
DAVID. It was a long time ago. *(a beat)* Sorry.… I'm … just a little nervous.
IMMIGRATION OFFICER. You're a little nervous? Wait. You just got here. What brings you back?
DAVID. This is my home.
IMMIGRATION OFFICER. Really? So what are you doing in New York?
DAVID. New York is just where I live.
IMMIGRATION OFFICER. How nice for you.

The IMMIGRATION OFFICER hands DAVID his passports.

IMMIGRATION OFFICER. Welcome home.

The IMMIGRATION OFFICER hands DAVID his passport. DAVID keeps walking. As he passes, DAVID looks back at the ARAB FAMILY in the other line. They are still being searched. The SOLDIER then motions for them to follow him. He leads them offstage and they pass right in front of DAVID.

DAVID looks back at the Garden. He looks back at BASSEE and JADI.

They hear a noise.

BASSEE. Shhh! Someone is coming.

JADI. Quick! Hide.

BASSEE. I'm tired of hiding.

JADI. Quick!! Bassee!! They will beat you.

BASSEE. They will beat me anyway. I'd rather not trouble myself.

JADI. They cannot beat you if they don't find you.

BASSEE. Where will you hide? Look around you. This place is not so big. Where can you possibly hide where they won't find you?

JADI. We have to at least try.

BASSEE. You can try if you like. I will sit peacefully and await whatever is coming to me.

JADI. You are a coward.

BASSEE. *I'm* not the one hiding.

JADI. You've given up. You refuse to try.

BASSEE. I refuse to be wasteful of my resources.

JADI. Enough talk. The time has come for action. *(looking around)* Where can I hide?

BASSEE. Enough. You are giving me a headache.

JADI hides behind a small rock. BASSEE watches mockingly.

JADI. How's this? Can you see me?

BASSEE. Only if I look in your direction.

JADI gets up and hides behind a tree.

JADI. How's this?

BASSEE. Good. Much better. No. Wait a minute. I can see you breathing. Can you hold your breath?

JADI holds his breath.

BASSEE. Perfect. Much better. Now stay like that for the rest of the day.

JADI holds his breath for as long as he can, but then deflates.

JADI. I won't last very long this way.

BASSEE. *(annoyed)* Too bad.

JADI. *(a new idea)* I have it.

JADI crawls underneath the bench that BASSEE is sitting on.

BASSEE. Really? That's your brilliant idea?

JADI. Don't talk to me. Don't talk to me.

BASSEE. Someone is bound to sit on this bench, you know.

JADI. So?

BASSEE. So you can't expect them not to notice you underneath their noses.

JADI. It's perfect. Think about it. People tend to see the person on top. No one ever thinks to look beneath. They'll only notice me if they are inclined to look beneath.

BASSEE. Or if I instruct them to look beneath.

JADI. You wouldn't do that. Would you, Bassee?

BASSEE. I may or may not. Either way, there's nothing you can do about it.
JADI. I would feel better if you told me you won't.
BASSEE. You shouldn't. Suppose I told you I won't and then I do.
JADI. Why would you do that?
BASSEE. Or what about this? Suppose I say I will tell, just to watch you squirm, and then I don't tell. What then?
JADI. Why would you do that?
BASSEE. To watch you squirm. The point is what I say now has nothing to do with what will or won't be.
JADI. Shhh. Here they come. I ask that you please not instruct them to look beneath this bench, and I leave my fate in your hands.
PAULA enters. She is youngish, innocent, and clearly a foreigner.
PAULA. Hello friend. May I sit?
BASSEE. You're asking me?
PAULA. You were here first.
BASSEE. That's something you don't hear every day.
DAVID. Where did you come from?
PAULA. I travel across the world. Meeting different people from different lands. They call me a goodwill ambassador.
DAVID. Oh Christ. This is gonna get messy, isn't it?
BASSEE. What do you care? You left us like this. So … go!
DAVID exits.
PAULA. I won't stay long. I just need a place to rest my weary legs for a moment or two.
BASSEE. Be my guest.
PAULA sits down. BASSEE watches her closely.
BASSEE. I have nothing to offer you.
PAULA. How do you mean?
BASSEE. Nothing to eat or drink. In order to honor you.
PAULA. Oh. No worries. Your hospitality is honor enough.
BASSEE. I have figs.
PAULA. Figs?
BASSEE. They grow in this garden. It's what I eat. It's all I ever eat. Would you like some?
PAULA. Oh. Okay. I'd be delighted.
BASSEE. Thank you.
BASSEE gets up to collect figs from the tree.
PAULA. Where is it that you come from?
BASSEE. Here.
PAULA. Ah. A lovely country indeed.
BASSEE. No. Not this country. I'm from here. This garden.
PAULA. Ah. But this garden is in this country.
BASSEE. According to some. But there are others that think different. Hold your hand out.
BASSEE places a handful of figs in PAULA's hand.
PAULA. My word. I've never seen figs quite like these before.
BASSEE. You'll also never taste figs quite like these. This garden has quite a reputation for its figs.

PAULA drops one.
PAULA. Oops.
PAULA starts to bend over to pick it up.
BASSEE. WAIT!!!!
PAULA. What?
BASSEE. Allow me.
PAULA. Nonsense. I'll get it.
PAULA bends down to pick up the fig, and promptly sits back up. She thinks for a moment and then bends down for a second look. She sits back up.
PAULA. Excuse me. I don't mean to be inquisitive. But is there by chance a man hiding underneath this bench?
BASSEE. Indeed there is.
PAULA. I see. And may I ask why he's hiding?
BASSEE. He thinks you've come to beat him.
PAULA. Ah yes. Very good. And might I probe a wee bit further and ask: Whatever would give him an idea like that?
BASSEE. It's been known to happen.
PAULA. I see. Might I assure him that I'm not in fact here to beat him?
BASSEE. You could try. I'm not sure he would believe you.
PAULA. You believe me, don't you?
BASSEE. I try not to believe anyone. I have knowledge of the past, and I keep an open eye towards the future.
PAULA bends down to talk with JADI.
PAULA. Hello.
JADI. Hello.
PAULA. I understand you're hiding underneath this bench.
JADI. That's right.
PAULA. And am I to understand that you're hiding on my account?
JADI. I am.
PAULA. Very good. We're making progress. And tell me one more thing. Are you hiding because you believe that I've come to beat you?
JADI. Yes.
PAULA. Fantastic! You see? This is how we avert conflict.
BASSEE. Well done.
PAULA. Thank you. You know, there is a simple solution to this problem.
JADI. Is there?
PAULA. Of course there is.
JADI. What is it, please?
PAULA. Well, I can simply put your fears to rest and assure you that I am most emphatically not here to beat you.
There is no response.
PAULA. Doesn't that give you the least bit of comfort?
BASSEE. With all due respect, ma'am, it's what they all say? We've never had a visitor that didn't end up beating us.
PAULA. I see. Well, that would cultivate certain insecurities, wouldn't it?
BASSEE. At this point, he may be more likely to trust you if you told him you *were* here to beat him. At least he would think you are honest.

PAULA. Excuse me, Mister. I've given it further consideration, and I've decided to come clean. I have every intention of beating you. Now come out and take it like a man.
JADI starts to cry.
JADI. No! Please! Please god!!! Protect me. Save me. I've suffered enough. Please don't beat me!!!!
PAULA. *(alarmed by JADI's reaction)* Oh no! No! Please, don't cry! I won't really beat you!
JADI. Why did you say you would?
PAULA. I was just ... kidding.
JADI. *(sniffling)* You were just ... kidding?
BASSEE. You have a sick sense of humor.
PAULA. I'm sorry I frightened you. If I really wanted to beat you, do you think the shelter of this bench would protect you?
JADI. I prefer to take my precautions. Ineffective though they may be. Makes me feel as though I'm doing something to help myself.
PAULA. Suit yourself. *(She eats.)* Mmm. *(She eats another.)* Mmm. These figs are better than any I've ever had.
BASSEE. Told you.
PAULA. I never knew figs could be this juicy before. You really must come out and have some.
BASSEE. Don't listen to her, Jadi. She's just trying to get you out of there.
PAULA. What?
JADI. Yup. I'm on to her tactics.
PAULA. My tactics? No. Please. You misunderstand me.
BASSEE. Honestly. I've never heard of anyone carrying on so about a bunch of figs. It's awfully suspicious.
JADI. Come to think of it, I am somewhat hungry. Would you mind lowering one or two of your figs down to me?
PAULA. Not at all.
BASSEE. Don't you dare.
PAULA. What? Why?
BASSEE. I picked those figs for you. Not for him. He lives in this garden. He can pick his own figs.
PAULA. It's quite alright. I don't mind.
BASSEE. I do.
JADI. Come Bassee. Have some compassion. I'm too frightened to come out.
BASSEE. Life requires necessary risk.
PAULA. Look. Why would I want to beat you? It seems to be counterproductive to my interests. I am a guest. I am counting on your good graces for hospitality. It seems I would remove myself from your good graces by beating you, does it not?
BASSEE. Your reasoning is flawed.
PAULA. Is it?
BASSEE. It's too simplistic. It doesn't take into account human capriciousness.
PAULA. Human what?
BASSEE. Today you may want to stay within our good graces. Tomorrow you may decide you'd like to dominate us.

PAULA. Dominate you? Never. I am a peaceful woman. I've devoted my life to helping acquire peace and equality for all.
BASSEE. Peace and equality for all as long as we supply you with free figs.
PAULA. Peace and equality for all regardless of whether or not you offer me any figs. Please, take your figs back. I don't want them.
BASSEE. You're giving the figs back?
PAULA. I am.
BASSEE. I gave those figs as a gift. In this garden, returning a gift that you've already accepted is a deeply hurtful insult.
PAULA. Well, I'm awfully sorry. But I will not be accused of trying to dominate your figs.
BASSEE. I am very insulted.
BASSEE and PAULA stand on opposite sides of the garden and avoid eye contact. They pout for a few beats. Finally, JADI emerges from under the bench.
JADI. Excuse me, Bassee. But if she won't eat the figs that you picked for her, do you mind if I do?
BASSEE. No sense in them going to waste.
JADI. Thank you.
JADI eats the remaining figs.
JADI. *(to PAULA)* Who are you?
PAULA. A stranger in a strange land.
JADI. What do you want?
PAULA. I'm here to spread the message.
JADI. What message is that?
PAULA. The message of peace, love, and hope for all of mankind.
JADI. Oh. *(considering)* That's a nice message. You are welcome to rest in our midst for as long as you wish.
PAULA. I am grateful.
JADI. If Bassee will not pick figs for you, I will be happy to do so.
PAULA. Tell me. Why do you trust me suddenly?
JADI. Anybody who turns down a gift, can't possibly be interested in stealing. But I don't recommend you stay long. Soon, they'll be back to beat us again. And if they think you are one of us, they are likely to beat you too.
PAULA. Who is likely to beat me? Who is it that you fear?
JADI. He that claims to own this garden.
PAULA. Why does he beat you?
JADI. If we knew, we might be able to remedy the problem.
PAULA. But surely we can surmise some kind of explanation.
JADI. Believe me, ma'am. We've tried for years. There simply is no explanation.
PAULA. This person who beats you. Does he have a name?
JADI. He goes by the name of Assav.
PAULA. Assav?
JADI. Yes.
PAULA. I see. Well. Come. Let us have a few more figs. And then let us rest. Tomorrow, I will seek out this Assav and see if I can't reason with him a little. Come, let us eat.
JADI. Come now, Bassee. We are all friends here. Let us eat and rest together.
BASSEE does not respond.

PAULA. Excuse me, Mr. Bassee. I am very sorry for insulting you. Please accept my apology.

A moment. BASSEE hesitates.

BASSEE. *(mumbling)* Your apology is accepted.

PAULA. Thank you.

JADI. Come, Bassee. That's all you're going to say?

BASSEE. What do you want me to say?

JADI. Did you not, likewise, insult our guest by accusing her of coming to dominate our figs?

BASSEE. I did not accuse her of anything. I simply proposed a hypothetical. And anyway, it wasn't I that hid under the bench when she arrived. If there is someone here who accused her of something, it is you, Jadi. Not me.

JADI. Of course, Bassee. It is never you who transgresses. It is always I. But surely if you search your heart, I'm sure you will find there is something that you can apologize for.

BASSEE. I refuse to participate in the custom of apologizing for its own sake. When I have something to apologize for, I will be the first to admit it.

PAULA. Come. I require no apology. Let us enjoy more figs. We have a long day ahead of us tomorrow.

JADI. Bassee, have you noticed? Today is not just another day. Today, we are no longer alone. At long last, there is someone else who cares.

Lights fade on the garden.

Lights up on a dingy hotel lobby in desperate need of renovation. There is no air conditioning. A fan blows in a futile attempt to cool the place down. MOTTI, the innkeeper, sits on a sofa with his arm around MOSHE, a guest. MOTTI takes a casual, personable approach to running a hotel.

MOTTI. Let me explain something to you. You called me yesterday. You said to me, I need a room. Yesterday mind you. Not in advance.

MOSHE. I gave you twenty-four hours' notice. That's not in advance?

MOTTI. In August? Not in this town. You don't believe me? Call every hotel. Ask every one of them who has rooms available for tomorrow night. They'll all laugh at you. But here, you call me, I say no problem. Now you've got complaints.

MOSHE. I carried my own bags to my room.

MOTTI. Who asked you to? You should have said something, I would have called someone to take them up for you.

MOSHE. I don't want to say something. That's what customer service is. Not having to say anything.

DAVID enters with his suitcase.

MOSHE. I get up to the room, the bed is not made.

MOTTI. Okay. Give me five minutes. I'll have the beds made up *chic-chak*.[5]

DAVID. Excuse me? Does someone work here?

MOSHE. There are no towels in the room.

MOTTI. Towels will make you happy? I'll get you towels. What's the problem to get towels?

DAVID rings the bell on the counter.

DAVID. Excuse me.

MOTTI. *(to DAVID, demanding)* A MINUTE!!!! *(to MOSHE)* In two seconds you'll have

all the towels you need. You want a bathrobe with our insignia? I'll send it up with the towels.
MOSHE. A bathrobe is asking too much. First let's see you produce the towels. And then we'll talk about bathrobes.
DAVID. Excuse me.
MOTTI. I said one minute. A little bit of patience goes a long way, friend. *(MOTTI stands up with MOSHE.)* Look. My point is this. You'll find this hotel can provide all the services you seek. We may not get it right on the first try. But give us a chance. By the time you leave here, it'll be home. Huh? Or you can take your chances and find another hotel. The appearance may be nicer, but to them you'll only be a client. Here, you're part of the *mishpacha*.[6] You understand? *(MOTTI guides him towards the exit.)* So go upstairs, take a cold shower. Put your feet up, and we'll take care of everything else, okay?
MOSHE. I need a towel.
MOTTI. Okay, okay. Go upstairs. Someone is following you up this instant with a whole stack of towels.
MOSHE. Just one will be enough to impress me.

MOSHE exits. MOTTI takes a moment to decompress after MOSHE leaves. He takes out a cigarette, and lights it. He inhales as though he derives the will to continue from this cigarette. DAVID just watches, incredulous that MOTTI feels a cigarette is more urgent than attending to him.

MOTTI. Okay. *Motek*.[7] Come. Tell me what I can do for you.
DAVID. I have a reservation.
MOTTI. Reservation? For when?
DAVID. Tonight.
MOTTI. Tonight? No. Sorry. It's impossible.
DAVID. What do you mean impossible? I have a reservation. I called last week.
MOTTI. Who did you speak to?
DAVID. I don't know. Some woman.
MOTTI. Ah. See? That is your problem. Do not speak to some woman, friend. Speak to me. What is your name?
DAVID. Green.
MOTTI. Green? Green what?
DAVID. David Green.
MOTTI. David Green?
DAVID. That's right.
MOTTI. *(looking through a rolodex)* There was a David Green that came to this country many years ago. You know what happened to him?
DAVID. What?
MOTTI. It's a long story. *(He finds the reservation.)* Here it is. David Green. I have a room for you for tonight.
DAVID. And tomorrow night.
MOTTI. No. Tomorrow night is impossible.
DAVID. What do you mean impossible? I called last week. My reservation was for—
MOTTI. Alright, alright, alright. And tomorrow night. What else do you want? You wanna move in?
DAVID. Does the room have air conditioning?
MOTTI. And a television.

DAVID. And what about a phone?
MOTTI. What phone? Who do you wanna call? You don't know anybody.
DAVID. You have food here?
MOTTI. Food? What do I look like? No food. But take the key. Go get settled in the room and come back down. I'll invite you to a beer. Okay? We're glad to have you with us, David Green. Welcome to the Chalom Hertzl[8] Hotel.
MOSHE re-enters angrily.
MOSHE. There is no water coming out of the faucet.
MOTTI. What water? Did you ask me to turn on the water?
MOSHE. You told me to go up and take a shower.
MOTTI. Okay. So I didn't think you'd do it right away. You have to tell me ahead of time to turn it on. I can't have people running amok with the water.
DAVID. It's water, not wine.
MOTTI. Habibi, in this country, wine is less expensive.
Lights down on the hotel lobby.
Lights rise on the garden.
BASSEE and JADI are on the bench. JADI is bruised up even more. BASSEE looks untouched. BASSEE applies a moist rag to JADI'S face.
JADI. Why me? Why is it always me?
BASSEE. Because you were hiding.
JADI. I was hiding because it's always me. You weren't hiding. They didn't touch you.
BASSEE. They didn't touch me because I was not afraid. What would they have accomplished? And anyway, I've gotten my fair share. Will you hold still?
BASSEE applies the rag again. JADI flinches.
JADI. It hurts. How did they know I was under the bench anyway?
BASSEE. What do you mean how did they know? They saw you. That's how.
JADI. They didn't see me. Not at first. They saw you. They were coming right for you. So what happened? What made them change their course?
BASSEE. What are you getting at, Jadi?
JADI. You told them I was under the bench. You told them to avoid getting yours.
BASSEE. Did you hear me telling them? Did you hear me say, "Hey. Don't beat me. Jadi is under the bench. Beat him instead." Did you hear me say that?
JADI. Perhaps you communicated without words.
BASSEE. Don't be ridiculous. I was prepared to stand my ground and accept a beating on your behalf. At the last minute, they discovered you under the bench and decided to make a point.
JADI. You were prepared to stand your ground and at the last minute you went, "Psst." *(pointing under the bench)*
BASSEE. That's ridiculous. Did you hear me go, "Psst." *(pointing under the bench, imitating JADI)*
JADI. I'm not suggesting you went "Psst." I'm just saying you made them aware that I was under the bench in order to avoid getting a beating.
BASSEE. How could I know I would avoid getting a beating by betraying you? They could have beaten both of us.
JADI. But they didn't, did they?
BASSEE. Jadi, honestly. I suppose next you'll suggest that I collaborated with Assav ahead of time. I'm sorry you got a beating.

JADI. And relieved that you didn't.
BASSEE. Well, of course I'm relieved. You want me to be sorry that I didn't suffer like you?
JADI. Yes.
BASSEE. Why should both of us suffer?
JADI. It's only fair.
BASSEE. It's only fair if both of us suffer?
JADI. It's only fair if we suffer equally.
BASSEE. I think it would only be fair if neither one of us suffered at all.
JADI. That would be my first choice. But since that's unrealistic, I would rather we both suffer equally.
BASSEE. What do you want to do? Take shifts?
JADI. Yes.
BASSEE. Assav's men would only beat the opposite person if only to make a point that they don't adhere to schedules.
JADI. And in so doing they would still be adhering to a more equitable schedule, wouldn't they? *DAVID enters and watches the garden.*
BASSEE. Come. Enough of this. I made you some soup. It's probably already cold.
BASSEE scoops out some soup into a tin container and hands it to JADI.
JADI. Thank you.
BASSEE. You're welcome.
JADI. It doesn't make up for my beatings though.
BASSEE. No. I didn't expect it would.
JADI drinks a bit of the soup and makes a slurping noise.
DAVID. How is it?
JADI. Delicious.
DAVID. Can I try some?
BASSEE. Piss off.
DAVID. That's not very nice. I'm hungry.
BASSEE. You're free. Find your own soup.
DAVID. Fair enough.
JADI. Bassee. I'm sorry that I was grumpy because you didn't get a beating also.
JADI drinks more soup. BASSEE watches him eat for a moment.
BASSEE. They were going to beat me, you know. Just before they delivered their initial blow, I looked at my feet. I couldn't look them in the eye. I think that's what gave you away. I'm sorry. I should have been more brave.
JADI. You don't have to be brave on my account.
BASSEE. I wish I were more brave on mine.
JADI. It's okay, Bassee. Soon the day will come when neither one of us will have to be brave.
BASSEE. In the meantime, more soup.
Lights up on a café. The place is empty. SHACHAR, the owner and a religious Jew, stands behind the counter leaning forward. He wears a yarmulke on his head and his prayer shawl fringe are visible over his pants. He has a rough appearance. Clearly, life has exhausted him. He wears an apron with cooking stains on it. DAVID sits at the table.
SHACHAR. Listen to me very carefully, *motek*. In this country, everyone is a thief. The guy who sells you schawarma. Thief. The guy who sells you water. Thief. The Prime

Minister. Thief. Everybody's a thief. The whole world is made up of thieves. Just try crossing the border. There, they're thieves and terrorists.

DAVID. Which border?

SHACHAR. Which border? Pick one. They're all the same.

DAVID. They're all the same.

SHACHAR. Everybody. Either they want to rob you, or they want to kill you.

DAVID takes out a pad and starts writing.

SHACHAR. What are you writing?

DAVID. "They're all the same."

SHACHAR. This is news to you? You're a Jew, aren't you?

DAVID. I live in America.

SHACHAR. And what are you doing in America, my brother? This is the homeland of the Jewish people. This is where you belong.

DAVID. Yeah. It's not so easy though, is it.

SHACHAR. Easy? Life is not easy. When *Moshiach*[9] comes, then it will be easy. At least you care enough to visit.

DAVID. "If I forget thee O Jerusalem..."

SHACHAR. "Let my right hand forget its cunning." Psalm 137, Verse 5. Unfortunately, this is Tel Aviv. *Yalla.* What are you eating?

DAVID. I don't know. What's good here?

SHACHAR. What's good? What do you like? *Schnitzel?*[10] *Sheeshleek?*[11]

DAVID. You have something more...

SHACHAR. More what? Spicy?

DAVID. Yemenite.

SHACHAR. Yemenite? You want Yemenite? What do you know from Yemenite? You're American.

DAVID. You have it?

SHACHAR. Listen, if Yemenite is what you want, you've come to the right place. Yemenite soup with meat, *chilbeh*, and *schug*.[12]

DAVID. I'll take it.

SHACHAR. Fifty shekels.

DAVID. I thought it was forty-one.

SHACHAR. You want it for forty-one?

DAVID. The sign says forty-one.

SHACHAR. For you I'll do it for forty-one. But only for you.

DAVID. Everyone is a thief, huh?

SHACHAR. You think I'm not included? I'm no better than anyone else. And why should I be?

SHACHAR produces a bottle of alcohol and pours two shots.

SHACHAR. You know what this is?

DAVID. Vodka?

SHACHAR. Vodka you drink in Moscow. This is Arak. You didn't serve in the army?

DAVID. No.

SHACHAR. Right. Maybe that's why you live in America. At least this will put hair on your chest.

He hands one to DAVID.

DAVID. No, thank you.

SHACHAR. What no thank you? I'm inviting you. Don't be shy.
DAVID takes it.
DAVID. Thank you.
SHACHAR. You're welcome. With joy and blessings, *motek*. Relax. Rest. Make yourself at home. And before long your mouth will be ablaze with the taste of my world famous Yemenite soup.
SHACHAR raises the shot glass. DAVID follows him.
SHACHAR. Yalla. L'Chaim. To your health.
They drink.
SHACHAR. Where are you staying while you're here, American?
DAVID. The Chalom Hertzl Hotel.
SHACHAR. The Chalom Hertzl? Wow. That place is a real shithole.
Back in the garden.
JADI. What did you put in this soup?
PAULA enters.
BASSEE. What does it taste like? Chicken.
PAULA. I thought you only ate figs, Bassee.
BASSEE. I found some chicken bones in a nearby trashcan. I was able to salvage the bones and make a broth out of it for Jadi.
PAULA. That's very resourceful of you. And who does the trash belong to?
BASSEE. It's trash. Does trash belong to anyone?
PAULA. Okay. Who *did* the trash belong to? Before it was discarded.
BASSEE. Well, I imagine Assav.
PAULA. I see.
JADI. Why the interrogation? Did you speak with Assav?
PAULA. I did not speak with Assav. No.
JADI. Oh?
PAULA. I spoke with Assav's secretary. Assav was away.
JADI. Oh.
BASSEE. And what did he say?
PAULA. She.
BASSEE. What did this person, say?
PAULA. No. Not this person. She.
BASSEE. Sh-e-e-e. What relevance is this person's gender?
PAULA. It's only relevant insofar as it's a fact.
BASSEE. It's only relevant insofar as you say it's relevant.
JADI. Bassee, please. Don't be cross with our visitor. *(to PAULA)* Please. What did she say?
PAULA. Well, we talked for quite some time.
JADI. Yes. You've been gone a while.
PAULA. And she gave me a new perspective on the whole situation. It appears it's not quite so simple as I thought.
JADI. What do you mean?
PAULA. Well, you guys aren't quite as innocent as you had me believing?
BASSEE. What?
JADI. Not so innocent?
PAULA. Are you?

BASSEE. Do you have any idea what's happened to us in the last 24 hours since you left? We were beat.

JADI. We?

BASSEE. Jadi was beat. Assav's men came here and beat Jadi. Look at his face.

PAULA. And what about you, Bassee? How did you manage to avoid Jadi's fate?

BASSEE. I didn't.

PAULA. Oh. So you were beat too?

BASSEE. No. I mean, I didn't avoid anything. I didn't have to. They didn't beat me this time. That's all.

PAULA. Why not?

BASSEE. I don't know. They just decided not to.

PAULA. Oh. Well that was considerate of them, wasn't it?

BASSEE. You don't believe me.

PAULA. Well, you have to admit. It does sound a little bit fishy, doesn't it? How do I know you didn't beat Jadi yourself?

BASSEE. Why would I do that?

JADI. Bassee didn't beat me up.

PAULA. I'm not saying he did. I'm only saying. I wasn't here. So I can't really know for sure, can I?

BASSEE. You didn't seem to doubt what we told you yesterday.

PAULA. I didn't have all the facts yesterday.

BASSEE. And what facts do you have today that causes you to doubt us?

PAULA. I have the other side of the story.

BASSEE. I see. I didn't realize that our beating was just one side of a larger story.

PAULA. Yes. Well that may be part of the problem here, Bassee. To every argument, there is a counterargument.

BASSEE. I see. And what is the counterargument for our abuse?

JADI. That we deserve it?

PAULA. That's not what I said. No human being deserves to suffer.

BASSEE. What then?

PAULA. Look. I'm not saying I believe this, but Assav's secretary seems to think that you murdered his father.

JADI. That's a lie.

PAULA. I'm not saying it isn't. I'm just saying that's what she said.

BASSEE. No. You're saying you believe it.

PAULA. I'm saying I believe it's a possibility.

BASSEE. You believe it.

PAULA. Well, I wasn't here, was I, so I can't possibly know for sure.

JADI. And anyway, our family has always lived in this garden.

BASSEE. Jadi!

JADI. What? It's true.

PAULA. So you did kill Assav's father?

BASSEE. Is that what he said? That's not what he said.

PAULA. I ask if you killed Assav's father, and his response was, "And anyway our family has always lived in this garden?"

BASSEE. So?

PAULA. So it sounds to me like a justification for violence.

BASSEE. No. Not a justification.
PAULA. What then?
BASSEE. An explanation.
PAULA. So you *did* do it. You murdered him.
JADI. We killed him. Not murdered.
BASSEE. Jadi! Enough.
JADI. What? I'm just saying.
BASSEE. You're saying too much.
JADI. I'm not afraid of the facts. Look. One day, Assav's father shows up with his family and claims he bought the land. We said, "What do you mean you bought the land?" From whom? Our father brought us here when we were small.
PAULA. I thought you said your family has always lived in this garden.
BASSEE. Our family, yes. Our lineage. Not so much us.
PAULA. So where did you live before that?
BASSEE. Our people wandered. From land to land.
JADI. They beat us everywhere we went.
PAULA. Why?
JADI. How should we know?
BASSEE. We were different. We stuck out.
PAULA. Did you try to fit in?
BASSEE. Why?
PAULA. To avoid getting beat?
BASSEE. Huh. That never occurred to us.
JADI. Is that what it takes to be treated like a human being? You have to be just like everyone else?
PAULA. It's a tactic.
JADI. We are unique.
PAULA. I understand. But being unique comes at a cost.
BASSEE. Before we came to this garden, we lived in the Land of Love and Acceptance.
PAULA. You were beaten in the Land of Love and Acceptance?
BASSEE. Relentlessly.
JADI. Before that our family dwelled in the fields of Hope and Understanding.
PAULA. And?
JADI. Same thing.
BASSEE. Our people lived behind locked gates. We were only allowed out for two hours every day.
PAULA. And before that?
BASSEE. We lived on the Island of Eternal Citizenship For All.
PAULA. And?
BASSEE. They revoked our citizenship.
PAULA. How long did your people wander?
JADI. *(thinking)* Quite some time.
PAULA. Thirty years?
BASSEE. A bit longer than that.
PAULA. Fifty years?
BASSEE. Two thousand years.

PAULA. TWO THOUSAND YEARS? Your family has always lived in this garden, except for the last two thousand years?
BASSEE. Yes, yes, two thousand years ago, this was the place to be.
PAULA. Oh this is unbelievable. You want me to buy into a story that goes back two thousand years? How can you even be sure they were your family?
BASSEE. Trust me. We can be sure.
JADI. We are of a very select line.
BASSEE. The point is, when our father brought us, there was nothing here. We planted these wonderful fig trees with our bare hands. And we lived in peace for many years. We didn't bother anybody and nobody bothered us. Until Assav showed up and started making trouble. Hostilities started to escalate, and to make a long story short…
PAULA. You killed him.
BASSEE. Our brother, yes. Assav's father came after him with a stick.
PAULA. A stick?
JADI. It was a sizeable stick.
BASSEE. Our brother defended himself and killed him.
PAULA. And what happened to him?
JADI. He was killed.
PAULA. Assav's men?
BASSEE. Probably. We don't know. We had never seen these men before, and we haven't seen them since. So, yes, my brother killed Assav's father. If it was a crime, he paid the price. So now what?
PAULA. Why do these things always have to go back thousands of years? God forbid we should be able to verify anything.
BASSEE. We were here first.
PAULA. That's a childish argument.
BASSEE. It's a childish problem.
PAULA. Is it really worth the daily beatings?
JADI. Where can we go where we won't be beat?
BASSEE. We are beat everywhere.
JADI. Nothing to *do*.
BASSEE. *Nothing* to do.
JADI. At least here we have food to eat.
PAULA. Look. Assav is offering to suspend the beatings.
BASSEE. Oh. Is that his offer? That's very generous of him.
PAULA. Do you want to hear his conditions?
BASSEE. There are conditions for not beating us? Tell him not to inconvenience himself. This garden is all we have, we're not leaving.
PAULA. No. He doesn't expect you will. Here's his counteroffer.
BASSEE. Here's a counteroffer. How about if they stop beating us?
PAULA. In exchange for what?
JADI. Why do we owe him something for expecting him not to beat us?
PAULA. He'll stop beating you, if you stop eating his figs.
BASSEE. *His* figs?
JADI. What are we supposed to eat?
PAULA. Something else.
BASSEE. Those fig trees belong to us. We planted them.

PAULA. That's the offer.
BASSEE. Great. So instead of beating us, he'll starve us. What difference does it make?
PAULA. You won't starve.
BASSEE. Oh no? Who will feed us? You?
PAULA. I'll help. Look, I know it's not perfect. It's a start. Just avoid eating the figs, and we'll keep negotiating.
BASSEE. This is not negotiating. This is acquiescing.
PAULA. It's just a start. We'll make things right. Just give it time.
BASSEE. How can you make it right? You don't even understand how it was made wrong.
PAULA. We'll make it better.
Lights up on DAVID's hotel room. He lies in bed wearing only shorts. He speaks to PAULA from his bed.
DAVID. You really think you're gonna straighten all this out?
PAULA. I'm trying. What are you doing?
DAVID. Trying to rest. But you're making too much noise.
DAVID gets out of bed and puts his clothes on.
BASSEE. Where are you going?
DAVID. For a walk. I'm not sleeping anyway. Go home, goodwill ambassador. You're not going to accomplish anything. And no one wants you here.
PAULA. I'll go when you go.
DAVID. This is my home.
PAULA. You really believe that?
Lights up on a marketplace booth. MAS'UD, 20s, a marketplace vendor, sees DAVID glancing at some of his merchandise.
MAS'UD. You need help?
DAVID. No no. I'm just looking.
MAS'UD. I will help you. I will give you cell phone. Very good deal. And if it breaks, bring it back anytime. I will fix it for free. No one-year warranty. No three-year warranty. Lifetime warranty. You come back any time, I will fix it for free.
DAVID. No no. I'm not from here.
MAS'UD. Where are you from?
DAVID. New York.
MAS'UD. New York?! I love New York.
DAVID. You've been there?
MAS'UD. No. But I see in movies. Very nice. Lots of water. Must be nice living on water.
DAVID. Well, I don't really live on water.
MAS'UD. New York is island, no? Water on all sides?
DAVID. Well, yeah. Manhattan is an island. But … um … I live in Astoria.
MAS'UD. Astoria? That's in Russia, no?
DAVID. Um … no. It's in Queens. Not far from the airport.
MAS'UD. Ahhh! JFK.
DAVID. Yes. That's right. Actually, I'm closer to LaGuardia, but you know, that's okay.
MAS'UD. You are lucky to be surrounded by water. We never see water.
DAVID. You're not very far from the sea.
MAS'UD. Yes, but we can't go there.
DAVID. No. I don't suppose you can.
MAS'UD. Please. Come sit for a minute.

DAVID. I don't need a cell phone.
MAS'UD. Forget cell phone. Just talking.
DAVID. Just talking.
MAS'UD. Why not?
DAVID. We don't really do just talking in New York.
MAS'UD produces two stools.
MAS'UD. Sit.
They sit.
MAS'UD. Please forgive me. I have no coffee to offer you. It's Ramadan.
DAVID. Oh no. Please. Don't worry.
MAS'UD. You don't drink coffee?
DAVID. No no. I drink coffee. But it's okay.
MAS'UD. Come back when it's not Ramadan. I'll have coffee for you and Baklawa. You know Baklawa?
DAVID. I've had it.
MAS'UD. Take some home to your girlfriend in New York. It's Arabic Viagra. Tell me. What brings you here?
DAVID. I'm ... just visiting.
MAS'UD. Ah. You are on holiday.
DAVID. Well ... uh ... actually ... I was born here.
MAS'UD. Here? Really? Where?
DAVID. Um ... just ... uh ... outside of Tel Aviv.
MAS'UD. And where does your family come from?
DAVID. My mother's family comes from Yemen.
MAS'UD. Yemen! Ahh. So you speak Arabic?
DAVID. Uhh. No. No, I don't.
MAS'UD. Ahh.
DAVID. What about you? Where are you from?
MAS'UD. My family? Originally from Yafo.
DAVID. You've been working here long?
MAS'UD. Me? This is mine.
DAVID. You own this business?
MAS'UD. I started it with my friend. He gave up and left.
DAVID. What does he do now?
MAS'UD. I don't ask. That's his business.
DAVID. So now you run this place all by yourself.
MAS'UD. All by myself.
DAVID. How old are you?
MAS'UD. Twenty-four. But I started when I was nineteen.
DAVID. Nineteen? Wow. That's a young age to start a business.
MAS'UD. Why wait?
DAVID. You didn't ... go to school?
MAS'UD. School? Of course. I finished. One of the best in the class.
DAVID. You finished at 19?
MAS'UD. Ahh. You mean, I didn't go to university.
DAVID. Well, yeah. That's what I meant by school.
MAS'UD. No. My parents couldn't afford to send me.

DAVID. Oh.
MAS'UD. You went to university?
DAVID. Yeah. Yeah. I went.
MAS'UD. Wow. Was it nice?
DAVID. Uh. Yeah. Yeah. It was nice.
MAS'UD. NYU?
DAVID. No. I ... went to school in New Jersey.
MAS'UD. New Jersey. Oh. Not as good as NYU.
DAVID. Uh ... well. It wasn't bad.
MAS'UD. It's still America. It must be nice to study in university in America.
DAVID. Yeah. *(a beat)* What's it like? Fasting on Ramadan?
MAS'UD. It's nice.
DAVID. It's not ... hard?
MAS'UD. No. Just from sunrise to sunset. When the sun goes down, we eat a big meal. It's nice. You should come. Eat with my family.
DAVID. With your family?
MAS'UD. Yes. We have a beautiful meal. You will see. Will you come?
DAVID. Uh ... maybe. I don't want to impose.
MAS'UD. No. My family will enjoy having you. They love to have guests.
DAVID. How many kids do you have?
MAS'UD. Me? No. I do not have kids.
DAVID. Oh. Your family?
MAS'UD. My parents. My sisters.
DAVID. Oh ... your family is your parents?
MAS'UD. Everybody!
DAVID. Oh.... I'm.... I don't know.
MAS'UD. It will be a great honor you're giving them. To have a guest.
DAVID. Do you live around here?
MAS'UD. No. It is a little far. I hope you don't mind. I live in Huwara.
DAVID. Huwara. Where's that?
MAS'UD. Palestine.
DAVID. Palestine.
MAS'UD. The West Bank.
DAVID. Right.
MAS'UD. A little far. But ... it's okay. We'll get there quickly. We don't waste time on Ramadan.
DAVID. Yeah. I bet.
MAS'UD. You know how it is to fast? Right?
DAVID. Me?
MAS'UD. You fast. Yom Kippur. No?
DAVID. Yeah. Yeah. Yom Kippur.
MAS'UD. Yes. I know.
DAVID. It's hard.
MAS'UD. It's ... a challenge.
DAVID. Yes. A challenge.
MAS'UD. But rewarding.
DAVID. Yeah. I guess so.

MAS'UD. You'll come? Our meal will be extra good today. The water in my village is flowing today.
DAVID. The water in your village ... doesn't flow every day?
MAS'UD. Every other day. The water is limited. The Israelis. They don't allow us to have it every day.
DAVID. Oh. You sure your parents won't mind? Having a guest? Unannounced?
MAS'UD. I told you it is honor. They will be happy. You are ... uncomfortable?
DAVID. Um ... a little.
MAS'UD. It is okay. My family is not surprised to have guests. We are Arab. In America, you call first, no?
DAVID. Yeah.
MAS'UD. Not here. I close at five. Come back then. We will go from here in peace. *Inshallah.*
DAVID. *Inshallah*? What ... what is that *inshallah*?
MAS'UD. *Inshallah*? Uh ... you know Jews say, *Bezrat Hashem*?[13]
DAVID. Yeah.
MAS'UD. Right. That's what it means.
DAVID. *Inshallah.*
MAS'UD. *Inshallah.*
Lights fade on the marketplace.
Lights rise on the garden, but now there is a thin string rigged about a foot off the ground bordering the entrance to the garden. BASSEE stands at the garden entrance contemplating the string. JADI sits on the bench diligently making chewing motions with his mouth. Every so often, he stops to swallow. Eventually, BASSEE notices.
BASSEE. Jadi.
JADI stops and looks at BASSEE like a deer in headlights.
BASSEE. What are you doing?
JADI. I'm very, very hungry.
BASSEE. Are you eating the figs? After you promised not to? After lecturing me on how we must at least try to be agreeable to Assav's terms? How we must work hard and do our part to achieve a durable agreement with Assav. And now you're eating the figs? Are you out of your mind? You don't think I'm hungry too?
JADI. Calm down, Bassee.
BASSEE. Don't tell me to calm down. I am starving.
JADI. I'm not eating the figs.
BASSEE. Then what are you eating?
JADI. I'm not eating anything.
BASSEE. Then why were you moving your mouth in that ridiculous fashion?
JADI. I was swallowing spit. I figured maybe my stomach won't feel so empty.
BASSEE. I'm eating the figs.
JADI. No. Bassee. Please. We must be strong. We must endure.
BASSEE. Endure what? Jadi? This is not a test of endurance. This is suicide.
JADI. If we break the agreement, Assav will end the negotiations and blame it all on us.
BASSEE. And if we adhere to the agreement, we die of starvation. Either way we lose.
JADI. We must have hope. We must trust in the negotiations. We cannot violate the agreement.
BASSEE. What agreement, Jadi? An agreement is a settlement where both parties give

something, and get something in return. We gave up our livelihood. We gave up our sustenance. And for what? What are we getting? Nothing. This is not an agreement, Jadi. This is surrendering.

DAVID and MAS'UD arrive at an Israeli checkpoint. They stand in line waiting for the ISRAELI SOLDIER to acknowledge them.

MAS'UD. Don't worry, Astoria. They don't make us wait long going home. Going in this direction is much easier.

ISRAELI SOLDIER #1. *Vakasha!*[14]

DAVID steps up and hands the ISRAELI SOLDIER his passport.

ISRAELI SOLDIER #1. *Amerikayee?*[15]

DAVID. *Ken*[16]

ISRAELI SOLDIER #1. *Medaber Ivrit?*[17]

DAVID. Not really.

ISRAELI SOLDIER #1. He's with you?

DAVID. Um … yes.

ISRAELI SOLDIER #1. Okay. *Shalom Aleichem.*

DAVID and MAS'UD pass the checkpoint.

MAS'UD. Wow. That was even quicker than I thought. You should come home with me every day.

DAVID. You go through the checkpoint every day?

MAS'UD. Ooh wah. Twice a day. And in the morning, it can take two hours. Sometimes longer.

DAVID. That's … inconvenient.

MAS'UD. Inconvenient? Going to the post office is inconvenient. These checkpoints make me hate living here. Maybe someday I'll move to Astoria. You have checkpoints in Astoria?

DAVID. Uh … no. But we have toll booths.

MAS'UD. Toll booths?

DAVID. Yeah. You know. Where you have to pay to pass through.

MAS'UD. You have to pay … to pass? Don't say that too loud. You'll give these Israelis ideas.

DAVID. What did he mean, that you're with me?

MAS'UD. You're an American. And a Jew. You're a person.

DAVID. You're not a person?

MAS'UD. To that soldier? I am less than an animal. But one day. Things will be different. *Inshallah.* Come. My mother's hummus awaits.

DAVID. Can I be honest for a second?

MAS'UD. Just for a second? Be honest always.

DAVID. I'm a little nervous. I'm worried that your family won't be so … happy to see me.

MAS'UD. Why wouldn't they be happy to see you?

DAVID. Cause.… I'm a Jew.

MAS'UD. You think my family hates Jews.

DAVID. Well … yeah? Kind of?

MAS'UD. Do you know what we hate, David? We hate living under Israeli occupation. We hate that the Israeli government targets Palestinian civilians. We hate that there is not a moment of peace for us. That there is no freedom. That's what we hate.

DAVID. I understand, Mas'ud. But I think if I was in your place, all of that would make me hate Jews.

MAS'UD. Our fight is with the Israeli government. Not Jews. Come, David. This will be a good experience for you.

MAS'UD and DAVID exits.

IN THE GARDEN, Paula falls onstage. She doesn't see the wire that has been rigged, and she trips on it. She takes a big spill.

PAULA. Ow!! Shit. What the hell?

PAULA looks back to see why she tripped.

PAULA. Goddamn it! Who put this wire here?

BASSEE. I did.

PAULA. Why?

BASSEE. It's part of my new project. I call it The First Line of Defense.

PAULA. Ow! I think I scraped up my knee.

BASSEE. I'm surprised how effective it is. I thought I was just trying to make myself feel better. But now I see. It might actually accomplish something.

JADI. Bassee. This is against our agreement.

BASSEE. I agreed to stop eating the figs. And I did, I'm starving. I did not agree to refrain from measures of self-defense.

PAULA. This is an act of aggression. Assav and his men are allowed to enter this garden. They should be free to do so without risking injury.

BASSEE. Assav's men only come to this garden for the purpose of beating us. They should not be free to do that without risking injury.

JADI. Bassee. We agreed to allow our friend to continue with the negotiations.

BASSEE. And we have. Who's stopping her?

PAULA. When Assav finds out about this wire, it will undermine my efforts. Bassee, you must take this wire down.

BASSEE. You must be crazy.

PAULA. Bassee, I have been making a great deal of progress on your behalf. Assav's secretary said he'd like to make another offer today. One that he was confident you'd like.

BASSEE. Assav's secretary. She still hasn't spoken to Assav directly.

PAULA. He's been busy.

BASSEE. What kind of mediator are you? It doesn't sound like Assav is taking you very seriously at all.

JADI. What's the offer?

PAULA. She didn't tell me. He's coming here to present it to you himself.

BASSEE. Assav's coming here?

PAULA. He'd like to talk with you directly. As a gesture of goodwill. But he won't have much goodwill for you if he trips on your wire.

BASSEE. We won't achieve goodwill from him if we let him push us around. Let him trip. It will show him that, starving or not, we know how to fight back.

JADI. Bassee, you are ruining our chances.

BASSEE. Our chances for what? We are worse off now than we were when these negotiations began.

PAULA. I have brought you food. Maybe it will help you listen to reason.

PAULA removes a cookie from her pocket. BASSEE snatches it out of her hand aggressively and starts eating it.

JADI. Do you have one for me?

PAULA. I could only get one. I figured you would share.

Jadi looks at Bassee.

JADI. *(asking him to share)* Bassee?

BASSEE stops eating the cookie. Reluctantly, he hands over the uneaten remnants to JADI. JADI eats the rest of the cookie, trying to savor every bite.

BASSEE. One lousy cookie? That's what you meant when you said you would feed us?

PAULA. No. I meant to feed you well. I spent hours cooking. I only picked up the cookie on my way over here. I figured you would appreciate some dessert to go with your meal. I used my last shekel to buy that cookie. I'm sorry.

BASSEE. So where is our meal?

PAULA. It was confiscated.

JADI. Confiscated?

BASSEE. By whom?

PAULA. Assav's men. As soon as I passed his estate, they said I was not permitted to smuggle anything in.

BASSEE. Bringing us food is smuggling?

PAULA. That's the word they used. I think they're afraid of weapons.

JADI. They're afraid? We have to starve because they're afraid?

PAULA. I'm sorry. I'm doing the best I can. Honestly, I am.

BASSEE. The wire stays up. And if Assav shows up here today, he's a dead man.

PAULA. No. Bassee, please. This is not the answer.

BASSEE. Why do I have to suffer so that someone else can feel safe?

PAULA. I don't have an answer for you. But today we meet with him. Today, we'll be face to face. He'll be forced to confront the suffering that he's imposed on you. He'll be forced to confront his actions. Believe me, suffering is your most powerful weapon.

BASSEE. My bare hands are more powerful.

JADI. Bassee, please. Give her a chance to meet Assav. Let her see for herself what kind of person he is. Violence is always an option if the negotiations don't work.

PAULA. Listen to him, Bassee. Once you resort to violence, you will never be able to resume negotiations. It won't end until we talk. Let's talk until we're blue in the face.

BASSEE. Then we'll be too weak to lift a finger. We have an opportunity now to show them who they're dealing with. We have to take it.

A 13-year-old BOY enters carrying a bunch of bananas. He trips on the wire as PAULA did and falls to the ground.

ASSAV. Oww!!!

The bananas go flying out of ASSAV's hand. BASSEE quickly rushes towards him and picks him up with force.

PAULA. Bassee, no.

BASSEE locks his arm around the BOY'S throat.

PAULA. Bassee, you've made a mistake. Let him go.

BASSEE. I haven't made any mistake.

PAULA. Bassee, look at him. He's just a boy.

BASSEE. This boy as you call him is Assav.

PAULA. *(confused)* What?

Pause. PAULA looks at ASSAV with shock.

BASSEE. Don't let his appearance fool you. He may be small. But he is powerful. And he's responsible for all of our suffering.
PAULA. Bassee, I will not allow you to hurt a child.
BASSEE. I don't think I'm giving you much say in this decision.
PAULA. If you don't let him go, Bassee, we're through. I'll leave you to fend for yourselves. No more negotiations. I'll let his men do anything they please with you.
JADI. Bassee, let him go. Let's hear his offer.
BASSEE. To hell with his offer. I'm making the offers now.
PAULA. Goddamn it, Bassee. If you don't let him go, I'll kill you myself!!!!

BASSEE thinks for a moment and then finally releases ASSAV. ASSAV regains his composure and recovers from being in BASSEE's grasp.

PAULA. Are you okay?
ASSAV. My leg hurts really bad.
PAULA. I'm sorry. Let me help you.
ASSAV. I don't need your help. Who put this wire here?
BASSEE. I did.
ASSAV. I should have known. Violence. That's all you understand, isn't it Bassee?
BASSEE. I understand starving. We have no food to eat thanks to you.
ASSAV. I feel terrible for you. But maybe you should have thought of that before you murdered my mother.
PAULA. Wait. Your mother? I thought your father was the one that was murdered.
ASSAV. Bassee's brother murdered my father. But Bassee murdered my mother. I am an orphan thanks to your friends.
PAULA. Is that true, Bassee?
JADI. We are entitled to defend ourselves.
BASSEE. Jadi!
JADI. What?
BASSEE. Enough.
PAULA. *(to BASSEE)* You didn't tell me that.
ASSAV. I'm sure there's a lot more to the story, they didn't tell you. Where are my bananas?
JADI. I have them.
ASSAV. Bring them to me.

JADI approaches ASSAV with the bananas.

JADI. May I keep one of them? I'm very hungry.
ASSAV. Put them in my hand.

JADI puts the bananas in ASSAV's hand.

ASSAV. I brought these bananas for you. Both of you.
JADI. That was very kind of you.
ASSAV. Would you like one?
JADI. Very much.

ASSAV holds out a banana to JADI.

ASSAV. Okay.

JADI approaches the banana, but before he can reach it, ASSAV pulls back.

ASSAV crushes the banana in his hand. He throws the flattened banana at JADI's face.

ASSAV. There you go.

JADI tries to salvage the banana. He tries to eat whatever part of it he can.

ASSAV. How about you Bassee, would you like a banana?

BASSEE. Yes I would.
ASSAV. Would you like it whole or mushed like Jadi.
BASSEE. However you see fit to give it to me.
ASSAV. Ask me to mush it for you.
BASSEE. Mush it for me.
ASSAV. Didn't your mother ever teach you to say please?
BASSEE. Please.
ASSAV. Please what?
BASSEE. Please, would you mush it for me?
ASSAV. Gladly.
ASSAV puts the rest of the bananas on the ground. ASSAV steps on the remainder of the bananas.
ASSAV. Enjoy.
ASSAV starts to exit.
PAULA. Wait.
ASSAV. What do you want?
PAULA. Where do we go from here?
ASSAV. I'm going back into my house, to take care of my leg that's probably broken now.
PAULA. Please. We have to let the past be the past. We have to look to the future. You came here to present an offer, didn't you?
ASSAV. Yes, I did.
PAULA. Well?
ASSAV. I no longer make offers. I make decisions. I will decide unilaterally how to handle this garden.
PAULA. Please. You have to consider the suffering of those who dwell in your garden.
ASSAV. I've spent a lot of time in the last few weeks considering their suffering. And then I was attacked.
ASSAV exits.
PAULA. You see what comes of violence, Bassee?
BASSEE. I see.
JADI. I see too. You should have killed him when you had the chance.
Lights down on the garden.
DAVID approaches a checkpoint on his way back from MAS'UD's home.
He takes out his American passport and hands it to YAEL, a different Israeli soldier. There is a second Israeli soldier, SHLOMO, nearby.
YAEL. Where are you coming from?
DAVID. My friend's house.
YAEL. Friend? You know someone who lives in Hawarrah?
DAVID. My friend Mas'ud. I was having dinner with his family.
YAEL. How long have you known this Mas'ud?
DAVID. I met him today.
YAEL. *(calling out to another SOLDIER)* Shlomo. Bo enah regah.[18]
SHLOMO. *Mah ha ba'ayah. Cvar Lilah.*[19]
YAEL. *Bo enah. Al teeyeh atzlan.*[20]
SHLOMO comes over. He looks at DAVID's passport.
SHLOMO. *Mah ha ba'ayah. Hoo Americayee, lo?*[21]
YAEL. *Ein lo Visa.*[22]

SHLOMO. *(to DAVID)* How did you get into this country?
DAVID. What do you mean?
SHLOMO. Your passport doesn't have a visa. How did you get in?
DAVID. Oh … uh.
YAEL. *Tees ta kel efoh she hoo nolad.*[23]
SHLOMO. You have another passport.
DAVID. Yeah.
   DAVID produces an Israeli passport. He hands it over to the SOLDIER.
YAEL. You see? This is the passport we need to see. Not this one.
SHLOMO. *(celebrating)* Ahh. You're Israeli. *Mazal Tov!*
DAVID. Well. I was born in this country.
SHLOMO. Okay. *Baruch Hashem.*[24]
YAEL. Now. Tell us again what you were doing in Hawarrah?
DAVID. I was having dinner with a friend.
YAEL. That's very nice. I'm afraid we can't let you through. You'll need to wait here until we get word from our superiors.
DAVID. Why?
YAEL. Because you're a citizen of the State of Israel. And you broke the law.
DAVID. What?
YAEL. Hawarrah is Area A. Israeli citizens are not permitted in Area A. You just committed a crime. Have a seat.
DAVID. How long do I have to wait?
YAEL. Our commanding officer is calling the police. They'll let us know if it's okay to let you through.
DAVID. What if they say it's not okay?
ISRAELI SOLDIER. Then an officer will arrest you and take you to jail.
DAVID. Jail?
YAEL. You broke the law, *Motek*. What do you want me to tell you? Relax. It won't be long, now. You want coffee?
   DAVID looks over at the garden and sees BASSEE who just looks right back at him.
BASSEE. And now?

LIGHTS FADE TO BLACK
END OF ACT ONE

ACT TWO

THE CHECKPOINT. DAVID is being held in a holding cell.
IN THE GARDEN, BASSEE and JADI are tied to the bench. They are now gagged.
DAVID is asleep in an upright position, leaning against the wall of the cell. He wakes up suddenly.
YAEL. *Boker tov, Motek.*[25] Pleasant dreams?
DAVID. I've been here all night?
YAEL. What can I tell you? It takes time. What do you want me to do? I didn't ask you to sneak off into Hawarrah.
DAVID. I didn't sneak.
YAEL. No. You wanted to eat falafel with your friend, Mochamed.
DAVID. His name is Mas'ud.

YAEL. Mas'ud? How nice. It'll be handy to know his name when he blows himself up on a bus.
DAVID. That's a really ignorant thing to say, you know that?
YAEL. Ignorant? The absentee Israeli is calling me ignorant. Do you serve in the army? Do you risk your life every day protecting this country?
DAVID. No.
YAEL. No. So don't call me ignorant. Enjoy your calm, peaceful life in America. And don't come here to teach me about terrorists. I see it every day. I know what it looks like.
DAVID. Look. Mas'ud's a good guy, okay? He's not going to blow himself up.
YAEL. Okay. So his neighbor, Ismail Jachalal. What difference does it make? And what are you doing visiting Hawarrah anyway? You know how dangerous it is?
DAVID. I was invited.
YAEL. You're a Jew.
DAVID. He didn't seem to mind.
YAEL. Wake up, American. Don't be so naïve. Where do you think you are, New Jersey? There are people here who want to kill you. Or worse. Kidnap you so that Israel will release more prisoners for your dead body. Don't be reckless.
DAVID. I'm not reckless. Mas'ud is okay. I trust him.
YAEL. I'm sure he is. But what about his neighbor? Do you trust him?
DAVID. I didn't meet his neighbor.
YAEL. And that's a good thing. Cause let me tell you how it goes. His neighbor Ichy Ayesh finds out a Jew and an Israeli is visiting his good friend's house. He makes one phone call, and before you have time to choke on your falafel you're a hostage for Hamas. Mas'ud and his neighbor are hailed as heroes for their efforts in jihad against the colonial Zionist regime, and you're wasting away in a basement wondering if today is the day Hamas hangs you in a public square. Meanwhile, my Mossad brothers are killing themselves trying to figure out how to find you. Except they don't know that you're not worth saving because you spend all your time feeling badly for a bunch of people who just want to kill you. You're lucky we arrested you. You know that? It's the safest thing that could have happened to you.
DAVID. So what. All Arabs just want to kill you? Is that it?
YAEL. Of course. I'm a soldier in an army that occupies them. Who knows? Maybe they will one day.
DAVID. And how does it play out? You risk your life, forever occupying an entire people?
YAEL. I do nothing forever. I do my duty for three years, and then I'm off to Argentina. Let it be someone else's problem.
DAVID. Right. So let it be your son who gets killed over here when it's his turn to serve. And his son, then his son, then his son. How does it end? When everybody's dead?
YAEL. It ends when Arabs care more about their freedom than they do about destroying Israel.
DAVID. Ahh. But Israel limits their freedom. So you're just perpetuating a vicious cycle. Don't you think?
YAEL. It must be nice to be an American. You sit over there thousands of miles away in your safe multiracial utopia. And you judge us as you watch on CNN how we make life hard for the poor Palestinians.
DAVID. No. I don't judge—

YAEL. It's easy to be a peacenik from thousands of miles away, Americano. Try being a peacenik here. It won't be so easy for you. Try living in Tel Aviv during the Intifada. Try sending your kids to school on a bus every morning wondering if this is the day that bus will blow up. Try wondering if you should send them on this bus or wait five minutes and send them on the next one. But you don't send both kids on the same bus. Oh no. That would be unthinkable. You put the 12-year-old on the 8:05 and the 9-year-old on the 8:15. That way you play the odds. Hedge your bets. Oh but wait a minute. Which child deserves to go on the 8:05 and which child deserves to go on the 8:15. I don't know. Which bus is giving off a darker vibe? Oh but wait a minute, if one of them is giving off a darker vibe, maybe you should switch them. Maybe you should put the 9-year-old on the 8:05 and the 12-year-old on the 8:15. And you make these calculations over and over again, driving yourself into hysterics, until you realize what you're really doing is choosing between your children. This is what it means to be an Israeli. These are the things we think about. And if patrolling the Palestinians in Hawarrah means someone doesn't have to work through these calculations, then goddamn it, I'm going to patrol them. If only to reassure myself that I'm at least trying my best to keep someone's child safe. Understand?

A PALESTINIAN FARMER steps up to the checkpoint.

YAEL. Time to work. Nice chatting with you.

YAEL holds his hands out to the FARMER. The FARMER hands him an ID. YAEL scrutinizes his ID.

We hear bells ringing in the distance.

DAVID. What are those bells?

YAEL. It's freedom ringing in the distance. *(a beat)* That was a joke.

DAVID. It was funny.

YAEL. It's Ramadan. They ring bells on Ramadan.

DAVID. Why?

YAEL. Why? How should I know? *(to the FARMER)* You? Tell him?

The FARMER does not respond.

YAEL. Nu? Are you deaf? I said tell him.

FARMER. Tell him, what?

YAEL. Why do they ring bells on Ramadan?

FARMER. How should I know?

YAEL. How should you know? You're not Arab?

FARMER. I'm Christian.

YAEL. You can go.

The FARMER does not move.

YAEL. You can go. You can go.

The FARMER exits the checkpoint.

DAVID. You let him go pretty easily. You're not afraid he'll blow himself up?

YAEL. He's not on my list. He's a farmer. He's going to work his land.

DAVID. He owns land?

YAEL. That's news to you? You need to get out more.

DAVID. So wait a minute. There's a checkpoint separating his house from his land?

YAEL. Apparently.

DAVID. That's ... ridiculous. I'm sorry. This whole thing is ridiculous.

YAEL. Ridiculous, huh? Okay. So it's ridiculous. But you know what? It's effective. There

hasn't been a single terrorist attack coming from this part of the West Bank in ten years. I'd rather be ridiculous and alive than reasonable and dead.
A phone rings in the checkpoint. YAEL answers it.
YAEL. *Ken? ... Lo.... Hoo Beseder?* Okay. *Efshar Lechashrer otto? Beseder. Besder Gamur. Yalla Bye.*[26] *(to DAVID)* That's it. I'm supposed to kill you now.
DAVID. What?
YAEL. They said you're a Hamas agent and I should execute you immediately. You have anyone you want to make a final call to?
DAVID is stunned and does not answer.
YAEL. Relax. I'm kidding with you.
DAVID. Jesus Christ. What is wrong with you?
YAEL. Sorry. It's just army humor.
DAVID. It's fucking sick is what it is.
YAEL. That's the thing about peaceniks. No sense of humor. You really think I would just kill a fellow Jew? Just like that?
DAVID. Maybe not a fellow Jew.
YAEL. No. But an Arab, huh? *(pause) Yalla.* You're free to go. Go home. Change your panties. I think you pissed yourself.
DAVID. Wait. I don't understand why I'm free to go just like that.
YAEL. Oho! Why ask? You ask too much. Just go. Don't ask why?
DAVID. I'm sorry. It's just strange. If I broke the law, I should be charged.
YAEL. We held you here all night. They figured you learned your lesson. Go home. You think the government has time to prosecute every Israeli who breaks the law? We have bigger fish to fry. Don't ask questions. Just go home. Where are you staying?
DAVID. The Chalom Hertzl Hotel.
YAEL. The Chalom Hertzl? Wow. That place is a real shithole.
DAVID. You're telling me.
YAEL. Stop going to Hawarra. Better yet, go back to America. If I lived in America, I would never come to Israel. This country's a mess. *Yalla. Shalom Aleichem.*[27]
DAVID exits.
Lights fade on the checkpoint.
Lights up on the garden. BASSEE and JADI are tied and gagged to the bench.
DAVID approaches BASSEE and JADI. They glare at him with hostility. DAVID rests his hand on BASSEE's shoulder.
DAVID exits, leaving BASSEE and JADI tied.
PAULA enters, carrying bags filled with goods.
PAULA. Look. I know we're not in the best situation here. But you have to remember you did take action against Assav. What did you expect him to do? The important thing is to stop being angry. Stop trying to plot against him. Do your best to forgive, and most importantly continue negotiating. That's what I've been doing. And you know what? It's working. Assav has allowed me to bring you food. You know what that means? No more figs. No more discarded chicken bones. I brought meat. I figured we'd have ourselves a little barbeque. What do you think about that?
No response.
PAULA. And if you really want to hear of the progress we're making, Assav has agreed to let me untie you while you eat? Huh? That's not nothing. Right? So let's celebrate. Look what I've brought for the occasion.

PAULA holds up bottles of beer.
PAULA. Not bad eh? I figured we could all use a drink after what's been going on in the last few weeks. So I'll just get you started on the beers, and then get the steak on the grill.
PAULA opens the beers. She wedges each beer between BASSEE and JADI's legs. She then prepares a small grill by pouring lighter fluid onto the charcoal.
BASSEE and JADI remain immobile, only now they each have an unopened beer balanced between their legs.
PAULA. What am I thinking? You can't drink your beers all tied up, can you? Assav made me promise that I would only untie you to eat. But, what the hell. The beer is part of the meal, isn't it? I'll untie you now. But only if you promise not to give me any trouble when it's time to tie you back up.
PAULA starts untying them.
PAULA. We have to make sure we abide by Assav's terms. Otherwise we jeopardize future negotiations. He needs to see that we want a resolution. That we're doing our best to work for one. That we're truly interested in a win-win situation and not just out to protect our own interests.
As soon as BASSEE is freed he slips his gag off. He takes his bottle of beer and chucks it across the garden.
BASSEE. Aaahh! That's what I think of your negotiations.
PAULA. Bassee?!
BASSEE. Before your negotiations began, I wasn't starving. I wasn't tied up all the time. Your efforts have only made matters worse.
PAULA. Bassee, I'm trying.
BASSEE. Then stop trying. We're better off without you trying.
PAULA. I see.
BASSEE. And as for bringing us drinks, bring us water to drink. We need water for sustenance. Not beer.
PAULA. I'm sorry. I thought you might like something to help you relax.
BASSEE. I DON'T DRINK!
JADI. Bassee is right. Enough is enough. We're tired of negotiations. I think the time has come to fight back.
PAULA. No, Jadi. Not you too. Don't you see fighting is only making matters worse?
JADI. There is nothing new about fighting. It's been going on long before your arrival here. Before you came, Assav's men had us beat every single day. We're not choosing whether or not we should fight. We're choosing whether or not we should fight back.
BASSEE. So you're ready to fight back, Jadi?
JADI. Yes, Bassee. Enough is enough. Paula, thank you for bringing us all this food. We are in your debt. Let us eat. And at the end of our meal, you should go. What Bassee and I must do now, you can't have any part in.
PAULA. No. I won't let you do this. I got involved to help you. Not to sit back and watch you turn to violence.
JADI. I'm afraid we're not asking for your permission. Go home.
PAULA. I'm going nowhere. I told Assav that I would take responsibility for you. I promised him that you would be tied up again—
BASSEE and JADI grab PAULA.
PAULA. —if he only allowed you to be fed properly.

They pick her up and carry her towards the bench.
PAULA. *(protesting)* I AM THE PEACEMAKER!!!
They sit her down and tie her up.
JADI. A battlefield is no place for a peacemaker. You'll have to wait until the war ends.
PAULA. No. You can't do this. Let go of me.
BASSEE. Until then, have a beer. It'll help you relax.
BASSEE tilts a sip of beer into PAULA's mouth.
PAULA. Stop it! Untie me this instant. Do you hear me?
JADI. We really do appreciate everything you've done for us, Paula. We just can't have you getting in the way of what we must do now.
BASSEE. I'm starving. How about you, Jadi?
PAULA. This is outrageous. What are you gonna do?
BASSEE. I, for one, am planning on having a nice juicy steak. But don't worry, there's plenty to go around. You can rest assured that we'll return your favor, and make sure you're properly fed. Let's see. What have we got here? A nice little grill.
BASSEE picks up the lighter fluid.
BASSEE. Oh, and this must be how you start the fire. Am I right? You just pour this right on?
BASSEE pours some of the lighter fluid on the charcoal.
BASSEE. There we go. Now what can we use to light the fire?
BASSEE looks in the bag.
BASSEE. Oh look. You brought matches. You just think of everything, don't you, Paula.
JADI. How about some more beer, Paula?
JADI pours more beer into PAULA's mouth.
BASSEE. You know, I never thought I'd say this. But at this moment, I'm so happy, I feel like celebrating. With a cocktail.
PAULA. I thought you didn't drink.
BASSEE. I don't.
JADI. But you do, right Paula? Drink. Drink, my friend. In good health.
JADI pours more beer into PAULA's mouth.
Lights down on the garden.
Lights rise on an outdoor bar. DAVID sits at a table with BASSAM, 40s, and ELAD, 30s. ELAD is in charge. He is in possession of a bottle of whiskey.
ELAD. David, Bassam. Bassam, David. Good, you met. We're doing shots. You too Bassam.
BASSAM. *(chuckling)* No no. I'm Muslim. I don't drink.
ELAD. Yeah. I know. I've noticed. *(BASSAM chuckles.)* Drinking me into the poor house all week. It's fine. *Sachten.*[28] Drink in good health.
The three take down a shot. ELAD promptly refills the three shots while recovering from his drink.
DAVID. No no. Come on. We can't drink so much. We're here to talk.
ELAD. We'll talk. You'll see how much easier we'll talk the more we drink. *(to BASSAM)* David is my cousin. He lives in America.
BASSAM. America? Where?
DAVID. New York.
BASSAM. Oh. New York. Very nice.
DAVID. And you? Where are you from, Bassam?

BASSAM. Nablus.

ELAD. What Nablus? Where's Nablus? Sh'chem. Not Nablus.

BASSAM. But my wife and child live here. My wife is an Israeli citizen.

DAVID. She's Jewish?

BASSAM. Of course not. She's Arab.

ELAD. She's an Israeli Arab.

BASSAM. She's a citizen. She can stay here. Me. I'm not allowed to be here.

DAVID. But you're married. Don't you get automatic citizenship when you marry a citizen? *(BASSAM laughs.)* You can't tell them you need citizenship to be with your family?

BASSAM. I can tell them. They don't care.

DAVID. So you're here illegally?

BASSAM. If they catch me, straight to jail. But what can I do? I need to work. To feed my family. Your cousin is a good man. He gives me a job.

ELAD. I'll drink to that. Another shot.

DAVID. No no, Elad. We've already had two. That's enough.

ELAD. *Ezeh* enough.[29] When was the last time you were here?

DAVID. When I was eight.

ELAD. When you were eight. 25 years ago. He comes every quarter of a century and he tells me that's enough. Drink now. I might not be alive in 25 years. *Yalla. L'Chaim.*
They shoot another.

DAVID. I need you to be able to speak clearly. What you have to tell me is very important.

ELAD. What do I have to tell you? I've got nothing to tell you.

DAVID. No. You've got plenty to tell me. Without slurring your speech.

ELAD. I'm telling you nothing.

BASSAM. Where are you staying while you're here, David?

DAVID. The Chalom Hertzl Hotel.

BASSAM. That place is a real shithole.

DAVID. I know. What do you do for my cousin here, Bassam?

BASSAM. I work in the kitchen.

ELAD. He does nothing. He's here for atmosphere.

BASSAM. I'm here so your cousin can say he has Arab friends.

ELAD. Listen to this guy. Friends. What friends, you're my employee.
BASSAM and ELAD chuckle. BASSAM pats the back of ELAD's neck.

DAVID. So you're a chef?

BASSAM. I would be. If this place wasn't a shithole.

ELAD. That's right. Bassam is the Muslim Jacques Pepin. We're limiting his possibilities with our Israeli cuisine.

BASSAM. That's right. Someone needs to teach you Jews how to eat. All you eat is schnitzel. You have schnitzel coming out of your asshole. You know schnitzel, David?

DAVID. Fried chicken breast.

BASSAM. It's Kentucky Fried Chicken.
DAVID laughs.

ELAD. Yes. But it's what you do with that Kentucky Fried Chicken that makes all the difference. Bassam is a real artiste. He brings a certain…

BASSAM. …*Je ne c'est quoi?*

ELAD. ...Palestinian flare to the schnitzel. Tell him how you make it.
BASSAM. I take the schnitzel out of the freezer, and I put it in the microwave.
ELAD. Yeah, but it's all about how you take it out of the microwave. Most people wait till it beeps. Not Bassam. He can sense the right moment that the schnitzel is ready. Not a second more.
BASSAM laughs.
BASSAM. Such a dick your cousin is. Allah keep you healthy, you smart ass.
ELAD laughs.
DAVID. You guys laugh a lot.
ELAD. What else can we do?
BASSAM. I'm an Arab living in a Jewish state. Laughing is the only way I know to survive.
ELAD. That's right. Without laughing Bassam would join Hamas.
BASSAM. I joined Hamas. They sent me here to blow your ass up.
ELAD. Nu. So what happened?
BASSAM. I tasted your schnitzel. I felt sorry for you.
ELAD laughs.
ELAD. I love this guy. He keeps me sane.
DAVID. So where do you stay when you're here?
ELAD. Oho!! More questions. My cousin doesn't laugh. He just asks questions.
DAVID. I'm sorry. It's hard for me to laugh.
ELAD. He's a peacenik.
BASSAM. He's an American.
ELAD. Americans are very concerned about Palestinians. It helps distract them from all the Iraqis and Afghans they're murdering.
DAVID. Oh fuck you, Elad.
BASSAM. Don't let your cousin push your buttons. Besides, in Afghanistan and Iraq, it's not murder. It's murder for oil. It's totally different. Palestinians have no oil. So Americans feel bad about raping us.
DAVID. Okay. I need another shot.
ELAD pours another round.
ELAD. *Yalla! L'chaim!*
DAVID. Okay. Can we be serious now?
BASSAM. You think I am not being serious?
ELAD. He is. This guy hates Americans. *Mashoo lo normally.*[30] It's why we get along so well.
BASSAM. Okay. Let's stop picking on the American. To answer your question, I stay with my family. In Al-Quds.
ELAD. *(correcting him)* Yerooshalayim.
DAVID. So every day you come from home and back, hoping you don't get stopped?
BASSAM. Hoping? No. You can't just hope. I avoid it. I blend in. I practice my Israeli accent. "*Mah nishmah?*"[31]
DAVID. Can't you help him get a work permit?
ELAD. Me? What do you want me to do?
DAVID. Tell them you need him here to work.
ELAD. I can help him, if he's in Sh'chem. Maybe. But if he's here illegally, and then I ask for a permit, they'll deny him and send him back to Sh'chem without ever hearing of another permit ever again. No. There's nothing I can do.

BASSAM. Nothing to do.
ELAD. It's a screwed up situation.
BASSAM. What can be done?
DAVID. Elad. Your turn.
ELAD. My turn? My turn what? What do you want to know?
DAVID. I want to hear some of your stories.
ELAD. Trust me. You don't want to know.
DAVID. I want to know.
ELAD. If I tell you some of my stories, you won't want to have me as a cousin.
DAVID. Elad. There is nothing you can tell me that will make me not want to have you as a cousin.
ELAD. Oh really?
DAVID. Seriously.
ELAD. I don't think you can imagine what I have to tell you.
DAVID. Try me.
ELAD. Try you? Listen to him. The peacenik wants to know. I tell him he doesn't want to know, he tells me he does. He wants me to teach him a lesson.
BASSAM. So. Teach him.
ELAD. See the problem with being a soldier is power. They put a lot of power in your hands, when they give you a weapon. It's great if you need to defend yourself. But it's not great when the people you need to patrol have nothing. They can annoy you. They can spit on you. They can even injure you a little. What are you gonna do about it? Shoot them? It's not exactly a responsible reaction for a decent human being. And so you're paralyzed. You have no recourse. And the more you do nothing, the weaker you're perceived by the people. The more annoying they become. Well one morning, I had enough. There was a little eight-year-old boy throwing rocks at me. Sure he was only eight, and sure they're only rocks. But rocks aren't nothing. They hurt. They cut the skin. They injure. They get on your nerves. Let's just say you would rather not have anyone throwing rocks at you. I told this kid to stop. I gave him three warnings. And then, it was time to teach him a lesson.

ELAD stops speaking. It's clear he would go no further if he was not encouraged to say more.
DAVID. So what did you do?
ELAD. What did I do? I picked him up. I stripped him naked. And I tied him to the top of my jeep. And then I drove all around the village, so that everyone could see him. Eight years old. No one throws rocks at you with a naked eight-year-old kid tied to your jeep. And everyone got the message that you don't throw rocks at a soldier.
DAVID. Jesus.
ELAD. You see? It's no good being a soldier. It's bad news.
DAVID. *(to BASSAM)* What do you think when you hear a story like that?
BASSAM. What do you want me to say? It's fucked up.
ELAD. You see what a horrible person your cousin is?
BASSAM. Some customers are coming. I better defrost the schnitzel.
BASSAM gets up and exits.
DAVID. He's a nice guy, Bassam.
ELAD. He's the best.
DAVID. You didn't have to tell that story in front of him. I didn't mean to force you into a confession. I just wanted to hear for myself.

ELAD. Are you kidding? I don't keep secrets like that from Bassam. I've told him lots of stories.
DAVID. And he still works for you?
ELAD. He doesn't blame me. He blames Israel. He blames the history. Somehow he doesn't blame me.
DAVID. It's so hard to take all of this in. I don't know how you live here.
ELAD. How I live here? I'm a Yemenite Jew. This is where I belong. Where do you want me to live? Yemen? Egypt? We tried that. It didn't work so well. So where? Spain, Poland, Germany. It was even worse there. You live in America. How's it going?
DAVID. So far so good.
ELAD. And where will you go when the Americans decide they've had enough of the Jews?
DAVID. Why would—
ELAD. It's happened everywhere else. Why wouldn't it happen in America? Because America is some magical place where everyone is equal. Except for Blacks. Oh, and Muslims. And gays. So … you don't think the Jews are next?
DAVID. And if they are, where do you think that's gonna leave Israel?
ELAD. I don't know. But that's why we have an army.
DAVID. With nuclear weapons.
ELAD. Exactly. We're going nowhere without a fight.
DAVID. Just like Samson.
ELAD. *Beedyook.*[32] We may lose. But we won't be the only ones.
DAVID. What a fucking nightmare.
ELAD. That's the nightmare we live in. What else can we do? Don't be so damn proud of your America, David. It's just another country where Jews are the minority living by the good graces of the goyim. This is your homeland. This is where you belong. Israel needs Jews. And Jews need Israel. As a wise man once said, "If you don't have a seat at the table, you're probably on the menu." Israel is our seat, David. It's our job to make sure Jews stay off the menu.
DAVID. Speaking of menus. I'm fucking starving.
ELAD. *(calling off)* Bassam. Bring some schnitzel.
Lights fade.
DAVID gets up from the table and turns his attention on the garden.
BASSEE and JADI are on the ground finishing their food. PAULA remains tied to her chair. But now she is also gagged.
BASSEE. What a meal!
JADI. Delicious. Thank you Paula. For putting together such a great menu!
PAULA tries to speak.
PAULA. Mmmm. Mmm. Mmm.
BASSEE. I'm sorry. What?
PAULA. Mmmm. Mmm. Mmm.
BASSEE. I can't understand you. Can you understand her, Jadi?
JADI. Are you kidding? I can't understand a word. It's such a shame we had to gag her. If only she had stopped lecturing us about attacking Assav, like we asked her to. Such a shame.
BASSEE. And now that we have our strength, time to fight.
JADI. Shouldn't we clean up first?

BASSEE. But of course. Paula, are you done with your beer bottle? Here, let me clear that for you. I have a very special way of disposing of beer bottles.
JADI. What is it?
BASSEE. I'll show you. First you take the bottle and you fill it with liquid.
JADI. Like water?
BASSEE. No. Not like water.
JADI. Good. Cause we don't have any water.
They laugh.
BASSEE. No. This method requires a liquid a bit stronger than water.
JADI. Like alcohol?
BASSEE. Closer.
PAULA. Mmmm. Mmmm.
BASSEE. What's that Paula?
PAULA. Mmm-Mmmm. Mmmm.
BASSEE. The lighter fluid? Now that is a wonderful idea, Paula. Thank you so much for thinking of it.
PAULA. Mmm. Mmmm.
BASSEE. I know. It's a bit dangerous. But not to worry. I'll be careful.
BASSEE takes the lighter fluid and pours it into the beer bottle.
BASSEE. There we go. Not bad. Now I just need a piece of cloth. Do we have one?
JADI. I only have what I'm wearing.
BASSEE. How about you, Paula? Do you have an extra piece of cloth? Let's see. You've supplied us with everything else that we need. Do you mind if we just borrow a little piece of your shirt?
PAULA. Mmmm. Mmmm. Mmm.
BASSEE. I know. It's not really fair. I would use my own shirt, but you see this is the only shirt I own. I imagine you have more shirts at home.
PAULA. Mmm. Mmm.
BASSEE. I'll just borrow a small piece. No more than necessary. I promise.
BASSEE tears off a strip of the bottom of PAULA's shirt.
BASSEE. There we go. You see? Very small. And it's for a good cause.
PAULA. *(growing in intensity)* MMMMMM!!! MMMMM!!!
BASSEE. Now you stuff the cloth in the bottle. (He does so.) See?
JADI. Now what do you do with it?
BASSEE. Now you wait till Assav comes out of his house and then you throw it at him.
PAULA. MMMMM!!!! MMMMM! MMMMM!!!!
BASSEE. What Paula? You say I'm forgetting something?
PAULA. MMMMM!!!! MMMMM! MMMMM!!!!
BASSEE. You say, I'm supposed to light the cloth before I throw it? I don't know. Sounds kind of dangerous to me.
PAULA. MMMMM!!!! MMMMM! MMMMM!!!!
BASSEE. Okay. If you insist. Do we have any matches? Oh. Of course we do. I almost forgot. We have the matches that Paula brought for us. You've been so useful today.
PAULA. MMMMM!!!! MMMMM! MMMMM!!!!
BASSEE picks up the matches.
DAVID. What are you doing?
BASSEE. Look who's back? What do you think we're doing?

DAVID. Don't do this. You'll lose.
BASSEE. But we won't be the only ones.
DAVID. PLEASE! DON'T!
BASSEE. You have a better way?
DAVID. No.
BASSEE. No! In other words: Piss off! Would you like to do the honors, Jadi, or should I?
JADI. I would love to do it.
PAULA. MMMMM!!!! MMMMM!!!!
BASSEE. Be my guest.
JADI takes the bottle and the matches and exits.
PAULA. *(hysterically budging and trying to free herself)* MMMMM!!!! MMMMM! MMMMM!!!! MMMM!!!! MMMM!
BASSEE. Shhh. It'll be fine. Everything will be just fine.
The lights start to fade as we hear the sounds of an explosion from offstage. Flashes of bright red bleed onstage as the lights fade to black.
We hear the sounds of police sirens. Lights up on a slightly inebriated DAVID walking down the dark street toward his hotel. He is stopped by a POLICE OFFICER.
POLICE OFFICER. Excuse me, can I help you?
DAVID. No.
POLICE OFFICER. Where are you going?
DAVID. My hotel?
POLICE OFFICER. Where are you staying?
DAVID. The Chalom Hertzl Hotel. I know! It's a real shithole.
POLICE OFFICER. No. It *was* a real shithole.
DAVID. What?
POLICE OFFICER. I'm sorry to tell you, the Chalom Hertzl is no more. A suicide bomb went off there earlier this evening.
DAVID. Holy shit!!!
POLICE OFFICER. Can I see your passport?
DAVID hands the POLICE OFFICER his passport.
DAVID. All my belongings were in that hotel.
POLICE OFFICER. All your belongings? How about 10 people who were killed, so far, including Motti, the innkeeper, may his memory be for a blessing.
DAVID. The innkeeper is dead?
POLICE OFFICER. 25 more in critical condition. Where are you from?
DAVID. New York.
POLICE OFFICER. You have an American passport?
DAVID. It was in the hotel.
POLICE OFFICER. Good. So now you're officially an Israeli. You'll have to find another hotel for the night. But at least you're alive. You're very lucky, my friend.
MAS'UD enters.
MAS'UD. *(calling out)* Astoria?
DAVID. Mas'ud.
POLICE OFFICER. Mas'ud? A friend of yours?
DAVID. Yes. Yes. He's a friend.
POLICE OFFICER. *Mee efoh atah, chaver?*[33]

MAS'UD. Huwarah.
POLICE OFFICER. *Te'udah vakasha?*[34]
MAS'UD produces his ID and hands it to the POLICE OFFICER.
POLICE OFFICER. *(to DAVID)* How do you know him?
DAVID. I met him in the *souq*.[35] He sells cell phones.
MAS'UD. I've been there 4 years.
POLICE OFFICER. *Medaber Angleet. Yafeh.*[36] Where were you tonight?
MAS'UD. I just came from work. I stayed open late.
POLICE OFFICER. *Dafka*[37] tonight. How convenient. And what do you know about what happened here?
MAS'UD. Nothing. I came because I knew my friend was staying in that hotel.
POLICE OFFICER. How sweet. And what can you tell me about the man who did this?
MAS'UD. Nothing.
POLICE OFFICER. Nothing? Are you sure?
DAVID. I told you, he's my friend. He's okay. He doesn't know anything about this.
POLICE OFFICER. Don't be so sure, David. When one terrorist strikes, other terrorists usually know about it.
MAS'UD. I'm not a terrorist!
POLICE OFFICER. No? How can I be sure?
MAS'UD. Because I told you.
POLICE OFFICER. We'll see.
The POLICE OFFICER exits.
MAS'UD. *(to DAVID)* I came as soon as I heard. Are you okay?
DAVID. Not really. I'm pretty shaken up.
MAS'UD. But you're not … hurt.
DAVID. No. I was in Jerusalem.
MAS'UD. *Al ham du lillah.*[38]
DAVID. You should get out of here. You don't want to be anywhere near what's going on.
MAS'UD. It's fine. I've got nothing to hide. I'll stay until I know you're okay.
DAVID. This is so fucked up. I could have been killed tonight.
MAS'UD. I know, David. You don't have to tell me.
DAVID. How does this happen, Mas'ud? How does a man just blow himself up to murder others?
MAS'UD. It's terrible, David. What can I tell you? But at the same time, when people can barely feed their families, when they have nothing, no life, no freedom, what do you expect them to do?
DAVID. What do I expect? I'll tell you what I don't expect. I don't expect them to murder innocent people. That's what I don't expect.
MAS'UD. I'm not excusing what he did, David. But … it's complicated. No?
DAVID. Is it? Innocent people staying in a hotel died tonight. For what? That should not happen. It's not that complicated!
MAS'UD. You're angry.
DAVID. Fuck yeah, I'm angry.
MAS'UD. And … do you get this angry when innocent Palestinians die?
DAVID. Mas'ud. Israelis don't blow themselves up in Palestinian hotels to murder innocent travelers.

MAS'UD. No. They don't need to. They have an air force, with American backing, to drop bombs on Palestinian schools and hospitals whenever they want.
DAVID. That is not fair, Mas'ud. Israelis are not targeting Palestinian schools and hospitals. Hamas shoots rockets at Israel from those very schools and hospitals.
MAS'UD. Okay. So just explain that to my Aunt Fatimah when my five-year-old cousin was killed in the last Israeli strike on 'Aza.[39] Maybe she'll understand if she hears it from you. Just tell her, "I'm very sorry you're grieving for your sweet five-year-old child, who knows nothing about terrorism and politics but just wanted to ride her bicycle down the street and play jump rope with her friends. We didn't mean for her to die. We were just trying to kill Hamas." Tell her that. You think she'll understand? "Oh you were trying to kill Hamas? Oh, I thought you were trying to kill my daughter. Oh, it's just a misunderstanding. No harm done." Is that what you expect her to say? Would you understand if it was your five-year-old?
DAVID. It's not the same thing.
MAS'UD. It's not? Why not? Because an Israeli life is worth more to you than a Palestinian?
DAVID. No. All lives are worth the same.
MAS'UD. Then why isn't it the same thing?
DAVID. Because Palestinians are creating the terror that Israelis are fighting.
MAS'UD. And Israelis are creating the humanitarian crisis that Palestinians are fighting. Don't you understand?
DAVID. We're not gonna agree on this, Mas'ud.
MAS'UD. No. We're not. And here's why. Because you're a Jew. And you get angry when Jews die. And I'm an Arab. I get angry when Arabs die.
DAVID. So what do we do?
MAS'UD. Nothing. Until people can learn to get angry when people die. Don't make the mistake in thinking we have to agree with each other, David. We don't. We just have to agree to give each other a fair chance at living.
TWO ISRAELI SOLDIERS storm on stage with large guns aimed right at MAS'UD.
SOLDIER #1. *(to DAVID)* Teetracheck mee Ha'Aravi. Teetracheck mee Ha'Aravi.[40]
Frightened, DAVID and MAS'UD put their arms in the air.
MAS'UD. Tera-gah! Tera-gah![41]
SOLDIER #2. Teestom et a peh. Al te da ber.[42]
SOLDIER #1. Americayee. Tseh mee sham.[43]
SOLDIER #1 forcefully pulls DAVID away from MAS'UD. They keep their guns pointed at MAS'UD.
SOLDIER #2. *(to MAS'UD)* Atah! Teered le mata.[44]
MAS'UD. Lo Aseetee cloom.[45]
SOLDIER #2. Teestom et a peh. Ani lo meesacheck eetchah. Teered le mata.[46]
MAS'UD drops to the floor and lays down with his hands over his head.
DAVID. *(to the SOLDIERS)* Excuse me. Please. He's a friend of mine.
SOLDIER #2. *(to MAS'UD)* Yesh l'cha neshek?[47]
MAS'UD. Ein lee.[48]
SOLDIER #2. Mee efoh atah?
MAS'UD. Huwarah.
SOLDIER #2. Teetpashet.[49]
MAS'UD does not respond.

Soldiers (Alex Weisman and Rachel Silvert) interrogate Mas'ud (Sami Ismat, right) and David (Adam Poss) in *The Victims or What Do You Want Me to Do About It?* by Ken Kaissar, directed by Michael Malek Najjar (photograph by Airan Wright).

SOLDIER #1 comes over and kicks MAS'UD. MAS'UD groans in pain.
SOLDIER #1. *Hoo Amar "Teetpashet." Lo?*[50]
DAVID. Stop it. Why are you hurting him?
SOLDIER #2. He's not listening to us.
DAVID. He doesn't understand what you said. Please. He speaks English.
SOLDIER #2. *(to MAS'UD)* You speak English?
MAS'UD. Yes.
SOLDIER #2. Good. Slowly take off your pants.
DAVID. Why? He said he has no weapon.
SOLDIER #1. Stay out of this, American. *(to MAS'UD)* Slowly take off your pants. This is your last chance to cooperate.
MAS'UD stays down and takes off his pants. He hands it to the soldier.
SOLDIER #1. Put it there.
MAS'UD tosses his pants aside.
SOLDIER #1. Take off your shirt.
MAS'UD takes off his shirt and slowly tosses it aside.
SOLDIER #1. Hands behind your back.
MAS'UD puts his hands behind his back.
SOLDIER #1 puts cuffs on him.
SOLDIER #2. Stand up.
MAS'UD stands up.
SOLDIER #1. Tell us your name.
MAS'UD. Mas'ud Hadawi.
SOLDIER #2 writes it down.
SOLDIER #1. Let's go.
MAS'UD. Please. I didn't do anything. I just came to check on my friend.
SOLDIER #2. Good. So you have nothing to worry about. We'll take you to ask a few questions. If you're clear, you'll be back in Hawarah by morning.
MAS'UD. Will they take away my permit to come here?
SOLDIER #1. Here? What do you need to do here?
MAS'UD. I have a business. Please. I have to feed my family.
MAS'UD tears up.
SOLDIER #2. Come with us.
The SOLDIERS take MAS'UD away.
DAVID. *(calling out to MAS'UD)* Mas'ud?
MAS'UD looks back at DAVID.
MAS'UD. And now?

DAVID. It'll be okay.
MAS'UD. Will it?
DAVID. *Inshallah.*
  MAS'UD exits. DAVID turns his attention to the garden.
  BASSEE is now gagged and tied to a chair that sits in the middle of a large, metal cage. PAULA stands outside of the cage. She holds a bag. She stands before BASSEE in silence for a few beats. She is not sure what to say. She removes BASSEE's gag.
PAULA. We are making progress.
  BASSEE does not respond.
PAULA. There haven't been any beatings in a while.
  BASSEE does not respond.
PAULA. I brought food.
  BASSEE does not respond.
BASSEE. What have they done with, Jadi?
PAULA. I don't know.
BASSEE. Yes, you do.
PAULA. I suspect. But I have no knowledge.
BASSEE. What else could they have done with him? Sent him to university? He's not coming back. That's certain.
PAULA. I'm sorry, Bassee.
BASSEE. You're sorry. He was the only family I had left.
  BASSEE starts to cry.
PAULA. You mustn't be angry. If your response is anger this will never end. You must learn to forgive.
BASSEE. I MUST LEARN TO FORGIVE? I'M STARVING TO DEATH … I LIVE IN A CAGE. I'M TIED TO A CHAIR.
PAULA. But anger is not the correct response. Only forgiveness will improve your situation.
DAVID. *(to PAULA)* ENOUGH! Stop talking. No one wants to hear it! Go home. No one wants to hear the sound of your voice anymore. Get out of here. And don't ever come back. You hear me?
PAULA. No. Let me do my job.
DAVID. What job is that?
PAULA. I am the peacemaker.
DAVID. I don't see you doing a very effective job.
PAULA. Don't give up on me. Give me a chance.
DAVID. Give you a chance to do what? What is there to do?
PAULA. I don't know. But I am filled with hope.
DAVID. It's not the only thing you're filled with. We're all tired of you. Please go.
  A beat.
PAULA. I'll be back.
  PAULA exits.
DAVID. God help us all.
  DAVID and BASSEE confront each other.
BASSEE. Thanks. She was really starting to get on my nerves.
DAVID. I know.
BASSEE. And now?

DAVID. Now. I'm leaving too.
BASSEE. You can't run from me, you know. I'll always be with you.
DAVID. Let me go. I can't do this anymore. There's nothing I can do to help.
BASSEE. So you're just gonna leave me like this. Tied up. Starving.
DAVID. What else do you want me to do?
BASSEE. How do they say?
DAVID. Who?
BASSEE. If you will it … it is no dream?
DAVID looks back at BASSEE. ASSAV enters and looks to DAVID.
ASSAV. Go ahead. What would you like me to do?
DAVID. You want me to tell you?
ASSAV. It's your dream, isn't it?
DAVID. Open the cage.
ASSAV uses a key to open the cage.
ASSAV. And now?
DAVID. Untie him.
ASSAV does so.
ASSAV. And now?
DAVID. Get him out.
ASSAV offers BASSEE a hand out of the cage. BASSEE takes it and steps out. BASSEE and ASSAV stand face to face looking into each other's eyes with hostility. ASSAV looks back at DAVID.
ASSAV. And now?
DAVID. Allow Jadi to return.
ASSAV snaps his fingers. JADI comes back and stands on the other side of ASSAV. BASSEE and JADI look at ASSAV menacingly, who is in between them. ASSAV looks at both of them. Tension rises. ALL THREE look back at DAVID with a challenging glare.
ASSAV, BASSEE AND JADI. And now?
Pause.
DAVID. Just … fucking kill each other.
DAVID starts to leave.
JADI. Are you serious?
DAVID. What else do you want me to say? It's what you all want, right? So do it. And get it over with.
ASSAV. Wait?
DAVID. What?
ASSAV. This is your dream?
DAVID. This is my nightmare. All I want … is to wake up from it.
BASSEE. We didn't need you for this.
DAVID. I agree.
JADI. We can't just keep killing each other.
DAVID. Well that's a new thought, isn't it?
ASSAV. Come up with a better dream!
DAVID. I can't be the only one who dreams. I'm tired. Maybe it's time for all of you to have a dream of your own.
DAVID gets an idea.
DAVID. Here.

DAVID crosses to the cage. He opens it.
DAVID. Get in.
No one moves.
DAVID. Get in or kill each other! That's your choice.
BASSEE and JADI get in.
DAVID. You too Assav.
ASSAV. Me?
DAVID. Now!
ASSAV gets in the cage.
DAVID crosses to the cage.
DAVID. Give me the key.
ASSAV hesitates.
DAVID. Give it!!!
ASSAV hands over the key.
DAVID throws it away. He then gets in the cage with the other three and shuts the door.
ASSAV. What did you do that for?
JADI. Now we're stuck.
DAVID. Damn straight.
BASSEE. How do we get out?
DAVID. Beats the shit out of me.
JADI. We'll starve in here.
DAVID. Yes we will.
ASSAV. We'll die.
DAVID. Probably.
BASSEE. All of us.
DAVID. So we better get busy.
JADI. Busy doing what?
DAVID. Dreaming. Not me. Not you. Not Assav. All of us. Go.
A look of panic comes over the four trapped in the cage.

Left to right: **Jadi (Kaiser Ahmed), Assav (Kaelan Strouse), and Bassee (Kroydell Galima) are locked in the cage by David (Adam Poss, foreground) in** *The Victims or What Do You Want Me to Do About It?* **by Ken Kaissar, directed by Michael Malek Najjar (photograph by Airan Wright).**

END OF PLAY

THE ZIONISTS

Zohar Tirosh-Polk

All rights reserved ©2018 Zohar Tirosh-Polk. ztp@me.com

About the Playwright

Zohar Tirosh-Polk was born in Brazil to Israeli parents. She grew up in Brazil, Israel and the U.S. Her plays, *Pieces*, *Land/Holy*, *Home/Front*, *The Zionists*, *Theo's Dream*, *Waltz*, *Fog*, and *Six*, have been produced and developed at The New Group, Magic Theatre, New Repertory Theatre, Silk Road Rising, The Lincoln Center Theater's Director's Lab, The Cape Cod Theatre Project, The Jewish Plays Project, Rising Phoenix Rep, the Lark Play Development Center, The Brick, HERE, among others. Her English translation of Hanoch Levin's play, *Those Who Walk in the Dark*, is published in *Wanderers and Other Israeli Plays* by Seagull Books.

A 2017–2018 LABA fellow, Zohar won the Jewish Plays Project's new play competition for her play, *Six*. She is a recipient of the Foundation for Jewish Culture's theatre grant and a commission from Highbrow Productions. She is the Israeli Dramaturg and Dialect Coach for the Broadway production of *The Band's Visit* directed by David Cromer. Zohar has a B.A. in literature and writing from Columbia University and a playwriting MFA from Brooklyn College. She lives in Brooklyn with her family.

— Essay —
Zohar Tirosh-Polk's *The Zionists*: Tracking Generational Trauma

Michael Malek Najjar

> "Maybe there will be new bridges instead of walls
> Maybe we'll learn to forgive
> Maybe there will be no more fighting."
> —Dory, *The Zionists*

Zohar Tirosh-Polk's *The Zionists* is an era-spanning, genre-bending play that opens with Sonya, a Zionist, asking her Tateh what it means to be a Jew. In many ways, the play grapples with that question over three distinct periods—the 1930s–1940s in Poland, Palestine, and Israel; 2006 in Jerusalem; and 2007–2010 in Jerusalem, Tel Aviv, and New York City. Each generation has suffered in their own way—Morris, Shemel, and Sonya in the 1930s, Sheila, Avi, Asaf, and Dory in the 2000s, and Boaz, Dan, and Yoram in the late 2000s. All are haunted by the ghosts of the Holocaust, of the dead in the Arab-Israeli wars, and by the death that accompanies the occupation. A band, appropriately named "The Zionists," occasionally interjects a hard rock song insisting "I'm HERE/I'm HERE/I'm HERE."

Tirosh-Polk, a New York–based Israeli playwright who was born in Brazil to Israeli parents, has seen her share of the Palestinian-Israeli conflict. She has lived through wars, intifadas, demonstrations, peace agreements, and was even in attendance at the rally where former Prime Minister Yitzhak Rabin was assassinated. When asked why she writes plays, she responded,

> I want to pose and explore complicated questions about Israel, Palestine, and the Middle East. I try to inspire my audiences to see/think/hear/feel/experience the region and its history in more complex, multi-layered, and sophisticated ways. I'm also interested in the ways the outside is a reflection of our inner lives, and if that's true, I'm curious about the "Middle Easts of our lives." How do we deal with the war-torn regions in ourselves? In our relationships?[1]

The Zionists attempts to encapsulate lives that were lived before *Aliyah*, or the immigration of Jews from the Diaspora to Eretz Israel, during the early years of the newly declared State of Israel, and later with the descendants of the first generation who must contend with the beauty and heartbreak of living in a country that is constantly beset by wars and uprisings. As the character Sonya says, "Life isn't honey. Let me tell you, it isn't. Even here, in the land of."[2] The ghosts of the past are everywhere, haunting the characters; even the ghost of Theodor Herzl, the father of modern political Zionism, appears by way of posters, books, and dreams.

The play contends with the horror of those killed, crippled, and disappeared. Each generation has suffered loss—in the Warsaw Ghetto, in the valleys of Lebanon, in the cities of Palestine, and even in a bed in New York City. Tirosh-Polk says she is "trying to track the way in which trauma trickles down through generations or learn about the role of trauma within the arc of the Zionist idea."[3] Despite the hardships endured by all of the characters in the play, Sheila, the ex-teacher turned painter, reminds us that there is beauty everywhere—if only we would take the time to look for it, no matter how difficult that may be. Is this play a tragedy or a hopeful missive? Perhaps the final sounds heard in the play provide the answer.

— Playwright Statement —
The Zionists—A Reckoning

As I sit down to write this essay, a few things are happening at once: the IDF killed over thirty people and wounded many during the recent Gaza protests. It is also Yom HaShoah (Holocaust Memorial day) today. And next week, Israelis will celebrate/note Israel's seventieth as Palestinians will continue to mourn the *Nakba*. Another day will pass under the Israeli occupation, as days have for the past fifty plus years.

Hard to make sense of it all. Is there a way forward? Are we trapped forever in this endless cycle of bloodshed and grief? Is there a way out? These are some of the questions that the characters in *The Zionists* and I struggle with.

Born to first-generation Israeli parents, I'm a product of Zionism. I carry within me its genesis, its enormous promise, and unfortunately, the lies it told and carried out and wherever it's heading now. My plays reflect a complex relationship with Israel and the Middle East. I often write about home as the ideal versus the reality of home. There's a vast gap that lives between the two: deep longing, disappointment, and immeasurable grief.

This is why I write plays; I try to reckon with and unearth complicated and painful truths about Israel. I hope to inspire my audiences to be braver, to look deeper. To see/think/hear/feel/experience Israel and its history in more complex, multi-layered ways.

The Zionists looks at Zionism's vibrant and sweeping ideology, its turbulent history, and current state, and asks—how did things get here? How did we start out as the eternally oppressed and ended up being the oppressors? How did we go from being hunted down to the ones doing the hunting? Perhaps the distance is not as far as one thinks, and if so, where is it all going? The play doesn't offer answers but, maybe, versions of coping or some insight. I do know that our lives are now forever bound together, and it is within the acceptance of this fact that we might find a new direction.

The Zionists' inclusion in this anthology is my prayer that we may come to these awfully polarized and deeply painful subjects with new eyes and an open heart. I hope that we could all, one day, find our way home. Inshallah, amen, peace.

— Playscript —

The Zionists

CHARACTERS

MORRIS GOLDENBERG—A 25-year-old man.
SHEMEL GOLDENBERG—His brother, 22, crippled.
SONYA EYLON (née GOLDENBERG)—Their sister, a Zionist.
SHEILA ISRAEL (née EYLON)—Her daughter, an ex-teacher turned painter, in her late 50s. She is warm and kind, a mother. She is now anxious and vulnerable. Though she hides the anxiety well, you'd be worried about her.
AVI ISRAEL—Her husband, a psychologist in his 60s. The opposite of Sheila or the thing that completes her; logical, strong, direct, he keeps it together. He is warm and funny. They're connected in all sorts of enmeshed and complicated ways.
ASAF ISRAEL—Their son. An officer in the Israeli army.
DORY ISRAEL—Their daughter, in her late 20s. A mixture of her parents, she vacillates between their extremes.
BOAZ ISRAEL—Their son, 20. A soldier in an infantry unit. More sensitive than he lets on. He has a way with the ladies.
DAN—Dory's boyfriend, late 20s, a doer.
YORAM—A soldier serving in the same unit as Boaz, 19.
BAND—A hard rock band.
A KIBBUTZ MEMBER
OFFICER
A LADY AT A DESK
PROSECUTOR

NOTES

* a new scene
— the other character is cutting off the sentence or train of thought
/overlapping
Time in this play moves back and forth between the following periods:
 Mid 1930s–1940s Warsaw, Poland, Palestine, and Israel
 2006 Jerusalem, Israel
 2007–2010 Jerusalem and Tel Aviv, Israel and New York City, U.S.
The scenes should flow easily and freely into one another; transitions should be seamless.
Unless otherwise noted, the characters in this play speak their minds. They don't shy

away from expressing themselves and will never shy away from a good argument. The band functions as a chorus throughout the play until the very end.

For my grandparents.

ACT ONE

I Want to Go Home

*

Stage goes dark; we're in a club. The music is loud, offensive almost, lights flash here and there but we can't see who's singing.
BAND. I tell you, I kick and scream looking for my way, way, way
I bite and fight, because I know, I know, I know
I shake and break and love and shove looking for my day, day, day
I cheat and beat because I breathe, breathe, breathe
I'm HERE
I'm HERE
I'm HERE
*

Winter of 1935, a small town in Poland. Sonya is writing a letter.
SONYA. My good Tateh,
I'm writing to you to show you my reasoning for leaving.
Please let me try.
   Pause
Recently, I came across a definition of what it means to be a Jew (I know, I know, you would say, "What sort of thing is this? A Jew is a Jew. A Jew is born to a Jewish mother and that is all." And I'm sure Reb Zaltzman would say, "A Jew is a boy who has been circumcised and a daughter who grew up in a Jewish Kosher home.") But this is the definition I found, Tateh: "A Jew: A person belonging to a worldwide group claiming descent from Jacob and connected by cultural or religious ties." I found this too: "A Zionist: A person belonging to a group seeking to reestablish a Jewish homeland in Eretz Yisroel, currently Palestine." The word Zionist comes from the word Tzeeyon, which is another word for our beloved Yerushalayeem, which is another way of saying Israel which was also named Jacob. Therefore, my good Tateh, in my mind, the way I see it, being a Jew means one *must* also be a Zionist. It is the same thing. Do you follow?
   Pause
I know, I know you'll say, "This is all bollocks that the schlemiels from them socialists are trying to sell girls like you," and that we shouldn't even think to go to Eretz Yisroel before the Masheeach comes.
   Pause
What if the Masheeach has come, Tateh? What if he was a man, flawed but visionary just the same? And what if he preached something, like our prophets?
What if it's time to go home, Tateh? Home!
   Pause
Besides, where else would you go when they come? Where else?

A poster of Theodor Herzl appears. Sonya kisses it.

*

2007. Lights on a spacious living room in one of the affluent suburbs of Jerusalem. There's a bedroom in the back and an entrance to a kitchen; a staircase leads to more bedrooms upstairs. There are quite a few paintings of flowers on the walls. Everything emanates warmth, comfort, and beauty.
Avi stretches in his chair.

AVI. It's good to be home. It's not that I don't like traveling. I do, but it's good to be home. Before we leave, I can't wait to get the hell on that plane and go. Then we get back, and I think: We could have just stayed home and saved a shitload of money.
To think we have to spend all that money and travel to only *then* realize home is where I wanted to be in the first place!
Sheila enters. She is holding a box.

AVI. Come on, Sheila, put this down.

SHEILA. Some trips are fun, though.

AVI. I didn't say they aren't. I loved Spain. The art, the food, and the wine was incredible. I loved every bit of it. The museums, the one about the Inquisition was really interesting./Don't you think?

SHEILA. —The Inquisition, it was awful! But the art was magnificent. Caravaggio's David holding Goliath's head still haunts me.

AVI. I wouldn't have taken you, if I had known.

SHEILA. Why? It was … important.

AVI. Good thing the kids weren't there. They would have whined the whole time.

SHEILA. Remember when we drove coast-to-coast in America with the kids? How did we do that? How did we get through that? I'll never forget that trip. Remember the thing Dory said when we got to the Grand Canyon?

AVI. No.

SHEILA. Avi!

AVI. I don't remember.

SHEILA. She was four years old. She stood in front of the Grand Canyon and said, "Something is broken here."

AVI. That one always had a lot on her mind. Not like Asaf, he just kept/…

SHEILA. —Stop it, Avi.

AVI. What? What did I say? Where are you going? You said—the children.

SHEILA. I know what you were trying to say.

AVI. Come on, Shuly, don't go there. That's why we went to Europe, so you'd enjoy yourself, right? I just don't want you sinking…

SHEILA. I hate when you say that to me.

AVI. I'm sorry I know it's getting hard with the first anniversary…

SHEILA. Avi!
AVI. I'm sorry.
Pause
Boaz will be home from the army soon, I promise.
SHEILA. I know.
Beat
AVI. Why don't you put it down, we agreed you won't do that anymore.
SHEILA. Yes, I'm just not sure…
Pause
AVI. Let's put it here. On the shelf.
Sheila looks at the shelf, then the ceiling.
AVI. What? The ceiling? Do you think it's going to collapse?
SHEILA. What if there's an earthquake? Or, I don't know, a rocket?
AVI. There's not going to be an earthquake.
SHEILA. … No, no, this is not good. This is complicated. I have to think, think.
AVI. Let's just put it on the couch for now.
She sits on the couch as if to examine it.
AVI. So?
SHEILA. No. Not sturdy enough.
AVI. Sheila!
SHEILA. I just want to be sure.
AVI. Here, let's put it on the table for now. It doesn't have to stay there. Just for now. The table is stable. *(He knocks on it)* Solid, see?
SHEILA. Hmmmm…
AVI. Just for now, Shuly. We can take it and put it somewhere else later. And if anything should happen…
SHEILA. Yes, what about that?
AVI. I will run and grab it, I promise.
SHEILA. Well, I guess, for now…
AVI. Yes, for now…
Avi very gently takes the box from Sheila and places it on the table. Sheila watches it for a few moments and continues to do so as she walks into the kitchen.
*

1935, Palestine. Two months after Sonya's letter. The song "Heena Ma Tov Uma Na'eem" is playing in the background.
SONYA. Tateh, Mamah, Mira'le, Morris, Shemel and Lea'le:
Sending my first postcard from the Holy Land to say we have arrived! We're staying in a small hostel outside Jaffa, in Tel Aviv. The British gave us trouble when we arrived on the boat but people from the movement intervened, and we are all right.
Pause
The air is sweet and salty at the same time and the sun is too bright. The people are rude but also, kind. It's a world away—no, it's worlds away, actually, it's a whole universe away and yet, I feel right at home.
Zion!
*

2007. The door slams and Dory and Dan walk into Avi and Sheila's home.
DORY. I hate this place, it's so fucking crowded!

DAN. Yeah, we looked for parking forever—
DORY. /Hi, welcome home—
SHEILA. Thank you, Honey—
AVI. /Did you find parking?
DORY. How was it?
SHEILA. Spain? Good, good—
DORY. /Oh, I'm glad.
DAN. Yes, it took a while—
SHEILA. /I'll go finish dinner—
DORY. Well, we did, after eight hundred gazillion times of going around the neighborhood.
It's just so fucking tight. Everyone trying to get a spot, and they fight you for it. Like they're going to kill you or something. Someone got out of their car and shouted at Dan. Animals. No room anywhere, no parking, nowhere to sit on the bus, I can't breathe!
AVI. When did you take a bus?
DORY. I didn't.
AVI. So why did you say there were no seats on the bus?
DORY. It was a metaphor.
AVI. I don't think it was.
DORY. What do you mean, Abba?
AVI. I'm just saying I don't think you used it as a metaphor. I think you used it as an example of what you meant, but you didn't really experience it. *(Pause)* You embellished.

DORY. Are you saying I've never had to fight for a seat on the bus? I was in the army, you know.
AVI. Your base was across the street.
DORY. So? I still had to take lots of busses.
AVI. Right.
DORY. I wasn't lying!
AVI. I didn't say lying. I said embellishing. I just don't think you were using a meta…
DORY. Stop it, Abba.
Sheila shouts from the kitchen.
SHEILA. Yes, stop it, Avi!
AVI. What? What did I say? To get to the bottom of things/
DORY. —It's just hurtful and unnecessary, that's all.
AVI. Unnecessary, that's what I meant!
DAN. This is cool, I like it.
Dan quickly points to a painting on the wall.
AVI. Yes, she's been painting again.
DAN. That's great. I like it. It's bleak.
Pause
SHEILA. Did he say there's a leak?
AVI. No.
SHEILA. I heard Dan say there's a leak. Is there a leak again?
AVI. No, no.
SHEILA. What did he say?
DAN. I just said—
AVI. He said your new painting is—
DAN. …Sleek. Really sleek.
SHEILA. Oh, thank god!
DAN. You're welcome. It's really nice.
SHEILA. Thank you, Dan. I'm trying something new.
DORY. Isn't it great that she's painting again?
DAN. Really great.
Dory collapses on the couch. Sheila walks in.
SHEILA. Just trying something. Don't get all excited.
There's food in the kitchen.
DORY. Oh, good, we're starving!
DAN. I'll go get some for us.
DORY. Thank you, motek.
SHEILA. How was the concert?
DORY. You know. **DAN.** It was good.
SHEILA. So-so?
DORY. No, it was okay. **DAN.** I thought it was great.
Dan exits to the kitchen.
SHEILA. What?
DORY. I said it was good. What do you want from me?
SHEILA. Just trying to understand if you liked it.
AVI. Art, like everything else, is very, very subjective.
DORY. What art?

SHEILA. I just want to get the whole picture.
AVI. That's hard to do, unless you were there, and even then…
DORY. What's with you, Abba?

Dan comes in from the kitchen with two plates of food. He walks over to the table where the box is.

DAN. Can I move this?

*

1937, a kibbutz in the north of Palestine. It's dark. Sonya is holding a letter.
SONYA. Mira'le,
Like I told you in my last letter, Menachem and I are up north now,
building a new kibbutz. This is very hard work.
We are sustained every day by our great thinkers and leaders:
Ben Gurion, Gordon, Hertzl, of course. We're doing our part to build a home for the Jews in Palestine.
In the kibbutz everything is shared, everything;
The clothes and the children and the food … even Menachem.
(You understand what I'm telling you, yes?)
  Pause
And the work. I love the work, don't get me wrong,
Just the twelve hours in the heat…. The Arabs make sure to let us know they don't want us and the British make our lives miserable.
  A noise is heard.
What was that?
  Pause
Who's there?
  Her gun is revealed.
Stop or I'll shoot!
  Sonya waits and listens, when she's sure no one else is there, she returns to the letter.
What was I writing? Mira'le, I'm not sure I'm cut out for this. I thought about going back to Poland, like Rivka.
  Pause
But how could I show up in Warsaw with my tail between my legs and Tetah…
  Pause
No.
I'm here to build a country and I'm going to do it, even if it kills me.
  Sonya looks at the letter and tears it up.

*

Back in the club. The band continues to play. It's dark and loud. We don't see their faces.
BAND. I tell you I kick and scream, looking for my pay, pay, pay
I take and make and bow and wow because I know, I know, I know
I eat and hit and wait and mate looking for my prey, prey, prey
I kick and scream because I live, live, live.
I'm HERE
Do you hear?
Do you hear?
I'm HERE

I'm HERE
I'm HERE
*

1941, in a back room somewhere in the Warsaw Ghetto. Morris and Shemel, Sonya's brothers, are talking. Shemel is in a wheelchair. Morris has a yellow star on his coat.
MORRIS. I'm sorry, Shemel.
SHEMEL. I'm all right. I can still stand up, brother. See? We'll wait for Sonya's letter.
He tries to stand, and then, collapses.
MORRIS. Shemel, please. Don't make this harder than it already is.
SHEMEL. Who made you god?
MORRIS. I am not god, Shem. And god isn't god either. There is no god, Shem. It was a lie.
SHEMEL. *(crying)* Don't.
MORRIS. It was, Shem. Look at us.
SHEMEL. You don't know. You don't know. We don't know what will happen tomorrow.
MORRIS. Yes, we do. That's why I'm doing this.
SHEMEL. What if there's a way? What if we can somehow get past the guards at the gate? What if Dr. Goldmeyer is going get us out, like he promised? What if Sonya finds us? We wrote her that letter.... What if she comes for us?
MORRIS. Where will you go, Shem? Where will you go now? And how?
They'll shoot you before you even get to the main road.
SHEMEL. Home. I want to go home.
MORRIS. There is no home, Shemel.
SHEMEL. There was home! There was warm food and a bed. There were Shabas dinners and clean sheets.
MORRIS. There was Mamah...
SHEMEL. There was Mamah. SO DON'T TELL ME IT WAS A LIE.
MORRIS. More like a dream.
SHEMEL. There was home. I was there once.
Pause, a shift
MORRIS. Yes, you were, my sweet brother.
SHEMEL. I don't want to do this.
MORRIS. I know.
SHEMEL. So let's not.
MORRIS. Better me than them.
SHEMEL. You will have to live your life knowing.
MORRIS. That I saved you from suffering.
SHEMEL. We don't know that!
MORRIS. You are the best little brother in the world. You're our pride and joy. Tateh's favorite. The best student in the chader. The smartest, the brightest, the quickest.
SHEMEL. The most crippled.
MORRIS. You are the light and nachaes of the Goldenbergs.
SHEMEL. Just a bit crippled and sickly.
MORRIS. You can do so many things. You did.
SHEMEL. *(shouting)* What help is it now, TELL ME?
MORRIS. Now is a lie too.
SHEMEL. We're in it.

MORRIS. We are. We are living a lie and I want it to end before it becomes a nightmare.
SHEMEL. It is a nightmare.
MORRIS. You're right.
SHEMEL. Let's wait until tomorrow.
MORRIS. They're taking all the sick ones tomorrow. They said. Better me than them.
SHEMEL. I'll take my chances./Let them take me.
MORRIS. /I won't.
SHEMEL. Who made you god?
MORRIS. God, god made me god. If god were acting like god, I wouldn't have to try and be him.
SHEMEL. I hate you.
MORRIS. Please, Shem.
SHEMEL. No, no. I want to go home.
MORRIS. I do too, Shem.
SHEMEL. I want to go home.
Morris takes a pill from his pocket and quickly puts it in Shemel's mouth. Morris makes Shemel swallow, choking him.
SHEMEL. I want to go home, I want to go home, I want to go home, I want to go…
He coughs and coughs and coughs and finally, silence.

*

2007. Lights on the living room in Jerusalem. Dory is watching the evening news.
DORY. All I'm saying is that if I hear one more person bring up the Holocaust as an excuse
I'll explode, that's all!
BOAZ. It's not an excuse. It happened.
DORY. Exactly, happened, past tense, it's over. Did you hear about Burg's book *The Holocaust Is Over; We Must Rise from Its Ashes*?
AVI. Well you know, some people say that a trauma like that would take decades—
DORY. It's been decades, it's fucking time they put it/
AVI. centuries to heal.
DORY. Sorry, I don't have centuries. I want to live my life.
AVI. I see your point. I understand.
DORY. The Holocaust this, the Holocaust that, maspeek! It doesn't give you the right to be an animal because sixty years ago you were persecuted.
BOAZ. We're still being persecuted. You know how many people want to kill us?
DORY. Yes, dumbass, I know.
AVI. Hey, watch your mouth.
DORY. I just said, I happen to know. I was at my own brother's funeral.
BOAZ. I wasn't talking about that. I was talking about Iran and Syria and you know.
DORY. And if one more person brings up Iran and Syria and then the Holocaust, I'll scream.
AVI. Maybe you just need to scream.
DORY. No, it's sickening, this pairing. Sickening, I can't take it.
BOAZ. That's because you don't know the real deal and those on the inside know what's going on and if you actually knew you wouldn't be talking like this. You'd be scared. Really scared.

DORY. I don't want to know. This is bullshit politicians make up so they can get re-elected. That's all.
BOAZ. Easy for you to say. It's not your job to keep this country safe.
AVI. Shhh, your mother is coming. No more politics!
Sheila walks in holding the box.
DORY. Hi, Ima.
SHEILA. Hello, my beautiful child. How are you? What are you going on about?
DORY. We're done, Ima.
SHEILA. Hello, another beautiful child. I see you're ready.
BOAZ. I have to go soon, Ima. I'm sorry.
SHEILA. I know.
DORY. You've been painting, Ima?
SHEILA. A little today.
Avi takes the box from Sheila and places it on the table.
AVI. She painted for a while and then read a book.
DORY. Which book?
SHEILA. *Altneuland* by Theodor Herzl.
BOAZ. Bo-ring!
DORY. Savta Sonya will be proud!
SHEILA. Yes, my dear child, your grandmother Sonya will probably be proud. Or she will scold me for not having read it yet.
DORY. For not knowing it by heart.
BOAZ. "Once a Zionist, always a Zionist."
DORY. I won't tell her.
SHEILA. Good.
A honk is heard from outside.
BOAZ. I'm sorry, I have to go. The guys are picking me up.
He picks up his duffle bag and gun.
AVI. It was so nice to have you home for a whole week.
SHEILA. A dream.
AVI. You have everything?
BOAZ. Yes.
AVI. Make sure to call. Your mother doesn't sleep well otherwise.
DORY. *(to Avi)* How do *you* sleep?
BOAZ. I will.
DORY. Don't kill anyone.
AVI AND SHEILA. Dory!
DORY. What, just saying, don't kill anyone.
BOAZ. Shut up, you don't know anything.
DORY. I was in the army, you know.
BOAZ. Yeah, across the street. That's more like a vacation.
DORY. At least I wasn't trained to kill people.
BOAZ. What do you think people do in the army?
DORY. Just be careful is all I'm saying.
AVI. Enough!
Another honk.
BOAZ. I have to go.

Avi and Boaz hug. Sheila hugs Boaz and she doesn't let him go. Dory remains sitting. Boaz breaks away and leaves. Sheila picks up the box and exits the room sobbing.
Pause

DORY. Is she taking her meds?
AVI. She is, but this is no time to disrupt the calm like that.
DORY. Like what?
AVI. You know what. Why do you have to upset your brother before he leaves?
DORY. I'm sorry if the realities of the occupation are upsetting to him.
AVI. You're still angry.
DORY. About what?
AVI. Your brother, everything.
DORY. Which one? The one who got killed in Lebanon or the one you sent to the Occupied Territories?
AVI. Dory.... Don't start.
DORY. You didn't need to sign the form. You know that.
You could have kept him from becoming a combat soldier. You are bereaved parents.
AVI. I'm working very hard to keep the calm here.
DORY. And how is that going for you?
AVI. What do you want from me, Dory? What do you want?
DORY. You let him go, you signed the form, you made her sign the form. You didn't have to. She didn't have to. So don't blame me for disrupting the calm. She's not going to sleep well as long as he's there.
AVI. He wanted to go! It's his life, his choices. We don't have the right to stand in his way because his brother died. He paid a heavy price as it is, losing his brother. We thought about it for a whole year, we talked about it for months and we made our decision to stand by him and allow him to live his life as he sees fit.
DORY. Occupying other people, you mean?
She wasn't in a state to make a decision like that. You made it, not her. And now she's a fucking mess, and you don't have a right to stand in his way?
Pardon me if I think it's your stupid pride because your friends ended up in Jerusalem in '67 while you were—
AVI. /I was recovering from an illness!
DORY. Exactly.
AVI. It has nothing to do with/
DORY. —Really, you're telling me that you didn't let him go fight because somewhere your ego about '67 and how they didn't take you back in '73 after you got sick, and your brother the famous general—
AVI. /This is some bullshit that Sonya put in your head.
DORY. You're the psychologist.
AVI. Shhh.... She's doing better! I'm begging you, don't make more problems.
DORY. Don't worry, Abba, I won't.
AVI. Dory...
DORY. My brother is your problem, not mine.
AVI. They're all my problem: your brother, your other brother, your mother, you.
DORY. I won't be your problem for very long.
AVI. Dory, I don't mean it like that.
Pause

You're angry all the time.
DORY. It's better than pretending not to be by trying to control other people.
AVI. Shut up, Dory, just shut up!
Sheila calls from the bedroom.
SHEILA. What happened?
DORY. Everything is fine, Ima!
AVI. Shit.

*

That night. Dory and Dan are in bed.
DORY. Dan???
DAN. Yes?
DORY. Are you asleep?
DAN. Not anymore.
DORY. Sometimes I have nightmares about World War II.
DAN. Did you have one now?
DORY. No.
DAN. So why did you wake me up?
DORY. Because I'm scared I will.
DAN. If you do, you can wake me up.
DORY. Okay.
Pause
Dan?
DAN. What?
DORY. I really don't want to have one, though. And sometimes I can just feel one coming.
DAN. Dory, it's 2007. Nothing bad will happen to you.
DORY. Once, when I was in high school, I dreamed that Geobbles or Gerrbeles or Goballs whatever his name was—
DAN. Yes?
DORY. Spoke to me and he said the war isn't over. And I told him he was dead but he said he wasn't really and nothing really ended, not the war and not the camps and that the Nazis—
DAN. It was a dream.
DORY. I told him the war is over and that he's dead but he didn't care. In my dream he was fat and had a cigar and recently I saw a picture and he was skinny and ugly.
DAN. See? It was a dream. It's over, Dor, really. It's over.
DORY. Sometimes when I feel a nightmare coming—
DAN. I'm here, Dory. I'll protect you.
DORY. When they come?
DAN. The nightmares?
DORY. The Nazis.
DAN. Who?
DORY. The Arabs.
DAN. Who?
DORY. Whoever is coming
DAN. No one is coming.
DORY. But the other day on TV I did see someone who looks like the real Goebbles or

Goballs or whatever his name was. Then I thought, what if they are among us, just walking down the street, like here.

Sometimes, when I feel a nightmare coming I open my eyes and tell myself all the horrible things I know happened. All of them, the trains and the gas stoves and the mozlemen and the no food and the children and the shots and the mass graves and the—

DAN. Okay.

DORY. So then I don't have to dream about it.

DAN. That's one strategy.

DORY. Do you ever dream about the Holocaust?

DAN. No.

Pause

All the time.

*

That night. Boaz and his unit mate Yoram on a break from patrolling in the Occupied Territories.

BOAZ. My grandfather was this big dude. He was the head of the Jewish Federation or whatever. He had a car in the 50s. No one had a car then. He had a driver too, and no one had a driver. They barely had anything to eat.

YORAM. What was his name?

BOAZ. Gershon Eylon.

YORAM. Never heard of him.

BOAZ. My grandmother was kick-ass too. She built a kibbutz and stuff, Sonya Eylon.

YORAM. Don't know her.

BOAZ. Look it up, like in the books, she's mentioned. There are pictures of her and stuff. I'm telling you, she's big.

YORAM. My father fought in '73.

BOAZ. Yeah, I know.

YORAM. That's why he hates Arabs.

'Cause he knows what's it's like, you know.

He says they all want us dead.

BOAZ. I don't know if I hate them/

YORAM. —What do you think, they don't want to throw us all into the sea?/

BOAZ. I mean, I guess I do, they blew up buses left and right.

YORAM. None of them want us here. They'd just wipe us out if they/

BOAZ. —But after they killed my brother...

YORAM. Forget it. If that happened to me, I would kill one every day if they'd let us. I have no problem just *(he motions)* taking one out.

BOAZ. I thought so too. But after I actually, you know, had to shoot...

YORAM. Oh yeah, that girl that got wounded.

BOAZ. Yeah, didn't feel good. Not that I wouldn't do it again.

YORAM. For sure, for sure, man.

BOAZ. So you know, I'm here, doing my duty, for my brother.

But I can't wait to go home.

YORAM. You are home my brother, this is home.

Just a few months left of this shit. You can do this.

We're in it together, yes?

BOAZ. Forever man. Forever.

*

Lights down, the room transforms, and the band appears. It's dark and loud. We don't see their faces.

BAND. Whaaaaaaaaaaaaaaaaaaa
Yeah, yeah,
More more more more
More of you
More of you
More of me
Wanting more of you
When it gets dark
Let me make my mark
Hear me roar, hear me bark
More, more more
It's all that exists
As this pain persists,
You
More of you
More of you
More of me
Wanting more of you
It's like a monster
It will continue to haunt her
More, more, more.
Whaaaaaaaaaaaaaa
Yeah, yeah, yeah

*

It's early 1947, Palestine. Morris is standing in Sonya and her husband Gershon's small room in the kibbutz. It's simple but clean. Pregnant Sonya enters slowly, nervously.

SONYA. Morris? Is that you?

Morris turns to her. He is silent.

SONYA. Morris, Morris, my Morris. Oh dear god, there is a god! Toda la'el!

Silence

Sonya hesitates, but then approaches him and hugs him. He doesn't move.

SONYA. You look ... good, Morris. Yes. Good.

Silence

SONYA. Say something, Morris, otherwise I'll plotz.

Silence

SONYA. What is it, my sweet brother?

Morris shakes his head.

SONYA. All right. We don't have to do it all today. I'm just happy I can lay eyes on you. That you are here. Healthy and well.

Morris shakes his head.

SONYA. But you are, Morris'le, you are. You are here and standing on two feet. The rest doesn't matter.

She pats him on the back, he freezes.

SONYA. You're home now. Now you're with me and Gershon. He's short but he's nice. And we will take care of you forever and ever. We will. And the rest, the rest doesn't matter, my sweet brother.

He lowers his head.

Because you're home now. Here in Eretz Israel. Here in the kibbutz and we will find work for you and you will take part in building our country. And we will take care of you. We are strong. Strong-willed. Not like our people there like sheep…

Morris raises his head angrily.

SONYA. What I mean is … we're strong here and we will not give up and we are together. Forever, my sweet brother. (*Pause*)

Will you not say a word to me?

He lowers his head.

SONYA. Besder. All right. No need. I'll bring you tea and we'll talk. How is that?

Morris shakes his head.

SONYA. Nu tov. I'll just bring you tea then, all right?

Morris agrees.

SONYA. I'm so happy I could scream. I couldn't sleep all week. I couldn't eat. I was so nervous. Just to get a glimpse of you. Just a glimpse…. When we got the letter from the Bureau for Locating Relatives my hands were shaking. I thought I would faint. How do you open a letter like that? I didn't want to open it. I was too scared. Luckily, Gershon opened it. He's short but he's helpful. Why am I talking? I'm just so nervous.

Pause

I should have made you all come with me when I visited in '38. Remember that visit, Morris? How Tateh lifted his eyes and his beard and saw me standing there? How I surprised you all? He cried and I cried and we all cried. And I brought you oranges. Some went bad on the boat but I still had a few and little Shem and Mira'le… (*pause, stopping herself*) I'll go bring the tea.

Sonya goes into the kitchen. She then, comes in with the tea and a cake.

SONYA. Here, sit, have some tea and a bit of cake. They gave me some flour from the kitchen. I begged them, even though it's not Friday. I made it especially for you.

He grabs three pieces, devours two, and hides one in his pocket. She watches him.

Pause

SONYA. (*trying hard to smile*) You like it, that's good. That's good.

She gives him more. He devours it.

SONYA.

I can't wait for little baby to come. If it's a girl, we'll name her Sheila.

Silence

SONYA. (*slowly*) Morris…. Can you just tell me about…?

Pause

You don't even have to talk, just yes or no.

Pause

Are they…? Will they…?

He lowers his head.

SONYA. No one?

He shakes his head, making his first sound.

SONYA. But…

He shakes his head again.
SONYA. Maybe we just don't know or we have to really look.
Morris shakes his head.
SONYA. No.
Sonya takes this in. Pause.
SONYA. Mira'le, please, Morris, Mira'le?
SONYA. Somewhere? Australia? You know a lot of them ran to Australia or Argentina?
He shakes his head.
SONYA. Please, Morris, please don't say this to me. Please.
Morris shakes his head.
SONYA. Please Morris, please, please.

*

2007, Jerusalem home. The same night as the scene in the Territories. Avi enters the living room in the dark. He turns a faint light on.
AVI. Shuly?
Sheila raises her head from the couch.
SHEILA. Mmm, what?
AVI. I was worried. I didn't see you in bed. It's the middle of the night.
SHEILA. I couldn't sleep, so I thought I would come out here.
AVI. Why didn't you wake me up?
SHEILA. I'm fine, Avi'le. I'm fine. I just couldn't sleep.
AVI. Maybe we should call Doctor Foer?
SHEILA. Really Avi, I'm comfortable here. I was falling asleep already.
AVI. Boaz will call, Shuly.
SHEILA. I know, I know.
AVI. What is it?
SHEILA. It's all right, Avi. How many ways can I tell you?
AVI. I'm just worried.
SHEILA. Don't be, I'm fine.
AVI. You want to sleep here?
SHEILA. Yes, yes. I'm comfortable.
AVI. All right. I'll be in the bedroom if you need me.
SHEILA. Thank you, my dear. Leave the light on, will you?
AVI. Good night.
SHEILA. Good night, darling.
Avi leaves. Sheila turns over on the couch. Pause, a long one. Avi turns the light off in the bedroom. Sheila listens. She waits. Then Sheila quietly gets up from the couch. She goes over to the dining room table where the box is. She watches it. She lifts it and puts it back on the table. She then brings it over to the couch. She sits on the couch and holds it. She caresses it. She then puts it under her, on the rug. She lies back down and covers herself with the blanket. She is going to sleep. The lights dim. Right before the stage turns dark, Sheila's hand reaches out from under the blanket. She grabs hold of the box, she opens it.

ACT TWO

GET ME THE FUCK OUT OF HERE

*

Sheila is standing at a lectern.
SHEILA. Flowers are an expression of joy and celebration, of immense sorrow.
They mark the seasons, the passing of time.
They remind us of our vulnerability, of our mortality, of home.
They tell stories.
They tell this land's story, which like everything else
here is often dramatic, exhilarating and also, horrifying. It's my honor to be here with you to share some of these flowers' stories, as they have inspired my paintings for years.
Pause
Thank you for having me.
The picture below is projected on a large screen.

SHEILA. This is the drone bee orchid, in Arabic, *nachla kabeera*, in Hebrew, we say, *dvoraneet gdola*. Strange looking, isn't it? It has a little fruit that has seeds in it. Thousands, hundreds of thousands of seeds. The wind spreads them but only very, very few survive.
Next, please:
SHEILA. This is the great snapdragon, or what we call the lion's mouth, in Arabic, *pa'am a sumakaa*. Fantastic pink, isn't it? And the texture of the leaves—wonderful. When we were kids, we used to squeeze the flowers right before they bloomed, and if you squeeze tight enough, a lion's mouth appears.

*

1948. We hear a part of the Israeli Declaration of Independence and the ecstatic celebrations that ensued.
SONYA. Did you hear, Sheila? Did you hear them cheering last night? We did it. We built a country. With our own two hands. With our sweat and tears. Our beloved Zion is ours. Our beloved Zion which is *Yerushalayeem* which is now *Israel* which is Jacob which is what we longed for two thousand years, is ours. We did it, Sheila'le. We did it. I'm so happy I could scream.
BOMB
Lights reveal a bomb shelter and a toddler.
(staying calm, almost) That was a loud one, wasn't it, Sheila?
Pause
It's going to be all right. We're going to be all right because we have to. And when you have to be all right then you just do whatever it takes.
You hear me, Sheila'le?
We must be strong now. We leave the past in the past. Over there, in Europe, we were weak. Now we have to be strong. No more tears. No more crying.
We have to be strong and live, you hear me, Sheila'le?
Another BOMB
It's all right. It's all right.
Pause
Last night I dreamed of wolves. I thought we all turned into wolves. No, no, don't cry.

It was just a dream.
> *Pause*

Maybe that's good. I don't know. Maybe that's what we must become in order to be: wolves. After all, his name was Benyamin Ze'ev Herzl, right?
> *Pause*

Look at Morris. How courageous he is. Defending us, not crying, but fighting.

Your father didn't go. He's more of a manager type, like Ben Gurion, short and smart.
> BOMB

Don't cry, Sheila'le. We don't cry. Your Uncle Morris will bring you a present when he comes back.

We built a country and now we have to protect it.

That's how it goes.
> *Pause*

Life isn't honey. Let me tell you, it isn't. Even here, in the land of.

*

> *Jerusalem home. Sheila is looking more disheveled and tired. The living room has been lived in for a few weeks now.*
>
> *Avi calls from the bedroom.*

AVI. What are you doing?

SHEILA. You don't have to check on me every second, you know.

AVI. Just wondering what you're up to.

SHEILA. Yeah and my name is Golda Meir.

AVI. What?

SHEILA. Nothing.

AVI. What were you saying?

SHEILA. I'm going to paint.

AVI. Oh, great!

SHEILA. Don't get too excited.

AVI. I'm just excited you're trying.

SHEILA. Yeah, yeah.
> *Pause*
>
> *Sheila gets ready to leave. Avi walks over to the staircase.*

AVI. Shuly, you left your book.

SHEILA. Which one?

AVI. The one you've been reading.

SHEILA. About Zionism?

AVI. Yeah; History of.

SHEILA. Oh, bloody hell, leave it there.

AVI. Maybe that's why you're so edgy.

SHEILA. Yeah, that's it! Blame everything on the Jews, why don't you?

> *Sheila leaves via the front door. Avi watches her. She returns immediately after.... She doesn't see him. Sheila searches for something, finds the box and takes it with her.*

AVI. It's got to go, Shuly.

SHEILA. *(startled)* I know, just not yet. I'm not ready.

AVI. Do you want me to call Dr. Foer?

SHEILA. I'm fine, really. Going to paint.

AVI. Leave it here, then.

SHEILA. I will, I promise I will. Just give me a few days.
AVI. Leave it, Sheila.
SHEILA. Can you get me my book?
AVI. Sure.
Avi goes upstairs. Sheila leaves with the box.
Pause
Avi returns.
AVI. Sheila? Sheila?
Pause
Shit.
*

Lights on Sheila at the podium.
SHEILA. Next, please:
SHEILA. You all probably know the crown anemone, in Arabic, *shka'ak nuama'an* or in Hebrew, *kalanit metzuia*. Voted yes, the quintessential Israeli flower a few years ago.
*

2006, a year earlier. Lights on a studio. Sheila and Asaf are looking at the unfinished painting of the projected image.
ASAF. Looks a little like two scary eyes staring right at you.
SHEILA. Where do you see that? I don't see that. It's a beautiful flower.
Vibrant, like you.
ASAF. Ima, stop it.
SHEILA. And see how attached they are? That's how I want to be. I want to come with you.
ASAF. Ima.
SHEILA. It's a war.
ASAF. It'll be over soon. A short Lebanon war not like the other one.
SHEILA. One thing I learned in this country is that you never know how long a war will last. So, I get to worry.
He takes a brush.
ASAF. Can I do this?
SHEILA. What about your uniform? I'm not doing another load!
He makes a few brush strokes on the canvas.
ASAF. Didn't I sit on a painting once?
SHEILA. Yes, with your naked behind, thank you very much.

ASAF. Sorry.
SHEILA. I should go find it and bring it to your brigade—to show them what you did to your poor mother.
ASAF. You won't…
SHEILA. I might just … you never know. Mothers who worry can lose their minds.
ASAF. Yeah, yeah, threats. I'm shaking over here.
Sheila paints his face.
ASAF. Not funny! You just said you're not doing another load—
SHEILA. Ready for battle.
ASAF. Ima!
Pause
SHEILA. I'll miss you.
ASAF. I'll be okay.
SHEILA. Please take care of yourself up there.
Asaf points to the painting.
ASAF. Is this right?
SHEILA. As long as you aren't sitting on it/
ASAF. —Very funny.
He points to the painting again.
ASAF. Is this right?
SHEILA. Yes.
ASAF. Sometimes you don't know, you know?
SHEILA. What do you mean?
ASAF. Sometimes you don't know if what you're doing is right.
SHEILA. I understand.
ASAF. So what do you do?
SHEILA. Well.… I try to ask myself what feels right.
And why things feel wrong. I try to listen and trust my intuition.
ASAF. Yes, that makes sense.
SHEILA. What did they tell you in officer training?
ASAF. "Just shoot."
SHEILA. What?
ASAF. Just kidding.
SHEILA. Not funny!
ASAF. They said to have a plan. Execute it, follow orders.
If there are problems, improvise, trust your instincts, listen.
Shoot when you have to.
SHEILA. Is that helpful?
ASAF. Yeah, I guess…
SHEILA. *(hiding her tears)* I'm going to get a towel for your face.
She leaves. Asaf stands in front of the painting for a moment.
Pause
Sheila returns holding another small painting and a towel.
SHEILA. Look what I found!
ASAF. I have to run. I love you, Ima.
SHEILA. Wait! Your face!

*

Split scene: 1951, Sonya speaks with another Kibbutz member, and 2006, an officer is at Sheila's door.

AN OFFICER. Mrs. Israel?

SHEILA. Yes?

AN OFFICER. Mrs. Israel, I'm so sorry.

SHEILA. No, no—you must have the wrong address.

AN OFFICER. Please, Mrs. Israel.

SHEILA. You have the wrong house.

AN OFFICER. Your son, Lieutenant Asaf Israel, was killed in Lebanon after his vehicle was hit by a katyosha rocket. *Sheila sits down.*

SHEILA. Avi.

SHEILA. Avi.

SHEILA. Aviiiiiiiiiii.

*

SONYA. Disappeared?

KIBBUTZ MEMBER. He didn't show up for his shift at the barn and we couldn't find him after that.

SONYA. He's probably asleep somewhere.

KIBBUTZ MEMBER. No, we looked all over.

SONYA. He'll show up. I'm sorry about the shift.

KIBBUTZ MEMBER. Look, Hachavera Sonya. We understand he is your brother and has had a hard time over "there" but we have a kibbutz to run and the work to think about.

SONYA. I'm so sorry.

KIBBUTZ MEMBER. We caught him stealing food from the kitchen the other day, too.

SONYA. I'm sorry.

KIBBUTZ MEMBER. And he started screaming when sirens went off at night. We couldn't get him to calm down.

SONYA. How can you blame him, Shraga?

KIBBUTZ MEMBER. Sonya, we can't have a kibbutz this way. What kind of an example is this to the children and the others? Not showing up at a shift? Stealing? Screaming?

SONYA. Shraga, I'll talk to him. Tomorrow, during four o'clock tea. I will.

KIBBUTZ MEMBER. We already brought it up to the dismissal committee.

SONYA. No, you didn't!

KIBBUTZ MEMBER. We're voting on Tuesday.

Lights on stage. The band appears. It's dark and loud and we don't see their faces.

BAND. Ahhhhhhhhhhh
The day you left
My world was torn
Apart
To pieces.
Don't go
Don't go
I miss you, Bro.
The day you left
Everything turned
Upside down and inside out
Don't go, don't go
I miss you, Bro. All the time.... All the time.... All the time...
*
   Lights on Sonya in 1954.
SONYA. He left, Sheila'le. Your uncle left. Before the animals could kick him out. Achvat acheem, they say. Brotherly love, they say. Don't they?
   Singing
Heene ma tov uma na'eem, shevet acheem gam yachad.
   Pause
Lo po. Not here.
Not him.
So he left.
I don't know where he is.
He won't tell me.
He didn't tell me a thing.
   Pause
Maybe I was too hard on him.
Trying to get him to join.
Join the kibbutz and the movement and be like everyone else.
Be a tsabra
I don't know.
He didn't say anything.
Even about Mira. So I asked for permission and went to Yerushalayeem.
Myself, to Yad Vashem.
   A lady at a desk appears.
LADY. Goldenberg Anna
Goldenberg Batia
Goldenberg Duvid
Goldenberg Fruma
Goldenberg
SONYA. Do you see it?
LADY. There are a lot of Goldenbergs, Miss. I have to go through all of them.
SONYA. Maybe she's not on the list, I said.
LADY. There are a lot of Goldenbergs. A lot.
Goldenberg Gina
Goldenberg Hans

Goldenberg Hans
Goldenberg Inga
Goldenberg Ina
Goldenberg Jacob
Goldenberg Jacob
Goldenberg Katherine
SONYA. What?
LADY. I know. That's what it says.
  Pause
Goldenberg Leon
Goldenberg Lydia
SONYA. I have to go.
LADY. I'm almost there.
Goldenberg Losha
Goldenberg—
SONYA. No, really, I'm going. My daughter.
LADY. Goldenberg Liliana
Goldenberg Max
Goldenberg Maxim
Goldenberg Miriam
SONYA. What?
LADY. Goldenberg Miriam.
SONYA. No, no that's not…
LADY. Goldenberg Mira. Auschwitz, May 14, 1943.
In black and white.
  Pause
It also says Goldenberg…
SONYA. That's enough, I said.
And I ran and ran and ran and ran and ran.
*

  Slide appears
SHEILA. This is called red everlasting, in Arabic, *dam el a'zal* or in Hebrew, *dam hamacabeem*.
In Israel, the flower is named after the Maccabees. A group of religiously devoted Jewish fighters who revolted against the Greeks. Rumor has it that wherever a Maccabee died, this flower grew in commemoration. In 1954, red everlasting was named the commemoration flower of the State of Israel.
*

  Dory and Dan are in their bedroom.
DORY. Dan—
DAN. Mmmmmm
DORY. Dan—
DAN. What?
DORY. Are you sleeping?
DAN. Yes.

DORY. I had a nightmare.
DAN. Sorry.
DORY. It was terrifying.
DAN. What, what.
I'm up now.
DORY. I was somewhere in Hertzliya.
DAN. There's nothing scary about Hertzliya, other than traffic.
DORY. Well, you know, Yigal Amir. But that's not what I dreamed about, I don't think. I was in Hertzliya in a house. I was trying to get back to Tel Aviv.
DAN. But the traffic was crazy.
DORY. And the people in the house knew I was there but they were generous and let me stay. Hide, I mean.
DAN. Hide?
DORY. I was trying to gather my things and leave. But somehow it was taking a long time and I knew it would be hard, no, almost impossible, to get to Tel Aviv because Tel Aviv was under siege.
DAN. Okay...
DORY. And I made up my mind I would walk to Tel Aviv.
So I was trying to get ready and get water and get all my stuff organized.
DAN. Well, just that would take two thousand years.
DORY. And as I'm about to leave, this woman, this Knesset member walks in the door and notices me. She's knows something is not right and the father is starting to get uncomfortable with me being there but she keeps questioning him and me and I can't leave, I can't get to Tel Aviv, it's been seized.
DAN. Wait, by who...
DORY. Armed militias.
DAN. Palestinian?
DORY. No.
DAN. Syrian?
DORY. No.
DAN. German?
DORY. No, no. Don't you see? It was us against them and I couldn't, I couldn't get to Tel Aviv. It was under siege.
DAN. You mean?
DORY. Yes.
DAN. Us.
DORY. Against us.
DAN. A civil war? That's fucking scary.

*

Boaz, Dory, and Avi are in the living room. Boaz is pacing and shaking.
BOAZ. He was outside his house. He started coming toward us
and I kept saying "Stop, stop where you are!"
And he wouldn't stop. He wouldn't stop and I told Yoram to shoot a warning shot
But ... whatever, he didn't.
And I kept saying "Stop" and he said,
"This is *my* house, this is *my* street."
DORY. Oh my god.

AVI. Let him speak!
BOAZ. I said: "Stop or I'll shoot!" But my M16 was stuck and I couldn't get the bullets to load. And he was coming closer and closer and Yoram ... whatever.
DORY. What?
BOAZ. It doesn't matter.
AVI. We're listening.
BOAZ. Anyway, Yoram finally passed me a grenade.
And I said, "Are you fucking crazy? There are people in there."
But this guy keeps saying, "This is my house, this is my street, this is my town," and keeps walking toward us and I didn't know if he was armed or was just going to explode or ... so I threw the grenade toward him and the house.
DORY. I don't want to hear it.
BOAZ. You need to hear it!
DORY. Your father needs to hear it.
Boaz walks toward Dory. Sheila enters but stays in the hallway, listening.
AVI. Stop it you two, stop it right now. Your mother will be back soon.
BOAZ. So, I'm the Palestinian man and you're me and I'm walking toward you and you don't know if I'm going to explode any minute or shoot you and I'm walking toward you
like this:
"This is *my* home
This is *my* street
This is *my* town
This is *my* land"
What would you do? Ha? I'm asking you?
Because...
DORY. I wouldn't be there in the first place.
AVI. Dory, I'm warning you, don't start!
DORY. *(to Avi)* What are you going to do, throw a hand grenade?
AVI. DORY!
BOAZ. This is real. Do you get it? This is real, not those things you talk about with your artsy friends at your cafés. This is real life.
DORY. You chose this, Boaz. And you let him.
AVI. I'm asking you to keep this down. And keep it civilized.
DORY. Nice word you chose, Abba—
civilized!
BOAZ. If I hadn't been there, that guy could have walked through some tunnel and gotten to one of your lefty pretentious artist friends' cafes where you sip cappuccinos and discuss the Occupation.
DORY. Well, luckily, we have a working wall.
BOAZ. Which you were against!
DORY. Because it's evil!
BOAZ. But it has kept you safe!
Beat.
DORY. So, what happened to the rest of the people there?
BOAZ. You don't want to know, so why are you asking?
AVI. We can't do this here. Your mother/

DORY. —I'm asking.
BOAZ. It would have been nice if you'd said: "I'm so glad you're safe, little brother. I'm so glad you didn't end up like our other brother. Thank you for protecting me, us. I'm here for you. What do you need?"
DORY. I DON'T WANT TO BE PART OF ANY OF THIS AND YOU BEING THERE MAKES ME PART OF IT!
BOAZ. GROW UP, you spoiled bitch!
AVI. BOAZ!!!
BOAZ. You are part of it. WE are in the mud.
We are in the swamp, the blood swamp.
All of us.
Pause
Five people were killed all together: two little girls, too. Deal with that.
Sheila retreats toward the door.
DORY. I can't listen to this!
BOAZ. Don't worry, they're going to put me on trial.
AVI. When?
BOAZ. Soon.
DORY. Oh, I'm not worried. I know how that's going to go.
BOAZ. *(shouting after her)* How would you want it to go? Tell me.
DORY. I can tell you all this: We're leaving!
AVI. I'm sorry? **SHEILA.** What?
Sheila enters.
DORY. Dan and I are leaving.
AVI. Dory, maybe we should do this later? Your mother is back now.
BOAZ. Of course you are.
DORY. He got a job and I'll study.
BOAZ. That's what traitors do, you know. Leave.
DORY. Or the righteous, depending how you look at it.
AVI. Have you thought this through, Dory? I mean—
SHEILA. Yes, honey, maybe give it some time?
DORY. Oh, I've thought it through. I can't be part of all this.
BOAZ. Now I'm to blame for you leaving too?
DORY. I leave that for the judge.
BOAZ. You are a bitch!
DORY. And you're a murderer.
Boaz approaches her. Avi stops him.
AVI. We're not going to do this in this house and not in front of your mother!!!
DORY. Only out there.
AVI. Get out, Dory.
DORY. With pleasure.
Dory starts to go.
SHEILA. Wait! Dory! Avi??? What are you doing?
Dory slams the door behind her. Boaz leaves too. Sheila grabs the box
*

Middle of the night. The living room has been completely sealed out with chairs, paintings, suitcases, ladders, and sheets. Sheila has settled in, for good.

AVI. Sheila!
SHEILA. Don't come near me! Stay away from the box!
AVI. I know, I know it's hard. I know it's hard about Dory leaving. She will be back, Dear. She and Boaz will be fine. He will be fine, his officer said.
SHEILA. Don't come in here! Stay away! Don't talk to me! I'm warning you!
AVI. Sheila, we're going to the hospital.
SHEILA. I'm not moving from here! You hear me? This is *my* home!
AVI. Sheila'le, it's me, Darling. It's Avi.
SHEILA. I don't care who you are! I don't know you!
Avi tries to enter the living room. Sheila grabs a knife.
AVI. (*pleading*) Please, Shuly. Please!
SHEILA. Bring me my children back!
AVI. Sheila, let's talk about this, calmly.
SHEILA. Then don't come in here. This is sealed territory.
Only the protectors of the box can enter.
AVI. Sheila, I beg you.
SHEILA. You hear me? Do you hear me! Don't come in here! I'm warning you! You've been warned! You've been warned! Do you hear me? Don't come near me! Don't touch me! Don't! Don't! Don't!
Avi gives up for the first time. He takes a cell phone from his pocket.
AVI. (*on the phone*) Hello?
Pause
Doctor Foer?
Yes, it's Avi, Avi Israel, yes.
Sheila's husband. Yes. It's bad.
Yes. I should have called before.
I'm sorry. I'm sorry I thought I could manage it.
No, no, it's bad.
Ambulance? Yes, please.
   (*Pause*)
Thank you.
   The lights begin to dim.
Hello, yes, her name is Sheila Israel
Number? She doesn't have one. Oh, ID number?
Sorry, I can't remember…
Wait, I think it's 01547662.
Age? Fifty-nine.
Prior history? Yes, long.
Come soon?
Thank you.
Thank you.
   He hangs up.

ACT THREE

To the Land That I Will Show You

*

Dory is writing an e-mail from New York City. It's fall of 2008.
DORY. Abba,
I just wanted to let you know that we are here and we're all right.
We found an apartment the other day. It's beautiful, small and
you know, really expensive. Dan is very busy working and I'm … I'm … enjoying getting to know the city before classes begin.
Pause
It's strange; everything is really loud but I can hear myself better.
Pause
I know you're angry with me.
I know what you're thinking:
We don't leave. We stay put. We fight.
I guess I'm not as strong as you.
Maybe I take after Ima in that way.
Or, who knows, maybe Sonya.
I'm sorry.
I had to.
Dory.

*

Lights on a military courtroom. A prosecutor cross-examines Boaz.
PROSECUTOR. Please state your name and your soldier ID.
BOAZ. Boaz Israel 5287878.
PROSECUTOR. Can you tell us what happened during the afternoon of Friday, September 7th?
BOAZ. I was patrolling the Casbah in Nablus with my friend Yoram Levy.
PROSECUTOR. Please continue.
BOAZ. It was hot and I asked Yoram for water from his canteen and as I turned to get it from him a Palestinian man came out of his house and started walking toward us.
PROSECUTOR. Then what happened?
BOAZ. We told him to stop but he wouldn't.
We told him we'd shoot but he wouldn't stop.
PROSECUTOR. What language did you speak?
BOAZ. Hebrew.
PROSECUTOR. Did you speak any Arabic?
BOAZ. I don't speak Arabic well but maybe Yoram said a few words. I don't remember.
PROSECUTOR. How do you know he understood you?
BOAZ. He spoke back to us and said that this is his house, his street, his home.
I kept telling him to stop and…
PROSECUTOR. And what?
BOAZ. And tried to fire a warning shot but my rifle was stuck somehow.
PROSECUTOR. What does that mean?
BOAZ. I couldn't shoot it.
PROSECUTOR. Why didn't your friend shoot?

Pause

BOAZ. I think he thought I was going to shoot a warning shot.

It all happened really fast.

PROSECUTOR. That's why you're a trained soldier.

Pause

BOAZ. So then the man kept walking toward us and I didn't know if he was armed or not.

PROSECUTOR. And then what happened?

BOAZ. My ... my friend passed me a hand grenade.

PROSECUTOR. So he didn't shoot, but passed you a hand grenade?

BOAZ. Yes. And then, as the man kept getting closer, I ... threw it at him.

PROSECUTOR. Did you know there were people in the house? Children?

BOAZ. I think I heard a few voices…

PROSECUTOR. You think? You think?

BOAZ. I wasn't thinking about any of that. That man was walking toward me and I didn't want to die because my mother already lost my brother in Lebanon.

PROSECUTOR. I'm sorry. I saw that in the letter your uncle wrote.

But there were people in the house. There were children.

BOAZ. I know.

PROSECUTOR. Some were killed; some were severely wounded.

BOAZ. I know. I was protecting my friend and myself.

PROSECUTOR. In Nablus.

BOAZ. I was sent there. I had official orders to patrol there.

PROSECUTOR. Yes, you did.

BOAZ. And an unidentified Palestinian was walking toward me.

I didn't think he wanted a hug, if you know what I mean.

I was protecting my friend and myself and my country,

as my brother had done.

PROSECUTOR. Do you think you deserve to be punished?

BOAZ. I think I've been punished enough, for a 19-year-old, Sir.

*

Sheila, Avi, and Boaz are at the hospital. Sheila is lying down, the box is next to her.

BOAZ. Ima.

Sheila doesn't answer.

I know you can hear me.

I didn't want to come home in another coffin.

AVI. Boaz, I don't think Ima is in a condition to have this…

BOAZ. I'm here. I'm alive. I did it for her.

Every day soldiers kill people. In checkpoints, in command cars, in houses.

Beat up, shoot, choke, whatever you want.

Ask anyone. You don't fucking want to see it.

But that's the truth. What do you think your "Saint Asaf" did in Lebanon?

Ha? You think he was playing catch?

Singing?

Having a beer?

You can kid yourself all you want.

I did what I had to do and I'm alive. THAT fucking makes me more a man than anyone.

Pause
Did I want to be there? Hell no.
Did I want to kill a whole family? No.
Never.
Will I have to live with this for the rest of my fucking life?
Yes.
But I am alive. On my two feet, and Asaf is not.
And I ... I came home to you, Ima.
And if you can't appreciate it, well—
Sheila shakes her head.
AVI. Why don't we have this conversation another time?
And just celebrate the fact that the trial went well and Uncle Benny was able to help. And that you're out of the army and that you can focus on what's in front of you.
Sheila shakes her head again.
BOAZ. That's exactly what I'm going to do and I'm not going to walk around apologizing to any of you or Dory or you, Ima. *(looking at Sheila)* I did it for you. I thought you'd be proud of me.
AVI. She ... is. We ... are. Of course ... we are.
BOAZ. I don't fucking want to hear about Dory's bullshit.
AVI. You don't have to worry about any of that now.
BOAZ. When is she getting out of here?
AVI. We don't know yet.
BOAZ. I'm not going back home.
AVI. I think you should, for a while. Dory isn't there. We're not there.
BOAZ. No. I'm going to see some friends and might stay on couches for a while.
AVI. We love you, Boaz. We're here for you.
BOAZ. My ass. It was always about Asaf and always will be. I'm getting out of here.

*

Sonya, now much older and Avi are outside Sheila's hospital room.
SONYA. When will they let her out of this place?
AVI. We don't know yet.
SONYA. What are they giving her? All kinds of poison?
AVI. Things to make her feel better.
SONYA. And you believe them?
AVI. Sonya...
SONYA. What do they know, these doctors ... nothing!
AVI. We have to help her stay comfortable.
SONYA. Life isn't comfortable. These days everybody wants to be comfortable.
Comfortable this, comfortable that. Comfortable bed, comfortable sweater,
comfortable car, comfortable shower, comfortable thoughts. When we came, nothing was comfortable. We didn't even know what that meant, comfortable. We knew about work, hard work and perseverance, but not about comfortable shmuftable.
Pause
Her life isn't comfortable. Her life is hell.
AVI. So why do you want her to suffer?
SONYA. I don't want them to give her poison.
AVI. This poison is keeping her alive.

SONYA. If she wants to live she will live.
All the rest is games.
AVI. How many times have we had this conversation?
Shuly is sensitive.
SONYA. We all are. When you don't have time for sensitive, you don't stay sensitive.
You stand on your feet, you work, you persevere.
AVI. You just told me yourself that her life is hell.
SONYA. My life was hell too.
AVI. You're strong, Sonya. You always were.
You're from a different generation.
SONYA. No, no, I just didn't have the luxury. We didn't have time. We were building something, a country, with our blood, sweat, and tears.
We were building the third temple!
Pause
And you know how we did it? How we built this country, how we dried the swamps and planted in the desert?
I'll tell you how we did it. *Together. Together.* Now everyone is on their own.
Going after the big car, and the big house and the big boobs and the big bank account. Nowadays you can't even knock on a neighbor's door for a glass of milk, or an egg. They make a face: "Why did you come, Sonya?" "Why didn't you tell us you were coming?" To each his own, or as they say it, a person to another person is a wolf. Not a pack but a lone hungry wolf. So of course she'll collapse.
Of course she'll want Valium.
AVI. She needs it, Sonya. Besides, together is only good if you're part of it.
Together works if you're not left behind, as you know.
That valium and other poisons, as you call them, are keeping her alive.
SONYA. You always spoiled her too much.
AVI. That's so unfair.
SONYA. Well, you too were spoiled. That's how it was with the *Yekkes* from Germany that came way before the war and had pianos in their houses and chocolate torte.
And you even got a little sick and didn't go fight in '67.
AVI. The doctors said visiting hours are over.
SONYA. You tell them her mother is here and I'm not going to leave until they let me see her.
AVI. The nurses are on a break and visiting hours are over.
SONYA. So what are you doing here?
AVI. I'm her husband and primary caretaker, as I have been for the last thirty years.
SONYA. I gave birth to her and built this country so you are going to let me see her.
AVI. I'm sorry you came all this way…
SONYA. Who cares about that? I'll just have to get on a bus and go back to the kibbutz, or whatever is left of it. Not like I'm going to Auschwitz.
AVI. Sonya!
SONYA. I'm just telling the truth, Avi, and now you are going to let me see her.
AVI. *(blocking her)* I don't think that's…
SONYA. *Trying to get past him.*
Sheila—
Shelia'le.

AVI. Sonya, I said/
SONYA. —I've come to get you, Sheila'le. It's time to go home.
Sheila motions to Avi to let Sonya come in. Avi sits on a chair in the room helplessly. Sheila is lying down by her box
SONYA. Do you hear, my Sheila'le? It's time to stand on your own two feet.
Pause
What is it? You're not talking now? Like your uncle Morris? He wouldn't say a word to me. You need to find your own strength, Sheila. You have to dig as hard as you can with everything you have and find it. You think I was always like this? No, no, I've become this. Life doesn't give you the option of giving up. Even Morris, even Morris didn't give up. He found his way in the end. His way, not mine. I know you two are made for a more refined world but I need you to take every goddamn refined gift you got and get up and get out of here. Asaf doesn't need you anymore and he really doesn't need you to be here. If you miss him, write him letters or paint him paintings or cry but get out of here. All of them don't need you here. Even Boaz, especially Boaz. And Dory.... I told her not to go, I told her we don't leave, we stay put, no matter what, but she had other ideas, that one.
Nu tuv, Sheila'le, it's time to get up now.
AVI. Sonya, stop it!
SONYA. I'm not leaving until you do.
AVI. Oh dear god.
SONYA. I'll help you. Come on. We'll do it together.
Sheila lets Sonya help her. Sheila stands up slowly. It is reminiscent of Shemel's rising, only Sheila remains standing.

*

Dory is writing an e-mail in New York. It's winter 2009.
DORY. Abba,
I'm writing again to say hello from a freezing New York City.
Pause
No, seriously, it's freezing.
Pause
I appreciate your updates about Ima, despite how short they are.
Pause
I miss home.
I miss Ima, I miss you.
Pause
It's too cold here. What was I thinking?
Dan is busy.
It's lonely. Really lonely.
What was I thinking?
Pause
P.S. I'm pregnant.
To herself
There's no way I'm sending that.
Delete.

*

Lights on a bench in a park.

YORAM. My brother.
They hug.
BOAZ. Thanks for meeting with me.
YORAM. You are family. Anything you need.
Pause
After what you did for me, brother. *(looking around)*
After taking responsibility for all of it and
never betraying me, ever. Anything you need, man.
BOAZ. Thank you.
YORAM. How are you?
BOAZ. Eh, you know, okay, I think.
YORAM. Don't let the bastards get you down, man. Don't let them.
BOAZ. No, no, I'm not letting anyone get me down.
YORAM. That's good.
BOAZ. Yeah.
Pause, awkward
YORAM. You know, I'm getting married soon.
BOAZ. So young.
YORAM. I love her. I'm happy.
BOAZ. Mazel tov.
YORAM. We want you to come live with us.
BOAZ. In the settlement?
YORAM. If you want to call it that.
It's home to us. It's beautiful.
And it's so much cheaper than Tel Aviv.
BOAZ. I never thought about that.
YORAM. You're family. And we want you as our family.
Not here in Tel Aviv with all the sinners.
BOAZ. Stop it. You're a sinner.
YORAM. I'm repenting, I'm learning, I'm finding myself
and my strength, and my Judaism and god.
I read the bible. You should too.
BOAZ. Stop it, Bro. I'm just looking for a couch for a while.
YORAM. I'm offering you much more than that, my brother.
You saved my life and I'm going to give you a life.
Happiness, a path. Out here there's nothing…
BOAZ. But my—
YORAM. Bring anything you want. Be who you are.
What's waiting for you out here?
Sins and pain.
We have answers.
We have a community. Brotherly love.
We have a path.
Heene ma tov uma na'eem,
Shevet acheem gam yachad…
BOAZ. I'll come for month. To stay on the couch.
YORAM. Whatever you want, my brother.

Whatever you want…

*

   Lights on Sonya who's ill in bed, she's frail.
SONYA. Tateh? Is that you?
Morris? Miral'e?
Who is there?
Who is walking in here?
Morris?
Are you coming home, finally?
Are you coming home to me?
Did you bring Shemel with you?
Morris, sit down, sit down,
I'll make you some tea.
And cake
But don't do that thing, Morris'le
You know, when you eat all the cake
It's embarrassing
Don't eat all the cake Morris,
We need to leave some for the others.
Here in the kibbutz
Everything is equal and everything is shared.
Hene ma tov ima na'eem
Shevet acheem gam yacha
Remember when Tetah used to sing it
And Mira sat next to me
And we held hands forever.
We're all survivors, my Morris
That's the thing you didn't understand.
We're all survivors
And Herzl is looking down at us
With his black beard
wishing it was white.
   Morris walks in. He holds Sonya's hand. Sonya dies.

*

   Dory and Dan are in bed in New York City.
DORY. Dan…
DAN. Come on, Dory. Enough.
DORY. I think…
DAN. What?
DORY. Something is broken here.
DAN. What?
DORY. It's broken.
DAN. What are you talking about?
DORY. There's blood.
DAN. Ohhh, ohh, ohhh.
DORY. Everywhere.
DAN. We have to get you to the doctor now.

DORY. A lot of blood….
DAN. It's okay, it's okay, I'm here. I'm calling an ambulance, I think.
DORY. That's what you get.
DAN. Stop it, Dory.
DORY. My punishment.
DAN. Stop it.
DORY. For leaving. We don't leave. Avi says: We don't leave. Sonya says: We don't leave.
DAN. Stop it right now. Let's try to get you clean and get into a taxi.
DORY. Something is broken.
DAN. We'll fix it. We will.
DORY. I can't fix it. It can't be fixed.
DAN. Let's go. We need help.
DORY. We need help.
DAN. Yes.
DORY. We need a lot of help.
DAN. Yes.
DORY. We don't leave.
DAN. It's okay, Dor. I'm here.
DORY. I'm not, I'm not here, I'm over there.
*

Light dim. We see the family standing in front of a grave.
AVI AND BOAZ. Yitgadal v'yitkadash sh'mei raba.
B'alma di v'ra chirutei,
v'yamlich malchutei,
b'chayeichon uv'yomeichon
uv'chayei d'chol beit Yisrael…

Epilogue
*

It's a year later. Sheila and Avi are out in the garden of their home.
Sheila is painting. Avi is reading her segments from a book. The box is next to them.
AVI. "Wild marjoram. The flower you make Za'atar from." How did we not know that? They say it grows everywhere but "in the late 90s and early 2000 was declared a protected wildflower since it has been overused for the creation of spices and medicine."
Pause, flipping through the book.
AVI. And this one, I wanted to read about this one to you: "Mount Tabor's Oak: One of the sturdiest *(fighting back tears)* and most steadfast trees, this oak has been around for centuries. The oldest oak was found in the Galilee *(struggles to continue)* and was measured to be five hundred years old. The oak can rise up to ten meters and its leaves are long and can reach five to ten centimeters. *(determined to continue)* One side is hard, the other more delicate. Its stem has been used for furniture, housing, sculptures, and other art endeavors." *(finally breaks down)*
Sheila watches him, comforts him.
SHEILA. It's all right, it's all right, I'm right here.
*

DORY. Abba and Ima,
Winter is finally over and we get out whenever we can, just for a glimpse of sun.
I wrote more. One piece inspired by that course I took called *Conflict (Non) Resolution*.

We read *Altneuland*, you know, Herzl's book, the one Savta Sonya loved so much. When he laid out the foundations for a Jewish State it all seemed so impossible, so out of reach, like a dream.

*

The band enters the stage. They're wearing yarmulkes and are carrying guns. They approach the microphones. Slowly, the lights come up and we see Yoram and Boaz.
YORAM. Welcome friends, welcome fellow Jews, welcome soldiers, and welcome all. It's an honor being here with you in the beautiful settlement of Kdumeem.
Let's go Zionists!!!
One, two, three…
THE ZIONISTS. I tell you, I kick and scream looking for my way, way, way
I bite and fight, because I know, I know, I know,
I shake and break and love and shove looking for my day, day, day
I cheat and beat because I breathe, breathe, breathe.
I'm HERE
I'm HERE
I'm HERE
I tell you I kick and scream, looking for my pay, pay, pay,
I take and make and bow and wow because I know, I know, I know
I eat and hit and wait and mate looking for my prey, prey, prey
I kick and scream because I live, live, live.
I'm HERE
I'm HERE
I'm HERE
Do you hear?
Do you Hear?
I'm HERE
I'm HERE

*

SHEILA. *(handing Avi the box)* Slide, please:

This is what our beloved homeland looks like in the late winter, early spring.
It's a breathtaking sight.
Pause
My uncle Morris, the Holocaust survivor, took me down south to see the *kalaniot* once before he left us and emigrated to Argentina and we never saw him after that.
This used to be my favorite image.
Pause
Now, it horrifies me. Blood, everywhere.
Pause
As a mother of a son who has been killed and of a son who has killed,
I've been in the "privileged" position of experiencing both dreadful, dreadful sides.
Pause
I have almost given up on all of it. I know you understand.

*

THE ZIONISTS. I'm here, do you hear?
Do you hear? I'm here!

*

SHEILA. It's an honor to speak here at the Bereaved Families Circle event. To join you, Palestinian and Israeli, Jewish and Arab bereaved mothers and fathers, sisters and brothers, children and grandchildren. It took me a long time to understand that we are all bereaved. I realized that if I could find the courage to join this Circle, maybe together we could transcend something, the pain, the perpetual pain.
Pause
With a lot of help, and loved ones, I was able to pick up a brush again.
I'm now working on finishing a painting I began with my son, Asaf before he was killed.
It's based on this image:

Two anemones joined together, in beauty and grief, in this land.
Pause
I wanted to share it with all of you.
May we all keep standing, continue searching, keep trying…
If we look hard, really hard, together…

*

DORY. So I'm working on a little version of my own *Altneuland*: "*The New Altneuland*" (typical vain me) of all the things that seem utterly impossible and out of reach right now.
You know, like: Boaz, peace, home.
Maybe there will be bridges instead of walls
Maybe we'll learn to forgive
Maybe there will be no more fighting.
Wasn't it Herzl who said: "If you will it is not a…?"
Pause
Oh, she's up.
I have to go. I'll send it to you when it's done.
We hear a baby crying.

END OF PLAY

PHOTOGRAPHS,
IN ORDER OF APPEARANCE

Portrait of Theodor Herzl on an old Israeli 10 shekel banknote (vkilikov, Shutterstock.com)

Old town and port of Jaffa and modern skyline of Tel Aviv, Israel (Boris Stroujko, Shutterstock.com).

Yoram (Adam Poss, left) and Boaz (Sean Wiberg) bond over their military service in *The Zionists* by Zohar Tirosh-Polk, directed by Jonathan L. Green (photograph by Airan Wright).

A wild orchid (Marco Maggesi, Shutterstock.com).

A purple snapdragon (ncristian, Shutterstock.com).

Red crown anemones in Ramat Gan, Israel (emkaplin, Shutterstock.com).

Red everlasting (Helichrysum sanguineum, aka red cudweed), Judean mountains, Israel (rontav, Shutterstock.com).

Spring poppies in full bloom (rontav, Shutterstock.com).

Red crown anemones in Ramat Gan, Israel (emkaplin, Shutterstock.com).

The cast of *The Zionists* by Zohar Tirosh-Polk, directed by Jonathan L. Green (photograph by Airan Wright).

Afterword

Diplomatically Speaking: Envisioning a Semitic Commonwealth • Jamil Khoury

Semitic: Relating to the ancient peoples of southwest Asia who spoke the Semitic languages, primarily Arabic, Hebrew, and Aramaic, as well as their descendants and Diaspora communities.

Commonwealth: A nation, state, or political unit, or a union of constituent states, united by tacit agreement of the people, and established for the common good.

Semitic Commonwealth: A nation or state, or a union of states and/or jurisdictions, located within the territory of 1947 British Mandate Palestine, and predicated respectively upon Jewish and Palestinian national identities and the right of self-determination.

In conceiving a collection of plays written by Arab and Jewish playwrights, the words "Semitic" and "Commonwealth" fused rather seamlessly in my mind. The idea of a polity that could satisfy the national aspirations of Palestinians and Jews, a bi-national, bi-narrative arrangement of sorts, adjacent, conjoined, or united, is one that's been vigorously debated for more than a century.

I've been known to suggest, somewhat humorously, that the theatre company my husband and I co-founded is America's only theatre company with its own foreign policy. Or, at the very least, a rather expansive definition of cultural diplomacy. Theatre makers can be policy wonks too. Chalk it up to my being an alumnus of Georgetown University's School of Foreign Service. But beyond the dramaturgical and aesthetic considerations of curating a play series, I'm compelled to ponder the political contours of my hoped for, yet hypothetical, Semitic Commonwealth.

I'm particularly intrigued by seven distinct scenarios (all of which I outline here) that, with many variations, have been envisioned and debated by politicians, diplomats, academics, activists, and dreamers alike. But prior to my presenting any bill of fare, I must clarify my decision to reference Jews and Palestinians, as opposed to Jews and Arabs or Israelis and Palestinians.

If Palestinian nationalism foregrounds a specifically Palestinian national identity within a broader Arab world context, and Zionism foregrounds a specifically Jewish national identity within an Israeli state context, then the central plaintiffs in this trial are Palestinians and Jews. (Full disclosure: while I'm generally wary of nationalism, I entirely recognize its potency and durability.) I'd be remiss not to add that there are other litigants in this discord: chiefly the United States, but also the European Union, the Arab and Islamic blocs, the Jewish and Palestinian Diasporas, and Russia.

Suffice to say, both populations are growing and neither will "disappear." Cynically speaking, they're stuck with each other. And ideally that's a good thing. But Israel's continued occupation of East Jerusalem, the West Bank, the Gaza Strip, and the Golan Heights, remains unjust, immoral, and anti-democratic, and the persistence of Palestinian statelessness remains unconscionable and untenable.

The policy objective thus becomes one of heedful accommodation: to advance goals of mutual self-determination and self-defense, to end military occupation and asymmetrical power (Israel over Palestine), and to achieve lasting security, dignity, and a just peace. Resolution may be postponed, but it's still inevitable, and remains highly incentivized by the world community. If the arc of history bends toward progress, then these ancient Levantine communities are poised for a windfall of prosperity.

In a Semitic Commonwealth, policies that regulate immigration, right of return, and refugee resettlement would be equitable and mutually sustainable. They would not privilege Jews at the expense of Palestinians, but would enable livable environments, sensible development, environmental responsibility, territorial contiguity, and unprejudiced allocation of resources. The commonwealth would guarantee universal access to religious and holy sites, and the preservation and protection of antiquities and archeological sites. Whatever "end of conflict" agreement the parties arrive at, Jerusalem will likely serve as either a unified capital or a shared capital, be it one based on sole jurisdiction, dual jurisdiction, or multiple jurisdictions.

As for the forementioned seven scenarios, they are as follows:

1. Two fully independent, sovereign, and cooperative states. This scenario would consist of a Jewish (Israel) state with a fully-enfranchised Palestinian community, and a Palestinian state (Palestine) with a fully-enfranchised Jewish community. Citizens of each state would enjoy equal rights under law, regardless of ethnicity or religion. There'd be free movement of peoples and goods between both states, and Arabic and Hebrew would both be recognized as official languages.

2. Federal or confederal states. A union of states, either Israel and Palestine or Israel, Palestine, and Jordan. In a federal system, each state would be separate but united under one central government for purposes of inter-state and external affairs (somewhat akin to the United States). In the confederal system, each state would be separate and free to exercise specified control over its internal and external affairs under the umbrella of a centralized governing authority with interstate and regulatory powers (somewhat akin to the European Union).

3. A binational Arab and Jewish state. This state would exist within a unified geographic territory (encompassing Israel, the West Bank, and the Gaza Strip), and would be the democratic homeland of both Jews and Palestinians, guaranteeing equal rights and responsibilities of citizenship to all. The two national communities would exercise far-reaching control over their respective internal and communal affairs (autonomy), but would govern jointly on matters of security, economy, diplomacy, state budget, national infrastructure, and land and resource management.

4. A multiethnic, secular, democratic state. A similarly unified geographic territory in which citizenship would be derived through residency, parentage, birthright, and/or naturalization, rather than ethnicity or religion, per se. Citizenship would be constructed around the individual, as opposed to national and reli-

gious group affiliations. Governance would adhere to the principle of one person, one vote. Arabic and Hebrew would be official languages, and Palestinian and Jewish cultures would define national identity.

5. Two parallel states. Again, a unified geographic territory in which two parallel state structures would coexist within the same borders, one for Jews and one for Palestinians. Citizens of either state could live anywhere they wish, including in the same building; but citizenship, voting, and governance of internal and communal affairs would correspond to national identity—Jews would be citizens of Israel and Palestinians would be citizens of Palestine. These parallel states would cooperate on matters of security, economy, diplomacy, national infrastructure, land and resource management, and in areas where laws and legal structures overlap.

6. One homeland, two states. In this scenario there would be two separate, geographically defined independent states, one Jewish and one Palestinian, with the combined territory of the states being recognized as the homeland of both Palestinians and Jews. In other words, Jaffa is in Israel, but it is recognized as part of the Palestinian homeland as well; likewise, Hebron is in Palestine but is also recognized as part of the Jewish homeland. Citizens of Israel could be residents of Palestine, and citizens of Palestine could be residents of Israel, so long as they abide by local laws and respect the national sovereignty of the state in which they reside.

7. A confederation of cantons. A canton is defined as "a subdivision of a country established for political or administrative purposes." Drawing on Switzerland's canton confederacy model, the land of Israel/Palestine would be divided into dozens of self-governing cantons, or districts, that would correspond largely to demographic realities on the ground. A unifying central government would assume many of the roles it is traditionally ascribed in the confederal system. Arab and Jewish communities could conceivably establish separate national cantons, as could secular and religious communities. Arab cantons could be established along Bedouin, Christian, Druze, and Muslim lines. Jewish cantons could be established along Ashkenazi and Mizrahi/Sephardic lines, or along secular, national-religious, and Haredi lines.

Scenarios three, four, five, and seven all present opportunities for a bicameral legislature, with a Jewish chamber and a Palestinian chamber; or, a tricameral legislature which would also include a joint Jewish and Palestinian chamber. The same logic could be applied to government cabinets and ministries. One could also imagine a co-presidency/co-prime-ministership or a rotating presidency/prime-ministership. Not to mention the potential for public and private sector joint ventures, and partnerships between cultural and educational institutions as well as civil society groups. You may say I'm a dreamer, but dreaming is an essential step in state building.

No doubt each of my seven scenarios contain elements both promising and problematic. And frankly, I don't have definitive answers. I wish I did. What I do know is that a scenario that ends Israel's dominion over Palestinians and guarantees human and civil rights to all is preferable to a status quo of oppression, racism, terrorism, and pervasive insecurity. And while the Jewishness of Israel, in all its vivid pluralism, has been celebrated for decades, we must also be mindful of the rich Palestinian mosaic, one that includes

Muslims, Christians, Druze, Baha'is and Samaritans (as well as Jews, if they opt for citizenship in a Palestinian state). In the Palestinian state context, efforts to privilege or elevate Islam over other faith traditions must be resisted. Shari'a should not be the basis or inspiration for Palestine's legal system and judiciary (as is the case in Egypt—with devastating consequences for Egyptian Christians).

Ours is a world in which the concept of the nation-state is becoming ossified in certain areas and dissolving in others; where religions and cultures continue to co-exist and separate; where nostalgia for past empires and lost territories challenges borders and complicates identities; where nativism and xenophobia are chipping away at multicultural democracies; where statist autocracies struggle to concoct idyllic "national narratives." In such a world, surely the great thinkers of Palestine and Israel can help us imagine creative new paradigms for governance and national expression.

The notions of sovereignty and shared sovereignty, jurisdiction and joint jurisdiction, independence and co-independence, as well as peoplehood, citizenship, identitarianism, land control, and resource management are all overdue for significant updates. I, for one, am hard-pressed to think of a conflict better positioned to yield new models for dynamic cohabitation and symbiotic coexistence.

Looking Back, Looking Ahead: Semitic Commonwealth in Art and Reality • Michael Malek Najjar

> "I believe the role of the playwright is to create public discourse about phenomenon which threaten us as individuals and communities. The playwright must ring the alarm, but the cathartic experience he offers must strengthen the spectator to face these threats more honestly, more courageously, and with deeper solidarity with others in his community."—Motti Lerner, playwright

In many ways I believe this project started fifteen years ago when Jamil Khoury asked me to direct his play *Precious Stones*. That play, which premiered at the Chicago Cultural Center in January of 2003, was the genesis of our collaboration which focused on the seemingly intractable Israeli–Palestinian conflict. For that production we cast two brave actresses—Roxane Assaf and Nicole Pitman—and asked them to play characters who they identified with culturally *and* characters they may have not identified with at all politically. This was a tall order, especially during the height of the second intifada which lasted from 2000 to 2005. It was during that production that we explored the possibility of "being in the other's shoes" both figuratively and literally. Despite the highly political nature of such a project, the artists and audiences reacted positively and we had some very passionate and interesting dialogues surrounding that production.

Over a decade later, the situation between Palestinians and Israelis has further deteriorated. The Oslo Accords have all but collapsed, there has been a wave of violent attacks throughout Palestine and Israel, the Israeli occupation (of the West Bank, East Jerusalem, the Gaza Strip, and the Golan Heights) continues into its fiftieth year, more settlements are being constructed, the separation wall has divided more land and families, the United States has virtually given up on the two state solution, and there is seemingly no end to the conflict that seemed solvable in 2000 after the Summit at Camp David. Furthermore, we've seen the rise of the so-called "Islamic State," the horror of the Syrian Civil War, a fractured and devastated Iraq, the slaughter and displacement of millions of people, the mass migration of refugees, the destruction of many ancient shrines and archaeological treasures, and further conflicts between many of the ethnic, religious, and cultural groups that inhabit the region. The Trump administration's move of the U.S. embassy from Tel Aviv to Jerusalem effectively undermines any Palestinian claim to the holy city as their capital, thereby dooming a two state solution. Tellingly, several Israeli officials have celebrated the Trump victory because, according to Israeli Minister of Education Naftali Bennett, "the era of a Palestinian state is over."[1] Israel has even changed the name of the new Western Wall train station to honor the American president.

What can a collection of plays possibly accomplish in dealing with the ongoing Palestinian-Israeli conflict? What is the point of art when real lives are being destroyed on a daily basis? How can a play have anything important to say about such a tragic and impossible situation? The answer: perhaps nothing, or perhaps everything. Beyond the tragic loss of human lives, the greatest loss in this conflict is the loss of empathy for the other. Somehow, both sides have found ways to delegitimize and dehumanize one another through war, propaganda, hate speech, and violent acts committed in the name of God, the state, or the homeland. This dehumanization has systematically destroyed the already tenuous relations between Arabs and Jews in the region, and has allowed heinous acts to be perpetrated on a daily basis. The extremists, it seems, have won the argument and the moderates are left hopelessly bereft.

The plays we presented here are an attempt by these playwrights and artists to *re-humanize* the other. The characters in these plays are, just like the rest of us, complicated and multifaceted individuals. They often act out of their worst, rather than their best, instincts and intentions. However, this "Semitic Commonwealth" is offering audiences a glimpse into the world not as it is, or the world as it should be, but rather as a dream of life that *might* be. Can we not take time to examine the wrongs that have been committed, and find constructive ways that we might be able to go on living with one another? Is there a way we can rise above our past and envision a better future? These are the questions Semitic Commonwealth posed and dared us to ask ourselves as citizens, as artists, and as dreamers both through the plays and the interactive dialogues that surrounded this event.

These six plays are written by six very different, yet very talented, playwrights. They each attempt to understand different aspects of this conflict. Motti Lerner's *The Admission* is a compelling play that examines the complicated and painful history of the horrors of war and how history haunts the present; Hannah Khalil provides a kaleidoscopic overview of decades of the conflict in her *Scenes from 70* Years*; Ismail Khalidi's *Tennis in Nablus* reimagines pre–1948 Palestine during the British Mandate; Mona Mansour's *Urge for Going* dramatizes the lives of Palestinians living in exile in Lebanon; Ken Kaissar's *The Victims* dramatizes two abstract yet entwined stories that conclude with a cage and a dream; and Zohar Tirosh-Polk's *The Zionists* transports us back and forth from 1930s Europe to contemporary Israel. These plays speak to us as artists, as scholars, as Americans who have a vested interest in this conflict, and as people who are helplessly watching the tragic events in the Middle East unfold. We chose these plays because we believed in these playwrights and their desires to attempt to capture in words and images the joys, griefs, triumphs, and suffering of the Palestinian and Israeli people.

Each of these playwrights offers a deeply personal and very powerful message about the pain they feel with this ongoing conflict as part of their lives. For most Americans, the Israel-Palestine conflict is a distant problem that is brought to our attention whenever events there spiral out of control; but when you grow up in an Arab or Jewish household the conversation about Palestine and Israel is ever-present. Many American Jews have taken trips to Israel while many Palestinians have either visited their relatives in Palestine (when they are allowed), or have visited Palestinian refugees in the surrounding nations. Whenever violence breaks out those of Arab and Jewish descent are seized with a terrible feeling of helplessness and grief, something not shared by others around them who have no ties to the land.

Is a Semitic Commonwealth possible? Could there be a day when tourists book a high-speed rail tour that travels from Jerusalem to Beirut, Damascus to Baghdad, Istanbul to Tehran? Can we imagine a time when all of us can look back at this Palestinian-Israeli conflict the way now we look back on the Hundred Years' War; as a horrific time of conflict that eventually found a solution rooted in a Middle Eastern Union (MEU)? Can we dare to envision such an ambitious future? Perhaps, after a just peace is achieved, and a truth and reconciliation commission can complete its work, we might be able to envision a time when these tragic conflicts are also a distant memory. It may take generations, but we must find hope now if that dream is ever to materialize. Until then we must fight for a vision of Palestine and Israel as a united land of peace, not as a land of perpetual war. Perhaps if we dream it, it might come to fruition.

Chapter Notes

Introduction

1. "Motti Lerner: Playwriting as Resistance to War," in Domnica Radulescu and Maya E. Roth, *Theater of War and Exile: Twelve Playwrights, Directors and Performers from Eastern Europe and Israel* (Jefferson, NC: McFarland, 2015), 151.
2. Peter Marks, "Motti Lerner's Controversial Play: 'The Admission' Gets Another Life." *The Washington Post*, 14 April 2014. https://www.washingtonpost.com/goingoutguide/theater-dance/motti-lerners-controversial-play-the-admission-gets-another-life/2014/04/14/c75458fa-c40f-11e3-9ee7-02c1e10a03f0_story.html?noredirect=on&utm_term=.e3114e5ef341. Accessed 18 June 2018.
3. Robert Skloot, "Directing the Holocaust Play." *Theatre Journal* 31 (1979): 528.
4. Susan Slyomovics, "'To Put One's Fingers in the Bleeding Wound': Palestinian Theatre Under Israeli Censorship." *TDR: The Drama Review: A Journal of Performance Studies* 35, no. 2 (1991): 34–35.
5. Radulescu, *Theater of War and Exile*, 152.

Motti Lerner's The Admission

1. Rochelle Davis, "Mapping the Past, Re-Creating the Homeland," in Ahmad H. Sa'di and Lila Abu-Lughod, *Nakba Palestine, 1948, and the Claims of Memory* (New York: Columbia University Press, 2007). Cultures of History. Web. 56. See also Susan Slyomovics, "The Memory of Place: Rebuilding the Pre-1948 Palestinian Village." *Diaspora: A Journal of Transnational Studies* 3.2 (1994): 157–68. Web.
2. The Jewish militia which was created to protect Jewish interests in Palestine in 1920. They were allied with the "Irgun" group in 1945. In 1948 the Haganah became Israel's army. "Haganah." *World Encyclopedia: Philip's Oxford Reference*. 2004. Accessed 25 Jan. 2017.
3. "Israel Defense Forces: Military Casualties in Arab-Israeli Wars (1948–1973)," www.jewishvirtuallibrary.org/jsource/History/casualties.html. Accessed 18 June 2018.
4. Davod Holzel, "'A More Honest Discourse.'" Washingtonjewishweek.com. Accessed 19 March, 2014.
5. Motti Lerner, "The Israeli–Palestinian Conflict—The Challenge for the Israeli Theater." www.writerintheworld.com/2016/04/13/motti-lerner-1/. Accessed 18 June 2018.
6. At least three Israeli historians wrote different versions of the conquest of Tantura: Benny Morris, Yoav Gelber and Ilan Pappe.
7. The Palestinian uprising against the Israeli occupation lasting from December 1987 to 1993.
8. Circumcision ceremony.
9. Hyssop.
10. Arab village near Jerusalem.
11. Head of a village.
12. The canopy under which a marriage is performed.

Hannah Khalil's Scenes from 70* Years

1. Kelly Wallace, "Sharon: 'Occupation' Terrible for Israel, Palestinians." *CNN*, 27 May 2003. www.cnn.com/2003/WORLD/meast/05/26/mideast/. Accessed 18 June 2018.

2. Walid Khalidi, "Plan Dalit: Master Plan for the Conquest of Palestine." *Journal of Palestine Studies* 18.1 (Autumn, 1988): 8. Web. 26 January 2017.
   3. Hannah Khalil. *Scenes from 70* Years*, 90.

Ismail Khalidi's Tennis in Nablus

   1. For more about this issue see Sarah Ozacky-Lazar and Mustafa Kabha, "The Haganah by Arab and Palestinian Historiography and Media." *Israel Studies*, 7.3 (Fall 2002): 45–60.
   2. Quoted in *One Palestine, Complete: Jews and Arabs Under the Mandate*, 1st American ed., by Tom Segev (New York: Metropolitan, 2000), Print. 9.
   3. Ismail Khalidi, personal interview. 26 January 2017.
   4. Naomi Wallace and Ismail Khalidi, "Preface." *Inside/Outside: Six Plays from Palestine and the Diaspora*, edited by Naomi Wallace and Ismail Khalidi (New York: Theatre Communications Group, 2015), xii.
   5. Rashid Khalidi, "The Palestinians and 1948: The Underlying Causes of Failure," in *The War for Palestine: Rewriting the History of 1948*, edited by Eugene L. Rogan and Avi Shlaim (New York: Cambridge University Press, 2001). Print. Cambridge Middle East Studies; 27.

Mona Mansour's Urge for Going

   1. Mona Mansour, "The Unspeakable Loss of Displacement." January 25, 2017.
   2. Martin Asser, "Obstacles to Arab-Israeli Peace: Palestinian Refugees." *BBC News*. 2 September 2010.
   3. https://www.unrwa.org/where-we-work/lebanon. Accessed 18 June 2018.
   4. "Lebanon's Palestinian Refugees." www.aljazeera.com. 4 June 2009. http://www.aljazeera.com/focus/2009/05/2009527115531294620.html. Accessed 18 June 2018.
   5. Shaul M. Gabbay, "The Status of Palestinians in Jordan and the Anomaly of Holding a Jordanian Passport." *Journal of Political Sciences & Public Affairs*, 5 February 2014, https://www.esciencecentral.org/journals/the-status-of-palestinians-in-jordan-and-the-anomaly-of-holding-a-jordanian-passport-2332-0761.1000113.php?aid=23346. Accessed 1 February 2017.
   6. Mansour, *Urge for Going*, Unpublished playscript, 2011, 45.
   7. Edward W. Said, Charles Bruce, Jimmy Michael and Alon Farago, *In Search of Palestine* (Princeton, NJ: Films for the Humanities & Sciences, 2005).
   8. "Palestinian Labour Force in Lebanon." *Visualizing Palestine*, http://visualizingpalestine.org/visuals/palestinian-labor-force-in-lebanon-facts-and-figures. Accessed 1 February 2017.
   9. "Palestinian Labour Force in Lebanon Restricted Professions." *Visualizing Palestine*, http://visualizingpalestine.org/visuals/palestinian-labour-force-in-lebanon-restricted-professions. Accessed 1 February 2017.

Ken Kaissar's The Victims

   1. Ken Kaissar, e-mail message to author, January 5, 2017.
   2. Ken Kaissar, "Playwright Statement," 181.
   3. Ken Kaissar, *The Victims or What Do You Want Me to Do About It?*, 203.
   4. Kaissar, Ken. *The Victims or What Do You Want Me to Do About It?*, 203.
   5. In a flash.
   6. Family.
   7. Sweetie.
   8. Hertzl's Dream.
   9. The Messiah.
   10. Breaded and fried chicken breast.
   11. Kebab-like meat skewers.
   12. Chilbeh is a Yemenite dip made of fenugreek. Schug is a spicy Yemenite condiment made of very hot peppers.
   13. Godwilling (literally with God's help).
   14. Please.

15. American?
16. Yes.
17. Speak Hebrew?
18. Shlomo, come here for a second.
19. What's the problem? It's night time already.
20. Just come here. Don't be so lazy.
21. What's the problem? He's an American, no?
22. He doesn't have a visa.
23. Look where he was born.
24. Thank god.
25. Good morning, sweetie.
26. Yes? No. He's okay? Okay. Can I release him? Okay. Okay, great. Alright. Bye.
27. Peace be with you.
28. Good for you.
29. What enough.
30. Something fierce (literally "something not normal").
31. How are you?
32. Exactly.
33. Where are you from, friend?
34. Identification please.
35. Marketplace. (Pronounced shook)
36. He speaks English. Nice.
37. Particularly. (A word used to point out serendipity or a coincidence.)
38. Thanks be to god.
39. Gaza.
40. Distance yourself from the Arab.
41. Calm down.
42. Shut your mouth. Don't talk.
43. American. Get out of there.
44. You. Get down.
45. I didn't do anything.
46. Shut your mouth. I'm not playing with you. Get down.
47. Do you have a weapon?
48. I don't have.
49. Take off your clothes.
50. He said, "take off your clothes." No?

Zohar Tirosh-Polk's The Zionists

1. Mona Mansour and Zohar Tirosh-Polk, "A Closer Look: Mona Mansour and Zohar Tirosh-Polk." *The Lark*. 29 April, 2016. www.larktheatre.org.
2. Zohar Tirosh-Polk, *The Zionists*, 250.
3. Zohar Tirosh-Polk, e-mail message to author, February 3, 2017.

Afterword

1. Andrew Blake, "Trump Win Means No Two-State Solution in Middle East, Israeli Official Says." *The Washington Times*. 9 November 2016. Web.

www.ingramcontent.com/pod-product-compliance
Ingram Content Group UK Ltd.
Pitfield, Milton Keynes, MK11 3LW, UK
UKHW050702160426
5217IPUK00038B/2010